*American Insurgents,*
*American Patriots*

# American Insurgents, American Patriots

## THE REVOLUTION OF THE PEOPLE

## T. H. Breen

Hill and Wang

A division of Farrar, Straus and Giroux

New York

Hill and Wang
A division of Farrar, Straus and Giroux
18 West 18th Street, New York 10011

Copyright © 2010 by T. H. Breen

Printed in the United States of America
First edition, 2010

Library of Congress Cataloging-in-Publication Data
Breen, T. H.
    American insurgents, American patriots : the revolution of the people / T. H.
Breen.— 1st. ed.
        p.   cm.
    ISBN 978-0-8090-7588-1 (hardcover : alk. paper)
    Includes bibliographical references and index.
      1. United States—History—Revolution, 1775–1783—Social aspects.   2. United
States—History—Revolution, 1775–1783—Committees of safety.   3. United
States—Militia—History—18th century.   I. Title.

E209 .B76 2010
973.3—dc22

                                                                2009042496

Designed by Jonathan D. Lippincott

www.fsgbooks.com

20  19  18  17  16  15  14  13  12  11

*For Lady Susan,*
*as always*

# Contents

# American Insurgents,
# American Patriots

# INTRODUCTION

# The Revolutionary World
# of Matthew Patten

Two years before the Declaration of Independence, a young, evangelical colonial population accomplished something truly extraordinary. In small communities from New Hampshire to Georgia, it successfully challenged the authority of Great Britain, then the strongest empire in the world. The vast majority of Americans have never heard the people's story. Instead, we have concentrated attention on the lives of a small group of celebrated leaders. Without the people, however, there would have been no Revolution, no independent nation. Confident of their God-given rights, driven by anger against an imperial government that treated them like second-class subjects, American insurgents resisted parliamentary rule, first spontaneously, as loosely organized militants who purged the countryside of Crown officials, and then, increasingly after late 1774, as members of local committees of safety that became schools for revolution.[1]

## I

A narrative of the people's Revolution includes Matthew Patten and tens of thousands of ordinary colonists like him who elected resistance over accommodation. Long before the Battle of Lexington in April 1775, British officials would most certainly have classified Patten as an insurgent. The term is not meant to shock the modern reader. Along with rebels, mobs, and rabble, contemporaries used the word "insurgents" to describe American colonists who openly defied parliamentary acts.[2]

For our purposes, the word brings greater clarity to an understanding of the coming of national independence. The patriots who are generally credited with mounting the Revolution were in fact the beneficiaries of rebellious insurgents who initially sparked resistance. Without tens of thousands of ordinary people willing to set aside their work, homes, and families to take up arms in expectation of killing and possibly being killed, a handful of elite gentlemen arguing about political theory makes for a debating society, not a revolution. Such reflections raise arresting new questions. How did it happen that so many Americans reached a point of mutual commitment to a cause? When did they do so? The answers, it turns out, were hiding in plain sight. During the two years that preceded the Declaration of Independence, Americans launched an insurgency that drove events toward a successful revolution. In the process, American insurgents became American patriots. By restoring the insurgents to the story we tell ourselves about the nation's origins, we gain greater appreciation of the achievement of the patriots.

Born in Ulster, Ireland, in 1719, Patten migrated to New England when he was only nine years old. Although the Pattens were tough-minded Presbyterians—the heirs of John Calvin—they seem initially to have had a hard time adjusting to the religious culture of the Boston area, then the heart of Congregationalism. One group of Scotch-Irish in America who eventually made their way north to Londonderry, New Hampshire, complained that they resented being labeled "Irish"—in other words, being lumped in with Catholics—"when we so frequently ventured our all, for the British crown and liberties, against the Irish Papists."[3] Memories of sacrifice and violence in the Old World were not easily forgotten in New England. Perhaps as a result of the religious prejudice experienced in Massachusetts, coupled with a widespread antipathy to Irishmen of all sorts, the Patten family moved to New Hampshire, where Matthew and his brother obtained a modest tract of land.[4]

The Pattens and their neighbors led a hardscrabble existence, coaxing small harvests from the rocky soil, supplementing what they received from surplus yields by engaging in other marginal economic endeavors throughout the year. Like so many Ulster settlers in this region, Matthew became a jack-of-all-trades, and according to one historian who has studied these people, he supported a growing family "through fishing, fur-trapping, land speculation, and the local linen trade and by bartering his varied skills as surveyor, carpenter, auctioneer, and scribe in return for goods, labor, or, less frequently, paper money or even scarcer hard cash."[5] In fact, the only thing that distinguished Matthew from other inhabitants in this struggling community was his diary, a remarkable chronicle of his life and work on the New Hampshire frontier. That the document survived at all is something of a miracle. The records of ordinary people such as Patten are always more at risk of destruction than are those of affluent families. Month after month he noted small business transactions, jobs that he and his sons performed, and events that marked the history of his own family.[6]

Patten's journal has special significance. It bears witness to the extralegal processes—the activities that in fact made the American Revolution a radical event—that drew marginal families into what colonists at the time recognized as "the cause of America." How much his political sentiments during the two years before independence reflected long-standing ethnic grievances against Great Britain remains unclear. Certainly, other Ulster migrants whose background paralleled Matthew's thoroughly disliked the English for the poverty and oppression they had visited upon the people of Ulster, Presbyterians as well as Catholics.[7] One Irishman living in Virginia on the eve of the Revolution reminded his brother in a letter published in a colonial newspaper, "You know why I left *Ireland*; you saw the miserable situation of my family, by a rise in my rent *to the double* of what was paid before, and by the enclosure of the *only ground* where I could graze my few cattle; you saw the numerous companions of my misery spoiled, insulted, and abused."[8]

The sense of wrong ran deep. One Hessian soldier who fought for the British declared that the Revolution was "not an American Rebellion; it is nothing more or less than an Irish-Scotch Presbyterian Rebellion."[9] He had a point. It would not be a great exaggeration to claim that the American Revolution was Ireland's revolution in America. Most of the time, however, the betrayals that had occurred in Ireland lay buried in the past, dry seeds of a shared identity, capable under certain conditions of energizing political resistance in a new land.[10]

What little we know about Matthew—other than whatever we learn directly from his diary—derives largely from a bitter fight he waged against the Reverend John Houston, a Presbyterian minister whose authoritarian views on church governance did not sit well with the members of the Patten clan. Houston had graduated from Princeton, and it is possible that he patronized self-educated men like Matthew. That would have been a huge mistake. The members of the Scotch-Irish community in Bedford, where the Pattens lived, insisted on a more egalitarian structure, and Matthew openly berated Houston as "Priest Houston." The minister countered by claiming that his tormentor had instigated "Strife & Debate, Confusion and Evil Work."

Patten gave as good as he got. He announced that Houston was "fitter to stand in the pillory than in the pulpit." As the increasingly personal controversy dragged on, even neighbors who supported Matthew were forced to admit that when he thought a matter of principle was involved, he appeared "Crabid as a Crab tree." The tiresome controversy suggests that Patten was a stubborn, even obsessive man who knew his own mind and defined the issues of the day in stark moral terms of right and wrong.[11]

The entries in Matthew's diary reveal that he came late, perhaps somewhat reluctantly to the revolutionary cause. His reticence did not signal that he favored reconciliation with Great Britain. At issue was making a living. Like other farmers, he did not welcome disruptions that took him and his sons away from normal chores. The first signs of local insurgency appeared in his chronicle in September 1774, which was some months after the Boston Tea Party and the passage of a series of punitive statutes known collectively in America as the Coercive Acts. One day Matthew noted that he had attended a town meeting where a group of Bedford men were planning to harass a suspected Tory in a nearby town. He must have known what they were up to, and if he had had serious reservations about their activities, he could have stayed home. But he did not do so. They urged him to join them in an effort to intimidate a lawyer who had challenged the legality of electing New Hampshire delegates to the Continental Congress. The pressure on Matthew to come forward at that moment was intense—an appeal to take a political stand that came from neighbors, relatives, fellow parishioners, and business associates who, according to Matthew, "insisted on my going with them and they told me I must and Should go and that if I did not, they would Visit me on which I said I would go."[12]

The mission succeeded. On September 20 "about 300 men assembled and chose a Commitie [*sic*]," Matthew explained, "who went to Mr. Atherton and he came to the people to the Court house [where] he Signed a Declaration [a public political apology] and Read it to the people who accepted it . . . the people Dispersed about Midnight without Doing any Out Ragious act."[13] Matthew had witnessed the coercive force of extralegal militant activities. A loose organization of Bedford men known as "the committee" was now prepared to punish dissent. Protest had transformed itself into insurgency, at least in southern New Hampshire.

A New Hampshire newspaper confirmed what Matthew had confided to his diary. It reported that some four or five hundred local men— a huge percentage of the county's adult male population—had forced Joshua Atherton to apologize for his interference in the election of delegates to the Continental Congress to be held in Philadelphia. This was a key moment in driving the Revolution forward on the local level. The journal described Atherton as an "Esquire," a person who may have fancied that superior education or personal wealth gave him the right to make political decisions for ordinary people. But in a revolutionary setting—and in very dramatic fashion—he discovered that such social assumptions no longer held. Patten and his friends humiliated Atherton, brought him down a peg, and reminded him that anyone "suspected of being an enemy to the liberties of America" could expect no sympathy from the insurgents.[14] After this political baptism, the simmering imperial crisis increasingly drew Matthew beyond the boundaries of Bedford. Like so many other ordinary Americans at the time, his political horizons were expanding. Perhaps even more significant, the diary reveals that without bothering to reflect on the abstract political theories that allegedly justified the rebellion, he now enthusiastically supported organized resistance to an oppressive government.

We can date the tipping point for Matthew and the Patten family with precision. This was the moment when they accepted armed violence as a necessary and legitimate weapon against the government's abuse of power. The early months of 1775 had been tense. Disturbing rumors about the movement of British soldiers circulated throughout

New England. Then, on April 19, more reliable reports reached the towns of southern New Hampshire that "General Gage's troops had fired on our Countrymen at Concord yesterday and had killed a large number of them." Matthew scribbled in his diary that the news was "Melancholy."[15]

The incident triggered a flurry of activity in the Patten household; young and old, men and women, all were caught up in the insurgency. The attack on the Lexington militia had killed people like themselves. An army of occupation was responsible. Matthew's son John and other men from Bedford decided immediately to join the military units preparing to march in support of the irregular forces in Massachusetts who had engaged the retreating British troops after Lexington and Concord and were now taking up defensive positions on the heights surrounding Boston. Matthew expressed pride when "our John and John Dobbin and my brother Samuel's two oldest sons set off and joined Derryfield men and about six from Goffstown and two or three more from this town under the command of Capt John Moore of Derryfield. They amounted to the No. of 45 in all." Matthew's daughters also responded to the revolutionary moment. "Our Girls sit up all night baking bread and fitting things for him [John] and John Dobbin." The boys returned safely in early May. But John Patten was not so fortunate later at the Battle of Bunker Hill. He sustained a serious wound, from which he recovered only after a long convalescence.[16]

While John served in the army, Matthew was busy strengthening the insurgency in southern New Hampshire. The actions of father and son force on us another truth in plain sight, long overlooked. Fielding an impromptu army of armed insurgents who must leave family behind requires thousands more willing to police the local communities. This may mean interrogation of a suspected Tory at a country bridge or searching out loyalist sympathizers, be they Crown appointees or long-time neighbors. On April 26, a few days after his son had departed for Massachusetts, Matthew noted that he had gone "at the desire of the town [Bedford]" to warn several leading figures in the resistance movement "to take Special care of Strangers and persons Suspected of being Torys Crossing the River [and] to Examine and Search [them] if they judge it needful." Gone now were Matthew's former scruples about militancy. He not only joined the Bedford Committee of Safety, he also cooperated with committees from nearby towns in hunting down ideological enemies.

Within these small communities, support for revolution was gathering momentum. On July 3, Patten reported traveling to Amherst "to judge Esqur Whiting for his being a Tory." Matthew could not resist mixing business with politics. On the trip to interrogate Whiting—like Atherton, a so-called esquire whom the committee brought down a notch—he carried a fat salmon that he sold to a friend. Four days later, representatives from four separate committees in the region gathered at Bedford "by the desire of [the] Bedford committee." They came to deal with Matthew's old adversary the Reverend Houston. The members of these committees—from Goffstown, Merrimack, Derryfield, and Bedford—heard the evidence against the minister and declared Houston "Guilty and confined him to the county without leave from the major part of one of the committees of the towns who judged him."[17]

Through the lens of Patten's diary we witness insurgency in small, scattered communities—communities that could not claim to have been the birthplace of a single celebrated Founding Father—evolving into a genuine war against Great Britain. Although Congress had not yet declared independence in early 1776—indeed, although the nation with which the Patten family so fiercely identified existed only in popular imagination—American soldiers were fighting British forces on several fronts.

John reenlisted in an ambitious but disastrously organized expedition against Canada in the spring of 1776. From this service he never returned. Matthew's long diary entry for May 21 exposed a parent's pain upon learning of the death of a child. In his case, grief served to reaffirm a commitment to the American cause; anger fueled a sense of political self-righteousness. Matthew's words remind us of something that is easy to forget. If they were to succeed in mobilizing popular support, revolutions required a lot more than reasoned debate over legal precedent. They had to arouse basic passions.

> I got an account of my John's Death of the Small pox at Canada and When I cam home my wife had got a letter from Bob which gave us a Particular account. It informed us that he was sick of them [the smallpox] at Chambike and that they moved him to

St Johns where they tarried but one night when they moved
him to Isle of Noix where he died . . . the Reason of moving
him was the Retreat of the army which was very perceipatate
and he must either be moved or be left behind . . . He was shot
through his left arm at Bunker Hill fight and now was led after
suffering much fategue to the place where he now lyes in defending the just Rights of America to whose end he came in the
prime of life by means of that wicked Tyranical Brute (nea worse
than Brute) of Great Britain. He was Twenty four years and 31
days old.[18]

## II

From the vantage point of the twenty-first century, we recognize the
members of the Patten family as American patriots. They were also insurgents. Perhaps because of our own insatiable curiosity about prominent American leaders, we have not paid much attention to the
revolutionary experiences of such people as Matthew and John. This is
a mistake. They should be restored to the story. If nothing else, they and
the insurgency they participated in have a lot to tell us about the popular origins of our own political culture, which we, in more modern
times, have too often taken for granted.

We should make clear at the start exactly what we mean by the
American Revolution. The sine qua non of our Revolution—indeed, of
any successful revolution—was the willingness of a sufficient number of
people to take up arms against an unelected imperial government that
no longer served the common good. This moment occurred in America
sometime in mid-1774. If we cannot explain why reasonably contented
colonists suddenly decided to resist the representatives of the king's
government, with violence when necessary, then we will not fully understand the revolutionary character of our own Revolution.

Insurgencies are not movements for the faint of heart. They certainly involve a lot more than a commitment to a set of intellectual
principles. What is demanded of us, therefore, is a greater appreciation
of the kinds of passions that have energized insurgencies throughout
world history. Our revolutionary lexicon will include popular anger and
rage, a desire for revenge, and a feeling of betrayal—harsh concepts,

perhaps, but ones that better reflect the actual revolutionary process than do those encountered in abstract histories of political thought.

The argument is not that the insurgents did not have ideas about politics. They did. But these were ideas driven by immediate passions; they were amplified through fear, fury, and resentment. Moreover, evangelical religion played a much larger role in motivating revolutionary resistance than most historians have recognized. In 1774 the Reverend Nathan Fiske, a respected minister in Brookfield, Massachusetts, explained the emotional calculus of revolution to a New England congregation soon after a British army of occupation closed the port of Boston to all commerce. Anger rather than enlightened debate defined the political moment. "When any act of injustice is practiced upon us," Fiske observed, "we feel ourselves injured, we feel ourselves imposed on and dishonored; and we cannot help feeling our resentments kindle, our anger rise, and our grief excited." Fiske identified the wellspring of successful political resistance. As he argued—using rhetoric that has for a long time gone missing from histories of the Revolution—"sometimes, when the injury is great or long continued, we feel the workings of revenge."[19]

Fiske's was not an isolated voice. Thomas Paine, for one, believed that such a visceral sense of wrong gave life to insurgency. In *Common Sense*—the most popular publication of the entire revolutionary period—he explained how anger could mobilize political discontent. He urged those Americans who in early 1776 still contemplated reconciliation with the rulers of Great Britain to "examine the passions and feelings of mankind." Could anyone at this late date really advocate reasoned negotiations with the enemy? To those who answered in the affirmative, Paine asked, "Hath your house been burnt? Hath your property been destroyed before your face? Are your wife and children destitute of a bed to lie on, or bread to live on? Have you lost a parent or a child by their hands, and yourself the ruined and wretched survivor?" If one could experience such atrocities and still accept the king and Parliament as legitimate symbols of political authority, "then, you are unworthy the name of husband, father, friend, or lover, and whatever may be your rank or title in life, you have the heart of a coward."[20]

Those who today torture the revolutionary record by trying to transform these people into partisans for narrow and selfish causes—as if the sole purpose of the Revolution was the avoidance of taxation—insult the memory of those who once imagined a more just and equitable structure of government. They demanded the kind of political representation that modern Americans celebrate. To be sure, the insurgents did not fight for democracy, but by inviting so many new participants into the political process on the local level and by rejecting a monarchical system of government, with its attendant aristocratic privilege, they transformed the colonial political culture. Thousands of Americans who had never before held office—indeed, who never even imagined that it was their right to do so—flooded into positions of leadership, and between 1774 and 1776 people from New Hampshire to Georgia invented new, highly effective forms of popular resistance. This ranks as one of the most creative moments in American political history.

## *III*

A populist history of the Revolution raises provocative questions about mobilization and commitment, about sustaining resistance within small communities. Imagine, for example, the political ordeal of a young farmer—for our purposes an anonymous individual—who lives in a distant and troubled land. One evening a neighbor approaches him without advance warning, perhaps in a tavern or public meeting place. He has known the man all his life. We might even stipulate that a cousin has married into the other person's extended family. On this particular occasion, however, the visitor seems apprehensive, speaking in hushed, conspiratorial tones. The subject of the meeting is political resistance.

The nervous spokesman announces that other members of the community—all of whom are familiar figures—have decided that they can no longer tolerate an imperial government in which ordinary people have no meaningful voice. The local representatives of the oppressive power must now be driven from office. The time has passed, he declares, for legislative petitions and constitutional appeals. More effective measures are called for. He notes that an extralegal committee has been formed to denounce and, if necessary, to punish individuals whom he describes contemptuously as "the friends of government." The situation is growing desperate. Weapons will be needed; villagers must receive military training. Both men understand that this is an invitation to join the insurgency.

Even to suggest that an imagined conversation of this sort has a legitimate place in a history of the American Revolution may seem irreverent, if not downright subversive. We have come to regard insurgency as a foreign and unpleasant phenomenon that does not apply to our own experience. The problem, of course, is that denial about the popular character of revolutionary resistance serves largely to distort our understanding of the nation's origins. For ordinary Americans confronting the crisis of imperial rule between 1774 and 1776, discussions about insurgency occurred all the time.

The men and women who became insurgents did not initially welcome armed confrontation with Great Britain. They came to political resistance slowly, reluctantly, declaring even as they took up arms against the empire that they wanted to avoid what Samuel Lane, a struggling New Hampshire farmer, called a "Most Unnatural Civil War."[21] At some point, however, they took the next step. They accepted violence against the imperial state as a legitimate form of political resistance.

General Thomas Gage would not have had much sympathy with our scruples about using the term "insurgent" to describe such people. As head of the British forces in America, he found that by mid-1775 — in other words, a full year before the Continental Congress declared national independence — Parliament's authority over the New England countryside had dissolved. He could fulminate against the rebels as much as he liked within the security of Boston, a port city occupied by thousands of British troops, but beyond its fortified perimeter, no one listened to Gage or to the scores of appointed Crown officials who had so assiduously tried to preserve the empire in America. The bonds that tied the colonies to Great Britain had for the most part evaporated by the closing months of 1774, at least in New England.

Into the political vacuum flooded a new kind of enemy. Gage reported to superiors in England that he faced ordinary farmers, armed and angry men prepared to use violence against the state. The Americans, he explained, "deriving confidence from impunity, have added insult to outrage; have repeatedly fired upon the King's ships and subjects, with cannon and small arms, have possessed the roads, and other communications by which the town of Boston was supplied with provisions." On the distant frontier of empire, Gage confronted a rising of the people. The colonists "make daily and indiscriminate invasions upon private property, and with a wantonness of cruelty . . . carry depredation and distress wherever they turn their steps." Government ministers in London convinced themselves that Gage exaggerated. They did not want to hear such disturbing intelligence, and in any case, like the military officers they dispatched to America, parliamentary leaders had no understanding of insurgency.[22]

The phrase "wantonness of cruelty" in Gage's letter catches our eye. The charge may strike us as an example of overwrought language aimed primarily at persuading the king and his advisers that they should crush the rebellion as quickly and as forcefully as possible. Gage's harsh assessment of "depredation and distress" seems at odds with our own celebration of the Sons of Liberty. After all, these are the men who in history books were able to march to victory over the British without ever resorting to the kind of violence that we normally associate with insurgency.

Dismissing Gage's account as an example of highly partisan rhetoric would be wrong. He knew what he was talking about. To understand his confusion and horror and to recapture the shadowy world of popular resistance to the British Empire, we might briefly consider two disquieting incidents. They provide insight into how the Revolution was experienced by people in small communities throughout America.

One event involved the administration of popular justice in a small New Hampshire village, then called Camden. Sometime early in 1774—again, a long time before the Declaration of Independence—John Taylor somehow managed to offend his neighbors. The details of his transgression remain obscure. The local records are fragmentary, perhaps purposely evasive. It seems that during the anxious months following the destruction of the tea in Boston Harbor, Taylor had voiced support for parliamentary policies. He may have openly counseled political moderation at a time when other colonists sanctioned armed resistance to the British Empire. Whatever he may have done, a group of local men and women decided to address the problem. The method they selected drew upon customs that could be traced back in histories of European agrarian communities more than two centuries.

John Steele and Moses Jewell forced Taylor to ride a wooden horse. The procedure, intended to humiliate the victim as well as to administer pain, involved placing Taylor on a long fence rail. After his tormentors had secured him on the horse, they bounced him up and down while other participants "beat & kicked [him] with Fists & Feet." The ride lasted fifteen minutes, leaving Taylor, according to later court testimony, "very much bruised." Before his neighbors grew tired, the ordeal took a particularly ugly turn—whether by accident or design, we shall never know—for a sharp edge of the fence rail cut deeply into Taylor's groin, leaving a "mortal wound on the private parts of his body of the length of six inches [and] of the breadth four inches." The precision of the measurement seems in itself curiously gruesome. Within a short time, Taylor bled to death. A political warning in an isolated community had ended in homicide.[23]

What distinguished the New Hampshire incident from peasant tradition—what made it in some sense a modern event—was its revolutionary context. Taylor may well have been an abrasive neighbor; he may even have taken advantage of them in business dealings. What led to his death, however, were his political beliefs. John Steele, Moses Jewell, Robert Blood, Jr., and Jane Steele appeared before a New Hampshire court for killing a man who apparently had not supported the American resistance to parliamentary taxation with sufficient enthusiasm. A diary kept at the time by a quite ordinary man indicates that the trial generated great interest throughout the region. People cared about the verdict.[24] In September 1774 the judges found John Steele guilty of manslaughter and the other three of abetting the crime. But they all escaped serious punishment. Steele petitioned successfully for "benefit of clergy," a feudal relic of a distant legal past that allowed him to be branded on his thumb and to forfeit some property. Since his neighbors elected him for a civil office in 1779, it does not seem that Taylor's death greatly compromised Steele's standing in the community. The other "yeomen"—and this included Jane—who had assisted Steele slipped away, forgiven by a revolutionary public for an insurgent act that somehow got out of hand.

General Gage had probably learned of a similar event that occurred in Halifax, Massachusetts, early in 1775. Insurgents had recently swept the countryside clean of all officials in the colonial establishment who remained openly loyal to the Crown. People who had not resigned royal commissions issued by Governor Thomas Hutchinson found themselves the objects of special attention. Daniel Dunbar refused to be intimidated. As ensign in the local militia, he would not stand down. However courageous he may have been in defense of principle, he was politically naïve. The colonists who during this period had taken it upon themselves to enforce revolutionary discipline soon visited him. Their identities were never disclosed; they appeared in the documents only as members of a "mob." They insisted that Dunbar surrender his colors, the symbol of his military office. When he failed to cooperate, his neighbors—he later claimed that he could identify several village selectmen as participants—broke into his house and, according to one report, "took him out, forced him upon a rail, and was held [down] on it by his hands and legs, and tossed up with violence." Dunbar had struggled to avoid the wooden horse, but the insurgents "seized him by his private parts to drag him on it, then beat him." After enduring two or three hours of torture, the hapless ensign agreed "to give his colors up to save his life."25

We may find the actions of the American insurgents between 1774 and 1776 distasteful. It is comforting to view them exclusively as American patriots arrayed behind George Washington in combat for nuanced principles concerning republican governance. But this seriously discounts their accomplishments and distorts the history of the Revolution. Revolutions do not sustain themselves through ideas alone. Just as there is no denying that when we open our eyes to it, the evidence of ordinary Americans mobilizing in response to parliamentary insults and an army of occupation, forging common bonds of sympathy throughout all thirteen colonies, and creating an infrastructure to support and drive forward revolution in the years ahead of the Declaration of Independence is overwhelming.

## *IV*

*American Insurgents, American Patriots* follows a rough chronological path. After describing the colonial society that spawned resistance and reviewing the actions of a British ruling class determined at a moment of imperial crisis to be tough whatever the consequences, we examine the spontaneous political rage that swept through the New England countryside during the summer of 1774. This was the time when thousands of ordinary people actively joined the resistance to Great Britain. Within a few short weeks they drove royal officials from their communities throughout Massachusetts and forced them to seek security within an occupied city.

During this period New Englanders first learned—or thought that they had learned—that the main British battle fleet had destroyed Boston. It made no difference that the story was false, a rumor that acquired credibility through repeated retelling. Within hours, a huge army marched toward the ruined port, determined to revenge what turned out to be an imagined atrocity. This massive insurgency—military units from four different colonies operating without clear command structure—caught the members of the Continental Congress off guard. The surge of popular militancy forced the delegates to adopt political positions more radical in character than they had envisioned when they first gathered in Philadelphia in early September 1774.

Even during the days of popular rage, American militants recognized that successful resistance required cooperation. Had unhappy colonists in South Carolina or Pennsylvania decided—as well they might have—to ignore New England's appeal for support, the rising of 1774 would have yielded pathetic results. Those who supported the insurgency had to forge ways to communicate effectively with other Americans who had not directly experienced the humiliating presence of British troops.

In dealing with this problem, ordinary Americans showed remarkable creativity. They turned an appeal for charity—an ambitious enterprise designed to support the poor and unemployed people of occupied Boston—into a huge political network. Distant strangers came forward with a few pennies or several bushels of grain for an "American cause." Gifts of this sort have never struck modern historians as part of the central story of political resistance. But it was. For many people, even the smallest tokens represented the first step in mobilization, not threatening in itself, perhaps, but a personal decision taken publicly that indicated the fabrication of a new political consciousness.

The key to expanding the insurgency was communication. Americans contemplated even at this early date the establishment of a new postal system that would keep their messages safe from the prying eyes of British authorities. And without newspapers—without a constant flow of news documenting that colonists in other places were advancing the revolution by protesting, denouncing enemies, enforcing boycotts, collecting money for Boston—it would have been impossible for the militants to construct during 1774 and 1775 the sense of mutual trust upon which organized resistance ultimately depends. It was through these channels of information that the insurgency generated a collective commitment to revolution.

The middle chapters ask how—during a second stage of insurgency—Americans managed to channel spontaneous rage into a viable movement for colonial liberation. During this period our Revolution could have turned into a bloodbath. In other political cultures throughout the world, violence has led to anarchy, and in these situations the very people who called for resistance against arbitrary rule have come to regret that they opened Pandora's box in the first place. Yet while many Americans feared that militancy could destroy the social fabric, it did not do so. To understand the containment of revolutionary violence— its use as a weapon against ideological enemies—we look not to congressional leaders, but rather to how the insurgents sustained and strengthened resistance on the ground. In small communities throughout the country, scores of men who previously had had no meaningful voice in political affairs served on local committees that during late 1774 and early 1775 became the de facto government.

Variously called committees of safety, or committees of safety and observation, these groups provided a revolutionary infrastructure. As they assumed the power to govern, however, they generally chose to observe rough legal procedures, warning and shaming enemies rather than killing them. In an impressively creative move, local committees throughout America transformed the Articles of Association—an act originally passed by the First Continental Congress in 1774 to enforce a boycott on British commerce with the colonies—into a kind of provisional constitution. By citing articles from the Association as justification for revolutionary action, the committees avoided the charge of behaving in an arbitrary manner. To be sure, loyalists never bought the argument, but it allowed the committees to manage the insurgency while minimizing the threat of anarchy. And of course, once so many ordinary people had experienced such a heady sense of social empowerment, they found it hard to turn back the clock to the days when aristocratic pretenders demanded deference.

Finally, we consider what the insurgents believed. What ideas gave meaning to the revolutionary experience? There is no need to scour ancient classical or Renaissance texts to find the answer. Ordinary people—the kinds of men who flocked to revenge the destruction of Boston—responded to ideas that justified immediate revolutionary action. They may not have read the works of the great English philosopher John Locke—many may not have even recognized his name—but they were quite sure that they possessed basic, God-given rights that protected them from arbitrary rule. Faced with a terrifying confrontation with Great Britain, they made "An Appeal to Heaven."

And during the spring of 1775 ordinary people turned in huge numbers to *The Crisis* to help understand why they had to resist Great Britain. It was a shrill, angry publication that spoke of God's demand for the revenge of injustice. By any measure *The Crisis* was a bestseller, exceeded in readership only by Thomas Paine's *Common Sense*, issued a few months later. But however powerfully it spoke to the American insurgents, *The Crisis* has been dropped from the story we tell ourselves about the Revolution. Our reconstruction of the world of Matthew Patten forces us to ask why.

# ONE

# The Face of Colonial Society

Hannah Leighton never sought notoriety. In 1835, in fact, one would have predicted that Hannah would die as she had lived, an obscure farmer's wife who had spent most of her days in Acton, a small village in Massachusetts. That was not to be. Because of a surge of patriotic enthusiasm that swept through early-nineteenth-century New England, people turned to Hannah to learn about their own revolutionary heritage. In her eighty-ninth year, members of this small community, most of whom had been born long after Americans first rejected British rule, asked her to tell them what had happened one extraordinary April morning sixty years earlier.

As a young woman, Hannah had been married to her first husband, Isaac Davis. He was the type of American whom the British never understood. In 1775 he was thirty years old, in good health, and, by the standards of the day, reasonably prosperous. He supported a growing family largely through farming. He supplemented his income as a gunsmith. At the time, neighbors seem to have regarded Isaac as a genial man with lots of energy. He was also an insurgent.

Despite her age in 1835, Hannah vividly recalled the events of April 19, 1775. One thing that helped focus her thoughts was the memory of being an anxious mother caring for several sick infants. The youngest child was only fifteen months old. The children suffered from "canker-rash," a potentially fatal condition. Although her own revolutionary moment may have begun with the noise of fussing babies, her

neighbors awoke to a much more ominous sound. Shouts of alarm re-
verberated throughout the sleepy community. A messenger from nearby
Concord appeared in the village, slowed down before Captain Joseph
Robbins's house, and, without coming to a full stop, beat on the corner
of the building with a large stick, yelling as he passed, "Captain Robbins!
Captain Robbins! Up! Up! The Regulars have come to Concord."

For Robbins, captain of the Acton militia, the news did not come as
a complete surprise. He had prepared for such a possibility. So too had
the other people of Acton. Fathers and sons had been training seriously
as soldiers for many weeks. If they entertained doubts about the seriousness of the British challenge, they had only to listen to the words of the
Reverend William Emerson. This highly regarded minister from Concord had recently delivered at the Acton church a fiery sermon that
seemed to endorse armed resistance against tyranny. He asked the parishioners to consider the full implications of 2 Chronicles 13:12, "Behold
God himself is with us for our captain, and his priests with sounding
trumpets to cry alarm against you."

Robbins immediately galloped off to the Davis home. Isaac had
been selected some months earlier as captain of the Acton Minutemen.
This special rapid-response force had been busy studying military tactics, and because Isaac was an accomplished metalworker, he had made
sure that his men were equipped with state-of-the-art bayonets and car-
tridge boxes. He had even set up a shooting range behind his house,
where the Minutemen practiced marksmanship. Davis was also the
kind of person who without effort inspires trust. As Hannah explained
many years later, "Between him [and] his Company, there was strong
attachment [and] unlimited confidence." She added, "He well knew
his danger, but was a stranger to fear."

As the sun rose, Davis's fellow soldiers turned up at his house. Nervous, no doubt a little frightened by the prospect that lay before them,
they made cartridges for their guns in Hannah's yard. Two hours passed
before they were fully prepared to march for Concord, which lay only a
few miles to the east. Hannah watched her husband closely, attentive to
subtle shifts of mood that only a wife could perceive. "My husband said
but little that morning," she recounted. "He seemed serious and thought-
ful; but never seemed to hesitate as to the course of his duty." Finally it
was time to move out. Hannah must have waved. Isaac paused. "As he

led the company from the house, he turned round, and seemed to have something to communicate. He only said 'take good care of the children,' and was soon out of sight."

The Acton Minutemen joined other soldiers who had rushed to Concord from the surrounding towns. No one was quite sure who had overall command of the Americans who were taking up positions on the edge of the village not far from the famed bridge. Colonel James Barrett eventually took charge, but he looked nothing like a proper soldier. Witnesses remembered Barrett dressed in "an old coat, a flapped hat, and a leather apron." The fidgety troops watched as the British searched Concord for weapons and powder. Smoke began to rise, suggesting that the enemy intended to burn the entire community. One lieutenant from Acton could stand it no longer and asked Barrett pointedly, "Will you let them burn the town?" Davis for one was ready to confront the enemy. He drew his sword, announcing to the assembled insurgents in what may have been his last recorded words, "I haven't a man who is afraid to go." The colonists loaded their guns and began marching toward the bridge. The British fired. One of the first volleys hit Davis in the chest. He probably died on the spot. Another shot killed his lieutenant.

What happened on April 19 is the stuff of legend. Enraged Americans dogged the retreating British units all the way to Boston. They administered a stinging defeat to an army of occupation. For Hannah, the events of the day profoundly transformed her life. She waited for hours for news from Concord. "In the afternoon," she explained many years later, Isaac "was brought home a corpse. He was placed in my bedroom till the funeral. His countenance was pleasant, and seemed little altered."[1]

For the people of nineteenth-century Acton, Isaac was a hero, a patriot who had died defending American rights and liberty. They were correct. Isaac was also a man whom we would now identify as an insurgent. Long before he led the Minutemen to Concord, he had accepted the possibility—even the necessity—of using armed violence against British authority. When he paused that morning and turned to Hannah, he probably considered parting endearments. Perhaps with his men standing nearby, he felt that such an open declaration of affection might be out of place, a sign of uncertainty. We shall never know. But whatever his thoughts may have been, we can imagine that he did in fact "have something to communicate." More than two centuries after the event, Isaac Davis asks us to reflect on how ordinary people—in families and small communities—became central figures in the overthrow of imperial rule.

Of the many surviving accounts of the fight, one in particular helps us to comprehend the mental world of Hannah and Isaac Davis. It highlights an unfamiliar language of anger and revenge; it takes on board the raw emotional energy needed to mobilize popular resistance. Writing as Johannes in Eremo in a Salem newspaper on the morning of April 20, the Reverend John Cleaveland announced, "Great Britain, adieu! No longer shall we honor you as our mother; you are become cruel . . . We have cried to you for justice, but behold violence and bloodshed!" As for General Gage, Cleaveland declared that the demands of the people of New England for revenge "will not be satisfied till your blood is shed, and the blood of every son of violence under your command."[2]

The Reverend Jonas Clark spoke to the people of Lexington exactly one year after the battle. Entitled "The Fate of Blood-Thirsty Oppressors," Clark's sermon invited a Lexington congregation to revisit the April morning when British troops first appeared. "They approach with the morning's light," he explained, "and more like murderers and cutthroats, than the troops of a Christian king, without provocation, without warning, when no war was proclaimed, they draw the sword of violence, upon the inhabitants of this town." The enemy shed "INNOCENT BLOOD" on the nineteenth of April. Americans courageously stood their ground, and Clark assured those who had lost sons and husbands—the Hannah Davises of New England—that the sacrifice had not been in vain. "Surely there is one that avengeth, and that will plead the cause of the injured and oppressed; and in his own way and time, will both cleanse and avenge their innocent blood."[3] Long after the nation had won its independence, Hannah, who bore nine children and survived to the age of ninety-six, continued to remind her neighbors of a time when American patriots had been insurgents.

# I

The insurgents who most often go missing from modern narratives of revolution were ordinary people. That adjective, "ordinary," should not carry erroneous connotations—suggesting perhaps that the men and women in the forefront of resistance were somehow mediocre or undistinguished. They were anything but. Other terms, however, are even less satisfactory. To label someone like Isaac Davis a common person or an average American, for example, implies that we possess statistical data that would make it possible to depict a particular colonist as in some meaningful way average. Such records do not exist. Davis and the other militiamen who appeared at Concord probably would have accepted an eighteenth-century terminology, which identified them as "middling sorts." For our purposes, however, "ordinary" works as well as any of the alternatives.

Whatever descriptive language we adopt, we should recognize immediately that we are dealing with a huge percentage of the colonial population on the eve of independence. The insurgents were generally drawn from white farm families—in other words, from a body of people who made up approximately 70 percent of the free inhabitants. What one newspaper reported for Pennsylvania in 1756 was broadly accurate for ordinary Americans as a whole, especially for those who lived north of Virginia: "The people of this province are generally of the middling sort, and at present pretty much upon a level."[4] This middling group of colonists pointedly did not include the large number of African Americans, most of whom were slaves. Nor did it embrace the 3 or 4 percent of the population whom we might classify as members of the provincial elite, the extremely small segment of American society that currently dominates our understanding of the coming of revolution. Like the elite gentlemen, these ordinary men and women made decisions that affect us all; unlike them, they lived in a world that has entirely slipped from popular sight. After 250 years, all that is readily apparent is that Hannah and Isaac Davis—and tens of thousands of people like them—drew upon the ideas and circumstances of their own time when they rejected imperial authority.[5]

The Davises came of age in a society that had experienced extraordinary population growth. Indeed, at least since the 1740s colonists had pushed the rates of increase almost to their biological limit. Benjamin Franklin, who, along with other accomplishments, was one of the first mathematical demographers, calculated that the American population was doubling approximately every twenty-five years. This finding meant that the number of people alive had increased some 125 percent between 1740 and 1770. The figures varied from region to region. The Middle Colonies such as Pennsylvania grew faster than did those in New England. But about the overall results, there could be no dispute. Franklin fully appreciated the impact that tens of thousands of German, Scotch-Irish, and English immigrants had had on expansion, but he rightly concluded that the key element in population growth was the high reproduction rates among people already living in British America. More couples were having more babies. Franklin claimed that the numbers reflected a lowering of the age of first marriage, a trend that allowed young mothers more years in which to bear children. Other factors were at work, of course. General economic prosperity, reliable supplies of food, and availability of cheap land also contributed to the peopling of the colonies.

When a population expands as fast as it did in America, the overall age structure shifts dramatically. Accelerated growth means that at any given time, a large percentage of the population will consist of young people. We know, for example, that throughout the Revolution about half of the total number of colonists were under the age of sixteen.

The implication of this youth culture for an account of the coming of independence is profound. General treatments of the history of imperial breakdown often begin in 1763, with the formal conclusion of the Seven Years' War, or in 1765, with the passage of the hated Stamp Act. Such narratives of political discontent assume a kind of momentum; discontent mounts year after year as king and Parliament refuse to address the colonists' grievances. But the logic of this slowly evolving story becomes strained when we realize that many of the insurgents of 1775 had been little children during the early 1760s.

John Patten, for example, the young New Hampshire man who died during the abortive campaign against Canada in 1776, had been eight years old when France and Great Britain concluded the Seven Years' War. He was only ten during the Stamp Act crisis. No doubt he and other even younger Americans learned about the significance of these events from adults. As Joseph Plumb Martin, a Connecticut farm boy who served in the army throughout the entire war, recounted, "I remember the stir in the country occasioned by the Stamp Act, but I was so young that I did not understand the meaning of it; I likewise remember the disturbances that followed the repeal of the Stamp Act, until the destruction of the tea at Boston and elsewhere; I was then thirteen or fourteen years old, and began to understand something of the works going on."[6] In short, many of the young insurgents who appeared at Concord had not taken part in previous confrontations with royal authority. Their knowledge of earlier controversies was secondhand. What young insurgents knew—in intimate and direct terms—was a sudden surge of popular violence that occurred during the summer of 1774 and culminated in the killing of Americans at Lexington and Concord. The point is not that the previous generations' conflicts with imperial policy were irrelevant. Rather, it was the case that they did not ignite the anger and passion that inflamed an insurgency.

Late colonial America was a small-scale society. Its approximately two million free white inhabitants had carved out farms and plantations over an immense territory stretching along the Atlantic Coast from the modern state of Maine to Georgia and at most several hundred miles inland. Although the stories we tell ourselves about the Revolution usually concentrate on events that occurred in cities—the Boston Tea Party or the debates of the Continental Congress in Philadelphia—an urban focus is misleading. Most provincial families lived in very small communities, often towns or villages of only several hundred inhabitants. Even such centers of intense revolutionary activity as Worcester, Massachusetts, and Wilmington, North Carolina, numbered fewer than two thousand people.

The overwhelming majority of the revolutionary generation spent its time on family farms, and meetings that brought neighbors together to address common affairs had to be scheduled around the demands of the agricultural calendar. Within these communities, no one was a stranger; families had long histories that, even when not openly discussed, were never forgotten. These were intimate, face-to-face settings— at church, the local store for imported goods, the county courts—in which few secrets, be they religious, political, or personal, were secure, and although ordinary Americans probably tolerated some idiosyncratic beliefs and behavior, they could bring powerful pressure to bear on dissenters who openly defied local norms.

In early America farm families were not economically self-sufficient. People like Hannah and Isaac Davis took for granted an impressive flow of manufactured goods that originated in England and were distributed throughout the eighteenth-century British Empire in ever-greater quantities. Textiles were the major import, about half of the total amount, and small rural stores from Georgia to New Hampshire offered customers — often on easy credit — a wide range of colorful and affordable fabrics. Metal items and glassware, medicines and children's toys transformed the consumer experience at mid-century. Indeed, this period was the first time in which the middling sorts of America, Holland, and England could select from among competing goods that promised anyone possessing even a little amount of money greater beauty, warmth, health, and status. On the eve of independence, Americans spent on average almost a third of their total incomes on imported goods.[7]

The availability of an exciting spectrum of manufactured goods imported from England provided an incentive to greater productivity. Of course, no family farm could afford to ignore the basic requirements of survival. Children had to be fed, animals cared for, and seed put away for future plantings. What was new for this generation of colonial Americans was a radical reorganization of family labor, so that more family members — wives, for example — engaged in producing surpluses that could be exchanged in the marketplace for manufactured items. Ordinary Americans may have prided themselves on having achieved a measure of independence in the New World, but every time they dealt with a merchant, they were reminded of the tenuous nature of that independence. Whether they produced tobacco or wheat, small farmers found themselves increasingly tied to a complex Atlantic economy. A change in the prices offered for American products in London, Glasgow, or the West Indies was a matter of huge significance in small provincial villages.[8]

One unintended consequence of this eighteenth-century consumer-oriented marketplace was a growing desire among ordinary people for news of the world. Newspapers entered the lives of ordinary Americans originally as commercial journals. At the beginning of the century Boston had the only weekly colonial newspaper, but by the time of the Revolution, scores of towns turned out papers. They carried advertisements for imported goods as well as stories about distant wars and royal ceremony. We do not know how many ordinary people were fully literate. The best estimate is that free white males in New England achieved very high rates of literacy, perhaps more than 80 percent. The women did not lag far behind. The southern colonies did not score as well, but even in Virginia and the Carolinas, newspapers enjoyed an impressive readership.[9]

During the early decades of the eighteenth century these publications tended to focus on general news from England and Europe, but as the imperial crisis became more threatening, colonists began to pay more attention to reports from other areas of British America. A medium that originally served the interests of Atlantic commerce took on a political character and provided Americans separated by great distances with a network through which they communicated a common revolutionary experience.

By the standards of contemporary Europe, white colonists enjoyed remarkable social equality. The process of settlement seemed to have removed two groups encountered throughout the Old World. The members of the aristocracy never found migration appealing; the desperately poor could not afford the trip. In every colony a provincial elite developed that had greater wealth than did the ordinary farmers. Great planters in the South and substantial merchants in the North lived not only well but also quite visibly. But as anyone who traveled the English countryside during the eighteenth century quickly discovered, the privileged Americans were parvenus compared with the lords and ladies who constructed huge Palladian mansions in places such as Kent and Essex. That, no doubt, contributed to the fact that while middling colonists deferred to those who had more wealth, doffing the cap and scraping the boot, they never accepted the notion that richer meant better.

When push came to shove in local matters, ordinary Americans certainly had no compunction about aggressively speaking out for what they regarded as their just rights. Thomas Anburey, a British officer captured during the Revolution, learned firsthand how little weight traditional social distinctions carried in Virginia. Anburey was witness when Colonel Thomas Mann Randolph, master of an estate known as Tuckahoe, was forced to entertain some local "peasants." Anburey reported that the men "entered the room where the Colonel and his company were sitting, took themselves chairs, drew near the fire, began spitting, pulling off their country boots all over mud, and then opened their business." How, the indignant British officer asked, could a great planter stand for such insulting behavior? Randolph patiently explained, "It was unavoidable, the spirit of independency was converted into equality, and every one who bore arms, esteemed himself upon a footing with his neighbour." He confessed, "No doubt, each of these men conceives himself, in every respect, my equal."[10]

However little respect these mud-covered Virginia farmers showed to Randolph, they would not have allowed such behavior in their own homes by a tenant, servant, or slave. People who were clearly dependent, or poor, or belonged to another race never dared to assume such an air of equality. The presence of so many enslaved African Americans in colonial society meant that whiteness in itself became a marker of special standing. This was the case not only in the plantation South, but also in New England and New York, where slavery persisted even in small country villages. At horse races and country taverns, in exchanges at the courthouse square or at militia training, white men could respect one another's "equality" precisely because black slaves were permanently excluded from such conversations.[11]

Ownership of land sustained the ordinary farmer's feisty sense of personal independence. One way or another, diligent families acquired sufficient acreage to support themselves and, in time, to participate in the consumer marketplace. Even though wages in urban centers were high, colonists preferred the agrarian life to working for another person. As one commentator noted in 1775, "In America . . . all sorts of people turn farmers . . . [There was] no mechanic or artisan — sailor — soldier — servant, &c., but what, if they get money, take land, and turn farmers."[12] One of the many reasons why British colonists and Native Americans engaged in almost perpetual war was that ordinary farmers insisted on pushing west from the coastal settlements into the Ohio Valley and the Appalachian South, where their almost insatiable desire for acreage sparked lethal conflicts. The frontiers of Maine and Vermont attracted other land-hungry colonists. Although in the pages of American history land speculators are usually reviled for sharp business practices, they performed an important economic function by making farms of modest size available to buyers who possessed little money or needed credit. Of course, as many colonial officials discovered after the Seven Years' War, squatters did not scruple about legal title. They established homesteads wherever they pleased and, when challenged, defended their right to every inch of land carved out of the wilderness.

Even those Americans who thoroughly disliked squatters—and this was a vocal group—accepted the notion that land and personal independence went hand in hand. Ownership promoted a spirit of possessive individualism; it served to make plausible a powerful grammar of political resistance. This core assumption about the structure of society helps to explain in part why ordinary people reacted so vehemently to parliamentary attempts to tax them without representation. They persuaded themselves that if they ever acceded to an unconstitutional tax—however small—they would soon find their land at risk. Arbitrary seizure was a slippery slope; today one might be forced to pay a few pence on tea, tomorrow one might lose the entire farm. The British dismissed such fears as unreasonable, hysteria founded on ignorance, but they missed a crucial psychological point. In colonial America, a well-developed culture of landed independence had the capacity to generate formidable political passion.

In the development of insurgency, evangelical Protestantism probably played an even more significant role than did the possession of land. In terms of understanding the world of Hannah and Isaac Davis—indeed, for comprehending the mentality of the great majority of ordinary people throughout America—the sudden and massive adoption of a new kind of religion that appealed more to the heart than to the head radically changed the character of colonial society. This assertion may not be welcome news to those who today prefer describing the members of the revolutionary generation as children of the Enlightenment—in other words, thoroughly reasonable men and women who carefully digested the works of various European political theorists before breaking with Great Britain. The assumption driving this depiction seems to be that reasoned arguments about politics and religious beliefs are incompatible. Alexis de Tocqueville, a brilliant early-nineteenth-century commentator on American society, knew better. Whenever he encountered an American, Tocqueville asked "if he thinks religion is useful for the stability of law and the good order of society; he immediately responds that a civilized society, but above all a free society, cannot subsist without religion. Respect for religion, in his eyes, is the greatest guarantee of the stability of the state and the security of individuals."[13]

Ordinary colonists confronting the British Empire did not see the world in dichotomous terms that separated political considerations from religious perspectives. The two spheres of human imagination overlapped, often reinforcing each other. Americans who became insurgents accepted scientific evidence; for the most part they did not put much stock in miracles. Earthquakes and fierce storms may have suggested that God was unhappy with their behavior, but natural phenomena of these sorts still had to be investigated. Colonial Americans followed the rhythms of commerce, performed modest agricultural experiments to improve crop yields, and took medicine when they felt ill. They did all these things without doubting the existence of a god who had the ability to intervene in political affairs.

Most American families who found themselves caught up in revolution were the children of the Great Awakening, a series of revivals that began during the 1740s and over the next four decades transformed the face of popular religion. Although many ministers championed evangelical religion at mid-century, the leading figure in the awakening of America was the Reverend George Whitefield, a young Anglican preacher from England who spoke to enthusiastic audiences not about church doctrines, but about intense feelings. He preached to whoever would listen. "Don't tell me you are a Baptist, an Independent, a Presbyterian, a Dissenter," Whitefield declared, "tell me you are a Christian, that is all I want."[14] He drew huge crowds. In Philadelphia and Boston many thousands came to hear him, an astounding achievement. These port cities had only fifteen to twenty thousand residents. The results in smaller country towns were equally impressive.[15]

Whitefield never claimed to be an original theologian. It was the drama of performance that riveted attention. In a voice so emotionally expressive that it provoked the jealousy of the greatest Shakespearean actors of the day, he asked people from all regions to put their complete faith in Christ, to open themselves to the experience of a "new birth," and to confess their utter dependence on an all-powerful God. It was a demanding message. But it worked. The impact of his visits amazed colonial commentators; they had never witnessed such a charismatic figure. Isaiah Thomas, the editor of a leading New England newspaper, reported "this celebrated itinerant preacher, when he visited America, like a comet, drew the attention of all classes of people. The blaze of his ministration was extended through the continent, and he became the common topic of conversation from Georgia to New Hampshire."[16] Whitefield's critics labeled him an anti-intellectual or a madman; they worried that his itinerancy would undermine established denominations and in his wake leave a trail of confusion, even spiritual anarchy, threatening the entire social order.

The consequences of the revivals were never as horrific as frightened conservatives predicted. They did have a point, however. No one who had personally witnessed Whitefield's enthusiastic reception could doubt that the religious landscape in America had changed forever. Leading revivalists invited ordinary people to challenge the authority, even the legitimacy, of their own ministers. Whitefield gave them a voice in religious affairs, and in congregation after congregation they spoke up as they never had done before. They demanded that their ministers demonstrate evidence of the new birth. They insisted that spiritual leaders preach from the heart, not from the book. And throughout America, from cities to frontier villages, they traveled to open-air prayer meetings where they begged the itinerants to tell them what they had to do to be saved.

The revivals came in waves, dying down and then returning with even greater intensity. Established churches were not immune to the force sweeping through the colonies. Lutherans and Congregationalists adopted evangelical techniques. So too did Presbyterians and Baptists. People who experienced the new faith often found that they could no longer endure listening to their old ministers. They turned their backs on friends and neighbors, becoming Separates or Universalists, and marked out different, purer paths to salvation. As might be expected, these groups were highly unstable, subdividing as soon as a member articulated a new, more radical form of spirituality. It is impossible to state with certainty how many Americans at mid-century experienced a new birth through evangelical Protestantism. Young people came forward in large numbers. Some adults reported repeated conversions. No region was spared.[17]

By the time colonial insurgents organized armed resistance to British rule, local revivals and divisions within congregations over the character of preaching had become so common that almost no one living outside the affected community bothered to comment. Ministers who wanted to keep their jobs accommodated to the new evangelical preaching style. Of course, critics continued to speak out against the revivals, warning that enthusiasm and feeling were not legitimate substitutes for traditional theology. Not a few loyalists blamed the entire collapse of British authority in America on radical Protestant ministers. Peter Oliver, a wealthy Boston Tory, thought that "the Black Regiment" stirred up resentment against Parliament. The ministers, he insisted, were unschooled, unprincipled, and dangerous. This "Set of Priests" were "a Disgrace to Christianity, & would have been the Opprobrium of even Mahometism."[18] In most small farming villages, complaints of this sort did not have much impact. The roads of America carried streams of itinerants. They defined religion in New England. They flooded the southern colonies. They brought word of the new birth to the backcountry.[19]

One particularly poignant description of this transformed religious landscape comes not from the pen of a celebrated evangelical clergyman, but rather from the diary of an ordinary woman who lived on a modest farm on Long Island, New York. During the late 1760s Mary Cooper seems to have been suffering from depression. A middle-aged mother of several children, she complained bitterly of a marriage gone bad. If she had had the opportunity, she would surely have divorced her husband. But legal escape was not an option. To assuage her disappointment and to flee occasionally from a suffocating domestic situation, she never missed a chance to hear one of the itinerant preachers who regularly passed through her town. These were extremely obscure figures; no one even recorded their names. In June 1769 she attended a Quaker meeting "where a multitude were gathered to hear a woman preach that lately came from England." Soon thereafter she heard a sermon delivered by an "Indian preacher." She hung on to the words of African American itinerants. Cooper reported listening to "some Indians and one Black man" preach an entire day. Only a week later she traveled to an evangelical service where "a Black man" delivered the sermon. Cooper's awakening reminds us that long after Whitefield first came to

America, people possessing no formal training were traveling from community to community. In this open, fluid environment, blacks and Indians—as well as scores of forgotten white itinerants—spoke powerfully to the religious needs of middling men and women, many of whom would come to reject imperial rule.[20]

Many itinerants who followed in Whitefield's wake expressed not the slightest interest in political affairs. The claim for religion's impact on the political culture is, therefore, more subtle. The revivals provided ordinary colonists with a persuasive, emotionally satisfying framework within which they interpreted ongoing political events. Evangelical religion gave meaning to everyday human experience; it was a template situated between the individual and an increasingly unstable external world. As a Philadelphia writer explained during the spring of 1774, "The man who refuses to assert his right to liberty—property—and life—is guilty of the worst kind of rebellion. He commits high treason against GOD."[21]

It is true that many Founding Fathers subscribed to forms of Deism. These educated gentlemen put their faith in a reasonable God of the Enlightenment. This bundle of ideas, which we associate with such figures as Benjamin Franklin and Thomas Jefferson, did not resonate convincingly with the militiamen who actually turned out to defend communities like Lexington and Concord. Nor did it reflect the religious beliefs of ordinary parents who encouraged children to support the insurgency. On July 31, 1775, for example, Lydia Gray wrote to her son Lieutenant Ebenezer Gray, who had just joined Connecticut troops on the American line outside Boston. She had recently learned "that you are preparing to meet the enemy, or to drive them from their new entrenchments. I could not hear it without some emotion of soul, although I firmly believe God is able to deliver and will deliver us out of the hands of these unnatural enemies in his own time . . . I would commit you into the hands of a just and merciful God, who alone is able to defend you . . . Trust in the Lord and be of good courage; the eye of the Lord is upon them that fear him; upon them that hope in his mercy . . . I am more afraid of our sins than of all the forces of our enemy." Lydia Gray signed her letter, "Your loving mother." Here is evidence of a religious culture in which the American victory at Bunker Hill could plausibly be compared to Old Testament stories about

God's special relationship with the Jewish people. "Had it not been the Lord who was on our side when such a number of troops rose up and surrounded our people, then they had swallowed us up quick when their wrath was kindled against us."[22]

Those who wish to posit a slow, simmering discontent among American colonists from 1765 forward run into a confounding fact: until the summer of 1774—even later for some people—a majority of white colonists expressed genuine pride in being members of the British Empire. Theirs was a loose political identity. To be sure, learned writers worried a lot about the precise character of the many possessions throughout the world that Britain ruled, and they speculated at length on whether the British had created an empire of conquest like the ancient Romans or something more modern, an empire of commerce.[23] For most Americans, however, such conjecture was not a matter of pressing concern. They thought that the British Empire—whatever its theoretical justification among European states—was a very good thing. And when pushed to expand on the sources of satisfaction, they put forward a series of political clichés about what made the British system preferable to that of the French or Spanish.

The British Empire, the colonists fervently insisted, brought liberty and prosperity to all the king's subjects. The explanation for such an achievement could be found in the unique history of the English people. The argument contained three separate strands. First, over many centuries—indeed, long before anyone seriously contemplated settling the New World—England had developed the famed balanced constitution. Contemporaries regarded it as one of the great marvels of the age. The Crown, the House of Lords, and the House of Commons represented competing interests within the political nation, and since each possessed an independent voice in the passage of law, they balanced one another's ambitions for greater power. The concept had many obvious flaws. Commentators regularly observed that the three parts of the constitutional structure were not in fact separate or balanced; they overlapped in ways that sustained the dominance of a landed elite. For Americans, however, the realities of everyday politics in London did not in the least compromise their faith in the balanced constitution. They were neither fools nor hypocrites. They simply ignored elements that did not sustain abstract theory and insisted that without the British constitution, they would become the slaves of distant tyrants.[24]

The second element distinguishing the British Empire of the eighteenth century from its European competitors was Protestantism. Religious confession energized national identity. An English person assumed an obligation not only to uphold the constitution but also to resist the spread of Catholicism. Not surprisingly, the seeds of England's dislike of Catholicism—an emotion that came close to mass hysteria—could be found in the history of the English Reformation. Henry VIII broke with the pope, and then his strong-willed daughter Elizabeth I turned back the Spanish Armada in 1588. The Spanish had intended to root out the religious heresy. Long after the threat of direct attack had receded, English people still imagined dark conspiracies designed to weaken the Protestant faith. Such notions acquired greater credibility during the seventeenth century, as a succession of Stuart kings either married Catholics, compromised themselves by accepting large subsidies from Catholic nations like France, or, in the case of James II, converted to Catholicism. None of this pleased the ordinary people. In 1688 England's ruling class sent James II packing—a defining moment known as the Glorious Revolution—and in his place invited William and Mary to accede to the throne. The new monarchs' major appeal was their unquestioned commitment to the Protestant cause.[25]

Eighteenth-century Americans wove anti-Catholicism into their own sense of being British. However deficient in charisma were the Hanoverian kings who for more than a century after 1714 held the British Crown, they defended Protestantism against its continental enemies. In America this commitment translated into a long series of wars against the French. When the British finally emerged victorious from the Seven Years' War in 1763, the colonists assured themselves that a Protestant God had supported British troops in the battle for Canada. Within this imperial framework it did not matter much whether one attended a Congregational, Anglican, or Presbyterian service, nor to what extent the leveling spirit of evangelical revivalism had swept up an individual or community. All Protestants qualified as proper British subjects.[26] And Catholics were implacable enemies. As the Reverend Jonathan Mayhew explained in a politically charged sermon delivered in Boston in May 1765, "Our controversy with her [Rome] is not merely a religious one . . . But a defense of our laws, liberties and civil rights as men in opposition to the proud claims of ecclesiastical persons, who under the pretext of religion and saving of men's souls, would engross all power and property to themselves, and reduce us to the most abject slavery."[27]

Commerce provided the third segment of imperial identity. Americans were convinced that what held the British Empire together, what gave it such strength throughout the world, was trade. Of course, the colonists welcomed redcoats during the conflict with France, but even as they expressed gratitude for military protection, they also observed that pocketbook concerns certainly added to the benefits of being British. Ever since the 1660s Parliament had insisted that a lion's share of American exports flow through the ports of the mother country. The so-called Navigation Acts enforced a policy known as mercantilism, which argued that the whole purpose of having colonies was to have them serve the economic interests of England. Although the colonists in America occasionally found it convenient to do business with the Dutch, they generally accepted the constraints on trade. Smuggling was always a marginal activity. After the 1740s the character of commerce within the Atlantic World shifted dramatically. Policy makers in London began to appreciate the colonists' growing demand for goods manufactured in Britain. As we have noted, Americans worked harder— increased the productivity of ordinary families—so that they could participate more fully in this new and exciting marketplace. By the middle of the eighteenth century, small farmers throughout America had become willing participants in complex networks of trade controlled by Great Britain.[28]

These positive elements had the inevitable effect of heightening the colonists' sense of their own importance within the empire. By the middle of the century they subscribed enthusiastically to a political identity known as British or colonial nationalism. After all, by their own lights they had made a significant monetary and military contribution to British campaigns against the French in Canada. They served a vital economic role within the empire. By purchasing manufactured goods in ever-increasing quantities, they helped reduce rates of unemployment in cities throughout Britain. Within the empire, they assumed that they were the equals of other subjects of the Crown, even those people who happened to live in Britain. A statement in the very first issue of a New Hampshire newspaper in 1764 reflects the Americans' strong assumption of self-worth within a burgeoning Atlantic World. Newspapers, declared the publisher, are the means by which "the spirited *Englishman*, the mountainous *Welshman*, the brave *Scotchman*, and *Irishman*, and the loyal *American*, may be firmly united and mutually RESOLVED to guard the glorious Throne of BRITANNIA . . . Thus Harmony may be happily restored, Civil War disappointed, and each agree to embrace, as *British Brothers*, in defending the Common Cause."[29]

The problem was that the English never really perceived the Americans—nor the Scots for that matter—in such favorable terms. They were people from the provinces who seemed different, in dress and accent, and were in some essential ways not quite English. The Reverend John Barnard, a minister from Marblehead, Massachusetts, encountered this phenomenon on a trip to England; the discovery that no matter how educated and charming he may have been, he remained an inferior Englishman in the eyes of his hosts made a lasting impression. After he delivered a sermon before a small country congregation in England, "an aged gentlewoman" engaged Barnard in conversation. "She asked me if all the people of my country were white, as she saw I was; for being styled in general West Indians, she thought we were all black." Having been corrected, she inquired "how long I had been in the kingdom. When I told her a few months, she said she was surprised to think how I could learn their language in so little time; 'Methinks . . . you speak as plain English as I do.'"[30] But Barnard was an exception. Not many Americans ever traveled to England, and in their ignorance of a double standard they imagined themselves—at least until Parliament began taxing them without representation—to be as fully British as any man who raised a glass and bellowed out "Rule Britannia."

British nationalism played out in curious ways in the colonies. Ordinary Americans turned George I and George II—the first two Hanoverian monarchs—into cult figures. Royal anniversaries and birthdays sparked effusive outpourings of affection for the monarchy. Indeed, the Americans seem to have thought much more highly of the kings and their families than did the British, who realized that these stolid monarchs preferred their native Germany to London. No doubt, then as now, Americans liked to follow powerful celebrities. It would be wrong, however, to declare the colonists' expressions of love for the reigning monarch as having no substance. As a symbolic figure of authority, the king's person was regularly invoked in courts of law. Many royal governors owed their positions to the Crown. Rather than being a burden, the rituals of monarchy generally reinforced colonial nationalism.[31]

But adoration of the monarch had limits. America was a monarchical society with an edge. When the king's representatives in the colonies clashed with various representative assemblies—a frequent occurrence—they quickly discovered that ordinary Americans almost always sided with their own elected officials. Americans took for granted the notion that power derived ultimately from the people.[32] For a long time that belief coexisted with fawning praise for the British monarchy. However, the growing political crisis within the empire after 1774 brought to the fore the populist side of the coin. A poignant example of this voice could be heard in the pages of a New London, Connecticut, newspaper. Reprinting a report that had originated in Charleston, South Carolina, the paper recounted that a minister there had recently been dismissed by his congregation "for his audacity in standing up in his pulpit, and imprudently saying, that mechanics and country clowns had no right to dispute about politics, or what King, Lords and Commons had done, or might do!!!." The preacher had forgotten a fundamental truth. He should have known that throughout the British Empire "mechanics and country clowns (infamously so called) are the real and absolute masters of King, Lords, Commons, and Priests: Though (with shame be it spoken) they too often suffer their servants to get upon their backs and ride them most barbarously."[33]

Whatever the theoretical foundation of government, in small inland communities—Acton, Massachusetts, for example—imperial authorities were in fact thin on the ground. From time to time one might encounter a royal governor or a customs collector, but such sightings were rare. British reformers understood the problem. Over the middle decades of the century they presented a number of plans for the creation of a genuine ruling class in the colonies, a kind of American aristocracy, but since Parliament never showed much interest in these schemes, the establishment of a special group with a vested interest in upholding royal authority went by the wayside.

One wonders how some of the men who became Founding Fathers—George Washington or Benjamin Franklin—might have responded to an offer of a privileged rank within the British Empire. However tempting such a plan might have been for some Americans, it did not materialize, and when ordinary colonists organized armed resistance against royal authority, the members of the local elites found themselves in an awkward social situation. Since they never received deference as pseudo-aristocrats, they had to find ways to speak convincingly to and for the people, and in these exchanges they often found that farmers staked out political positions more radical than those voiced by the members of the colonial gentry whom the people had elected to the provincial assemblies and the Continental Congress.

# II

Before 1760, nothing about the American people suggested that they would break violently with an imperial system that for so long had defended them against Catholic states, brought to modest American households a stunning array of consumer goods, and promised liberty under the balanced constitution for British throughout the world. From this perspective, it is surprising that these people became insurgents. It is even more amazing that deeply rooted ties and identities came undone so swiftly during the final two years of imperial rule in America.

Only a few years earlier, British writers claiming special expertise in colonial matters confidently predicted that Americans could not possibly unite. It seemed far more likely that they would turn on one another rather than on Great Britain. In 1759, for example, the English traveler Andrew Burnaby dismissed as ridiculous fears in Britain that Americans might contemplate independence. He drew attention to "the difficulties of communication, of intercourse, [and] of correspondence." For Burnaby, it was obvious that "fire and water are not more heterogeneous than the different colonies in North America."[34]

Although such observers were not fools, they misinterpreted the evidence. They exaggerated the significance of regional squabbling and ignored the very elements that not only eroded traditional bonds and identities but also sparked armed resistance to imperial authority in the name of an "American cause." Burnaby and others failed to appreciate how many ordinary colonists were young people who took a large measure of social equality for granted, who had been schooled to believe that they possessed fundamental rights, and who viewed the world through a religious lens, replete with powerful notions of divine justice, personal responsibility, and political revenge.

The great mass of ordinary people, the sine qua non of a successful insurgency, did not imagine that they were engaged in a genuine revolution, at least not at first. They struggled to find a name for the conflict that disrupted their lives. The most common term used after 1774 to describe the shift from complaint and petition to actual violence was "civil war." In late June 1775, for example, a South Carolina committee of safety issued a circular letter to "Fellow Citizens" in which it called the battles of Lexington and Concord the start of an "American civil war."[35] Sometimes Americans added a curious adjective, claiming to be involved in an "unnatural civil war." Samuel Lane, a New Hampshire farmer, went further, depicting the events that had overtaken his family as a "Most Unnatural Civil War."[36] The notion that they had entered into a genuine civil war revealed, among other things, that Americans believed they confronted their enemies as equals. The adjective "unnatural" suggested, of course, a painful sense of grievance. Like children mistreated by an abusive parent, the colonists persuaded themselves that Britain was acting in a manner unworthy of a mother country.

No American who joined the insurgency accepted the notion that the colonists were rebels. The word carried highly negative connotations. Rebels resisted lawful authority; they were classed among criminal groups such as bandits. To the very end of the colonial period Americans insisted that they were fighting to uphold the British constitution. It was the British who had corrupted legislative processes that had an ancient and honorable history. "I declare it before God, the congregation, and all the world, and I would be glad if it reached the ears of every Briton, and every American," declared the Reverend John Allen of Boston, "that it is not rebellion to oppose any King, Ministry, or Governor, that destroys by any violence or authority whatever, the Rights of the People." Allen drove the point home, arguing, "It is no more rebellion for the people to stand up for, and maintain their rights than it is to breathe in the free air."[37]

During the final run-up to independence, British officials came to appreciate the ability of an infuriated populace to undermine the fabric of imperial government. While the British did not have much respect for the American militia, the people were an entirely different matter. Swept up by unthinking passions, the people had the ability at any time to bring routine administration—the business of courts, for example—to a standstill. The challenge for the British was to explain why so many ordinary colonists would join an insurgency. Madness seemed an obvious answer. From this perspective, irresponsible organizers such as Samuel Adams had stirred up a popular frenzy. Joseph Galloway labeled them "American demagogues."[38] Manipulated by crude propaganda and lies, the people had surrendered reason. The very intensity of their commitment revealed just how little they really understood about the complex constitutional issues at stake. In 1775, for example, loyalists in Worcester, Massachusetts, announced that their neighbors who were preparing for war were guilty of "ignorance, distempered brains, heated imaginations, infatuated blindness and delusions, &."[39] Peter Oliver, a Boston Tory who wrote a venomous history of the American Revolution, agreed. "As for the People in general," he announced, "they were like the Mobility of all Countries, perfect Machines, wound up by any Hand who might first take the Winch."[40]

Loyalist hostility to the unthinking masses was predictable. More surprising were the deep reservations about popular resistance expressed by various members of the colonial elite. Like Oliver and his friends, they complained that the ordinary people had no independent judgment and as a consequence were easily led by radical spokesmen. In 1774 Gouverneur Morris, a suave figure who later gave stylistic polish to the final draft of the United States Constitution, commented on a large protest meeting in New York at which the local gentry were trying to convince the middling and lower sorts obediently to follow patrician leadership. Morris thought it a losing proposition. "The mob begin to think and to reason," Morris reported. "Poor reptiles! It is with them a vernal morning; they are struggling to cast off their winter's slough, they bask in the sunshine, and ere noon they will bite, depend upon it." He feared—as did other colonial gentlemen—"that if the disputes with Great Britain continue, we shall be under the worst of all possible dominions; we shall be under the dominion of a riotous mob."[41]

Not a few well-to-do Americans worried that insurgency might open a political Pandora's box. Ignorant men and women would become uppity. They would no longer defer to those who assumed it was their right to make decisions for others. Alexander Graydon witnessed the danger firsthand. A well-connected young man from Philadelphia, he tried with mixed success to recruit common soldiers for the American cause. "At all times, indeed, licentious, levelling principles are much to the general taste, and were of course popular with us," Graydon grumbled, "but the true merits of the contest, were little understood or regarded."[42]

The people's detractors had other complaints. They told themselves that ordinary Americans—especially those who lived in colonial ports— wanted not only to liberate the colonies from parliamentary tyranny but also to erode the many privileges enjoyed by their social betters. No one seriously thought that the people were scheming to redistribute property or burn down the mansions of the rich. The fear was rather that if ordinary men and women got it into their heads that they had as good a right to make political decisions as did their wealthier and more educated neighbors, then the traditional social order would be in jeopardy, a situation that would invite anarchy.[43]

One of the more strident attacks on popular politics came from the pen of James Iredell, a member of a prominent North Carolina family who rightly saw himself as a leader of the American cause. But when ordinary people in the region had the audacity to challenge his brother-in-law for elective office, Iredell lost control. In a statement titled "Creed of a Rioter," Iredell projected onto the poorer planters the words "I am a sworn enemy to all gentlemen. I believe none in that station of life can possibly possess either honor or virtue." He was just warming to the task. A second principle of the people, Iredell claimed, was "I believe the best way to have a good understanding is never to cultivate the mental powers, and that the most ignorant in appearance, are in fact the most knowing." And finally, this imagined self-centered lout declares, "I think that man alone a Whig [a supporter of the American cause], who has sagacity enough to mind his own interest, resolution enough to plunder his neighbors, who views the storm coolly at a distance, and discovers his principles by getting honestly drunk and abusing *gentlemen*."[44]

Colonists such as Isaac Davis paid little attention to such fulmination. Ignorant and self-absorbed individuals of the sort that annoyed

Iredell could not have possibly sustained armed resistance against the empire. Complaints about the political shallowness of the people — then and now — deflects attention from more significant questions about the wellsprings of popular motivation. The small North Carolina planters who so annoyed Iredell may not have held their own in a learned debate with a gentleman about political theory or constitutional law. But they knew full well why they came forward, first as supporters of boycotts and signers of petitions, then as soldiers in local militia units, as persons who refused to serve on juries in courts where the judges held royal commissions, or as members of committees charged with ferreting out America's enemies. At each step in a process that led ultimately to armed violence, they thought about what they were doing.

The Reverend Nathan Perkins understood what was on their minds. In a powerful sermon delivered in Connecticut on June 2, 1775, "To Soldiers, Who Went from West Hartford, in Defense of Their Country," Perkins observed, "Most of you are strangers to the dreadful horrors of battle. An army drawn up in battle array, the roaring of cannon, the smoke and confusion, the cries of the wounded, groans of the dying, and all the dreadful horrors of battle are things to which you have not been accustomed." Why then, he asked, should they risk death? "You have everything to inspire you with undaunted fortitude. You fight not for your daily bread — nor for four-pence sterling a day, but for your lives, your property, your native land, your dearest friends, your just rights, all you hold dear as men and sacred as Christians, your ALL. If these motives do not fire your souls in your country's cause, what can!"[45]

During the months leading up to Lexington and Concord, the colonists sensed a growing strength in numbers. As individuals, they reasoned about rights and oppression, about sacrifice, but as the movement gained momentum, they began to experience an exhilarating feeling of solidarity. The Reverend Nathaniel Niles understood how protest took root on the community level. "Acts are composed of seconds, the earth of sands, and the sea of drops, too small to be seen by the naked eye," he reminded his Newburyport congregation soon after the British navy blockaded the port. "The smallest particles have their influence. Such is our state, that each individual has a proportion of influence on some neighbor at least; he, on another, and so on; as in a river, the following drop urges that which is before, and every one through the whole length of the stream has the like influence." The insurgency began not with a familiar cast of American leaders, but with the people. In a time of crisis, as Niles reminded them, "We must begin with the weight we have."[46]

# III

The chapters that follow narrate the chronology of insurgency. They explain how the angry insurgents of 1774 channeled resistance into an elaborate infrastructure of revolution that respected a rule of law and demanded a government capable of addressing their interests. It is a complicated story involving many thousands of Americans who often left only fragmentary and incomplete accounts of their thoughts and actions. Fortunately, in total the record is rich enough to tell their story in full. Before we do so, however, it is worth pausing over one insurgent who, by virtue of his actions and resolve on behalf of insurgency, became indisputably an American patriot before being erased almost entirely from our collective story.

Samuel Thompson made other people, especially those who fancied themselves his social betters, uncomfortable. He still has that capacity. Born in 1735 to a Scotch-Irish family, he owned a modest tavern in Brunswick, an inland community in what would eventually become part of the state of Maine. Although Thompson has slipped from the pages of the history of the Revolution, he sparked a crisis during the spring of 1775 known as "Thompson's War," a moment of insurgency that exposed the raw, violent side of popular resistance to the British Empire.[47]

Thompson could have come from any colony. He was a product of his times, a representative man. Dr. David Ramsay, a revolutionary officer who wrote an account of the Revolution, observed in 1789 that "The great bulk of those, who were active instruments of carrying on the revolution, were self-made, industrious men. Those who by their own exertions, had established or laid a foundation for establishing personal independence, were most generally trusted, and most successfully employed in establishing that of their country."[48] Thompson fit Ramsay's general description. He managed to support a large family in a community that offered meager economic opportunities.

Social distinctions counted for little in Brunswick. In terms of manners and education, Thompson would not have stood out from most of his neighbors. What separated him from these people, in fact, was his ability to articulate forcefully what was on their minds. Although his detractors in Falmouth called him uncouth, Thompson unquestionably exercised a kind of charismatic leadership within this small town of 876 residents. What these qualities were remain obscure. His physical appearance certainly did not inspire respect. Contemporaries reported that he was "short, stocky, [and] opinionated." Others were more uncharitable, using words such as "portly" and "corpulent." But however he carried himself, everyone rated him an extraordinarily impressive speaker. They said this even though whenever Thompson became excited—a regular occurrence—he stuttered quite noticeably. It was the passion of his pronouncements that riveted public attention. His oratory was characterized as "impetuous, noisy, and sometimes even furious."[49] Wit and intelligence, no doubt, helped elevate him above the level of populist demagogue.[50]

Thompson proclaimed an absolute commitment to social equality. The source of this principle may have been Universalism. People of this religious persuasion took inspiration directly from the Bible. They taught that it is God's purpose, through the grace revealed in Jesus Christ, to save every member of the human race from sin. Universalists accepted no institutional authority beyond the locally gathered congregation, and when a local minister preached doctrines that ran counter to those held by the majority of his parishioners, he lost his job. Within these churches one person's opinion deserved as much respect as another's. Thompson often responded to questions—not only about British policy—with the observation, "It is all right in the great plan."

We should not treat these words lightly. They are the stuff of radical resistance. Such a belief can give a person a powerful sense of moral certainty; those who resist the plan or who fail to see the logic of the divine blueprint deserve little sympathy. When great plans become guides to revolutionary politics—as they have repeatedly over the last several centuries—they encourage the violent suppression of dissent. Whatever his perception of the great plan may have been, Thompson deferred to no one. When a person who thought highly of himself exclaimed that if Thompson had had a proper education, he would have been a great man, Thompson replied, "If I had your education, I could put you in my pocket." On another occasion a member of the Massachusetts General Court expressed pity for Thompson's lack of formal learning. To which Thompson observed, "If I have no education perhaps I can furnish some ideas to those who have."[51]

In 1774, news that Parliament had closed Boston to all commerce and restructured the government of Massachusetts Bay marked Thompson's own revolutionary moment. His anger focused initially on people who seemed slow to demonstrate their support for the American cause or, worse, who suggested that the British might have a point. Thompson raised a group of vigilantes—probably members of the local militia—who took it upon themselves to enforce a boycott of British imported goods and to expose ideological dissenters. Their methods shocked moderates who still insisted that well-meaning gentlemen like themselves could resolve the constitutional differences with the mother country without violence.

The insurgents of Brunswick favored stronger measures. They physically beat suspected loyalists. One target almost drowned while being interrogated about his politics. Thompson and his followers forced another opponent to dig his own grave; not surprisingly, when the insurgents pointed their guns at his head and urged him to prepare for his own death, the man experienced a dramatic patriotic conversion. The terror spread through neighboring towns. Anglican ministers came in for especially harsh treatment. It is no wonder that one person at the time described Thompson as "running over with zeal and patriotism."[52]

Reports from Lexington and Concord that reached Maine in late April 1775 convinced Thompson that Britain had declared war on America. And without much reflection he decided that the attack on the Massachusetts countryside called for an appropriate response. Writing from Brunswick to the head of the committee of safety at Cambridge, Thompson announced that "having heard of the Cruill murders they have don in our Province, makes us more Resolute than ever, and finding that the Sword is drawn first on their side, that we shall be animated with that noble Spirit that wise men ought to be, until our Just Rights and Libertyes are Secured to us. Sir, my heart is with every true Son of America."[53] Unlike John Patten, Thompson did not march off to

Boston. Instead, he devised his own plan in Maine to revenge what General Gage had done, and in the process of launching a guerrilla action against the British navy, he hoped to embarrass the merchants of Falmouth who still seemed eager to appease the enemy.

Without receiving orders from higher-ranking officers—not even those who spoke for the new provisional government of Massachusetts—Thompson decided that he would capture HMS *Canceaux*, a small British warship that provided protection for those in Falmouth who supplied General Gage's troops in Boston with food and fuel. The vessel was under the command of Lieutenant Henry Mowat, a tough officer who proved himself a worthy opponent for the indomitable Thompson. The insurgents thought that they might be able to take the *Canceaux* by surprise. The plan involved hiding sixty Americans on a barge and—after maneuvering it next to the British ship—launching a successful strike. It all came to naught. Someone alerted Mowat to the danger before Thompson's group had made much progress.

Without having a clear backup scheme, Thompson's irregulars began taking up positions on May 8 in the woods near Falmouth. They wore no uniforms. Their only mark of identity as insurgents was a sprig of spruce attached to their hats. For their standard they raised a pole that still had branches at the top. The men milled about, grumbling that the citizens of Falmouth did not have the courage to make a proper stand. Then Thompson's little army had an extraordinary piece of luck. Unaware that the Americans were lurking nearby, Mowat and another British officer came ashore for a meeting with local leaders, and as they were walking though town, Thompson seized them. In exchange for the two officers, Thompson demanded that the *Canceaux* immediately depart from Falmouth waters.

The British, however, showed not the slightest interest in bargaining with the insurgents. The officer left in charge of the ship threatened to bomb the town. To which Thompson responded, "Fire away! Fire away." He declared that for every shot the *Canceaux* fired, "I will cut off a joint," a threat of his own to dismember Mowat piece by piece. The terrified townspeople rushed to save their possessions. One witness reported that the confrontation "frightened the women and children to such a degree that some crawled under wharves, some ran down cellar and some out of town. Such a shrieking scene was never before presented to view here."[54] The leading gentlemen of Falmouth came to Thompson, begging him to stand down, and when he seemed unwilling to compromise, several local spokesmen promised that if he let Mowat return to his ship on parole, they would take Mowat's place as prisoners. The parties sealed the deal; Mowat left the woods of Maine, never to set foot there again. He claimed that he feared for his life—a fair, if cowardly, assessment of the situation.

Thompson's insurgents took their disappointment out on the townspeople, stealing goods and liquor from those who had spoken in favor of avoiding violence. According to one report, "The soldiery thought nothing too bad to say of the Falmouth gentry. Some of them were heard to say as they walked the streets yesterday, 'this Town ought to be laid in Ashes.'"[55] On May 10 Thompson's War was over. The leaders of Falmouth apologized profusely to Mowat, and in a letter to the Provincial Congress of Massachusetts they complained that insurgency was no way to resist the British. "We are afraid that if any number of men at any time, and in any manner, may collect together, and attack any thing, or any person they please, every body may be in danger."[56]

The incident at Falmouth had several unexpected results. In October, Mowat reappeared in the harbor. Resistance to British rule had spread to other towns on the Maine coast, and Mowat was determined once and for all to stop the insurgency. Despite the townspeople's assumption that he came as a friend, the *Canceaux* bombed the defenseless community. Marines came ashore and burned what the cannons had not already destroyed. As the *New-England Chronicle* reported on November 23, "The savage and brutal barbarity of our enemies in burning Falmouth, is a full demonstration that there is not the least remains of virtue, wisdom, or humanity in the British court; and that they are fully determined with fire and sword, to beggar and enslave the whole American people."[57] The British learned a little late in the day that punishing insurgency—especially by attacking innocent people—is usually counterproductive, turning moderates into radicals and enhancing the reputation of the local resistance forces.

However much some gentry leaders disliked Thompson, the Provincial Congress of Massachusetts thought highly of his patriotic zeal; to the disgust of those who thought that good breeding and college education should translate directly into military command, Thompson received an appointment as a brigadier general. A short piece that appeared a few years later in a Boston newspaper helps us better understand his popular appeal. In an address before the members of his brigade, he declared "that there had been Stories reported that the Officers and Soldiers in his Brigade were against him; therefore, if it was the case, he never would rule over a People, if he could not rule in their Hearts, therefore desired the commanding Officers to try a vote." Not one officer cast a negative ballot. When he learned the result, Thompson pledged to the Maine soldiers, "I never will forsake you." The person taking down Thompson's words that day wrote, "It was enough if he could at his Death see his Country Free, and it was a Pleasure to Die for the Rights of this People rather than submit to the cruel Hand of Tyranny, and if we go back we Die twice." Thompson asked only one concession from his troops. If on "the Day of Battle" he held back, "Slay me . . . for it will be just."[58]

After the Americans had won independence, Thompson returned to Maine, held many elective offices, and, as a delegate to the Massachusetts ratifying convention in 1788, spoke passionately against the Constitution of the United States. He demanded annual elections for senators and congressmen. When his critics chided him for his radicalism, Thompson responded, "We cannot have too much liberty." He was particularly bothered by the Constitution's failure to outlaw racial slavery in the new republic. As a revolutionary insurgent, he had fought for equality, and after sacrificing for independence, he asked those who remembered Thompson's War, "Shall it be said, that after we have established our own independence and freedom, we make slaves of others?"[59] Once again he had spoken truth to power. Perhaps for this reason obscurity was his reward. Thompson had the honor of having a single gun battery bear his name. It was in a fort constructed in the late nineteenth century to protect the citizens of Maine from possible attack during the Spanish-American War.[60] This is hardly sufficient. It is time to reconsider the stories we tell ourselves about our own Revolution and to restore Thompson and thousands of other American insurgents to our revolutionary history. For absent these patriots in the wings, there would quite possibly be no revolutionary history to celebrate.

# TWO

# Ghost Stories in a Time of Political Crisis

During the long summer of 1774 a surge of civil disobedience transformed the political landscape of colonial America. The initial wave of resistance to British policy swept through the country towns of central and eastern New England, escalating grumbling dissatisfaction about imperial affairs into political rage. This is not a chronicle of disgruntled artisans rioting in the streets of Boston, New York, and Philadelphia. Rather, the story turns on ordinary people in small farm communities rejecting the claims of British authority long before the Continental Congress issued a declaration of independence. Within a short time— roughly from May to October—colonists living in villages outside Boston purged the region of royal officeholders. This was the birth of an insurgency. Within months, other Americans living in distant places proclaimed their support for the New Englanders who violently defied the empire.

At the time, no one could plausibly have predicted such an abrupt intensification of popular resistance. The Boston Tea Party in December 1773 triggered the change. It did so, however, in a roundabout way. Dumping the tea into the harbor was a serious legal matter. About that, no one in Britain or America had the slightest doubts. The major concern—in Massachusetts, at least—was how Lord North and his allies in Parliament would react. Several months passed before the colonists learned the extent of their punishment. In a series of statutes known as the Coercive Acts, Parliament—like so many other uncertain imperial powers over the centuries—decided that provocation of this sort justified an overwhelming show of toughness. The punitive legislation closed the port of Boston to all commerce except for coastal trade in basic supplies like firewood, restructured the Massachusetts government in ways that curtailed free speech in town meetings, and filled the colony's council with Crown appointees determined to restore law and order to the troubled commonwealth. To enforce the new system, the Crown dispatched to Boston an army of occupation under the command of General Thomas Gage.

Like news of the 9/11 attack, the destruction of Pearl Harbor, and the bombing of Fort Sumter, word of the Coercive Acts elicited outrage throughout the population. Colonists believed that the punishment for the Tea Party was totally out of proportion to the alleged crime. The legislation represented nothing less than an act of vengeance. Within the realm of public opinion, Britain's decision to employ the military to impose the hated policy demanded a response. It was as if the king and his councilors had gone out of their way to insult men and women who had nothing to do with the destruction of the tea. These colonists equated British policy with personal humiliation, a condition that many of them associated with slavery. The attack on traditional rights seemed so excessive, so unreasonable, that to explain Boston's plight, Americans entertained conspiracy theories about evil, grasping rulers in London.

Not surprisingly, people who before this moment had not paid much attention to the imperial conflict suddenly did so. They experienced an awakening of political consciousness. In this electrified atmosphere Americans found ways to express their anger through actions that would forever destroy British authority beyond occupied Boston. Some individuals took tepid steps, small sacrifices in the name of a common cause; others followed more violent paths. However the Americans worked out the calculus of resistance, their actions represented the effectual start of the Revolution.

# I

Americans, grown to maturity thinking of themselves as subjects of the British Crown, found it hard to sever the bonds of political identity. After May—in other words, when colonists became fully aware of the substance of the Coercive Acts—the possibility that trust had been misplaced or betrayed by a corrupt Parliament slowly dawned on ordinary people. The strain of redefining allegiance must have been nearly unbearable, especially for men and women who had known prosperity under the imperial system. It beggars the imagination that the members of the Patten family or Isaac Davis and his young wife did not discuss such unsettling topics in the privacy of their own homes. About such exchanges, of course, we remain ignorant. They left no record of troubled conversations about what it meant to sacrifice for an American cause at a time when America as a separate polity did not exist.

Fortunately, one curious contemporary text exploring the emotional dimensions of political obligation during a trying time has survived. To describe this bizarre work, published in Boston in 1774, as a surrogate for the personal testimony that has gone missing or was never recorded would be an exaggeration. However, we must make do with the evidence that is available, and the story of the three political spirits is in fact as entertaining as it is telling.

The tale claimed to be a factual account of an American-born gentleman who continued to live the good life even during British occupation. The full title of the piece provided a marvelous sense of the anonymous author's style and purpose. He wanted to achieve something at once playful, serious, and frightening.

THE WONDERFUL APPEARANCE OF AN ANGEL, DEVIL AND GHOST TO A GENTLEMAN IN THE TOWN OF BOSTON, IN THE NIGHTS OF THE 14TH, 15TH, AND 16TH OF OCTOBER 1774, TO WHOM IN SOME MEASURE MAY BE ATTRIBUTED THE DISTRESSES THAT HAVE OF LATE FALLEN UPON THAT UNHAPPY METROPOLIS, RELATED TO ONE OF HIS NEIGHBORS THE MORNING AFTER THE LAST VISITATION, WHO WROTE DOWN THE NARRATIVE FROM THE GENTLEMAN'S OWN MOUTH; AND IT IS NOW MADE PUBLIC AT HIS DESIRE, AS A SOLEMN WARNING TO ALL THOSE, WHO, FOR THE SAKE OF AGGRANDIZING THEMSELVES AND THEIR FAMILIES, WOULD ENTAIL THE MOST ABJECT WRETCHEDNESS UPON MILLIONS OF THEIR FELLOW-CREATURES.

The narrative commences soon after the complacent gentleman— never identified by name—had returned to his lodgings after a bout of heavy drinking. His companions happened to be officers in the British Army. Since he came from one of the founding families of New England, one might have expected him to choose his friends with greater care. But reflective judgment was not the gentleman's strong suit. Feeling a little unsteady, he staggered back to his room and fell into bed. Around 2:00 a.m. a rapping noise at the window awoke him in a fright. The sound announced the arrival of an Angel, who burst into the room radiating a blinding light. Peeking out from under the blankets, the gentleman saw that the Angel wore a sword and carried a scale of justice. Frightened out of his wits, the gentleman called out, "Friend, from whence came you? —What business have you with me?"

The Angel ignored plaintive questions, took a seat in a comfortable chair, and, considering the circumstances, adopted what might be described as a genial bedside manner. "Arise man from your bed—put on your clothes—take a chair and seat yourself down by me," he commanded. "I have something to communicate of the greatest importance—your temporal—your eternal welfare are interested in it." The Angel's assignment was to warn the gentleman that sometime during the next night he would confront Beelzebub, who wanted to discuss imperial politics. The Angel noted ominously that Satan had scheduled the appointment only after it had become known that this particular American collaborator had betrayed his "country for unrighteous gain."

The next day, the gentleman tried his best to maintain an outward show of calm. British soldiers he encountered on the street joked about being drunk the night before. Despite such bonhomie, the man remained nervous. Even someone suffering from a hangover does not take lightly the prospect of conversing with the Devil. To be on the safe side, he decided to spend the afternoon preparing. He diligently "read over the late acts of parliament respecting this [Massachusetts] government." The exercise yielded no political insight. He could find nothing objectionable in the Coercive Acts. "Upon the most critical observation," he confessed, "I could not discover . . . that the parliament had any design of distressing the people of America; they [the members of Parliament] only meant to correct the errors and rectify the behavior of a few factious and disobedient individuals, who have trampled upon all

law and government, and therefore, it became absolutely necessary for
the Supreme Legislature of the nation to put a final period to such
abominable enormities as have been committed by those *Sons of Violence.*" For the general reader who might have harbored doubts about
supporting resistance, the author pointed out in a footnote that the
gentleman had articulated the Tory position, behavior that seemed particularly unwise on the eve of a meeting with Satan.

A punctual Devil appeared in the man's room precisely thirty minutes past midnight. Unlike the Angel, Beelzebub was all business. "My
purpose," he announced, "now is to converse with you concerning the
crimes you have been guilty of towards your country, the punishment to
which you have exposed yourself, and the certainty of your not escaping
it, if you continue in the same course you have for years past." Although
the Devil presumably did not require a detailed accounting—after all,
he probably had compiled a full list of political sins well in advance of this
nocturnal visit—he still peppered the gentleman with questions. "Pray
Mr. _____, how came you to be such an enemy to your native country?"

The gentleman sputtered that the Devil was mistaken. He insisted
that he had always championed the welfare of the country. He had
urged Americans to obey the Stamp Act in 1765, to pay the Townshend
Duties in 1768, and to make monetary restoration for the tea so recently
destroyed. While others rioted and protested, he had counseled obedience. What more could be expected of a law-abiding colonist? Such
perverted logic stunned the Devil. "Your system of politics, friend, will
never do—So far are you from discovering a regard to your country, that
I am now convinced you are one of its greatest enemies."

Satan did not quite know how to handle the situation. The man's
thoroughly rebarbative beliefs would ordinarily have won the Devil's
admiration. Here was a worthy minion. But something about the gentleman's pathetic lack of political self-awareness must have touched a
soft spot in Satan's evil heart. How could the Prince of Darkness dispatch such a feckless person to the fiery pit? And so, out of a weird sense
of compassion, the Devil gave the Tory a second chance. Although the
odds were great that the hard-drinking man would end up in Hell, he
still had time to reform. "I conjure you to desist, before it be too late,
from pursuing these cursed plots, which tend to the destruction of that
country to which you are under the greatest obligations—Ask forgiveness of all you have injured, and make them all that restitution you are

able, lest I come again and snatch you away e're you are aware." With that advice Satan was gone. The choice seemed clear enough. Support the American resistance or be damned for eternity.

The political ordeal continued for a third night. This time "the GHOST of one of my deceased ancestors" visited the man's chambers. The old Puritan did not pay as much attention to personal appearance as the Angel had done: he wore "a long white gown, and his hair [was] much disheveled." Unlike the Devil, the Ghost had no interest in interrogation. He had come to deliver a lecture to his "degenerate offspring." If the gentleman had bothered to study New England history—always a good thing—he would have known that he had sprung "from a reputable family, some of whom were driven from the place of their nativity [Old England] by persecuting hands—they, with many others, for the sake of enjoying that liberty which was denied them at home, were content to leave everything else that was dear behind, and seek it in the inhospitable wilds of America." The original migrants to New England had gathered strength of character by killing "savage beasts, and still more savage men."

From the Ghost's perspective, the point was clear. Earlier generations had not sacrificed so much blood so that a self-indulgent traitor could undermine the heritage of liberty. What was more, in 1774 the English were just up to their old despotic tricks. After hearing about this past, the man responded pitifully that he thought he was doing the right things. But he now realized his political sins. The Ghost seemed skeptical. Before vanishing, he echoed Satan's words, warning that if acceptable behavior did not come soon, the man who had betrayed America would be punished.

The story's narrator concluded with a general admonition of his own. He claimed that he did not know whether the collaborator had experienced a genuine political conversion. In the larger scheme of things, however, his reformation did not matter. The three spirits had had a more compelling purpose. They had spoken to the people, he affirmed. Genuine Americans were now obliged to step up and be counted for liberty. The account of one complacent gentleman's reeducation "may prove a solemn warning to all into whose hands this Relation may chance to come, not to be guilty of that capital crime, *Treason against the State*, lest, e're they are aware, they plunge themselves into remediless ruin."[1]

For the purpose of better understanding a political environment that would bring forth insurgency—a forgotten world of "the sons of violence"—the emotional content of the story is of great significance. The Angel, the Devil, and the Ghost did not speak a language of abstract political theory. Drawing effectively on familiar assumptions of a highly religious culture, they advanced arguments that stressed moral obligation. Betrayal of friends and ancestors involved something more than errors of political logic. Such acts entailed sin; they deserved retribution. As a newspaper advertisement in the *Massachusetts Spy* for *The Wonderful Appearance* proclaimed, the narrative contained "a solemn warning to all those, who, for the sake of aggrandizing themselves and their families, would entail the most abject wretchedness upon MILLIONS of their fellow-creatures."[2] The value of this political ghost story is that it opens up the mental framework in which families like the Davises decided to join their neighbors and sacrifice for an imagined solidarity that the Devil as early as 1774 described as "your country."

## *II*

Midnight conversations among family members about political betrayal would have amounted to little more than loose talk, had it not been for shortsighted decisions made in London. It was there that a sequence of extraordinarily misguided judgments about American affairs set off a chain reaction that within a very short time forced ordinary colonists as well as complacent gentlemen to make hard choices about political responsibility.

Reports of the destruction of the tea in Boston reached the imperial capital in the dead of winter in 1774. For the king and Parliament the news represented the last straw in a long series of misunderstandings and provocations. They conveniently ignored the fact that the East India Company—the owner of the drowned tea—was a bloated, corrupt business organization that had recently received special favors from the government to avoid bankruptcy. From the perspective of the British administration, the American controversy had been brewing for more than a decade. Neither patience nor accommodation had successfully defused the tensions, and now, faced with an insufferable insult, Parliament decided to enforce imperial policy with unprecedented rigor. Frustration gave the use of military power almost irresistible appeal.

This dramatic shift in administrative strategy—a product of arrogance and ignorance—was a crucial element in the development of colonial insurgency. Bold solutions that made sense to the leaders of Parliament at this moment helped create the very situation that they most hoped to avoid, a massive rising of Americans prepared to employ violence against the state.

The men who governed Great Britain during the American Revolution were products of a comfortable political culture that discouraged innovation. Not surprisingly, when compared with other figures who had provided leadership when England faced serious crises, Lord Frederick North, 2nd Earl of Guilford, and the members of his cabinet seem profoundly mediocre. Whatever their personal talents, they were not inclined to challenge traditional assumptions about the character of the British Empire—about the relation between the American colonies and the mother country—and their intellectual rigidity blinded them to the possibility of reforming a system that no longer worked.

To describe these men as inordinately corrupt or, as some contemporary critics insisted, as evil conspirators scheming to undermine the British constitution, would be incorrect. As a group, they muddled along in Parliament from session to session without a suggestion of larger purpose, showing almost no capacity for imaginative schemes. As one political rival observed of North, he "had no system or plan of conduct, no knowledge of business." It certainly was no secret that North "often confessed his incapacity, and from a consciousness of it, pretended a willingness to resign."[3] He never did step down, however, at least not until the final British defeat many years later.

Whatever North's faults, George III supported the man he had selected to serve as chancellor of the exchequer through the entire American conflict, an expression of personal loyalty that revealed the king's sense that the compliant North would never put forward creative ideas and thus force the monarch to think about topics he would surely find disagreeable. North and his allies in Parliament had one additional advantage that members of the opposition could not afford to ignore. They entered each debate secure in the knowledge that they controlled an overwhelming majority in Parliament, and however much dissenters insisted that the current government was leading the nation to ruin, the critics never had enough votes to challenge the chancellor's position.

One fundamental political idea bound the members of Britain's ruling class together. Even the least perceptive among them accepted as a matter of patriotic pride that the sovereignty of Parliament was the greatest achievement of the age. So fervently did North and his followers defend this principle that they could not comprehend why the Americans would ever raise the slightest doubts about Parliament's absolute right to legislate for the king's subjects wherever they might happen to live. It made no difference that many British people were not in fact allowed to participate in parliamentary elections. The legislature — the House of Commons and the House of Lords — still represented their interests regardless of whether they actually had a vote.

The colonists rejected this argument out of hand. It contradicted their own political experience. When they protested, however, they always faced an uphill fight. They were contesting more than a century of English history and tradition. In 1688 the members of the propertied elite grew so weary of James II's authoritarian practices that they sent him and all his Stuart heirs packing, and in a bloodless coup known as the Glorious Revolution, they brought William and Mary to the throne. By accepting the restraints of a genuine constitutional monarchy, the royal couple ended years of political turmoil, and during the eighteenth century a newly sovereign Parliament guided the country to commercial prosperity and imperial domination. What seemed to the Americans mulish attachment to principle impressed the British as a necessary defense of the constitution.[4]

As North's government summoned the resolve to enforce parliamentary sovereignty in the New World, it gathered intelligence about the political situation on the ground, or so it claimed. Reports from America received close attention, especially from the Earl of Dartmouth, secretary of state for the colonies since 1772, but no one seems to have asked hard questions about the reliability of this information. On March 7, 1774, when North discussed the "copies of all Letters, &c., received from *America*, relating to the disturbances there" that his administration had put before Parliament — materials that supposedly made the case for taking strong punitive action against Boston — he drew attention to their rudely insulting quality.

The ministry had few facts to offer about the men who had actually destroyed the tea. Instead, it condemned a pattern of offensive rhetoric.

The chancellor described the packet of documents justifying tough action against Boston as containing "inflammatory fugitive pieces, handbills, alarms, resolves of town meetings, and minutes of Council." North observed "all the printed and circulated trash were plentifully larded with the fashionable phrases of 'desperate plans of despotism; ministerial designs to ruin their liberties; slavery; galling fetters; forging infernal chains; encouraging popery; despotic rule,' &c. &c."[5] As for the precise character of colonial resistance to North's policy—lists of the names of people who had actually participated in the Tea Party, for example—the bundle of American papers did not have much value. That, of course, was not their purpose. Members of Parliament, who owed their seats to British electors and not to American protesters, had already made up their minds about the pressing need to establish—in the king's words—"the just dependence of the Colonies upon the Crown and Parliament of *Great Britain*."[6]

Even less useful in assessing what was happening on the ground in America were the numerous letters from the royal governors and other royal officeholders. This stream of correspondence from the colonies should have generated a high degree of skepticism.[7] After all, these Crown appointees had their own reputations to defend. If they confessed candidly that the situation in the colonies had suddenly and massively deteriorated—indeed, was on the verge of spinning out of control—they would have opened themselves to blame for the collapse of imperial authority.

And so, like many beleaguered officials who over the centuries have been dispatched to distant and rebellious posts, they sought to put the best face on the situation. The governors did not trade in outright dishonesty. Rather, they presented inconvenient facts in ways that masked the depth of popular discontent in America. They counseled a resolute though limited response to the destruction of the tea. A show of military force, they thought, should be just harsh enough to bring the colonists to their senses. Thomas Hutchinson, a royal governor of Massachusetts who returned to London early in 1774, mastered the self-serving language of royal bureaucracy. After a series of inept decisions that alienated most of the people in Massachusetts, he put forward as his expert opinion, "I see no prospect . . . of the government of this province [Massachusetts] being restored to its former state without the interposition of the authority in England." The message played well among North's followers, and with rare exception, no one in the cabinet thought to inquire whether Hutchinson had interpreted what was occurring in Massachusetts to suit his own purposes.[8]

However dubious the sources of intelligence from America may have been, they framed strategic discussions at the highest levels of government. North and Dartmouth were under immense pressure to take bold action. Many of their supporters in Parliament believed that an earlier ministry headed by the Marquis of Rockingham had made a major mistake by repealing the Stamp Act in 1766. In the opinion of the more chauvinistic figures among North's backers, compromise on the principle of parliamentary sovereignty had only encouraged the Americans to abuse British authority. Indeed, by showing weakness in 1766, British rulers had practically invited the colonists to destroy the tea in Boston Harbor. One did not have to pore over the American papers to see the logic of the argument. "The decline of British influence in America may be dated from the repeal of the Stamp Act," claimed one author who styled himself "An Officer of the Army." He declared that "ever since that fatal period, a spirit of democracy has been gaining ground in the country: the concessions made by Great Britain on that occasion, were considered by the colonists as more the result of apprehension and diffidence, than a generous intention of atoning for an act of injustice."[9] For people who viewed politics in terms of sellouts and insisted that history provided clear lessons on the need to be tough with enemies real and imagined, the decision to employ military force was never in doubt.

North swam with the political current. He persuaded himself that a handful of American troublemakers had fomented a crisis to advance their own radical agenda. To be sure, these mob leaders seemed to enjoy the support of the urban working class. The agitators, he believed, could also count on the backing of the local Congregational clergy. But from the perspective of London, these groups presented relatively minor problems. The king and his cabinet ministers assumed that by isolating the rabble-rousers from the rest of New England, they could restore order. In other words, they felt confident that the ordinary people who lived in the countryside would quickly back down. Nothing in the early intelligence reports suggested the possibility of widespread insurgency. Moreover, the beauty of such a limited and focused response to the destruction of the tea was that it would not further drain the British treasury and force an increase in domestic land taxes, a move sure to antagonize a ruling class that already felt it was paying enough to the government. A small number of British regulars stationed in Boston, in cooperation with a naval blockade, would demonstrate not only that Parliament was serious about punishing lawbreakers but also that it had no intention of instituting an American policy that would cost grumpy British taxpayers a lot of money.

North initially thought that his ministry might best achieve these goals by transporting the Boston ringleaders to London for show trials. Deprived of the support of friends and neighbors who would never convict a person for resisting taxation without representation—even if that meant destroying property owned by the East India Company—the American firebrands would face English judges prepared to deal severely with criminals of this sort. The proposal served another purpose. Although North enjoyed huge majorities in Parliament, he anticipated that such leading opposition speakers as Edmund Burke would harshly criticize North's colonial policy in the House of Commons. Even if they lacked the votes needed to stop legislation, orators of Burke's ability could score points "out of doors." Hostile public opinion might not be able to bring down the government, but in London it presented the chancellor with problems he preferred to avoid. He urged the king, therefore, to order the arrest of the treasonous Americans without involving Parliament in the matter.

The Crown's legal advisers would have none of it. In a carefully crafted statement the law officers observed that while North was surely right in wanting to punish someone for the latest American incident, he was not justified in ignoring basic legal procedures. The depositions that had been gathered in Boston simply would not sustain "the charge of High Treason." Dartmouth interpreted the ruling as a clear setback. He reported that the lawyers had found that "it would be difficult to establish such a connection between the acts of the body of the people, and the destruction of the tea, as to leave no doubt of the propriety and effect of bringing over the persons charged to be tried here." Although North backed down, he never voiced concern over how his plans for a show trial had threatened the fundamental principles of the British constitution. The defense of order and property in far-off colonies apparently justified authoritarian schemes. "With respect to punishing the individuals," he wrote, "that is the object most desirable [but] . . . the nature of our law . . . the distance of places . . . make it difficult to bring to justice persons who have been guilty of disobeying the authority of this country."[10]

For better or worse, in early March it fell to Parliament to pass the punitive legislation that the chancellor and his king desired. The ministry choreographed the debates in both houses of Parliament with great care. On March 14, North opened the discussion of American affairs with a long speech that cunningly avoided mention of specific provisions. Rather, he employed his position as first minister to stir up resentment. He reminded his colleagues of Boston's total disregard for English law. According to one person who witnessed North's speech, the chancellor openly declared that "he thought the inhabitants of the town of *Boston* deserved punishment." He recognized that "perhaps it may be objected, that some few individuals may suffer on this account who ought not; but where the authority of a town had been, as it were, asleep and inactive, it was no new thing for the whole town to be fined for such neglect." North cited several precedents for such a blanket correction — all of them of questionable relevance — and then, sensing the weakness of the administration's argument, he asserted, "*Boston* had been upwards of seven years in riot and confusion."

The city had disrupted commerce; its citizens had attacked the collectors of customs. It soon became clear that North had no intention of chastising specific troublemakers. He demanded retribution from an entire population, from men and women who in fact had nothing whatsoever to do with the destruction of the tea, from persons who still supported the principle of parliamentary sovereignty, from children and pensioners, from dockworkers and sailors. In North's eyes all of them were guilty of treasonable behavior for no other reason than that they happened to live in Boston.

The chancellor reminded the members of Parliament that he would have preferred to try the ringleaders in an English court, but alas, all the king's men in Boston had not been able to identify a single criminal organizer. And so, noting that the Americans had exhausted the nation's patience, he asked the Commons to demonstrate its unshakable conviction that patriotic Britons would not tolerate the destruction of private property, the interruption of trade, or the rejection of Parliament's absolute right to rule the distant colonies. In closing, North "hoped that all would agree with him, both peers, members, and merchants, to proceed unanimously to punish such parts of *America* as denied the authority of this country. We must . . . punish, control, or yield to them."[11] It was an effective speech, especially since North was not noted for his oratory. Like other leaders over the centuries who have had a weak hand to play, the first minister had worked upon the emotions of well-meaning, underinformed legislators who did not want to appear spineless at a moment of national crisis.

North quickly transformed rhetoric about lawless Bostonians into harsh measures, known collectively as the Coercive Acts—or, in the colonies, as the Intolerable Acts. The name one chose depended on one's ideological perspective. Although the ministry shepherded four separate pieces of legislation through Parliament, only the first two Intolerable Acts merit close attention in a history of American insurgency. These statutes radically altered the character of popular resistance throughout the colonies. In New England they had a more immediate impact. North's tough policy enraged ordinary men and women who before this time had distanced themselves from protest against the empire.

The Boston Port Act sailed through both houses of Parliament, becoming law on March 31, 1774. Among other things, it stipulated that after June 1 the city would be closed to all commerce. The Royal Navy took responsibility for enforcement. The statute also designated Salem as the official port of entry for Massachusetts Bay, a decision that in practice meant that everyday necessities had to be transported overland at considerable additional expense from Salem to Boston. Everyone anticipated that the bill would generate large-scale unemployment, since without maritime traffic, employers had no reason to hire workers to unload cargoes or repair merchant vessels. The punishment fell disproportionately on the poor. North suggested that if the city came up with a plan to pay for the East Indian tea and apologized for the assault on private property, the king might see fit to liberate Boston from a parliamentary act designed to cripple its economy. The precise terms of atonement, however, were teasingly uncertain. During the debate the first minister informed the Commons, "The test of the Bostonians will not be the indemnification of the East India Company alone, it will remain in the breast of the King, not to restore the port until peace and obedience shall be observed in the port of Boston."[12]

A second Coercive Act, signed into law by the king on May 20, bore an innocuous title that belied its ambitious intent. From North's perspective, the Massachusetts Government Act responded to a number of long-standing annoyances, the most vexing being the colony's excessively democratic political culture. The Massachusetts charter, originally granted by William and Mary in 1692, allowed the members of an annually elected house of representatives to nominate the men who sat on the council. The group served as an upper house of the colonial legislature, which was supposed to advise the royal governor about pressing matters of state. Governor Hutchinson and others had long objected to this mode of selection. The councillors seemed too close to the house of representatives, and when push came to shove, they generally sided with the popular assembly. As North explained, "I propose, in this Bill, to take the executive power from the hands of the democratic part of Government."[13] Moreover, officials appointed by the Crown thoroughly disliked the colony's town meeting system, which gave ordinary people the opportunity to debate freely sensitive political topics. The Government Act not only limited the Massachusetts communities to a single town meeting each year—and that devoted to routine business— but also took the nomination of council members out of the hands of the house of representatives.

North and others who shared his assumptions expressed confidence that these reforms would soon return the colonists to a proper sense of obedience. They believed that the council—filled now with "mandamus councilors" appointed by a writ of mandamus [or "we command" in Latin] from the king—would faithfully back the royal governor during confrontations with an unruly people. Changing the structure of the Massachusetts government made good sense in a distant imperial capital, where democratic practices were often confused with public disorder. Considering how fiercely North and his friends defended the inviolability of ancient British institutions, however, it is striking how little regard they had for the constitutional traditions of Massachusetts. They never considered how deeply attached the colonists might be to familiar forms of local government or how angrily they would react to imperial planners for whom local political customs were just another irritant.

Surviving notes from the parliamentary debates show that the prospect of punishing Boston encouraged the baying of the imperial hounds. Speaker after speaker came forward to condemn the Americans and to demand that they be taught a hard lesson about the need to obey orders from London. It is difficult to imagine that they would have employed such extreme rhetoric if they had been discussing the king's subjects who lived in Britain. The colonists fell into a lesser category. One member of Parliament insisted that the American situation justified severe measures. During a reading of the Port Act he drew attention to "the flagitiousness of the offence in the Americans, and therefore was of opinion that the town of Boston ought to be knocked about their ears, and destroyed."

Although other speakers dissociated themselves from talk advocating the actual destruction of Boston, they too were in no mood to compromise. Negotiation with the Americans was a waste of time. With a prescience he little appreciated, one proponent of the Port Act informed his legislative colleagues that "the Americans were a strange set of People, and that it was in vain to expect any degree of reasoning from them; that instead of making their claim by argument, they always chose to decide the matter by tarring and feathering." Another advocate of tough action blamed the colonists for their plight. After all, because of their stubborn resistance to parliamentary taxation, "we were drove to the wall."[14]

Even though passage of the Coercive Acts was never in doubt, a few speakers raised troubling questions about implementing such a punitive policy. Rose Fuller explained that Britain would never be able to commit the resources needed to pacify the Americans. North's many supporters in the Commons, he believed, called for toughness without taking into proper account that bellicose rhetoric seldom generated obedience. It was obvious that the Port Bill "could not be carried into execution without a military force." What, Fuller wondered aloud, would happen if the administration dispatched a small number of troops—just enough soldiers to make a political point. The answer seemed clear. "The Boston militia would immediately cut them to pieces." Fuller then asked what would occur if North sent a larger body of regulars, say six or seven thousand men. "The Americans," he observed, "would debauch them, and that by these means we should only hurt ourselves." Another dissenting voice begged Parliament to give up "idle ideas of superiority . . . for that country which is kept by power, is in danger of being lost every day."

Others took up the same theme. Although few colleagues lent them a sympathetic ear—indeed, to the majority, they sounded unpatriotic—

their predictions came to pass. They understood that military coercion is often counterproductive to the political ends it seeks to achieve. William Dowdeswell, a member of an opposition group, warned that the Port Act will "soon inflame all America, and stir up a contention you will not be able to pacify." George Johnstone, a former governor of West Florida and presumably a person who knew what was happening on the ground in the colonies, informed Parliament, "I now venture to predict to this House, that the effect of the present Bill must be productive of a General Confederacy, to resist the power of this country."[15]

During this session of Parliament, Edmund Burke energetically opposed North's policies. Contemporaries justly regarded him as a gifted speaker. His interventions wove erudition and wit into penetrating argument. When he rose to speak in Parliament, even long-standing adversaries listened carefully to what he had to say. Burke often went on for several hours. When he noted from time to time that perhaps he had exhausted the patience of his audience, his auditors begged him to continue. This was politics as a mode of entertainment. On this occasion Burke challenged North's judgment on American affairs. The Port Act was redolent of failure. "Have you considered whether you have troops and ships sufficient to enforce an universal proscription to the trade of the whole Continent of America?" he asked. After exposing the shallowness of North's vindictive policy, Burke closed with a stinging pronouncement: "This is the day, then, that you will go to war with all America, in order to conciliate that country to this; and to say that America shall be obedient to all the laws of this country."[16]

This was also the moment when the opposition—weak though it obviously was—might have been expected to advance a constructive policy of its own. But North's detractors never could bring themselves to do so. Their inability to rethink the fundamental principles of imperial rule doomed their criticism of the administration to a kind of sustained whine. In his own speech attacking the Port Act, Burke refused to grasp the nettle. "I wish to see a new regulation and plan of a new legislation in that country," he thundered, "not founded upon your laws and statutes here, but grounded upon the vital principles of English liberty."[17]

Considering the gravity of the situation, Burke must have known that his advocacy of abstract principle did not constitute a practical scheme for governing the American dominions. Indeed, the Rockingham group with which Burke identified promoted a concept known as "sleeping sovereignty."[18] It maintained that Parliament in theory possessed complete legislative sovereignty over the entire British Empire, but unlike North's followers, the Rockinghamites vowed never to use force in defense of Parliament's undoubted right to rule in all cases whatsoever. This was a distinction without a difference. At the end of the day, whatever talents Burke may have brought to the debates over American policy, he really did not have anything of substance to offer. Like his political rivals, he remained wedded to a political idea that the colonists had already rejected.

About one point Burke was correct. The Coercive Acts served to inflame the American situation. Anyone possessing even superficial knowledge of the growing tensions between the colonists and the North administration would have predicted at the very least that people in Boston would again take to the streets. But this time around, an accelerant was added to the political equation, one that increased anger and misunderstanding. The Americans learned about North and his supporters largely from essays—perhaps best characterized as highly partisan opinion pieces—that originally appeared in British newspapers. These journals made no attempt to report events in an objective manner. They did not hire reporters. Rather, many of them hammered away at the alleged corruption of the current administration. The *Kentish Gazette*, for example, announced on June 11, 1774—just about the time that the Boston Port Act went into effect—"Nothing can be more truly Machiavellian in our Ministry than their first endeavoring to sap the liberties of our settlements abroad. Every act, however injurious to freedom, loses its horror by repetition. Thus by progressive steps, and the pleading of precedents, we may expect shortly to see all of our most valuable privileges taken away from us, without so much as feeling their loss, till their restoration is irremediable."[19]

Printers throughout America picked up this virulent prose. None worried about plagiarism. They selected items that had the greatest market appeal. This flood of imported essays attacking North encouraged Americans to conclude that their cause enjoyed broad support among the British people. Their assessment of political conditions in the mother country was, of course, based on a fundamental misunderstanding. The swift and enthusiastic passage of the Coercive Acts in

Parliament might have suggested to them how limited sympathy really was among those who actually wielded power in the empire, but during the summer of 1774 the colonists read what newspapers printed. They mistook commentary that claimed to reflect British public opinion for political reality, and the signals Americans picked up from these sources set off alarms that justified in their eyes taking extreme measures to preserve basic rights and liberties. And thus, at the moment that Parliament chose to ratchet up the imperial crisis, both sides operated under serious misperceptions. The British government assumed that ordinary Americans would soon turn their backs on a few urban troublemakers; the Americans believed that the cabinet—perhaps even the king himself— subscribed to an evil conspiracy.

North tried to calm members of Parliament who seemed nervous that the country was sliding into an open-ended military commitment. They feared that a British army in America would cost the British taxpayers a huge amount of money. But the chancellor allayed their concerns. During debate over the Boston Port Act he insisted that he did not foresee the need for a large force. "The good of this Act is that four or five frigates will do the business without any military force," he argued. North even asserted his desire "to enforce a due obedience to the laws of this country . . . without bloodshed."[20]

Whether North believed what he told Parliament can never be known. He may have withheld significant information from skeptical legislators. As David Hartley, a member of Parliament, claimed, "The highest authority of government was made of, to inculcate opinions, which when put to the test, have proved totally unfounded; we were told, that the disturbances in America, were only the tumults of a deluded mob, misled by a few designing persons; that the appearance of a slight military force, to sustain the civil power, would soon quell all disturbance."[21]

On February 4—more than a month before the chancellor presented the first major Coercive Act—the king had a private conversation with General Thomas Gage. The ministry was looking for an energetic, experienced military officer to replace Hutchinson as governor of Massachusetts. The exchange went well. Gage impressed George III as especially talented, since he told the monarch precisely what he wanted to hear. As the king later recalled, Gage said that the Americans "will be

Lions, whilst we are Lambs, but if we take the resolute part they will undoubtedly prove very meek." The king concluded that he could work with this person. Indeed, Gage possessed the "character of an honest determined man."[22] The general sailed for Boston on April 18. He carried a copy of the Port Act, which had become law less than three weeks earlier. British ships also transported about three thousand regular troops to Boston. Within a very short time, the king's handpicked general was begging for reinforcements.

## III

Gage's arrival in Boston on May 13, 1774, may have struck spectators as a bizarre throwback to an earlier, happier time. For almost a century, colonists had greeted new royal governors—the king's personal representatives in America—with a formal ritual that amounted to political theater. The entire welcoming ceremony was designed to celebrate provincial loyalty and respect.[23]

Gage landed at Boston's Long Wharf, where, according to a local newspaper, "a number of his Majesty's Council, several Members of the Commons House of Assembly, many principal Gentlemen of this town, and the Governor's, or Cadet Company under arms" greeted him. The formal procession, led by an official displaying Gage's commission from George III, snaked its way through Boston—up from the docks, along a route that only a few years earlier had been the scene of bloody clashes with British authorities, and, finally, to the Council Chamber. Although Gage was aware that in March 1770—in an infamous event known as the Boston Massacre—British troops had shot several civilians, he believed that such incidents demonstrated that urban militancy could be contained through force. He had no appreciation that the countryside might be the problem. With the benefit of hindsight he might have been better advised to land in New York or Philadelphia, cities where fewer painful memories of violence lingered.

As the governor passed along King Street, various local military units saluted. The colorful triumph included a "Troop of Horse," "Company of Artillery," "company of Grenadiers," and "several companies of Militia." At the Council Chamber, Gage listened while someone read the royal commission. And then, after a brief swearing-in ceremony, he issued an official greeting from the balcony of the State House, "which was answered by three huzzas, a firing of cannon from the batteries . . . and three volleys from the respective companies." The entire assembly retreated to Faneuil Hall, where it enjoyed "an elegant entertainment," punctuated not surprisingly by a large number of laudatory toasts.[24] Gage exited the festivities in a carriage and spent the night in Province House.

The issue of the newspaper that chronicled Gage's first day on the job also carried a sobering report that should have given the governor pause. At the very least it might have alerted him to the possibility that many American soldiers and spectators who had cheered during his walk from Long Wharf to the State House had simply adopted the outward forms of imperial loyalty.

The second article described a provincial city seething with discontent. The journal announced that the "freeholders and other inhabitants of the town" had just met to discuss the "cruel edict of the British Parliament." They could hardly believe that North's government had actually closed a great port. He seemed to have forgotten that the British Empire owed its "opulence, power, pride and splendor" entirely to free commerce. By punishing Boston, therefore, the minister had found a way to harm all subjects of the Crown, wherever they happened to live. The newspaper made it clear that the people who attended the meeting had been in no mood to reason about economic policy. They were angry. In one sputtering outburst they declared that the "injustice, inhumanity and cruelty of the act . . . exceed all our powers of expression."[25]

Although he had pledged to George III to act like a lion in America, Gage found himself in an impossible situation. News of the Port Act had reached Boston before his arrival. People had already begun to contemplate resistance. Gage tried the best he could to interpret the politics of the street. On May 19—only a week after the convivial gathering at Faneuil Hall—he wrote in confidence to Lord Dartmouth, "I hear from many that the Act has staggered the most presumptuous . . . [and] minds so inflamed cannot cool at once, so it may be better to give the shock they have received time to operate."[26]

Gage had no choice but to wait. Instructions he received from London were ambiguous, even contradictory. Dartmouth had advised Gage only a month earlier that the king himself expected the general "to quiet the minds of the people, to remove their prejudices, and by mild and gentle persuasion to induce such a submission on their part to this law and such a proper compliance with the just requisitions it contains as may give full scope to His Majesty's clemency."[27] And what, Gage may have wondered, would be expected of a military officer if the people did not submit? Dartmouth had the answer. "To what further extravagance the people may be driven," he explained, "is difficult to say. Whatever violences are committed must be resisted with firmness, the constitutional authority of this kingdom over its colonies must be vindicated, and its laws obeyed throughout the whole empire." If Gage was too soft, too appeasing, Americans might listen to "dangerous and ill-designing persons" who Dartmouth assumed were busy promoting "ideas of independence."[28] As the general sought to establish his authority, British troops poured into Boston. Gage felt certain that if nothing else, an army of occupation would encourage "the friends of government."[29]

Political ideology divorced from a deep sense of injustice generates only learned discussion, not popular resistance to imperial authority. For ordinary Americans, the reality of enforcement—the experience of actually living under a military regime—meant that arguments over unconstitutional legislation took on a heightened emotional quality. They were energized now by a palpable sense of shock and fear. Americans who found themselves in this highly charged political environment did not abandon or discount ideas about rights and liberty. These principles meant more to them now than ever before.

As the complacent Boston gentleman learned from the Ghost of History, the tough new imperial policy made it extremely hard to maintain a neutral stance. Troubled times demanded commitment. After all, North's policies had introduced notions of cruelty into the political equation. When Samuel Adams learned of the Port Act, he exclaimed, "For flagrant injustice and barbarity, one might search in vain the archives of Constantinople to find a match for it."[30] The rhetorical thrust of these complaints was not the restoration of the famed balanced constitution or reviving ancient republican virtue. Rather, people spoke of suffering and humiliation, and they contemplated retaliation and revenge. As one writer in the Salem newspaper observed, the mother country no longer deserved that name. Great Britain had revealed itself "more cruel than Sea-Monsters towards their young ones! Her Measures tend not only to dissolve our political union to her as a branch of the British Empire, but to destroy our affection to her as the Mother State. We have petitioned, prayed, pleaded, argued &c. with her, but all in vain; she is like the deaf Adder that stops her ears, she won't hear!—What must be done?"[31]

Popular writers framed the crisis in shrill, often uncompromising language. Someone who signed a newspaper essay "The PREACHER" understood the rhetorical demands of the times. He played upon themes of religious and regional responsibility. "It has been an animating consideration in every succeeding period of New England that God has ever smiled upon this People, and in all their Distresses hath appeared for their relief." Sounding much like the Ghost of History, he lectured newspaper readers: "From the first Settlement in 1620 to this Day, God has frowned upon the Enemies to the Rights and Liberties of this Country; those who have been influenced by *Satan* to be active and plotting against them, have come to disgrace and ruin, and remain on Record as Monuments of Divine Vengeance." The message was clear. If New Englanders continued to trust in God, "He will tread down their Enemies and cause Liberty to triumph over all her Foes in America."[32] While the PREACHER stopped short of urging colonists to take up arms against the government, he discouraged obedience to authorities who were in league with the Devil.

Popular anger about the Port Act often focused on Thomas Hutchinson, the previous royal governor of Massachusetts, who appeared to have sold out the Americans to gain the smiles of distant courtiers. Just as the hated legislation went into effect, the *Massachusetts Spy* proclaimed his name "an execration, and a curse, a hissing, and a proverb of reproach, to all future generations." When people in Newport, Rhode Island, learned of Hutchinson's supposed death in early June 1774—he in fact lived for several more years—they fantasized that just before he died, Hutchinson had a vision: "America, rising up before him, the blood streaming from the wounds she had received from the hands of this vile, barbarous parricide, cried—revenge!"[33]

Sometimes appeals for resistance appeared in the form of a secular catechism. This contrivance marked a significant development in the communication of grievance on the popular level. The performance was religious—as if a minister were inviting parishioners to give a formal response to a reading of the Psalms—but the content of the exchange focused entirely on the political crisis at hand. One two-page publication designed specifically for a broad readership demonstrated how writers—almost all of them anonymous—approached the problem of addressing angry people in a persuasive manner. The piece appeared in late May 1774 under a singularly uninviting title: "The following DIALOGUE being conceived, in some Measure, calculated to advance the Cause of FREEDOM, in the present critical Situation of Affairs, is for that Purpose presented to the PUBLIC." The author began with what may have appeared an open-ended question. "What think you of the Act of Parliament for shutting up the Port of Boston?" It immediately became apparent that the catechist deemed only one answer acceptable. "It appears to me an unconstitutional and tyrannical Act, and that a Submission to it will greatly endanger the Liberties of America."

When the naïve colonist in this exchange suggested that the residents of Boston might pay for the destroyed tea and get on with their lives, he learned that such conditions "are too humiliating and oppressive, to be yielded to, by Men who have a Sense of the Blessings of Freedom, and who possess the Means of securing them." The exchange did not turn on abstract philosophic or legal terms. The author wrote of personal humiliation. "If the Parliament of Great Britain are allowed to bring their Laws upon your Farms and your Soil, to regulate your internal Policy, and snatch from the honest Proprietor his peaceable and well earned Possessions," he warned, then "adieu to Liberty and all the Train of Blessings that attend her!" The "DIALOGUE" returned at the end—as did most productions of this sort—to the issue of political responsibility. What were ordinary colonists expected to do? "In the Cause of Freedom, in the Defense of our Liberties, every Struggle and Effort for Victory and Relief should be made." Perhaps for the moment colonists might propose plans to help Boston or support a boycott of British goods. These were timely measures. But whatever their response, he observed, Americans should remember, "There are Men who think it laudable, and their Duty, to die in the Defense of their Liberties."[34]

# THREE

# Revenge of the Countryside

If emotional rhetoric in the newspapers had been General Gage's only problem, he might have weathered the storm. That did not happen. Discontent ran deeper than either he or the members of North's cabinet realized, and as the days of summer passed, people living in small communities throughout New England began to discuss the imperial crisis in unprecedented ways. It was as if popular perceptions of cruelty and the shock of occupation empowered ordinary farmers for the first time to confront hard questions about political resistance.

Enforcement of the Boston Port Act dramatically exacerbated tensions throughout New England during the summer of 1774. Ordinary people were profoundly insulted by the notion that Parliament would punish an entire region for a single assault on tea owned by the East India Company. Many concluded that the imperial government intended to enslave all Americans simply because they happened to live in America. But resistance turned on more than imagined conspiracies. The implementation of the act stoked popular grievance. After June, all goods intended for Boston had to be landed in Salem, where officious customs collectors inspected every item and demanded a flood of new paperwork that greatly slowed the flow of commerce. Beyond insult and irritation, there was now a visible army of occupation. The number of British troops stationed in Boston increased almost daily, and no one doubted that they—as many as three thousand well-trained regulars—could at a moment's notice be deployed against the recalcitrant colonists.

These daily annoyances transformed the political climate of New England. Before 1774, the records of the great majority of towns throughout the region contained no hint of anxiety about a looming imperial crisis. To be sure, people living outside Boston followed the political news, but they tended to regard the controversy as somehow distant from their own immediate concerns. That changed, however, after the Coercive Acts were implemented.

People in Farmington, Connecticut, signaled just how quickly. They organized a bizarre protest, which revealed that popular resistance no longer emanated solely from Boston. On the morning of May 19 a "Hand-Bill" invited residents of this small community to participate in an event designed at once to honor "the immortal Goddess of Liberty" and to execute "the late infamous Act of the British Parliament." Sons of Liberty were expected to attend. A newspaper report claimed that a crowd of nearly one thousand gathered in the evening, to witness the erection of a huge pole "consecrated to the Shrine of Liberty." Soon thereafter someone read the Boston Port Act, and it was then "sentenced to the flames, and executed by the hands of the common hangman."

Even the act's fiery death failed to satisfy the inhabitants of Farmington. Without a single voice raised in opposition, they resolved that "the present Ministry, being instigated by the Devil, and led on by their own wicked and corrupt hearts, have a design to take away our liberties and properties and to enslave us forever." They condemned "the insults offered to the town of Boston" and urged "those Pimps and Parasites who dared to advise their Master to such detestable measures, be held in utter abhorrence by us and every American, and their names loaded with the curses of all succeeding generations." The Farmington ritual closed with a powerful secular invocation: "Do thou great LIBERTY inspire our souls! And make our lives in thy possession happy! Or our deaths glorious in thy just defense!"[1] More than two years before the Declaration of Independence the local people of Farmington gathered, debated, and on their own raised the prospect of political martyrdom, a major step on the road to insurgency.

On June 2, New London hosted an equally dramatic condemnation of the Port Act. This Connecticut town—long a center of radical religion—marked the day that "the cruel Edict" was scheduled to go into effect, ordering "the Bells of the Town . . . to Toll a solemn Peal." People in the community also nailed the hated act to "the Town House Door," which they had draped in black cloth. Normal business stopped. In fact, "the Shops in Town were all shut and silent; their Windows covered with Black and other Ensigns of Distress." In the early evening residents gathered in front of the town house, where someone read the entire act. A town official explained to the assembly, "We are now, my brethren, to determine whether we will tamely submit to every Act of cruel Oppression or indignantly reject . . . with manly resolution . . . every instance of unjust power." Among other resolutions that they approved, the members of the group declared themselves "determined, as far as we are able, to stand fast in the liberties wherewith God has made them free."[2]

A meeting held in nearby Windham raised the political temperature even higher. On June 23 the town concluded that the Coercive Acts represented "virulent efforts to break down the great barriers of civil society." When confronted by such oppression, the villagers discovered that "words fail and the English language is deficient." How, they asked, could anyone describe the East India Company as a victim of popular violence? Everyone knew that this evil corporation had "spread destruction over the eastern world," murdering "millions by sword and baleful famine." It was time to set the record straight. "The Spanish barbarities in Mexico, and the name of Cortez sink in everlasting oblivion" when compared to the "more recent superior cruelties . . . in the late annals of their [British] rapine and cruelty."[3] The town's protest— like those of so many of its neighbors—turned entirely on emotional revulsion. The community did not adopt shrill vocabulary simply for effect. Anger energized first local and soon regional protest.

Other towns joined an unprecedented conversation about how best to deal with a common threat. To be sure, ordinary farmers gathered initially in their own communities with neighbors and family members. No sooner had they passed resolutions supporting Boston and pledging resistance to parliamentary oppression, however, than they sent a copy of their decisions to the nearest journal, where it appeared as a news story. Although the original spark for these local discussions may have come from Boston's appeals for support, the emotional energy came from the people themselves. As the men who had attended a meeting in Wrentham, Massachusetts, on June 3 well understood, the pressing source of concern was an "act of the British parlement of an unparreled [*sic*] nature, by a fleet and Army, thereby . . . destroying and rendering the Charter of this province a useless piece of waste paper."

The possible use of military force in civil matters raised acute fears that contemporary decision makers would be advised to take seriously; these fears directly fueled an insurgency that became a successful revolution. The people of Wrentham, for example, truly believed that Britain's goal was the reduction of "the inhabitants of this province . . . to nothing short of the miserable and deplorable State of Conquered Slaves."[4] A gathering in Gorham, Maine (then still part of Massachusetts), captured the popular rage as well as any formal document surviving from this period. With stunning bluntness, these hardscrabble farmers resolved that "we of this town have such a high relish for Liberty that we, all with one heart, stand ready sword in hand, with the Italians in the Roman Republick, to defend and maintain our rights against all attempts to enslave us, and join our brethren, opposing force to force, if drove to the last extremity, which God forbid."[5] Lord North probably would not have been able to locate Gorham on a map. It is doubtful Gage had knowledge of these self-styled Italians in Maine. For British authorities to dismiss them without a second thought would have been easy. We should not do so. After all, over the next two months people like these purged the countryside of royal officials.

Popular reaction to occupation sparked an even more significant political development. Americans began to appreciate that simply because they were colonists in an empire, Parliament had relegated them to a second-class status. In the eyes of those who ruled them, they were not quite British. This mental process has been repeated scores of times over the last two centuries as subjects of European empires in Africa and Asia became painfully conscious that imperial officials perceived them as lesser beings. As Frantz Fanon and other voices from the Third World have reminded us, a growing consciousness of difference—a sense of being judged inferior by the standards of the mother country—held the seeds of resistance and ultimately of a new, powerful nationalist identity.[6] Certainly, the American colonists—like their counterparts in modern times—were highly attuned to the felt slight of being deemed second class. As the king's subjects living in America, they demanded "*all* the liberties of Englishmen," but as the author of a "Letter to the

Inhabitants of Massachusetts Bay" reminded them, "*because you are colonists*, you can pretend no claim to them."7

The Reverend Samuel Williams framed his critique of the Coercive Acts in precisely these terms. Parliament's oppressive statutes, he claimed, had invited Americans to rethink what it meant to be a colonist. In *A Discourse on the Love of Our Country*, delivered late in 1774, he observed, "Our peculiar situation as *Colonists*, requires that we should also view the spirit and tendency of our general system of government, as it relates to the *Parent State*." In earlier times, Americans had willingly accepted colonial status. Everyone agreed that "the mutual interests of both, evidently require[d] that an infant colony should be strongly attached to, and in a proper degree dependent upon the state from which it sprang." If anything, they had proved their forbearance.

Williams scoured history books. He could not find another imperial system in which distant colonies had remained steadfast as long as the Americans had done. "The colonies and distant provinces of other states, have almost ever been uneasy; complaining of the treatment they have received, and murmuring at the restraints they have been kept under," he explained. Nothing of this sort had occurred in the American colonies. From initial settlement to the conclusion of the Seven Years' War, the British Empire had inspired pride. As he recounted, "We were so far from entertaining the idea of opposition to Britain, that the very name of Whig and Tory, Court and Country party, was scarce known among us."8 What was perceived in a colonial setting as cruel punishment for the lost tea not only sparked widespread popular anger but also set ordinary people to questioning the burden of dependency.

# I

Effective political resistance generated more than angry words. After all, condemnation of parliamentary oppression was one thing, organized protest in support of these principles quite another. Throughout New England, families such as that of Isaac and Hannah Davis considered how they might demonstrate to friends and neighbors that they did in fact reject the new imperial policy. This was not a process that generated a single response such as assaulting a local equivalent of the Bastille. People confronted a broad range of possibilities, some more dangerous than others. If we concentrate only on incidents of explosive violence, we miss the less dramatic expressions of defiance that accompanied and sustained insurgency.

Within this framework, disaffection with British rule did not carry all before it like a huge political tsunami. Some colonists stopped drinking tea; others joined vigilante groups roaming the New England countryside. The point is that within this society, publicly forgoing the pleasure of a favorite hot beverage was as much a revolutionary act as forcing a royal appointee to resign. Both were declarations of disaffection. Even more important to our understanding of how ordinary Americans became revolutionaries is recognizing that those who took little steps—refusing to purchase British imported goods or calling for the creation of a Continental Congress, for example—created a climate that encouraged other people to adopt more coercive ways to preserve liberty.[9]

As the crisis deepened, many Americans came to view a boycott of British manufactured goods as the most promising way to force Lord North to adopt a more conciliatory policy. In June, soon after the Port Act went into effect, the Boston town committee advanced such a plan, and people in many towns declared their willingness to sacrifice consumer pleasures for a greater political good.[10] Like other communities, Biddeford expressed enthusiasm not only for nonimportation but also for tough enforcement on the local level. The inhabitants of this village in Maine voted to support "a Universal Withdrawment of our Commerce with the Island of Great Britain until the aforesaid Oppressive Acts of Parliament shall be Repealed." They anticipated that a national congress would eventually sanction a general boycott, and with that possibility in mind they warned in July 1774, "We further Resolve that if any Person among us shall Demean himself Contrary to any Plan that shall be Laid for our Deliverance by the Congress and agreed to by this and the Majority of the other Towns in the Province, we will have no Society, Trade or Commerce with such Person, But will Esteem and Treat him as an Enemy to his Country."[11]

Residents of Glastonbury, Connecticut, agreed, announcing that they would happily accept a no-trade scheme, since "we . . . are resolved to exert ourselves to the utmost of our power in every lawful way to oppose, resist, and if possible defeat the designs of our enemies to enslave us."[12] No doubt, even in these communities some colonists secretly sipped tea. But they did so at a personal risk. They could be publicly exposed, shamed by neighbors. Ordinary household goods suddenly acquired extraordinary political resonance. Private decisions in the marketplace revealed where one stood on political issues. Swearing off British goods probably did not represent a major challenge for most New Englanders, but acts of this sort had the capacity to draw strangers together in a cooperative enterprise that, although not particularly onerous for the individual consumer, did mobilize public opinion at a time of crisis.

Calls for a congress of representatives from all of Britain's thirteen mainland colonies offered another fairly undemanding form of resistance. Such a meeting, of course, made a lot of sense. A gathering of distinguished Americans provided a highly visible forum for addressing the king and Parliament in a way that promised a possible relaxation of imperial tensions. Town meetings throughout New England voted to support the initiative, which came to be known as the First Continental Congress. Within a full spectrum of popular responses to the Coercive Acts, this one may strike us as rather timid, especially when compared with more violent activities. Within the context of the times, however, moderate schemes—the public execution of an act of Parliament or the forgoing of tea—had significant implications for the general politicization of ordinary colonists. Those who appealed for a congress understood that it was in fact an extralegal body. It had no standing either in the British constitution or in parliamentary statute. Although almost no one advocated independence during the summer of 1774, enthusiasm for a congress revealed that many people had already begun to think in terms of an American or continental cause. This broad shift in thinking about political identity—still in its earliest stages—not only helped to corrode the bonds of empire but also encouraged others to engage in more provocative forms of resistance.

The problem with focusing attention almost exclusively on the Continental Congress is that it discounts other, more subversive choices that people were making in their own communities. While colonial assemblies selected leading planters and lawyers to participate in the Congress at Philadelphia, ordinary New Englanders were busy dismantling imperial authority. These more aggressive moves were aimed almost entirely at the Massachusetts Government Act, which colonists regarded as oppressive and unconstitutional. They vowed no longer to obey orders from officials who held commissions under the system now headed by General Gage. According to one newspaper statement signed by more than one hundred individuals from towns scattered throughout Massachusetts, the people faced a choice between "LIFE & DEATH, or what is more, FREEDOM & SLAVERY." The signers declared, "as men, as freemen, as Christian freemen, united in the firmest bonds," to oppose "every civil officer now in commission in this province, and acting in conformity to the late act of Parliament." The cutoff date was July 1, 1774, the moment the Government Act went into effect. The group warned, "If any of said officers shall accept a commission under the present plan of arbitrary government, or in any way or manner whatever, assist the governor or administration in the assault now making on our rights and liberties, we will consider them as having forfeited their commissions, and yield them no obedience."[13]

During the summer of 1774, scores of communities throughout Massachusetts likewise voted to no longer transfer tax revenues to Harrison Gray, a treasurer of loyalist sympathies. The people made this extraordinary decision in town meetings. In other words, it was again on the local level that they most effectively challenged the legitimacy of the new imperial plan of government. Marblehead provided good insight into this profound reassessment. "A full Meeting" of the town directed the clerk to enter into the official records "such persons as should by the Province be considered and published as 'Rebels against the State,' and to the Constables and Collectors to pay to *Henry Gardiner*, Esquire, moneys which they then had, or in future might have in their hands, belonging to the Province." The inhabitants explained that henceforth everyone should ignore "the late Treasurer *Gray* being treated with the contempt due to one on the Rebel list."[14]

An even more significant breakdown of traditional authority occurred in the colony's militia units. In company after company, local officers resigned their posts rather than accept commissions issued by Governor Gage. Stepping down from positions of leadership did not mean that the militia no longer trained on a regular schedule. "The town of Marblehead," for example, "have agreed that their regiment of militia shall turn out four times in a week, with arms and ammunition according to law, in order to perfect themselves in the Military Art."[15] Local officers simply pretended that the Government Act had no impact on their relation to the men who served as soldiers.

Gage thought the revolt within the colony's military could be traced to the ordinary troops who had politicized the militia. He explained to Lord Dartmouth, "The officers of the militia, have, in most places, been forced to resign their commissions, and the men choose their officers who are frequently made and unmade."[16] In Worcester County—the most radical area in Massachusetts—"a Convention of Committees" sparked a major change in the command structure, voting in late August 1774:

> Voted, That it be recommended to the military officers in this county that they resign their offices to their respective Colonels.
> Voted, That the field officers in this county resign their offices, and publish such resignation in all the Boston newspapers.
> Voted, That it be recommended to the several towns in this county to choose proper and a sufficient number of military officers for each of their towns.[17]

Gage was fully justified in concern about the rebellion within the militia. As early as 1774—almost a year before the battles of Lexington and Concord—New Englanders anticipated confrontation with British regulars. At that moment they would have to be able to count on local military units. As the Reverend Jonathan Parsons, a Presbyterian minister in Newburyport, Massachusetts, explained in a published sermon, the colonists must be prepared to "repair our injuries at the point of the sword, for if one man may defend himself and his rights against an assailant, much more may a whole country defend themselves when their rights are invaded, because the concern is greater." Drawing on a powerful strain of evangelical Protestantism, Parsons sanctioned the taking up of arms. "In such case," he observed, "the spirit of Christian benevolence would animate us to fill our streets with blood, rather than suffer others to rob us of our rights." The men serving in the militia must surely know that "if old friends are disposed to be terrible . . . then it becomes us to take up arms and use them in the nature of a remedy."[18]

The courts of Massachusetts also generated extraordinary popular anger. The colonists took pride in their legal system, but as the protest against the Coercive Acts escalated, the people concluded that by restructuring the provincial government, Parliament had fatally compromised the institutions of justice. They feared that judges who received commissions after the Massachusetts Government Act had gone into effect would enforce oppressive and unconstitutional laws. To avoid that possibility, they closed the courts. No central revolutionary body within the colony organized these actions. Fear and resentment energized the closing of courts throughout the countryside, and as newspapers reported these events, the popular assault on the judges accelerated. As Gage informed Dartmouth in early September, "Civil Government is near its end, the Courts of Justice expiring one after another." The governor entertained the idea of marching regular troops to Worcester to protect the justices, but advisers in Boston discouraged such a bold move on the grounds that the force he had available was insufficient to provide security throughout the colony, and "after all, no Jurors would swear in; that it was needless laying fines, which they could not do on Grand Juries, there being no law for it in the Province; and, withal, it would be in vain, the refusal being universal."[19]

And so, made painfully aware of the impotence of imperial authority, Gage read the newspapers, which carried descriptions of massive intimidation. "We hear," noted one typical journal announcement, "that several Thousand People were collected from the Towns in the Neighborhood of Springfield, on Tuesday last, with a full Determination to stop the Proceedings of the County Court which was to sit in that Town on that Day."[20] Large numbers of people participated. "We hear that near 6000 men assembled at Worcester, on Monday and Tuesday last, and prevented the Inferior Court from sitting there," claimed another gazette in September.[21]

Occasionally, real personalities broke through the veil of anonymity that characterized reports of resistance. The opening of the superior court at Boston on August 30 was such a moment. We encounter here people who in the name of a higher political principle refused to recognize the legitimacy of an institution they perceived to be an instrument of general oppression.

The event began with a ritual designed to celebrate the majesty of the law. According to one witness, "The Chief Justice, Peter Oliver, Esquire, and the other Justices of the said Court, together with a number of Gentlemen of the Bar, attended by the High and Deputy Sheriffs, walked in procession from the State House to the Court House, in Queen Street." After the justices had taken their places, the clerk presented the names of those selected for this session to serve as grand jurors. That is when the protestors suddenly broke with the traditional script. First, the foreman refused to be sworn. Others followed his example. "The question being put to them all severally, whether they would take the oath," noted one reporter, "they one and all refused; and being asked whether they had any reasons to offer for their thus refusing, they answered they had."

The rebellious jurors presented the justices with a written statement that they asked to read out in open court. Not surprisingly, Oliver had no intention of providing the jurors with a forum for protest. But his opposition did not matter. The jurymen marched to the nearby Exchange Tavern, "where they unanimously voted that, in order to justify their refusal to the world, their aforementioned reasons should be printed in the public papers." Point by point they defended their conviction that the judges themselves had undermined constitutional law. In a powerfully worded final section, they announced they had refused the oath "because we believe, in our consciences, that our acting in concert with a Court so constituted, and under such circumstances, would be . . . betraying the just and sacred rights of our native land . . . which we look upon ourselves as under the most sacred and inviolable obligations to maintain, and to transmit, whole and entire, to our posterity."

The published statement included the names of twenty-two jurymen who resided in seventeen different towns. Their refusal to take the official oath was a genuinely revolutionary act. By standing up to royal appointees, they demonstrated that the old order was swiftly crumbling, at least in Massachusetts. Others joined them. A clerk for the Middlesex County court who had originally issued a juror list for the sheriff now came forward to "ask the pardon of all my Fellow Countrymen." Even though he was an old man with a large family to support, he resigned a post he had held for thirty-eight years—as an expression of his opposition "to all the attempts the British Parliament have made to subjugate the colonies to the most abject, cruel and oppressive slavery."[22]

During the summer of 1774 the people of New England created a

meeting culture, an essential ingredient of revolution. They made individual decisions about civil disobedience—closing the courts, diverting
local tax monies to a trusted treasurer, refusing orders from militia officers who had accepted commissions from the new government—within
groups. Towns discussed how best to respond to the crisis; counties
brought representatives together in support of the spreading protest. The
meeting culture made it very difficult for dissenters—skeptics as well as
committed loyalists—to resist pressure applied by organized neighbors.

And one did not have to attend a meeting to experience the excitement that accompanies popular mobilization. As soon as the members
of a community voted to defy the Coercive Acts, they reported their actions to a newspaper. The spread of such news helped persuade scattered groups that they were part of a larger movement that they called
the American cause. As the *Essex Gazette* observed, "The News-Papers
from all Quarters, in every British American Colony, so far as we have
yet received Intelligence, are chiefly filled with Accounts of Meetings and Resolutions of Towns and Counties, all to the same Purpose—
complaining of Oppression, proposing a Congress, a Cessation of
Intercourse with Great-Britain, and a Contribution for the Relief of the
Poor of Boston."[23] In August, the lieutenant governor of New York, a
Crown appointee, alerted Dartmouth, "From a view of the numerous
resolves of the people in all the Colonies, which appear in every newspaper, your Lordship might be led to think a stupid fatal hardiness
intoxicated the whole."[24] The writer assured Dartmouth that many
Americans still remained loyal, but of course, to the colonists who pored
over the journals, it seemed as if a spirit of resistance had indeed "intoxicated" the whole. The news assured angry militiamen, taxpayers,
and jurymen that whatever happened, they were not alone. To be sure,
they had not resorted to violence, but small rebellious steps contributed
to a political atmosphere favorable to insurgency.

# II

During the last weeks of August 1774, political rage throughout Massachusetts took on a more menacing aspect. At that moment popular resistance became violent. Without a clearly defined command structure,

thousands of anonymous farmers from small inland towns took the law into their own hands and within a short time had dismantled imperial authority outside Boston, now an occupied city surrounded by irregular colonial forces.

The breaking point came on August 9, when Gage announced the names of the individuals appointed to the council under the provisions of the Massachusetts Government Act. Dartmouth anticipated that publication of the list of twenty-four people would stir up trouble. Neither he nor Gage had had the leisure properly to vet the various suggestions put forward, and in the rush to curtail what they called the democratic element in the Massachusetts constitution, they selected persons they hoped could be trusted to implement a tough new colonial policy. On June 3—before the public release of the names—Dartmouth had confessed to Gage, "It would have been a great satisfaction if, in the choice of the persons recommended to the King to be of the new Council, we could have procured more perfect and satisfactory information both of the characters and connections of the principal persons in the colony qualified for such a trust; but the case would admit of no delay."[25] Dartmouth's inability to collect more reliable intelligence proved of secondary importance. Simply naming these people—known as mandamus councilors—put them in harm's way. Imperial oppression was now given real names and personalities. It had inescapably fastened itself on to specific colonists who suddenly had a lot to answer for. Overnight, they became targets of popular wrath.

Appointees residing in Boston were safe enough, but since Gage did not have sufficient troop strength to secure the towns outside the capital, the councilors who lived in the countryside were forced to look out for themselves. This at a time when Gage reported to Dartmouth, "It is agreed that popular fury was never greater in this province than at present."[26] How the governor acquired information about the people's anger was not clear. He may have read the newspapers or had agents in the field. Whatever his sources were, they proved accurate. The "inhabitants of the 5th parish in Gloucester," for example, described themselves as "being few in number, and chiefly poor fishermen, [who] have not time nor skill in the studies of politicks." But the appointment of a new council made insurgents of them. In a piece that appeared under the title "The Fish Hook and Fowling Piece," they declared, "we have in our colonies, many stupid villains endeavoring to aid in fastening on our necks and that of our posterity the yoke of bondage . . . How warm we feel; good God, our trust in thee. Our fowling pieces are ready while our fishing lines are in hand."[27] A writer from New London asked readers, "whether there is any Native Inhabitant of the Massachusetts Colony left . . . base enough to accept the empty title of Councilor, on the new fangled constitution? And if so, whether it ought to be considered in any other light, than an unnatural child, aiding an assassin to rip up his mother's bowels? And ought [he] not be shunned and abhorred more than an inhabitant of Hell?"[28] The Massachusetts Government Act had the unintended effect of declaring open season on anyone who dared accept a commission from the Crown.

Timothy Paine was one of the first to fall. He had long played the part of the country gentleman in central Massachusetts. A graduate of Harvard College, he served in a number of judicial posts, dabbled in real estate, and married a very wealthy woman who happened to be his stepsister. Although he insisted that he had never asked to become a mandamus councilor, his name appeared on the official list. The popular response came quickly. Early on the morning of August 27, companies of men appeared on the Worcester Commons. Estimates of their number varied wildly, but the best guess was about fifteen hundred, a figure roughly equal to the town's entire population. The visitors, who apparently did not carry arms, milled around for several hours, and at about nine o'clock they elected a committee of representatives to speak with Paine at his house, not far from the Commons. He received the group as cordially as one might expect in the circumstances, asking them to explain their business. They demanded not only that he resign from the new council, but also that he provide the representatives with a written statement of his intentions.

The whole business annoyed Paine, who expected ordinary people to show him proper respect. But there was little he could do. As he explained laconically in a letter to Governor Gage, "I found myself under a necessity of complying." As soon as Paine had scribbled out his resignation, the committee demanded that he read the paper to the entire body of fifteen hundred men waiting on the Commons. Paine feared for his life, but the representatives of the "people" assured him that he would be safe. On the way to the town center he "met with no insult" except that some members of the assembled farmers demanded that he "walk with [his] hat off when [he] passed through them."

The hat incident suggested that for the people, more than Paine's public resignation was at stake. The men who had traveled to Worcester Commons took the occasion to humiliate a person who had perhaps behaved over the years as if he believed himself superior to the ordinary lot. A spirit of equality demanded that he appear before them bare-headed—as an ordinary colonist. At that moment, no one—most especially not Paine—inquired by what authority this spontaneously formed assembly claimed to speak for the people. There had been no plebiscite. No doubt an extraordinarily large turnout provided powerful evidence that the crowd really did represent the people. At the end of the day, however, it was merely a rhetorical device. By assuming this voice, insurgent groups legitimized—perhaps to the very people they claimed to represent—attacks on Crown officials. Paine was lucky. The farmers judged his performance acceptable, and within a short time they dispersed. Paine, however, remained in shock. Writing to Gage, he observed, "You see an open opposition has taken place to the Acts of the British Parliament . . . [the] people's spirits are so raised they seem determined to risk their lives and everything dear to them in the opposition, and prevent any person from executing any commission he may receive under the present administration."[29]

Residents of Hingham identified Joshua Loring as the commodore. During the Seven Years' War he had received a commission as captain in the British navy and had served with distinction during campaigns on Lakes Champlain and Ontario. During those exciting times he had come to love the empire. Although his loyalist sentiments were no secret, the political nightmare that began at midnight on August 29 must have come as a surprise. A loud pounding on the front door awakened his family. Loring threw open an upstairs window and "saw five men disguised, their faces blackened, hats flapped and with cutlasses in their hands." When asked who sent them, the insurgents answered that they "came from a mob." And they demanded that Loring resign immediately from the new council. After it became clear that the commodore had no intention of stepping down, a spokesman warned that the group would return the next night to obtain satisfaction. But before departing, sixty or more men gathered on the road fired their guns.

Loring had seen enough. He fled to Boston, leaving his frightened wife and son to deal with the night visitors. When the men did return, they insisted on an audience with Loring himself. The son played for time, but the leaders, still with "faces blackened and cutlasses in their hands," cut off negotiation. They noted that they had now gathered twice at Loring's home. Their patience was running out. According to Loring, they told his son "to beware of the third" visit, for if a public announcement of resignation did not soon appear in the newspaper, "the consequences . . . would be very severe, that his house should be leveled to the ground, and many other of the like threats." All this time a crowd of several hundred men armed with clubs lined the road, screaming threats and drumming loudly on a fence. In a stunning understatement, Loring explained that the noise "was designed to intimidate." The tactic worked. Even without having to destroy the house, the people successfully drove another mandamus councilor from the countryside.[30]

Lieutenant Governor Thomas Oliver tried to check the popular rage. He succeeded no better than had Paine or Loring. Oliver explained his ordeal at the hands of the people in a long, painful letter to Dartmouth. Before the eventful morning of September 2, he had enjoyed a life of ease. His father had bequeathed him a large plantation on Antigua, and after graduating from Harvard, Thomas lived a comfortable life in his adopted home in Cambridge. Although he did not practice law as friends had expected, well-placed patrons—including Thomas Hutchinson—rewarded the amiable Oliver with a number of lucrative government posts. When Gage became governor of Massachusetts, Dartmouth asked Oliver to serve as lieutenant governor. In addition, he received an appointment as a mandamus councilor.

His moment of reckoning began early in the day. As he later recounted, "a large body of people to the amount of 1500 came down from the country without arms, consisting of landholders of this county, marching through this town." The prospect of confronting so many outsiders did not initially worry Oliver. He knew, of course, that the Government Act had destabilized imperial authority outside Boston. "Your lordship will have heard," Oliver explained to Gage, "that the commotions of the people upon the alterations of government had risen to such a pitch in this province that several gentlemen of the Council declined taking their seats at the Board." But the men filtering into Cambridge did not fit Oliver's notions of the kinds of people one would classify as troublemakers or rabble. They spoke well. No one offered insults. "I perceived they were the land-holders of the neighboring towns, and was thoroughly persuaded they would do no harm." After discussing the pressing issues of the day, Oliver reaffirmed his judgment that these outsiders were "no mob, but sober, orderly people, who would commit no disorders." This was a dramatic example of confronting the enemy and not recognizing them as such. He failed to appreciate that ordinary farmers had become insurgents.

The early arrivals who drifted into Cambridge expressed the fear that General Gage was preparing to send regular troops to pacify the countryside. When Oliver learned the source of their concern, he gave his personal assurance that the redcoats would remain in Boston. He dispatched a message to Gage warning that deployment of soldiers would be "attended with the most fatal Consequences, and particularly to your Excellency's Most Obedient Servant." Oliver's actions merely postponed the real business of the day. With each passing hour, more and more men from the region entered the town. Driven perhaps by anger as well as curiosity, they crowded into the open space around Oliver's house. By midafternoon the number of protesters had reached "three or four thousand," and perhaps of greater concern, "one quarter part [were] in arms." A committee of five selected out of the body of the people demanded that Oliver resign his position as councilor. When he charged them with ingratitude—apparently for his discouraging Gage's troops from marching to Cambridge—they calmly asked him "to consider the consequences of refusing the demands of an enraged People."

Oliver bravely exclaimed that he preferred death to humiliation. His histrionics had no impact on the intended audience. The people expressed growing impatience. They peered in the windows of Oliver's house, "calling for vengeance against the Foes of their Liberty . . . [and] I could hear them from a distance, swearing they would have my blood." Oliver's wife and children were crying in the next room. Finally he signed the forced resignation, adding, no doubt to save his own reputation with the imperial establishment, a defense: "My house being Surrounded with four thousand People, in compliance with their commands I sign my name." Neither Gage nor Dartmouth blamed Oliver for retreating to Boston. They agreed with him that it was "unsafe to remain longer among a People, who in such a state of frenzy, were governed by no principles, but blindly led, or impelled by a set of wicked seditious Levellers." Oliver and his family eventually moved to London.

During the American siege of Boston in 1775, his grand house in Cambridge—a symbol of imperial privilege—served as a hospital and command post for Connecticut soldiers who promised to do the structure no harm.[31]

The dismantling of the newly structured imperial government quickly gained momentum, spreading throughout the province and encountering almost no organized opposition. Only within the fortified perimeters of Boston could anyone safely perform the duties of a mandamus councilor. But outside the capital itself, no region was secure. Put another way, spontaneous popular efforts to intimidate Crown officials occurred in all areas. None seemed more committed or more radical than the others. Daniel Leonard, for example, fled to the protection of Gage's army after he learned that plans were circulating in Taunton "to deal with me." These were no idle threats. In late August "about five hundred persons assembled, many of them Freeholders and some of them Officers in the Militia, and formed themselves into a Battalion before my house." Leonard informed Gage that "they had no Fire-arms, but generally had clubs." Perhaps the armed insurgents arrived later, for at around 11:00 p.m. he reported that those with guns "fired upon the house with small arms and run off."[32]

A body of some three thousand men demanded that Timothy Ruggles, another mandamus councilor, leave the town of Dartmouth, and when he finally decided to depart, he discovered that the people had mutilated his horse. Samuel Danforth and Joseph Lee capitulated at the first sign of violence. Both submitted oral and written resignations to the people. Danforth, who described himself as a person of "advanced age," wrote out what he had already stated "to a great concourse of people." In the statement he pledged "not to be any way concerned as a Member of the Council at any time hereafter." Lee had not wanted to resign, but as he informed Gage, the new imperial government "has so universally inflamed the minds of the people of the Province and excited such tumults and disorders . . . as threatens a Catastrophe greatly to be dreaded . . . I am therefore obliged to submit to the Rage of the times." In Plymouth, "the indignation of the people" against George Watson, another mandamus councilor, was so palpable that they walked out en masse from church on a Sunday morning, announcing that they could not worship alongside someone supporting "despotism" and "the Popish religion

[in] this country."³³ High sheriffs and other court officials joined the forced exodus from the Massachusetts countryside.

The number of people involved in these incidents in Massachusetts reveals a lot about the developing insurgency. How many Crown officers were driven from their homes is hard to determine. Several score seem to have fled to Boston during the summer of rage. Far more significant, however, are the figures for popular resistance. Although frightened mandamus appointees probably exaggerated the size of the crowds, they were certainly correct in reporting that thousands of ordinary farmers had participated in confrontations with imperial authorities throughout the colony. Only religious revivals had so dramatically and so publicly generated numbers of this size. And for the most part the militants showed little concern about preserving their anonymity. Paine and Oliver knew full well the townsmen who demanded their resignations. The beleaguered officials also knew that there was nothing they could do to stem the tide.

The popular rage burned just as strongly in neighboring colonies. In early September 1774 Abijah Willard, another newly appointed councilor, journeyed to western Connecticut on business. As soon as he reached the town of Union, he expected to meet two lawyers from Windham. They were there, but to his surprise, they loudly condemned Willard for being "a Traitor to his Country." The charges provoked the people living in the area. About four hundred of them kidnapped Willard, carried him to Brimfield, and organized a tribunal, which sentenced the prisoner to hard labor at the Newgate Prison in Simsbury. The group had no sooner set off for the jail than Willard decided to sign an oath declaring his contempt for the Massachusetts Government Act. He acted just in time. When a Captain Davis of Brimfield attempted to intervene on Willard's behalf, the people "stripped him and gave him the New Fashion Dress of Tar and Feathers." According to intelligence that Gage received, Willard's journey home to Lancaster was almost as difficult as what he had already endured. Communities along the road turned out to insult the hated councilor. Some angry colonists "even put [arms] to his breast with threats of instant death unless he signed a paper the contents of which he did not know or regard."³⁴

Although the mandamus councilors found themselves the main focus of public rage, other figures in the countryside—many of whom did not even hold commissions from Gage—became targets for vengeance. The largest group consisted of leading Massachusetts lawyers and merchants who had publicly thanked the previous royal governor Thomas Hutchinson for a job well done. Their motives varied. Some claimed that conciliatory rhetoric might serve to promote a more constructive relationship with Parliament. Others were sincere loyalists who believed that a number of radical troublemakers had misled the people about imperial policy.

Whatever their thinking may have been, composing a congratulatory letter to Hutchinson as he sailed from Boston for London and then publishing the signed texts in regional newspapers constituted a serious error in judgment. The notices contained scores of names. Since the people blamed Hutchinson for the Coercive Acts, they proclaimed his enthusiastic supporters traitors to the American cause. And their identities were now a matter of public record. One newspaper lectured Hutchinson—now long departed from the colony—"If the curses of a whole people can have any effect, you will never have another peaceful moment . . . your name [will be] handed down, for an execration, and a curse, a hissing, and a proverb of reproach, to all future generations." Another piece in the *Essex Gazette* observed that the world was full of people "who pay religious worship to the Devil thinking, and designing, by such means, to flatter, cajole, and keep him in good temper." It seemed that the compliments lately paid to Hutchinson fell into this category.[35]

Of the many signers of the Hutchinson addresses who suffered popular retribution, Francis Green may have had the most harrowing experience. In late July, pressing legal matters necessitated that he travel from his home in Massachusetts to various towns in Connecticut. It probably did not help his reception that Green intended to collect overdue debts. Reports that he had praised Hutchinson spread throughout the area, and soon after he and a companion engaged rooms at Carey's Tavern in Windham, an angry crowd collected. At first the people merely shouted for Green to make an appearance. Between nine and ten o'clock in the evening one organizer informed him that if he had not left the community by six o'clock the next morning, he should "beware of the consequences." Good to its word, the group reappeared the next day. Church bells rang out an alarm; a cannon was placed before the tavern door. Finally, a few local protesters broke into Green's rooms, forcing him to get out of town without further delay. The ordeal was not over. Messengers ran ahead of him, warning people in the next towns that a hated Hutchinson supporter would soon pass through. In Norwich guns were fired and voices in the crowd were heard to say, "Let us go and fetch the cart," a frightening reference to tarring and feathering. In the end, the people were content simply to throw Green into his own carriage, and as he drove off, the residents lined the road, tossing stones and trash at the vehicle.

When Gage later complained directly to Governor Trumbull of Connecticut about Green's humiliation, some men implicated in the attack responded that what had happened in Connecticut was none of Gage's business, and in any case, they reasoned that Gage should have been aware that "it is well known that Governor Hutchinson is considered by all the Colonies as the principal agent who procured the Act for blocking up the port of Boston, and the other distressing Acts, and that it is the general sense of the whole Continent that those Acts are unconstitutional and oppressive." Green's politics provoked the assault. He should certainly not have been surprised when the people declared his "personal presence . . . disagreeable." Trumbull, who had been elected rather than appointed to office, read the temper of the times better than did Gage. He explained to the Massachusetts governor that he had investigated Green's charges, "and find that others, well knowing the affair do put a very different face and color on those transactions."[36]

In the district of Maine the violence of the summer of 1774 visited individuals whose major transgression amounted to little more than expressions of support for British authority. Local farmers in Gorham took it upon themselves to harass suspected loyalists, and a group of about thirty to forty of them—probably members of a loosely organized militia unit—decided that Dr. Abiathar Alden had been insufficiently enthusiastic about American resistance to the Coercive Acts. It made no matter that Alden lived in Scarborough. The vigilantes forced him out of his house, placed him on a convenient hogshead, and demanded he recant his objectionable principles. To help him make up his mind, every militiaman pointed a gun at him. They warned that he would experience instant death if he should refuse. Not surprisingly, the frightened physician confessed his alleged sins. He had been wrong to speak in favor of

Parliament; he had erred in opposing the resistance of the people to despotism. At the end of Alden's ritual apology his tormentors ordered him to shout, "[I] am very thankful for my life."

A few days later the Gorham militia learned that one of Alden's friends had supplied Gage's troops with materials needed to build military barracks. Richard King, who had aggressively endorsed the Stamp Act a few years earlier, was compelled to stand on a table and read a statement of contrition to the assembly. But King did not quite get it right. During his confession he observed that a very few Americans scattered over a huge territory had anything to hope for in a contest with the first nation of the Old World. Although this assessment of the American prospects seemed reasonable enough, the insurgents condemned the argument. They reportedly rattled their weapons in disapproval, and their captain demanded, "Down upon your knees, Sir, and erase that sentence; these soldiers can't endure the sentiment." Having obtained satisfaction, the visitors finally dispersed, but the man who defended the empire fell into depression. He died a few months later—supposedly of madness—and among his papers someone discovered a document containing a summary of his true political beliefs. "Our only Safety is in remaining firm to that Stock of which we are a Branch," he wrote, "and as a Prudent Man that guards against a Pestilential Air when a plague is in the City, so should we guard against those false Patriots of the present day who advise us to resist." In a final cry borne of incomprehension of the insurgency, he prayed, "Great God prevent our madness!"[37]

## *III*

These scattered incidents upset traditional narratives of the American Revolution. It is tempting, therefore, to dismiss the outbursts of popular rage as isolated cases that in no way detract from a familiar chronicle that leads directly from the destruction of the tea in Boston Harbor to the meeting of the First Continental Congress in September 1774. That would be a mistake. However disturbing the rising of an angry countryside may be, it cannot be ignored. To be sure, American insurgents did not destroy homes or murder royal officials in their beds. To take from this the notion that the American Revolution was a reasonable, largely intellectual affair, while other world-changing revolutions were defined by massive violence, is to miss the point.

Within the context of the lives of the colonists, assaults on councilors and other officials of the Crown had no precedent. Thousands of ordinary people—most of them farmers—were drawn into a political situation that required them to make hard decisions. Again, numbers were important. The individuals who pressed into Worcester or Cambridge to demand resignations from the hated mandamus councilors gained a sense of empowerment simply by seeing so many other people willing to come forward in support of a common cause. And purging the region of prominent representatives of the Crown was in itself a major accomplishment. Public resignations and confessions eroded the psychic bonds of empire. Every time a councilor was forced to step down, it became harder for Americans living in small communities to remain neutral or, like Richard King, to question whether resistance had any chance to succeed. The night visits and acts of terror revealed— if nothing else—the impotence of Gage's government. A misguided policy of toughness had demonstrated not only that the British were not really all that tough, but also that the Americans were more determined in their resistance than either they or their rulers had imagined at the start of the crisis.

Dartmouth failed to appreciate the real test facing the New England insurgency. At issue was not whether Gage could overwhelm popular resistance in Massachusetts, Connecticut, and Rhode Island with a larger army. The most pressing question for the Americans during the summer of 1774 was whether ordinary people in other colonies would support the rising in New England. As Samuel Adams explained to Richard Henry Lee, the challenge is whether "the people of America consider these measures [the Coercive Acts] as an attack on the Constitution of an individual Province, in which the rest are not interested, or will they view the model of Government prepared for us as a system for the whole Continent."[38] Implicit in Adams's query was the realization that—for New England at least—there was no turning back. The Ghost of History would have been proud.

# FOUR

# *Reaching Out to Others*

The political hopes of the men who drove the Crown appointees from the Massachusetts countryside could easily have been dashed. One has only to contemplate the very real possibility that other Americans could have condemned the insurgents of central New England as irresponsible troublemakers who had foolishly provoked the British military. Many colonists of Tory persuasion did just that. Which begs the question: Why should anyone living outside the region have concluded that the cause of New England was legitimately the cause of America?

The success of the Americans in reaching out to one another owed a lot to the creation of effective networks of communication. These systems linked distant strangers—people from South Carolina and Virginia, for example—with those New Englanders who during the initial burst of enthusiasm had challenged the legitimacy of Crown officials. The dissemination of information about local incidents of resistance or about ordinary colonists who had experienced severe hardships in the name of American liberty served to promote bonds of sympathy, the key to effective mobilization.

Newspapers—a relatively innovative form of communication in eighteenth-century provincial society—helped persuade colonial readers that no matter where they happened to live, they had a personal stake in what occurred in Boston. During 1774 and 1775 an unprecedented exchange of political intelligence gained momentum, and long before the Continental Congress got around to declaring independence, a surge of shared information convinced Americans that they could in fact trust other Americans whom they had never met.

Shared experience of resistance should not be confused with the content of formal political pamphlets. These publications have long dominated our memory of the American Revolution. Almost everyone has encountered a brilliant essay penned by such figures as John Dickinson, Thomas Jefferson, or John Adams. And well they should. These works contained powerfully innovative ideas about natural rights and republican theory. Educated leaders responded to the writings of other educated leaders and in the process developed abstract arguments about political liberty and advanced constitutional claims in the manner of well-trained lawyers. But this information—however valuable it may have been in shaping congressional deliberations—was not the stuff of collective revolutionary experience. As Isaiah Thomas, the highly successful editor of the *Massachusetts Spy*, explained, "common sense in common language is necessary to influence one class of citizens, as much as learning and elegance of composition are to produce an effect upon another."[1]

The point is not that the ordinary colonists who supported the insurgency were lowbrow or anti-intellectual. They most certainly were not. Rather, we are concerned with the actual communication of personal political experience. On this level, newspaper stories about distant communities organizing to resist Great Britain carried an emotional charge that is absent from the learned pamphlets.

The collective sense of common purpose that strengthened the insurgency was the product of mutual sympathy. It derived not only from the dissemination of information about resistance but also from how people interpreted that information even if they had not witnessed the events being described. If these reports had seemed patently disingenuous or painfully self-serving, they would not have had much impact on the loyalties of distant strangers. For political information to become a powerful mobilizing force—as it did during the two years before independence—it had to spark the sympathy of colonists living in other areas. It also had to raise the possibility that what had happened to the people of Boston could happen to other Americans.

Shared knowledge, therefore, assumed a grasp of the basic facts—the punitive character of the Coercive Acts, for example—as well as an empathy for the suffering of others who did not seem all that different from one's own neighbors. The emotional content of political intelligence encouraged people to act on what they thought had happened to others. This was precisely what occurred throughout America on the eve of independence. Colonists reading about events in Boston persuaded themselves that ordinary people who lived there were suffering for all Americans. Their cause was the cause of any person capable of compassion for the victims of political oppression. As with other insurgencies in more modern times, the ability to imagine the condition of strangers—again, a function of effective communication—provided the emotional foundation for united resistance.[2] As an author writing under the pen name Amicus Patriae asked the people of New Hampshire during the summer of 1774 in response to appeals to help the workers of Boston, "Will not such communications of charity strengthen the bonds of society, and endear us to each other? And when a firm union is thus cemented, happy our mutual affection, in the increased cultivation of our lands, in our frugality and economy, we shall securely bid defiance to all the enemies of our peace."[3]

# I

By creating a foundation of shared experience, newspapers played a key role in sustaining the American insurgency. They linked scattered communities at a moment of revolutionary decision. Publishers not only reported local events, they also established effective ways to distribute these stories to readers living in distant places. Otherwise, news would still have been news, but it would have remained local news.[4] Within a highly volatile context, insurgent networks drew strength first from reports of organized resistance to British authority and second from the broad dissemination of this intelligence to scattered communities throughout colonial America.

Newspapers did not have a long history before the Revolution. Early-eighteenth-century attempts to establish profitable journals in Boston and New York yielded only modest results, and squabbling between partners or the death of a talented printer frequently led to the closing down of an entire operation. The journals focused for the most part on commercial matters. The arrival and departure of ships figured centrally in these pages. Sensitive political topics usually caused more trouble than they were worth in terms of added readership. Although a savvy publisher might include essays lifted from the London papers, he or she—a number of publishers during this period were in fact women—generally concentrated on official government announcements and advertisements for goods just imported from Great Britain. And a printer who failed to obtain the patronage of the royal governor or the colonial legislature faced bleak financial prospects.

The character of newspapers began to change after the passage of the Stamp Act in 1765. Imperial tensions fueled a popular demand for information about parliamentary policy. By the early 1770s about forty-two colonial newspapers were in operation. They circulated in the large port cities, but journals also appeared in smaller towns such as Newport, New London, Norwich, Worcester, Annapolis, and Wilmington. Since literacy rates were high and since ordinary people could afford the price, newspapers were able to reach a wide social spectrum of readers. As Silas Deane of Connecticut wrote in 1776, almost all free colonists had "some Education," and even "the very poorest" consulted "Gazettes & political publications, which they read, observe upon and debate in a Circle of their Neighbors."[5] The *Boston Evening-Post* also noted the growing interest in political intelligence. "We, who are at a distance from the metropolis," the editor explained, "have no other way of being conversant with the political world than the Newspapers; therefore it is our constant practice to peruse them."[6] Some readers, of course, turned to the journals to learn more about the latest fashions or gossip related to the members of the royal family, but regardless of their intentions, more and more people on the eve of the Revolution were purchasing newspapers to obtain political information about a world beyond their own communities.

To meet the demand for news, publishers increasingly carried overtly political material. Essays taken from the London press often had a strident character. They made no attempt accurately to report what was happening in Parliament or at the court of George III. Rather, more like partisan pieces found in editorial sections of modern newspapers, they exposed the conspiracies and moral corruption allegedly to be found in the imperial capital. On the inside pages, one encountered the proceedings of colonial town meetings—and later, of the committees of safety—and although these formal accounts of local actions taken in defense of American rights dispensed with the rhetorical passions encountered in the purloined essays, they provided readers with a reliable index to the state of popular resistance.

How Americans interpreted what they read is hard to gauge. Some evidence suggests that they absorbed the news with a surprisingly uncritical eye. In 1775 an Englishman who had recently visited the colonies recounted, "I have been frequently in the country, and had many opportunities of conversing with the country people; *'they say we had sooner die than be made slaves; it is a pity the King of England was turned Papist,'* and a great deal of such stuff." When the traveler insisted that such stories were pure nonsense, Americans refused to believe him. "They seemed surprised at my talking in that manner, and were quite enraged. *'What* (said they) *do you know better than the newspapers? Are we not to believe what they tell us?'"*[7]

To claim that newspaper publishers during this period set about consciously to create a new political identity or spread a spirit of nationalism would be grossly ahistorical. In 1774 the men and women who ran journals still thought that the imperial crisis might be resolved to the satisfaction of the colonists. But even if they did not advocate independence, they sensed not only a pressing need for broad intercolonial cooperation, but also the central role that newspapers could play in energizing resistance beyond a single region such as New England. They certainly appreciated that newspapers provided the most promising means for overcoming regional differences. Put another way, they understood that if the colonists were to have any chance of holding their own against a hostile Parliament, links that promoted mutual trust had to be forged. In 1774 the *Connecticut Gazette and Universal Intelligencer,* published in New London, for example, instructed Americans on how communication might strengthen resistance against Great Britain. After all, this writer observed, the imperial administration intended to divide and conquer. "Had the colonies from the first, been united," the editor argued, "those acts of parliament of which we complain, would never have been passed, nor so much as an attempt that way; but the northern and southern colonies, intent on their own particular affairs, were in [a] degree, strangers to each other, and consequently inattentive to their general and common interest."[8]

The journals invited new kinds of conversations; they facilitated a reaching out to potential insurgents at a moment of crisis. During the summer of 1774 the publishers of the *Essex Gazette*, a Salem, Massachusetts, paper, seemed amazed by the power of the press to mobilize ordinary readers. "The News-Papers from all Quarters, in every British American Colony, so far as we have yet received Intelligence, are chiefly filled with Accounts of Meetings and Resolutions of Towns and Counties, all to the same Purpose—complaining of Oppression."[9]

Newspapers depended on the postal service to distribute copies beyond the towns or cities where they were produced. Benjamin Franklin, a brilliant entrepreneur as well as world-class scientist, understood this complementary relationship, and soon after he established himself as Philadelphia's most successful printer in the 1730s, he worked hard to obtain an appointment from the Crown as head of the colonial post office. It was a lucrative arrangement. The same riders who carried the royal mail distributed Franklin's newspapers, thus generating two sources of income. But the system suffered from several problems. Beyond the major cities, the postal system was not only unreliable but also riddled by corruption.

On the eve of revolution, Hugh Finlay received orders as the surveyor of the post roads on the continent of North America to provide a full and candid appraisal of the royal post. His tour from Canada down through New England and eventually to the Carolinas was a nightmare for a man, who seems under normal circumstances to have been a grouchy character. It did not help that the journey occurred at a time when the colonists were speaking out bitterly against parliamentary taxation. Late in 1773 Finlay arrived in Newport, Rhode Island, where, he discovered, "were any Deputy Post Master to do his duty, and make a stir in such a matter, he would draw on himself the odium of his neighbors and be marked as the friend of Slavery and oppression and a declared enemy to America." The situation in the South was even worse. When he reached New Bern, North Carolina, Finlay encountered the local newspaper printer, who confessed that he still collected fees for the post office even though he had long since resigned his post.[10]

Finlay touched on the second problem with the royal postal service in America. Established by act of Parliament during the reign of Queen Anne, the system's administrators in Britain regulated fees and appointed colonial officers. Like the customs office, it was part of the imperial establishment. The whole structure worked well enough so long as Parliament largely left the Americans to their own devices. But after the 1765 Stamp Act, "no taxation without representation" became the rallying cry, and some disgruntled colonists took the position that the postal system was in fact just another instrument for the collection of unconstitutional revenues.

The entrepreneur William Goddard brilliantly linked reform of the postal system to the distribution of newspapers in the name of American rights. It must be admitted that he hardly seems to have fit even the loosest definition of an insurgent. He never employed violence against Tory sympathizers. Indeed, it is doubtful that he even owned a firearm. What is more, he never succeeded at his scheme. But in a history of how ordinary people sparked a revolution, Goddard legitimately stands with the likes of Samuel Thompson, Isaac Davis, and Matthew Patten. Several years before the signing of the Declaration of Independence, Goddard clearly articulated—in ways that drew others to the same conclusion—the demonstrable fact that a more secure, more efficient postal system might be a key element in advancing American resistance to the British Empire.

Goddard was born in New London, Connecticut, in 1740. His father, a physician, also served as the local postmaster. More significant for the boy's later development, his mother, Sarah Updike Goddard, had learned the printer's trade. As a young man, Goddard moved from town to town, usually as an apprentice assisting various individuals who happened to know a good deal about newspapers and the postal system. His early work experience included short stints at New Haven, Providence, and Woodbridge, New Jersey. In 1762 he founded the *Providence Gazette* with his widowed mother and his sister Mary.

Like many enterprising people, Goddard could not resist taking a chance on a larger commercial center, where competition encouraged innovation. In Philadelphia, he entered into an agreement with two wealthy partners. For him this deal was a dream come true. In 1767 he established the *Pennsylvania Chronicle and Universal Advertiser*, a journal that adopted a bold new format. The design, apparently inspired by the popular *London Chronicle*, incorporated a much larger, four-column layout, thus breaking with the more cramped three-column format used by his rivals. Although these changes drained scarce capital, Goddard took pride in the product, and in the tough Philadelphia market he went head-to-head with such veteran printers as David Hall and William Bradford.[11]

However impressive Goddard's talents as a newspaperman may have been, he found it impossible to satisfy his partners, men of conservative temperament who constantly second-guessed how Goddard ran the *Chronicle*. When he decided that he could not stand their carping for another moment, he took the dispute to the public in the form of a shrill, no-holds-barred attack.[12] It may have felt good to even old scores, but for a man of limited financial resources, biting the hands that had fed him was not a prudent decision. Goddard came away from the dispute with a reputation of being edgy, irascible, and perhaps even unreliable. His prospects did not look promising when he moved once again, this time to Baltimore, where, supported by his sister, he tried to salvage his career as the publisher of the *Maryland Journal and the Baltimore Advertiser*.

No sooner had Goddard set up his presses in Baltimore than he announced plans for an American post office. Several elements seem to have sparked the proposal. First, he found obtaining the most recent Philadelphia newspapers more difficult than he had anticipated. Explaining delays in turning out the first number of the *Maryland Journal*, he growled, "It was impracticable to print such a one as would suit this Part of the Country, without establishing a RIDER from Baltimore to Philadelphia, to set out from the last-mentioned Place early on Monday Morning, and to arrive here on Tuesday Evening, whereby I should receive the Massachusetts, Connecticut, New-York, Pennsylvania, and sometimes the British and Irish Papers, and to be enabled to publish the JOURNAL, with the freshest Advices, deliver it to the Customers in Town, and forward it to Annapolis and the Lower Counties, on Thursday Morning, several Hours before the Arrival of the King's Post."[13]

Second, Goddard learned that Lord North had punished Franklin by stripping him of his position as head of the royal post in America. Franklin's public humiliation resulted from the discovery that he had leaked highly compromising letters originally written by Thomas Hutchinson, the despised royal governor, to the leaders of the resistance in Boston. Goddard may not in fact have been personally saddened by the misfortune of an old rival. He did sense, however, that Franklin's disgrace might translate into a splendid business opportunity for someone willing to come forward with a bold scheme. Goddard threw himself into the enterprise. Leaving his sister in charge of the *Maryland Journal*, he began his campaign for "an American Post Office on constitutional principles" early in 1774—more than two full years before the Continental Congress formally declared independence.

Goddard's announcement initially appeared as a broadside, a one-sheet format designed to reach a wide audience. In urban areas, broadsides were used among other things to call working people—mechanics and laborers—to political meetings. The full proposal also ran in major newspapers. In his statement, Goddard advanced three major arguments supporting his plan, all of them aimed specifically at colonists who had already begun to define themselves as Americans. In extraordinarily blunt language, he declared that parliamentary corruption and a ministerial plot to curtail colonial rights made it imperative to establish "an American Post Office." Time was short. Parliament, he insisted, viewed the royal post as a tempting source of revenue, and because the Americans enjoyed no representation in that body, they would soon find themselves paying exorbitant fees for letters and newspapers sent through the mail. "By this Means," Goddard explained, "a Set of Officers, *Ministerial* indeed, in their Creation, Direction and Dependence are maintained in the Colonies, into whose Hands all the social, commercial and political Intelligence of the Continent is necessarily committed, which at this Time, every one must consider as dangerous in the extreme."[14]

Rhetoric of this sort resonated throughout the colonies. Joseph Reed, a well-to-do moderate who in early 1774 was still writing to the Earl of Dartmouth in hopes of preserving the imperial order, noted that the royal post office drew criticism from all quarters. "There is no Act of Parliament which has been more universally submitted to than this: all objections hitherto have given way to the convenience of the thing." Goddard had hit upon a key grievance. According to Reed, the royal post "has become a most exorbitant tax upon all trade and business." Complaining did no good. When people objected to the "rudeness and incivility" that they encountered in the post office, administrators turned a deaf ear and thus persuaded patrons that all they could expect was "insolence and ill behavior."[15]

Goddard developed a second, much more original argument linking the "American Post Office" to the needs of the insurgency. The resistance movement required secure and independent sources of intelligence, but so long as the British were in a position to interfere with the free flow of communication, they could keep Americans ignorant about the political activities of other Americans. "It is not only our letters that are liable to be stopped and opened by a Ministerial mandate, and their contents construed into treasonable conspiracies," Goddard observed, "but our newspapers, those necessary and important alarms in time of public danger, may be rendered of little consequence for want of circulation." To disrupt crucial channels of information would not be difficult, Goddard warned. "Whenever it shall be thought proper to restrain the Liberty of the Press, or injure an Individual, how easily may it be effected?"[16] An anonymous letter published in Boston early in 1774 tied Goddard's proposal even more directly to the mobilization of political opposition. The author of this letter assured his readers that vigilant colonists would back Goddard's post office plan, since it preserved the "intelligence and information on which our very existence as a free people depends."[17] The creation of a secure intelligence network promised greater secrecy, the bedrock of resistance movements and the very thing the British rightly feared.

Goddard's third argument for the American post office had a very different thrust. The promotional statement simply took for granted that the colonists did in fact have common interests and grievances that might serve as a source for a powerful new identity. In this instance, assuming something that was by no means certain proved to be a clever rhetorical strategy. During the early months of 1774 no one seriously advocated national independence, yet at this critical moment Goddard's plan invited Americans to think of themselves as Americans, to overcome parochial interests, and to welcome a "free and safe Communication throughout the whole extent of English America." According to one Connecticut newspaper, Goddard's scheme had the capacity to "unite all the friends of America in one common bond of alliance."[18]

During the spring of 1774 Goddard took to the road, drumming up support for the American post office with the enthusiasm of an evangelical itinerant. He traveled first to New England, reasoning that this embattled region might be more receptive to his appeal for free and independent communication than the South, where British troops had not attempted to enforce the Coercive Acts. He took his case directly to the people. In each town, he met with the members of local committees of correspondence. In fact, he organized a masterful marketing campaign. Newspapers chronicled his success; letters appeared in the columns of journals endorsing his plan and urging the people of other towns to circulate subscription papers as soon as possible. On March 17, 1774, for example, a Boston paper praised Goddard, who "has long been noted as the proprietor and employer of a very free press." It insisted that in "every measure taken to demonstrate that in so glorious a motion for the recovery of American liberty, Boston will by no means fall short of the most sanguine expectations of her honest countrymen."[19]

In quick succession during March and April, Goddard visited Salem, New London, Newburyport, and Portsmouth. The people of New Hampshire thought the creation of "a constitutional conveyance of intelligence" a splendid idea.[20] New Yorkers expressed genuine interest in the plan. The momentum was building. "We hear from New-London, Norwich, Newport and Providence," explained one writer, "that the plan for the total abolition of the Parliamentary Post-Office in America, by the establishment of new Constitutional Posts, and Post-Offices, in the several Colonies, meets with general approbation, and will undoubtedly be patronized by every friend to American Freedom, not only in those towns, but throughout the Continent." Goddard's supporters assured the public that "the friends of liberty in the Southern colonies" would come forward as soon as they knew for certain that networks of riders were operating throughout New England and the Middle Colonies.[21]

Goddard's ambitious plan crashed soon after he returned to Baltimore. His own enthusiasm outran his ability to organize such a vast system. More was involved in the collapse, however, than complex administrative problems. Goddard's enemies—elite gentlemen who found his blunt style and fiery commitment to American liberty abrasive—began a whisper campaign that called his honesty into question. One story claimed that a constitutional post rider assigned to the route between Philadelphia and Baltimore had absconded with a large sum of money. The charge turned out to be false, but the damage had been done.[22] Another letter appearing in Williamsburg noted that Goddard had a dodgy reputation in Philadelphia and suggested he was a charlatan hiding behind a veil of patriotic rhetoric.[23] A New York loyalist noted that Goddard "is only supported by a Set of licentious people of desperate Fortunes whose sole Consequence, nay even Dependence, is on their fishing in troubled Waters." In short, he spoke for the ordinary people. "Men of property both in and out of Trade hold him and his Scheme in the greatest Contempt and Abhorrence, as tending to disturb the public peace and Tranquility of America."[24]

Not until July 26, 1776, did the Continental Congress finally address the need for safe channels of communication. Goddard lost out again. The delegates awarded the post office to Franklin, and he assigned the day-to-day operations to his son-in-law, Richard Bache. However frustrated Goddard may have been by this turn of events, he could at least take satisfaction from having appreciated long before the Founding Fathers the insurgents' need for large-scale networks of intelligence.

# II

What sort of information did Goddard's supporters imagine would circulate broadly among Americans of very different backgrounds? A possible answer can be found in a remarkable assemblage of letters written more than two centuries ago. This unlikely source provides splendid insight into the creation of a new political culture. One might be forgiven, of course, for not immediately appreciating their significance for a history of popular resistance. After all, the correspondence contains hundreds of separate entries, most of them describing gifts of food and money. Each letter in turn occasioned a polite thank-you note.

The collection documents the extraordinary work of the Boston Committee of Donations, a group that at a moment of extreme crisis managed to translate simple acts of charity into a broadly shared commitment to resist British policy. Like other organizations in more modern times that have understood how sympathy can generate political energy, the committee persuaded distant strangers that the cause of Boston was their cause. They convinced people who might have greeted New England's confrontation with British authorities with hostility that the men and women of this great port were in fact not very different from their own friends and neighbors in the Carolinas, the Chesapeake, or the Middle Colonies. Although the members of the committee came from well-to-do families, they tapped into a familiar and popular language of Christian charity that resonated powerfully among ordinary colonists not yet directly threatened by the British military. By making modest sacrifices in the name of a country that did not yet exist, Americans forged palpable bonds with others to create a new solidarity. The thank-you letters provide moving testimony that radical politics occurred outside formal congresses. Philanthropy injected real passion into the debate over the character of resistance, and the little tokens of shared concern sent to Boston—a sheep or bushel of corn—help explain how American insurgents created a powerful infrastructure for resistance and, ultimately, rebellion.

When Parliament closed the port of Boston to waterborne commerce and dispatched an army of occupation to punish the rebellious colonials, Americans do not seem to have contemplated turning humanitarian efforts to relieve the suffering people specifically to political ends. That move came later—an unintended consequence of the initial outpouring of charitable concern. The Port Act, which went into effect on June 1, 1774, had a devastating impact on working families. Within a few weeks, people in Boston reported serious difficulty in obtaining firewood. The basic necessities of daily life had to be transported overland, a slow and expensive process. In early August the *Boston Gazette* reported, "More than sixty days have expired, since Boston, by a late Edict of the British Parliament, has been besieged by a British Fleet and Army, and its trade annihilated." The results of this punitive policy rapidly became evident. "The inhabitants now receive that insult and damage, which was never experienced in the hottest wars we have been engaged in with France and Spain, and their allies." The writer observed that the full story of Boston's pain "may in future be told by some able historian," but with his own eyes he could see that food and fuel were scarce. The poorest people experienced the greatest hardship. "What further cruelties we are to suffer we know not," he explained, "but whether America, or even this single Town, is in this way to be brought to the feet of Lord North, with the full surrender of their inestimable rights and liberties, time only can determine."[25]

Efforts to reach out to other Americans at this moment required more than horrific descriptions of atrocities and injustice. Such reports mattered, of course. They mattered a lot. But the relief of Boston depended on more than stories of cruelty. The rhetorical challenge facing the leaders of the resistance in Massachusetts involved not only persuading distant strangers that ordinary people in Boston suffered at the hands of an unconstitutional military regime, but also convincing them that these men and women were suffering for them.

The appeal drew upon a familiar Christian vocabulary, for in this situation genuine sympathy—the passionate belief that a few innocent people in Boston were martyrs for an American cause—grew out of an imagined solidarity. The Boston Committee of Correspondence employed this theme. Writing to political supporters in Worcester County, Maryland, it proclaimed, "It is our interest as well as our duty, in this day of general calamity and distress, to commit our course unto that God who judges righteously. In short, in our own apprehension, we carry our lives in our hands, every day . . . We are not intimidated; our enemy doth not yet triumph over us. By the help and blessing of God, we shall not only persevere, but shall be crowned with success in our endeavors to preserve the rights and liberties of *North America*."[26] The authors understood that unless Americans could make the emotional leap, could assume somewhat ungrammatically that they are "us," then there was always a chance that those in other regions might hold back.

Put in crudest terms, talk alone provided no guarantee of solidarity. The transformation of general expressions of caring into meaningful support involved tangible acts of sacrifice. As one group in Maryland declared, "Words are said to be cheap, but it is universally allowed, that when a man parts with his money, he is in earnest."[27] The political seal of support demanded a symbolic offering in the name of the people of Boston. The gift may have amounted to only a few pennies. The value of the contribution was not the point. By coming forward with a donation, even ordinary Americans—those whose political conversion was absolutely necessary to sustain the insurgency—could plausibly claim that they had advanced a broader movement. In their own small way they had registered a pledge to resistance. This was the logic that turned charity into a powerful vehicle for political mobilization.

The relief of Boston required a level of managerial complexity unprecedented in colonial society. The effort involved not only the collection of money and goods on a massive scale, but also the creation of a series of public works projects. The whole enterprise got off to an impressively swift start. On June 17, 1774, the Massachusetts House of Representatives, aware that General Gage was about to dissolve the colonial legislature, called upon the people of the province to provide relief for the inhabitants of Boston "in such way and manner as shall be most suitable to their circumstances, till the sense and advice of our sister colonies shall be known."[28] For many decades, indigent men and women had received assistance from the Boston Overseers of the Poor, but as soon became clear, the Port Bill presented the city with a much larger challenge than the overseers had ever faced. The town meeting wisely appointed a new body of twenty-six men who comprised the committee of donations. The group included such well-known figures as Samuel Adams, Joseph Warren, Josiah Quincy, and John Adams. In a mission statement published in many newspapers, the committee announced that it intended "to receive Donations for the charitable purpose of relieving and employing the Poor, suffering by means of the Act of Parliament, commonly called the Boston Port Bill." The members promised to carry out their business in an open and responsible manner. "The Committee," they declared, "consider themselves at all times answerable to their Constituents, and as particularly accountable to their munificent Benefactors, who ought ever to have all reasonable satisfaction touching the disposition of their Charities."[29]

Even by modern standards, the committee took on an extraordinarily difficult assignment. The most pressing task was simply to assess the dimensions of the problem. How many people had actually been thrown out of work by the closing of the port? Of these, how many were in truly desperate straits? Gathering this information proved taxing. For ten consecutive afternoons they interviewed inhabitants who argued that they had a legitimate claim to charitable assistance. The committee asked "all classes of People suffering by the Port Bill to lay their circumstances before the Committee, that the distressed might (if possible) be employed in their several occupations." The numbers were overwhelming. As the organizers reported to a generous group from New Castle, Delaware, "This much we can say, that before the Port Bill, the annual charge for support of the Town's poor was about twenty-five hundred pounds, our lawful money. But the number of the poor, by means of the *humane* Port Bill, is doubtless increased in a twofold, if not threefold proportion, and considerable numbers, who, three months ago, lived very comfortably, are now spending on the little they had laid up against a rainy day."[30] Many of the newly distressed described themselves as "Mechanicks and Laborers." This segment of the workforce became the central focus of the relief effort.

The committee identified two problems of immediate concern. First, the members realized from the start that Americans living in other regions viewed cooperation of this sort with considerable skepticism. During the previous decade, when Americans attempted to organize continental boycotts of British imports, the leaders of the major ports grumbled that other cities were cheating. Rumors circulated widely that the merchants of Boston or New York secretly purchased British goods while publicly proclaiming their support for economic resistance.[31] With such memories still fresh, the committee insisted that neither its own members nor the town of Boston expected to profit from gifts directed specifically to the unemployed poor, who were of course the true victims of British oppression. Transparency seemed the best way to counter "slanderous reports." The committee opened its financial register to "candid enquirers" so that doubters could at any time review "all the Donations as they are received, and from whom, together with a fair record of all matters which come before the Committee."[32]

The second troublesome issue involved the character of the people who truly deserved relief. The committee promised to help only ablebodied laborers who had lost paying jobs as a result of the Port Bill. The charity claimed no interest in funding chronic layabouts or infirm individuals traditionally supported by the Overseers of the Poor. What the mechanics and laborers of Boston needed was work, not handouts, and so instead of parceling out donations directly to the unemployed as doles, the committee translated many contributions into cash, which in turn underwrote ambitious public works projects. It was a shrewd decision. For a very long time, colonists had distinguished between the ablebodied poor—morally upstanding people who through no fault of their own had fallen on hard times—and lazy individuals who were responsible for their own economic hardships. Something more was at stake, however, than merely providing assurance to potential donors that their contributions would not be wasted. By focusing on the suffering of the able-bodied, hardworking victims of political oppression, the charity's directors encouraged a sympathetic response from similar types of people throughout America. After all, what kind of person would refuse to assist humble Bostonians who during happier times had toiled and saved so diligently? Framed in such poignant terms, the presentation allowed distant strangers more readily to picture the unemployed workers as thoroughly decent and honest people, people not unlike themselves. This imaginative projection went a long way toward making the charitable appeal a stunning success.

Considering the constraints under which it operated, the committee put forward an amazing range of projects. The members observed that in normal times they would have preferred sponsoring the construction of a new bridge over the Charles River or perhaps building a much-needed hospital. But with British troops occupying the city, such civic improvements had to be postponed. As the committee reminded potential donors, "Miserable is the state of that Community who have the *Forms* but not the *Powers* of good Government, but much more miserable are they who have *neither*."[33] And so, in its attempt to create real jobs—as well as to generate income to help sustain an ongoing relief effort—the charity encouraged repaving Boston's streets, digging a public well, and erecting a model house for sale. They promoted the manufacture of shoes, nails, rope, and small ships. The committee purchased a stock of wool, flax, and cotton that it distributed to worthy spinners, and for those who did not own them, "looms for weaving . . . baizes and shirt-cloth."[34] The major focus, however, was the brick works, which organizers optimistically predicted would employ at least eighty men. As with the other activities, the plan called for selling the products—in this case bricks—to cover some of the cost of hiring even more deserving poor people.

These bold enterprises had absolutely no chance, of course, if Americans living outside Boston failed to come forward with donations. The committee gambled that its appeal would generate a favorable response. The risk was very great. At stake was not only the welfare of those thrown out of work but also the viability of a broader resistance movement. As "A Friend to American Liberties" reminded newspaper readers in June 1774, "there are thousands . . . which depend wholly on their daily work for their bread, and are now reduced to distress for want of employment, and are not able to support their families." The question before the colonists, therefore, was whether they would "enjoy plenty and see our brethren suffer in *our own* cause, and we not relieve them when it is in our power? The love of ourselves, the love of our country, and the love of GOD and religion calls for our assistance!"[35]

A Friend need not have worried. The floodgates quickly opened. Hundreds of donations were on their way. Ordinary men and women accepted the argument that the poor of Boston were in fact suffering for an American cause. This was a crucial moment in a revolution of the people. The members of an elite committee had initially issued a call for assistance. The affirmative answer that they received, however, came overwhelmingly from middling sorts who acted out of compassion. By coming forward to relieve the suffering of others, they were drawn into the insurgency.

One early example—perhaps the first of its kind—reveals how mobilizing the American people through charity worked. A donation from Windham, Connecticut, announced that this community of farm families had decided to come to the aid of Boston. The act was completely voluntary; it emerged from a serious debate among people on the local level who found themselves caught up in an imperial crisis not of their own making. Their gift reached Boston in late June 1774. Like so many other contributors, the inhabitants of Windham felt obliged to explain—perhaps to themselves as much as to the committee of donations—why they were willing to make a sacrifice for the unemployed workers. Those who had attended the town meeting reported that they looked "with pity, mixed with indignation . . . [on] the cruel and unmanly attacks made by the British Parliament on the loyal and patriotic Town of Boston." And what, they inquired, had the working poor done to deserve such treatment? Their only crime had been openly defending the "fundamental principles of the Constitution."

It is significant for our story to point out that the inhabitants of Windham were moved by more than political theory. The assault on fellow colonists—victims of oppression—generated real anger. They responded to Boston on an emotional level. "When we reflect that it is this for which you are suffering such horrid cruelties, for which your streets have been stained with blood, and for which you now feel the horrors of a military government," they declared, "we [are] overwhelmed with a conflict of tumultuous passions, and filled with that manly ardor which bids us join you hand in hand, and suffer with you in the common cause." Death, they concluded, was preferable to "that low, servile state, which is evidently planned for us." Windham's farmers begged the people of Boston to have courage. "We know you suffer, and feel for you."

In this heated state, they voted to send a flock of sheep, admittedly not of the highest quality, but the best they could obtain on short notice. When the animals arrived, the committee of donations dispatched a letter of gratitude. The inhabitants of Windham had kindly come to Boston's relief by sending "two hundred and fifty-eight sheep."[36] A few Tories tried to undermine the show of generosity by claiming that the committee actually had paid for the sheep. But the report was a lie. As the *Boston Gazette* noted, "How weak, how false, how little and how low!"[37]

Pledges to help the poor workers of Boston exceeded even the most optimistic expectations. The flow of gifts followed the sea routes of imperial trade. People in every mainland colony contributed to the cause. Residents of Savannah, Georgia, worried that, in comparison with other Americans, they had been a little slow joining the effort, but adopting a better-late-than-never position, they informed the committee on June 26, 1775, "There are many among us, who sincerely espouse the great cause contended for by you; & who ardently wish that the noble stand you have made in defense of these rights, which as men, and British subjects we are entitled to, may be crowned with success." To show their solidarity, they transmitted sixty-three barrels of rice and 122 pounds sterling.[38]

Donations were dispatched to Boston from as far away as the Caribbean islands, Canada, and London. As might be expected, the vast majority of goods and money originated in New England, and by the end of the summer of 1774 it was clear that the plight of Boston's unemployed laborers had touched the hearts of many thousands of people who are not ordinarily included in the traditional narratives of the coming of the American Revolution. About the wide geographic distribution, there can be no doubt. The committee's own records contain letters of gratitude mailed to scores of distant communities. In addition, many newspapers published a weekly report—a kind of box score of political responsibility—listing either the town or, in some cases, the individual offering support. If nothing else, such accounts injected a spirit of competition into the whole enterprise, for various groups strove to demonstrate that they were just as committed to helping Boston as were other Americans. "We Rejoice," declared the inhabitants of Stonington, Connecticut, "to see so many of the neighboring Colonies, and even Towns, vying with each other in the liberal Benefactions to the distressed, injured Town of Boston."[39]

The contributions varied immensely in character and value. On July 18, 1774, for example, "Twenty Gentlemen" living in South Carolina contributed "205 tierces of rice." (A "tierce" contained about forty-two gallons.) Alexandria, Virginia, shipped 38 barrels of flour, 150 barrels of wheat, and a large sum of cash. The inhabitants of Monmouth, New Jersey, provided 1,200 bushels of rye as well as another 50 barrels of flour. Other communities gave cattle, sheep, corn, firewood, codfish, peas, flax, brandy, and butter. One man declared that the Boston laborers needed several hundred head of cabbage. An inspired contribution came from New York City. According to a newspaper, a gentleman volunteered ten pounds sterling and "the best pipe of Brandy in his distillery, valued at 28 pounds." When other New Yorkers questioned the appropriateness of the brandy, the donor responded, "The generosity of the Virginians & Carolinians &c. was great and honorable with respect to food," but he thought that such "glorious sufferers for the common good ought to drink as well as eat."[40] And perhaps the most surprising gift came from "the Aboriginal Natives of Christian-Town on Martha's Vineyard." The Indians collected more than two pounds sterling for people who might not have been so generous had the situation been reversed.[41]

Much of this material found its way to Newburyport, Marblehead, or Salem, ports in Massachusetts still open to commerce. The New England contributions generally traveled overland. Even those who did not send food or cash helped the cause as best they could. In a note marking the arrival of 105 sheep from Pomfret, Connecticut, the *Boston Gazette* praised "the Taverners on the Road [who] were so kind as to refuse receiving any Payment for Entertainment or Forage."[42] Cash often proved harder to transmit. A committee in rural Bucks County, Pennsylvania, collected large sums of money. Since colonial society had not yet developed convenient ways to transfer funds of this sort, the committee simply dispatched a messenger to Philadelphia, where he contacted Samuel Adams, then a Massachusetts delegate to the Continental Congress, and, after putting the bundle of money in Adams's hands, asked him to see that the cash actually reached the suffering poor of Boston.[43]

Communities throughout America collected funds in different ways. East Hampton, New York, "laid a Tax upon the Town sufficient to raise *One Hundred Pounds* New York Currency, for the support of the industrious Poor in Boston."[44] More commonly, local groups distributed subscription papers to individual households. The family responded by declaring how much money or goods it could spare for the unemployed workers of Boston, and once the decision had been made, it returned the form to an organizing committee as a pledge of future delivery. Newspapers, for example, announced that "a Subscription is also set on Foot in every Parish through the County of Suffolk, on Long Island" for the purpose of gathering "Grain, Flax, &c."[45] A member of a committee in Chestertown, Maryland, announced that "subscription papers are sent out into the country, and I dare say will be filled up to a large amount. Those who cannot give money, can give corn. The people of Boston need not be afraid of being starved to a compliance."[46] An official town meeting in Lebanon, Connecticut, concluded with only one dissenting vote that it was the duty of every resident to contribute "to the Relief of those poor and distressed Inhabitants of said Boston." This assembly immediately formed a committee made up of selectmen "to receive the charitable Donations of such as are disposed to contribute."[47] The freeholders of Anson County, North Carolina, adopted much the same procedure, as did the members of the Albany, New York, Committee of Correspondence. The Albany overseers complained that some of the outlying districts had been tardy in rendering accounts of donations, and they urged the subcommittees in those localities to "use their Influence for the more speedy collections thereof."[48]

Colonists often stressed the voluntary character of these gifts. That claim may have been accurate, but we should recognize that ordinary people must have been under great pressure to conform to the will of the majority. Moreover, the subscription papers were public documents, in the sense that everyone in the area would have known precisely whether a household supported Boston and how much it was willing to sacrifice for the common good. In August 1775 the committee of safety in Bucks County punished a man by forcing him to confess: "Whereas, I have spoken injuriously of the distressed people of the town of Boston . . . I do hereby declare, that I am heartedly sorry for what I have done."[49] Other committees investigated reports that certain persons had "obstructed the contribution for the Relief of the Poor of Boston," and in Portsmouth, New Hampshire, William Pottle, Jr., was roughed up by a crowd for voting in a town meeting against "supplying the suffering Poor in Boston."[50] But there was another side to the story. Communities remembered who had come forward. In January 1777 a man was called before New York's Commission for Detecting and Defeating Conspiracies. He need not have feared. A certain Isaac Roosevelt testified that the person in question surely was a friend of the American cause, since a few years earlier he had cheerfully contributed five pounds for the support of Boston's poor.[51]

In general, however, the outpouring of sympathy seems to have been sincere and spontaneous. The appeal for support resonated powerfully even with people who had very few possessions to contribute. But they still wanted to do something, to demonstrate that however modest their belongings, they were eager to do whatever they could for the victims of British oppression. A letter from the small village of Durham, New Hampshire, revealed how deeply the imagined suffering of Boston's poor affected a group of struggling farmers. In November 1774 they apologized to the committee of donations for offering such a modest gift. We send only a few cattle, they observed, and a "small sum of money, which a number of persons in this place, tenderly sympathizing with our suffering brethren in Boston, have contributed towards their support." They went on to explain, "What you herewith receive, comes not from the opulent, but mostly from the industrious yeomanry in this parish. We have but a few persons of affluent fortunes among us." However limited their resources, the people of Durham had given their decision serious thought. "This is considered by us," they insisted, "not as a gift, or an act of charity, but of justice, as a small part of what we are in duty bound to communicate to those truly noble and patriotic advocates of American freedom, who are bravely standing in the gap between us and slavery."[52]

Although these widely scattered communities may not have been aware of the revolutionary implications of their actions—they insisted that they wanted only to help the suffering poor—they were in fact laying the groundwork for a vast political network. We are witnessing the creation of a huge charitable infrastructure that had obvious political possibilities. Between June 1774 and the summer of 1775, ordinary Americans learned how to collect supplies quickly and efficiently and to transfer them to distant places where they were most needed. These are not organizational skills that we should take for granted.

The astonishingly positive response to the needs of Boston's poor marked the moment when many ordinary people, from Georgia to New Hampshire, openly cast their lot with resistance. The committee's appeal brought people together in small groups not only to pledge sheep and corn but also to discuss before neighbors their thoughts about the imperial crisis. Of course, given Parliament's growing intransigence, such troublesome topics were bound to surface. The charity, however, forced the issue, crystallizing inchoate feelings and encouraging people—who had before this time largely avoided political matters of such consequence—to signal through votes and gifts exactly where they stood. A surge of sympathy sparked hundreds of local conversations about anger and sacrifice, about responsibility and identity. If discontented Americans spoke passionately about rights and liberties, they did so not in a language of theory, but as *felt* rights and *felt* liberties, elements embedded in their own experience, that seemed seriously at risk in Boston. What is more, feelings took on tangible, and public, form—goods sent, sentiments publicly declared. During these exchanges—among friends and neighbors, between local representatives and the committee of donations—a messy bundle of belief and emotion congealed into something we recognize as collective revolutionary knowledge.

An emergency town meeting held in Lebanon, Connecticut, on July 18, 1774, helps us to understand how reports from Boston could transform abstract notions about constitutional rule into a passionate commitment actually to do something about an immediate problem. The participants conducted a kind of teach-in that encouraged members of the community to explore, as they had not done before, the full dimensions of their own political beliefs. The turnout was impressive. Some "three Hundred respectable Freeholders" took part in a discussion sparked initially by "the most alarming and dangerous Situation of American Liberties . . . and to consider what we ought to do for the Relief of Boston."

After the inhabitants had carefully examined the issues at stake, they concluded that "the Controversy now subsisting between the Parliament of Great Britain and the English American Colonies, respecting the Rights and the Liberties of the latter, is a Matter and Cause of the most important and interesting Nature, that can affect our Minds, next to our own everlasting Welfare." An external crisis forced them to interrogate ideas and assumptions about their relationship to a wider imperial world. They praised their ancestors for leaving seventeenth-century England, where they had been persecuted, "to explore and settle a new World." Townsmen asserted that they enjoyed the same rights as the king's subjects living in Great Britain and therefore felt justified in condemning the Coercive Acts, which clearly compromised those very same rights.

At this point in the meeting, a crucial shift occurred. As people talked of general propositions, emotions became more heated. It was as if they suddenly realized that they had not come together simply to discuss rights and liberties as political theory. They were angry. The rights and liberties that needed defending belonged to the suffering poor of Boston, real men and women with whom they identified. Their discussions reaffirmed the active belief that Boston's cause was in fact their cause. What we encounter on the local level is the fabrication of a powerful sense of political solidarity; worried Lebanon farmers willed a new category into existence. For them, it seemed entirely reasonable to declare that those who lived in Boston were suffering "unparalleled Hardship and Distress . . . for their having been ever forward and resolute in Defense of their and the common rights of the Colonies." Within this context, Lebanon had a duty to contribute "to the Relief of those poor and distressed Inhabitants of said Boston." Donations raised in the town served as the tangible seal of a new solidarity.

This mental process would be repeated throughout America. It generally started with an articulation of first principles and quickly turned to a passionate commitment to strangers who happened to be the unemployed workers of Boston. Aware of the importance of communication in the spread of revolutionary knowledge, the people of Lebanon not only entered their resolves into the official "Records of the Town"—a message of resistance for future generations—but also inserted them in the *New London Gazette*.[53]

Like the Lebanon townsmen, a group in Wilmington, North Carolina, affirmed its ideological commitment to American resistance by making a gift to "the distressed inhabitants of the town of Boston." Stories of suffering had brought forth an extraordinary outpouring of sympathy throughout the Cape Fear region. On July 21, 1774, spokesmen for Wilmington informed the committee of donations that it had "loaded a sloop with provisions." They declared that these supplies should be directed specifically to "the indigent inhabitants of Boston, who, by the late oppressive Acts of Parliament, are now deprived of the means of procuring their subsistence by their daily labor and honest industry." The people in Wilmington who organized this assistance described the cargo as "inconsiderable in its value." But, as they appreciated, monetary worth was not the point. In this case, it really was the thought that counted. The North Carolina sacrifice—however modest it may have been— carried emblematic political value. The members of two very distant communities had managed to establish a bond of resistance through charity. Wilmington's representatives hoped that recipients in Boston would interpret the donation exactly as it was intended, not only as "testimony" of humanitarian concern for real people who were out of work, but also as Cape Fear's support for "the cause in which they now suffer."[54]

In Durham, New Hampshire, the Boston crisis provoked an even more searching exploration of the connection between political belief and revolutionary action. The inhabitants of this farming community perceived the suffering of the poor in highly religious terms. In a letter to the committee of donations drafted on November 21, 1774, they expressed confidence that the "superintendent gracious Being, whose ears are ever open to the cry of the oppressed, in answer to the incessant prayers of his people, [will] defend our just cause, turn the counsels of our enemies into foolishness . . . and make those very measures, by which they are endeavoring to compass our destruction, the means of fixing our invaluable rights and privileges upon a more firm and lasting basis."

As in other towns throughout America, Durham's residents realized that parliamentary measures designed to punish a specific port had promoted a new, powerful sense of solidarity. These self-described industrious yeomen observed, "We are pleased to find that the methods by which the ministry sought to divide, have happily united us, and by every new act of oppression, more and more strengthened union." Talk of mutual ties turned minds to the nature of political responsibility. The results were astonishing. Serious discussion about the state of imperial affairs caused Durham's residents meeting together to stake out more radical positions than they would probably have done as individuals. Indeed, the very act of examining current issues led to a realization that the defense of the common cause would most likely require more than words, certainly more than a small gift of money. They were ready, announced the townsmen of Durham, "to give our lives and mingle our blood with yours, in the common sacrifice to liberty." Their ancestors had immigrated to the New World to escape political despotism. Now there was nowhere to flee. "Before we will submit to wear the chains of slavery, [that] a profligate and arbitrary ministry are preparing for us," they declared, "we are determined upon an emigration through the gate of death, in hope of inheriting the fair land of promise, and participating with our forefathers in the glorious liberty of the sons of God."[55] British authorities would have been wise to pay closer attention to this kind of rhetoric. Long before anyone fought a pitched battle, these Americans had accepted the possibility that they might in fact have to die to liberate other Americans from tyranny. That distressing insight constituted the core of collective revolutionary knowledge.

Lebanon organized a particularly dramatic response to the appeal to help Boston's suffering poor. Throughout the day of June 1, 1774, "the Bells of the Town early began to Toll a solemn Peal," normal business stopped, and people hung "Ensigns of Distress" from their windows. In the evening a large group of inhabitants gathered to discuss the "cruel Edict" that threatened to throw so many honest laborers out of work. The event seemed a spontaneous expression of general concern. It certainly was not an official town meeting. According to a newspaper report, "a respectable Number of Freeholders of the Place and Others (upon short notice) appeared at the Town House, where the [Port] Act was publicly read, and observed upon."

The Lebanon assembly held an unscripted discussion of the looming political crisis. One can almost see various individuals rising to ask questions or state opinions. This was the seedbed of revolution. The community was digesting news, confirming rumors, sharing fears and doubts, and, during the course of these conversations, discovering that neighbors with whom they may never have talked about such sensitive matters were prepared to resist the empire. As one speaker explained, "The occasion of our meeting is interesting and solemn . . . We are now, my brethren, to determine, whether we will tamely submit to every Act of cruel Oppression or indignantly reject . . . every instance of unjust power." This man—the records do not provide his name—suggested how the people might best channel their anger. He proposed, "We do all at this time, heartily sympathize with our Brethren in Boston, in the scenes of distress which this day opens upon them." The inhabitants of Lebanon would send assistance.

Mobilization, however, required more than sensitivity for the pain of others. Like so many other Americans at this moment, the Lebanon speaker gave sympathy a political face. What energized resistance was the conviction not only that laborers in Boston were suffering but also that they were suffering for Lebanon. "We consider them as suffering under the hand of ministerial vengeance for their noble exertions in the cause of liberty—the common cause of all America," he observed. And as a result, "we are heartily willing and desirous to unite our little powers in whatever General Measure shall be thought best for the security and permanency of the just rights and privileges of our country."[56] The significant point here in contemporary terms is that revolutionary commitment in Lebanon flowed up from the people; unless ordinary colonists had discovered new sources of solidarity—on their own, in local settings—then the elite leaders who traveled to the Continental Congress would have been left talking among themselves.

Other communities added their voices to the growing chorus of resistance. On June 29, 1774, the inhabitants of Killingly, Connecticut, recorded that they had met to take "into consideration the dark and gloomy clouds which hang over and threaten the liberties of this, our native country, in general; the distressing circumstances of Boston, in particular." One can almost feel the authority of the empire slipping away in this small village. Two years before the signing of the Declaration of Independence, the residents of Killingly were thinking in terms of "our native country." They decided to send a few sheep to Boston and boldly announced that the town was "well united, and determined to maintain its privileges at the risk of lives and fortunes, and ready to contribute to the necessities of those called to suffer."[57]

In August the nearby town of Brooklyn contributed 125 sheep to the

Boston martyrs. After debating among themselves, the inhabitants drew political inspiration from Scripture, for from their perspective, the sheep were the appropriate gift to cleanse the sins of despotism. The animals, they claimed, will help Boston to resist "an ambitious and vindictive minister by the blood of rams and of lambs." And what was more, "if that do not answer the cure we are ready to march in the van, and to sprinkle the American altars with our heart's blood if occasion should be."[58] At the distance of more than two centuries, it is hard to know how one could better capture the thoughts of ordinary people at the political tipping point. The distress of real men and women in Boston—members of families much like their own—had transformed grumbling and complaint into a commitment to take up arms against Great Britain.

General Gage monitored the flow of donations into Boston. He found himself in a difficult situation. It was clearly in his own interests to assure Lord Dartmouth and other leaders of Parliament that the Coercive Acts had in fact brought the people of the city to their knees. Writing on July 20, 1774, he observed that the punitive legislation had had a negative impact on one important industry—the manufacture of rum—forcing it to curtail production. "Materials wanted to carry on trades, I am told, begin to fail and the carrying molasses and rum twenty-eight miles by land is found not to answer as well as it was expected it would." At the same time, he picked up troubling indications that the local workers were more resilient than anyone in London had anticipated. However much the local economy was hurting, the people themselves did not seem the least bit discouraged. Gage concluded that "assurances of assistance from the other colonies" had engendered a sense of false optimism. "South Carolina," he informed Dartmouth, "has sent some rice for the support of the people here . . . and a few sheep it's said has been sent from some other place." In his eyes these gifts were insufficient to relieve Boston for the long term. "Resources of this kind," he insisted, "are too precarious to be depended upon and must fail." In any case, he believed that donations came only from "some disaffected persons," not from official sources such as the governments of the other provinces.

Just as he was concluding this self-serving letter, Gage added an insight about the character of popular political mobilization, which neither he nor his superiors fully understood. "The great object here has been to persuade the other colonies to make the cause of Boston the common cause of America," he explained.[59] He was correct. What imperial authorities had not yet taken on board was the fact that ordinary people in hundreds of small communities had already made that decision. For at least a year after Gage penned this report, the committee of donations was still receiving money and goods from Americans along the entire Atlantic Coast who fully appreciated the link between charity and political resistance.

Tory writers did their best to undermine Boston's appeal for assistance. They targeted the committee itself, arguing that the leaders of the city had hoodwinked ordinary colonists. Some reports warned that "the Donations of our *sympathizing brethren* are so numerous and valuable, that *Boston* will grow rich from the Charities of their public Friends." Without an awareness of inconsistency, some Tories described the assistance as "trifling." Others insisted that the committee purchased grain and livestock in the countryside, sent these supplies to Boston, and then announced to the world that the American people were prepared to sacrifice for Boston. One rumor advanced a much more complex conspiracy. In this telling, Americans living in other regions provided food and cash to keep the Boston revolutionaries quiet.[60]

These aspersions did not make the slightest difference. The goods continued to flow into the city. In January 1775 Samuel Adams defended the committee's integrity. His letter ran in most colonial newspapers. He specifically denied that the members of the committee drew a salary for their work. "So satisfied are they of their own *disinterested* motives and conduct in this regard," wrote Adams, "that they can safely appeal to the omniscient Being for their sincerity in this declaration." He urged Americans to ignore "the enemies of *Truth and Liberty.*" And he reminded the skeptics that the committee's books "are open for the inspection of such as are inclined to look into and examine them."[61] No evidence survives to indicate that anyone accepted the offer.

## III

Colonists lived in a far more open, interactive society than most modern Americans realize. Even in small, largely self-contained villages, they welcomed news about distant strangers. This intelligence sparked far-reaching debates in hundreds of communities about basic political values, about the nature of political responsibility, and about the possibility that their "country" was no longer a meaningful part of the British Empire. Of course, many people strongly disagreed. A few loyalists tried to shape public opinion. Many other Americans remained neutral, waiting and watching, hoping to discover how the political winds were blowing. But opponents and doubters always found themselves on the defensive.

While loyalists whined about lost chances, innovative colonists such as William Goddard and the members of the committee of donations experimented with unfamiliar forms of communication. At least two years before national independence they had established networks linking small villages with other small villages. The swirl of messages—about resistance and mutual obligation—created a situation in which ordinary men and women could construct a new political identity. Through a developing consciousness of others, they became something different, less British, more American. It was an exhilarating experience. As one letter published in a newspaper exclaimed, "We have the pleasure to assure our readers, that as far as our intelligence has hitherto extended (since the news of the Boston Port Bill) that is from New Hampshire to Williamsburg in Virginia, it appears by all our letters and advices, that all our colonies breathe the same spirit, and seem actuated by one soul."[62]

The inhabitants of the community of Brooklyn, Connecticut, stated the same point even more powerfully. In August 1774 they observed, "The public virtue now exhibited by the Americans, exceeds all of its kind that can be produced in the annals of the Greeks and Romans. Behold them from North to South, from East to West, striving to comfort the Town of Boston, both by publishing their sentiments in regard to the present tyrannical administration, and by supporting their poor with provision."[63] Two years before independence, ordinary Americans had found the means to share the experience of revolutionary resistance.

# FIVE

# The Power of Rumor:
# The Day the British Destroyed Boston

The delegates to the First Continental Congress almost immediately faced a terrifying political prospect that has seldom drawn the attention it deserves. The fifty-five men who traveled to Philadelphia represented the best and brightest of provincial society. When they gathered in Carpenters' Hall on September 5, 1774, they had no precise idea how best to deal with an angry king and Parliament, yet they assumed that they were fully capable of guiding the colonists through a severe imperial crisis. After all, these were America's leaders, members of a grand fraternity that we now revere as the Founding Fathers.

During the first weeks of their deliberations, however, something unsettling occurred. Events did not unfold as the delegates expected. Congressmen quickly discovered through a series of bizarre events that the people had actually gotten out in front of their leaders. Popular politics on the ground forced the delegates to endorse a policy far more provocative than anything they might have anticipated before setting out for Philadelphia. The story of how the people drove the Revolution forward—and in the process marginalized moderate figures still hoping for reconciliation with Great Britain—turns on a frightening rumor that triggered an equally frightening response. The congressmen learned that in a horrible preemptive attack, British forces had destroyed Boston, then the third largest city in America.

# I

The mysterious radicalism of the first Congress centers on a largely forgotten document known as the Suffolk Resolves (September 17, 1774). Taking its name from the county in Massachusetts where it was originally drafted by a convention of town delegates, it was carried to Philadelphia by Paul Revere. Congress had assembled only a few days earlier, and little about the privileged social background of the colonial delegates would have suggested that this particular body would have paid the slightest attention to such a shrill call for resistance to British authority. Among other things, it advocated the right of subjects to nullify parliamentary statutes that they deemed unconstitutional.

To describe this as a radical doctrine would be an understatement. The notion that ordinary people could decide for themselves whether to obey the laws of Great Britain seemed an invitation to anarchy. No one at the time seriously wanted to encourage every man to do as he liked without regard for the common good. Rather, the Suffolk convention staked out an extreme position as a way to communicate its uncompromising opposition to the Coercive Acts. The second resolve, for example, announced, "It is an indispensable Duty which we owe to GOD, our Country, Ourselves and Posterity, by all lawful Ways and Means in our Power, to maintain, defend and preserve those civil and religious Rights & Liberties for which many of our Fathers fought, bled, and died."

The full text, widely circulated in the colonial newspapers, stated in no uncertain terms "that no obedience is due from this Province [Massachusetts] to either or any part of the Acts above mentioned, but that they be rejected as the attempts of a wicked Administration to enslave America." The leaders of the resistance movement also urged the people to ignore officials who had accepted a commission under the despised Massachusetts Government Act. Of course, that particular horse was already out of the barn. The authority of the Crown had been effectively dismantled in the Massachusetts countryside before Suffolk issued its resolves.[1]

After Congress had endorsed the full statement on September 17—a process that occurred with amazing speed—Americans of loyalist persuasion wondered whether the Philadelphia delegates had taken leave of their senses. To those counseling accommodation, it seemed utter madness to encourage massive civil disobedience at a moment when there still appeared to be a chance that moderate leaders on both sides of the Atlantic might devise a plan to resolve the imperial controversy and thereby contain the spreading insurgency. One critic insisted that by adopting the Resolves, Congress "gave such a blast from the trumpet of sedition, as made one half of America shudder." Another insisted that the document "contained a complete declaration of war against Great Britain."[2]

In *A Friendly Address to All Reasonable Americans*, Myles Cooper, an outspoken New York loyalist, argued that the Suffolk Resolves were the work of "rebellious Republicans," and he demanded to learn why Congress had given comfort to "these hare-brained fanatics." Cooper spelled out in lurid detail how Congress had betrayed the true interests of "reasonable Americans." "When the news arrived at Philadelphia, that the people of Suffolk had OPENLY REVOLTED FROM THEIR ALLEGIANCE to the King and his government," Cooper recounted, ". . . the Congress, in whom we considered as the faithful guardians of the safety, as well as rights of America, were disposed to enter into a league offensive and defensive, with its worst enemies the New-England and other Presbyterian Republicans." Hinting broadly that there was a radical conspiracy afoot—he later claimed that the Presbyterians and Independents had somehow been responsible—he reported that Congress intended to unleash the dogs of war.[3] Another less flattering explanation published in *Rivington's Gazette* described the colonial representatives in Philadelphia as having been dead drunk the day they approved the Suffolk document.[4]

Although no one today seriously maintains that strong drink explains why Congress supported the Resolves, the puzzle remains unsolved. Why did an assembly of elite gentlemen—many of them deeply suspicious that New Englanders were bent on provoking open hostilities with Great Britain—approve a shrill statement calling not only for nullification of the Coercive Acts but also for large-scale military preparations? One answer revives notions of conspiracy. The central figure in this backroom narrative was Samuel Adams, a cunning radical who allegedly traveled to Philadelphia determined to persuade Congress through charming guile and procedural legerdemain to endorse the aggressive measures taken by the people of Massachusetts in opposition to North's punitive policies. In this elaborate scheme, the Suffolk Resolves amounted to little more than a rhetorical move on a political chessboard. The very intemperance of the statement allowed the crafty Adams to claim that although he counseled moderation, things were getting out of hand in Massachusetts, and unless Congress was willing to take bold measures to preserve American unity, he could not guarantee that armed violence in Massachusetts could be avoided.[5] As Joseph Galloway, an outspoken royalist from Pennsylvania, claimed many years later, the popular leaders in Congress misled the people "by every fiction, falsehood, and fraud" and thereby aimed "to incite the ignorant and vulgar to arms."[6]

The problem with this argument is that it reduces one of the most radical documents of the revolutionary era to a mere expression of political intrigue. In this explanation for the Suffolk Resolves the people remain an abstraction or, at best, an exaggerated threat employed by Adams and his friends to drum up more enthusiastic support for Massachusetts. But in point of fact the people were not party to Adams's scheme. Nor were they rhetorical phantoms raised up conveniently to frighten moderates in Philadelphia. During the first week of September the insurgency in New England took on a life of its own. A rising of unprecedented size alerted congressional leaders that the people were quite capable of making their own history.

## II

The story of popular radicalism on the national stage took an unexpected turn just as the distinguished members of Congress began arriving in Philadelphia in late August and early September. Americans from all regions regarded these men as the last best hope for reconciliation with the Crown. Contemporaries who greeted them in Philadelphia treated them as celebrities. One writer in particular captured the surge of excitement and hope that marked the occasion. Christopher Marshall, a well-connected local figure who kept a diary called the *Remembrancer*, recorded the entry of each colonial delegation into the city. The first group appeared on August 9, passengers on a packet ship that had sailed out of Charleston, South Carolina. It brought Henry Middleton and Edward Rutledge to Philadelphia. The pace of arrivals quickly picked up. On the twenty-second, more congressmen from South Carolina arrived. The New Hampshire representatives took up residence at the end of the week. August 29 was especially busy. "Came to town," Marshall observed, "Hon. Thomas Cushing, Samuel Adams, Robert Treat Paine, and John Adams, delegates from the Province of Massachusetts Bay, with whom came in company, from New York, John Rutledge, delegate from South Carolina, who took his passage to New York." Two days later more delegates flooded into the city from New York, New Hampshire, Connecticut, Maryland, Delaware, and "some from this Province."[7]

However great the public's anticipation of the meeting may have been, the first days did not turn out as anyone expected. Instead of encountering adoring crowds, delegates heard the tolling of muffled bells. It continued for hours. All the major churches joined the somber chorus. For contemporaries schooled in interpreting the sounds of bells, the muting signaled alarm, danger, and sadness. On September 6 Robert Treat Paine scribbled in his diary, "Bells muffled rung all P.M." Caesar Rodney, a delegate from Maryland, noted, "The Bells were muffled & kept ringing." Connecticut's Silas Deane informed his wife, "The Bells Toll muffled & the people run as in a Case of extremity they know not where, nor why."[8] How, one wonders, did an occasion that promised so much joy give way so swiftly to fear and mourning?

As the delegates soon learned, the bells announced that British forces had just bombarded Boston. The early reports were vague and confused. Some accounts claimed that ordinary people had been shot down in the streets; others insisted that the city had been shelled, even destroyed. One can only imagine what went through the minds of the congressmen, tired after their long journeys and not certain just how best to deal with a hostile king and Parliament, as they contemplated the implications of such violence and destruction. For these leaders— as for later leaders of the United States who learned of the attacks on Fort Sumter, Pearl Harbor, and 9/11—time stopped.

Some surely assumed that the leveling of the great port meant that war with Great Britain could no longer be avoided. Others worried about family members who might have been killed or forced to flee to the countryside as refugees. On September 8 John Adams wrote to Abigail, not knowing at the time whether she was safe. "When or where this Letter will find you," he began, "I know not. In what Scenes of Distress and Terror, I cannot foresee. We have received a confused Account from Boston, of a dreadful Catastrophy. The Particulars, We have not heard. We are waiting with the Utmost Anxiety and Impatience, for further Intelligence."[9] Silas Deane informed his wife on the seventh that an express rider had just arrived from New York "confirming the Account of a rupture at Boston . . . I cannot say, that all Faces, gather paleness, but they all gather indignation, & every Tongue pronounces Revenge."[10] The tales of "the Troops and Fleets cannonading the Town of Boston" so unsettled the members of Congress that they decided to postpone normal business.

The relief that Adams and his colleagues experienced when they learned that the British had not in fact destroyed Boston lasted only a short time. Rumors of bombardment soon gave way to much more unsettling reports from New England that a huge American army intent upon revenge was prepared to settle the imperial dispute without waiting for directions from Congress. To understand how a false story transformed scattered insurgents—the people who had effectively nullified British authority in the Massachusetts countryside during the summer of 1774—into a massive popular instrument of resistance requires reconstruction of the curious conditions that allowed a rumor to get out of hand.

After the people of Massachusetts had forced so many Crown officials to seek safety in Boston—especially the hated mandamus councilors—it seemed just a matter of time before Gage would attempt to reassert British authority beyond the city. Loyalist sympathizers fed him intelligence—only some of which was reliable—about the activities of the insurgents. Gage paid particularly close attention to information related to stores of powder and arms. On September 1, acting on a tip, he dispatched 260 redcoats under the command of Lieutenant Colonel Maddison to Quarry Hill in Charlestown, where they seized several hundred barrels of gunpowder, and without encountering any opposition, they transferred these materials to a British fort. They also commandeered two small cannons found in nearby Cambridge.

The British success—however modest—embarrassed the local militia units. Some Americans complained that an aging American officer,

William Brattle, had actually invited Gage to remove the military supplies, a charge he angrily denied. In a short published statement dated September 2, Brattle proclaimed his innocence and begged the insurgents to try to appreciate that his royal commission compelled him to obey a direct order from Gage, the governor and commanding officer of Massachusetts. They did not do so. "Upon the whole," Brattle explained, "the Threatenings I have met with, my Banishment from my own Home, the Place of my Nativity, my House being searched, though I am informed it was without Damage, and the Sense of the People, touching my Conduct, &c. for the present cannot but be grievous." However much he protested that he was "a Friend to my country," he had irrevocably lost the trust of the community.[11]

News that Gage's troops had taken the gunpowder spread rapidly, spawning an explosive rumor. People who had not been anywhere near Quarry Hill claimed that the British had shot down six Americans who attempted to resist the raid. Although it was too late to defend what had been lost, hundreds of American insurgents swarmed into Cambridge. Many more were part of a large group who had already gathered and who were determined to force Thomas Oliver to resign his position as mandamus councilor. However angry the militants may have been, they had not developed a coherent plan of resistance. To avoid unnecessary provocation, they left their firearms in safe places outside of the town. They milled about, therefore, "armed only with sticks." No doubt they assumed that their presence in such large numbers would discourage Gage from further operations outside Boston. As one witness remembered the events of September 2, several thousand colonists who were "not of the rabble, as ministerial hirelings have been disposed to speak, but of the respectable freeholders and free men of the adjacent towns, collected at Cambridge."[12]

Even at this point a major confrontation might have been avoided. But as luck would have it, an accident occurred that no one at the time could possibly have foreseen. Just as Oliver seemed to be making headway with the representatives of the people, Benjamin Hallowell rode into town in an open carriage driven by a trusted servant. With the exception of Thomas Hutchinson, the previous royal governor of Massachusetts, no public figure was more despised than Hallowell. He served the Crown as a commissioner of customs, a position that constantly brought him into conflict with colonial merchants. During the Stamp

Act riots of 1765 a mob had torn his house down, but this experience had only served to redouble his efforts to enforce parliamentary taxes. In one letter written in 1774 he complained that Americans enjoyed too much access to the speeches made in the House of Commons by opponents of Lord North. This stream of information served only to inflame passions. Hallowell believed that if the ordinary colonists bothered to reflect rationally about their situation within the empire, "we should very soon have order and good government again." But the hour was late. "The frenzy is now so great," he concluded, "that reason is entirely out of the question."[13] And so, fearing that the insurgents would humiliate him at his country home on that fateful September 2, Hallowell decided to flee.

When he arrived at Cambridge, he had no idea that thousands of insurgents were pressuring Oliver to resign his office in Gage's government. Hallowell halted his carriage for just a moment at the edge of the swelling crowd. Perhaps he wanted to take a measure of its mood; perhaps he was simply curious. Whatever his thinking, he made a mistake. He should have driven through the town at top speed. Someone—probably Isaiah Thomas, publisher of the fiercely pro-American *Massachusetts Spy*—pointed him out to the crowd as "an enemy to the country and an high Tory." There were cries to kill him. In a state of panic, Hallowell drove off toward Boston. According to one witness, "the sight of that obnoxious person so inflamed the people that in a few minutes about one hundred and sixty horsemen were drawn up and proceeded in pursuit of him on the full gallop."

The wild chase was on. After only a few miles, however, most pursuers turned back. As one of their leaders observed, the business with Oliver had brought them to Cambridge, and racing after Hallowell was a waste of time. Not everyone got the message. Witnesses reported "about 8 or 10 would not go back but continued the pursuit." One particularly swift rider, described only as being "of a small stature," overtook the carriage, calling out cleverly but disingenuously, "Stop the murderer, the Tory murderer, he has killed a man." Hallowell drew a gun and would have killed the American had the weapon not misfired. He then leaped from the vehicle onto an especially fleet horse belonging to his servant. This time he escaped. Hallowell "cast a knot on the reins," and with "a pistol in each hand," the hated Crown appointee rushed through the

British checkpoints at the edge of Boston, screaming like Henny Penny that a huge insurgent force was on its way to "destroy all friends of Government." At this moment the gallant horse collapsed. Hallowell, however, kept going. "He ran on foot to the [military] camp, through which he spread consternation, telling them he was pursued by some thousands, who would soon be in town."[14]

What happened next remains murky. Gage's officers, who had a reasonably good sense of what was occurring in Cambridge, appear to have discounted Hallowell's hyperbolic predictions. Gage had spies disguised as sailors gathering intelligence from the nearby towns, and they did not support Hallowell's ravings. Still, his dramatic arrival generated a lot of unusual activity in the main barracks, and spotting this, American agents immediately warned the members of insurgent committees in nearby communities that the commotion might signal preparation for a general assault on Cambridge. Even though Gage had no intention of launching an attack, the possibility of British retaliation sparked a much more potent rumor that rapidly took on a life of its own. As one observer reported, "The alarm was communicated to Dr. Roberts then at Charlestown ferry, who having a fleet horse, brought the news in a few minutes to the [American] Committee then at dinner; the intelligence was instantly diffused, and the people, whose arms were nearest, sent persons to bring them, while horsemen were dispatched in both ways, to gain more certain advice of the true state of the soldiery."

The key leaders of the resistance quickly established that no troops had in fact left Boston. But it was too late. By that time the swiftest riders had already carried the false information to towns throughout Rhode Island, Connecticut, and western Massachusetts. Even at that early stage, there were indications that the ordinary people of New England were ready to fight. Witnesses noted that the insurgents had never before demonstrated "greater fervor and resolution."[15] It was striking that men like Hallowell did not anticipate the coming storm. Recovering from his own narrow escape, he whined that the British had missed a splendid chance to crush the rebels. Showing remarkable insensitivity to the situation on the ground—a chronic blindness afflicting the agents of empire—he asserted that "two companies of the King's troops would have drove them [the Americans] to the places from whence they came."[16] The next few days would reveal the foolishness of such advice, for Hallowell's ride had sparked a spontaneous mobilization of ordinary farmers who, if given the opportunity, would have massacred Gage's entire force.

Fast riders carried the news throughout New England. The process of telling and retelling the story of what had happened at Boston inevitably encouraged exaggeration. One Connecticut journal observed that everywhere the people were "prodigiously enraged, they having been informed that a party of soldiers had marched to Framingham, to seize the powder of that town, and had killed 6 of the inhabitants outright."[17] In New London, a much more alarming account circulated. In this community Gage's repositioning of several companies of redcoats within Boston sparked a report that "regular troops and ships of war were cannonading the town of Boston, and massacring the inhabitants without distinction of age or sex." It was this version of the tale that "flew like lightning." The journal estimated that within thirty-six hours the information had reached "more than one hundred & seventy miles in extent." The residents of nearby Saybrook, Connecticut, learned at about the same moment that Boston had been totally destroyed "by the regular forces and ships of war."[18] It is noteworthy that no one seems to have expressed the slightest skepticism about the intelligence. One might have expected that colonists would have asked why the British would have wanted to destroy a city where several thousand soldiers were quartered or how those troops had managed to redeploy before the main battle fleet opened fire. The terrible news was certainly unwelcome, but it apparently came as no surprise to the scattered towns where insurgency had already taken root.

The popular response to the news from Boston was nothing short of spectacular. Everywhere men spontaneously fetched weapons, and with almost no thought given to how best to organize a huge people's army, they marched north and east to defend the capital of New England. "It is surprising and must give great satisfaction to every well-wisher to the liberties of his country," exclaimed one journal, "to see the spirit and readiness of the people to fly to the relief of their distressed brethren." The reflexive mobilization had no precedent in this society. "The unshaken fortitude and determined resolution to conquer or die, which appeared in all ranks on the arrival of the news, would do honor to veteran troops," the report continued. "In many towns almost every man

able to bear arms marched for their relief; in others it was equally difficult to repress the ardor of the people."[19] In another Connecticut town
"a large body of men voluntarily appeared to enroll themselves to march
forthwith for the relief of their distressed brethren, and were all properly
equipped for battle and on their march before noon."[20]

A more detailed account of the popular reaction to the communication from Boston has survived from Windham, a town in eastern
Connecticut with a long history of radical politics. Though at the time
of writing the author knew that the British had not attacked Boston, he
noted that when they first heard the rumor, the people of Windham
thought "the alarming news . . . undoubtedly to be authentic." And they
reacted with an outpouring of anger. The piece, which was signed
"HARMONIUS & ARISTOGITON," explained that "the most tumultuous and opposite passions seemed to take possession of every breast;
on the one hand pity, for the cruel fate of Boston and her murdered
sons, on the other rage and determined vengeance, on their murderers."
Without guidance from anyone outside the community, ordinary farmers prepared to punish the British troops. "Couriers were immediately
dispatched to every quarter, with the most surprising expedition," he
observed. " 'To Arms! To Arms!' was the universal cry.—Instantly nothing was seen, on all sides, but men, of all ages and characters, cleansing
and burnishing their arms, furnishing themselves with provisions and
warlike stores . . . gentlemen of rank and fortune, exhorting and encouraging others, by their advice and example, and the very women
lending their helping hands, with the utmost readiness and assiduity, to
expedite the march, which began in a few hours from the receipt of the
intelligence." Soon the roads leading out of Windham were crowded
with scores of armed insurgents. Almost no one talked, so great was the
concentration on the task at hand.[21]

Reports of the sudden mobilization of so many troops sparked the
curiosity of the Reverend Ezra Stiles, a child of the Enlightenment who
would one day serve as the president of Yale College. The whole episode merited close examination, and like a modern journalist, he set out
several weeks after the popular rising to find out exactly what had happened. As luck would have it, Stiles was traveling through eastern Connecticut in mid-November when he encountered a Mr. McNeil, whom
Stiles identified as a moderately well-to-do trader from Litchfield. As

they talked on a road near Norwich, Stiles discovered that during the early days of September, McNeil had been lodging in Shrewsbury, a village not far from Boston, on the very night that the Americans first believed that the British had killed six colonists. Here was an "Eye Witness" to history.

What exactly had the merchant seen? Stiles asked. The minister could barely contain his excitement. McNeil told Stiles, "he never saw such a Scene before—all along were armed Men rushing forward, some on foot, some on horseback, at every house Women & Children making Cartridges, running Bullets, making Wallets, baking Biscuit, crying & bemoaning & at the same time animating their Husbands & Sons to fight for their Liberties, tho' not knowing whether they should ever see them again." Stiles demanded to know whether ordinary Americans showed genuine courage. Were these people serious about resisting oppression? Perhaps, Stiles suggested, when the raw troopers saw their wives and children weeping, they had second thoughts about taking up arms against the Crown?

On that point McNeil had no doubts. Everywhere he encountered "a Spirit for revenging the Blood of their Brethren & rescuing our Liberties." But it had not been the men who most impressed McNeil. The women joined the insurgency with wholehearted commitment. "The Women kept on making Cartridges, & after equipping their Husbands, bro't them out to the Soldiers which in Crowds passed along & gave them out in handfuls to one and another as they were deficient, mixing Exhortation & Tears & Prayers & spiriting the Men in such an uneffeminate Manner as even would make Cowards fight." Indeed, upon reflection, McNeil added, "If anything the Women surpassed the Men for eagerness & Spirit in the Defense of Liberty by Arms." These women understood full well that their sons and husbands might be killed in battle. This was war. "They expected," McNeil recounted, "a bloody Scene."[22]

Other Americans exchanged stories—mostly the stuff of pure invention—about how at the moment of crisis individuals had shown extraordinary courage in the face of almost certain death. A Pennsylvania journal, for example, printed an anecdote submitted by a "correspondent" about "a feeble old man about 83." When the younger men of his town turned out to fight the British, he followed along. At some point, however, his neighbors asked him to return home, since "he would expose himself to danger without any prospect of doing service." The aged warrior ignored the appeals. When pressed to explain his stubborn behavior, he "gave them an answer worthy of an old Roman. It is true, says he, my arm is feeble and my strength gone, but I can do some good, [as] I may happen to receive the ball which would otherwise destroy a younger and a better man."[23] Before we disregard the anecdote as the stuff of chest-thumping hyperbole, we should pause to consider the sorts of people who eagerly traded such tales of excess zeal and a willingness to die for cause and comrades. No doubt the tale contained an element of symbolic truth. The New Englanders who rushed north to avenge the destruction of Boston persuaded themselves that they too were prepared to die.

The New London newspaper offered readers an unusually rich collection of heroic stories. In one neighboring town the minister stepped down from the pulpit and led his armed parishioners on the march to Boston. Another body of men prepared to join the defense, but as they were assembling, they discovered that "they had no stockings and shoes, and other clothing sufficient for such a journey." A clever militia captain quickly solved the problem. He "went into the meeting house, and, by the consent of the people, took as many stockings and shoes, and other clothing from the people present, as supplied those, who were willing to venture their lives, in defense of their country." No sooner had the soldiers sorted out the borrowed footwear than they rushed north to save their beleaguered countrymen. In yet another Connecticut community the spirit of resistance so energized the people that even after the young men had departed for Boston, the remaining residents "armed themselves with scythes, fixed on poles, and marched off in that manner." Everywhere the women were as committed to the defense of liberty as the men. "In many places," the New London editor recounted, "the women assisted their husbands and sons, in preparing for their march, with as much coolness and deliberation, as they performed the ordinary offices of the family."[24]

News of the bombardment reached Israel Putnam at his home in Pomfret, Connecticut. An officer of the militia in a nearby town had alerted him to the crisis at eleven o'clock on the morning of September 3. How this man—one Captain Keyes—learned of the Boston tragedy reveals how rumors spread in this society. It seemed that an unnamed person heard—from whom was never stated—that the British had attacked the city. Skeptical that such an event could possibly have occurred, he dispatched his son to Massachusetts to discover whether the reports reaching Connecticut were reliable. The young man galloped north to Grafton, about thirty-five miles outside Boston, and there he spoke with various people he encountered on the road. They all testified that Gage had in fact attacked Boston. When the son returned with confirmation of everyone's worst fears, the father ordered him to go immediately to Carter's Tavern in Dudley, "where one Mr. Clarke of Woodstock, a trader, happened to be." Clarke passed the story to Keyes, who went to Putnam "with the strongest assurances of the truth and reality of said report." The news then radiated out from Putnam's farm, for Putnam himself scribbled a note to Captain Aaron Cleveland telling him of the British assault, which he claimed commenced when "the Men-of-War and Troops began to fire upon the people last night at sunset." Six Americans had been killed.[25]

It was not surprising that Putnam became the focus of the emergency mobilization. He had become something of a folk legend in his own time. Born to very poor parents in Salem, Massachusetts, in 1718, he had moved to northeastern Connecticut, where he managed to turn an unpromising piece of property into a successful farm. Although he never received a formal education, he worked hard. Putnam was also wonderfully coordinated, and when the young men of the region staged games— much like modern track-and-field events—he always emerged the winner. But it was his extraordinary courage that most impressed commentators. People recounted how he had once drubbed a Boston bully—who enjoyed a huge size advantage—in a fistfight. The favorite tale—one repeated by Putnam himself—involved a ferocious wolf that regularly killed the farm animals of the area. The local farmers tried their best to slay the terrifying "she wolf," but the beast always managed to outwit her pursuers. Putnam took up the challenge. He tracked the wolf to a den, which was described as an extensive underground cavern. The group attempted to smoke the wolf out of its lair. After this strategy failed, Putnam decided that someone would have to be lowered by rope into the den and then shoot the wolf before it mauled the intruder.

Putnam descended alone into the pit. And sure enough, he soon emerged victorious, having shot the wolf just as it was preparing to tear him apart. David Humphreys claimed in a biography published in 1788 that he included all the details of the wolf episode "because they contain a display of character." Perhaps they conveyed more than Humphreys intended. To be sure, Putnam was brave. But he was also stubborn, and even those who gave him respect knew better than to test his patience.

During the Seven Years' War, Putnam's irrepressible courage as well as his ability to command earned him the praise of senior British officers. He repeatedly put himself in harm's way. No one complained about his rapid rise through the ranks of the provincial army, and when peace returned to North America after 1763, Putnam—much like George Washington—stood out among the colonists as a person possessing both military ability and combat experience. Even on the eve of the Battle of Bunker Hill, such leading generals in the British forces as Thomas Gage urged Putnam to accept a commission from the Crown, but however much he admired his old allies in the war against the French, he supported the American cause. His endorsement of the news from Boston in September 1774 transformed a rumor into certainty. If Putnam was willing to march in defense of liberty, then who would dare contradict the one authentic military leader in the region. Soon after receiving Captain Keyes's report, Putnam ordered a general mobilization, and on the first Sunday following the destruction of Boston, every Congregational minister in Connecticut read Putnam's letter to the faithful.[26] It was reported that he declared that he and his men "shall glory in having a share in the honor of ridding our country of the yoke of tyranny, which our forefathers have not borne, neither will we."[27]

In one town the call to arms exposed deep ideological differences that almost cost a local minister his job. The Reverend John Smalley of New Britain complained bitterly to anyone who would listen that he resented the disruption of his normal Sunday sermon. People kept popping in and out of the church, talking about the crisis at Boston and urging all able-bodied men to appear that afternoon for a general muster. Smalley suspected that the story would soon be exposed for what it was, a product of exaggeration and fear. As he explained in a Connecticut newspaper, "As to what was said on occasion of the muster [day], considering the extreme incredibility of the news we had in itself—considering how it came—and that it was so long altogether unconfirmed—considering also, what a handful of regular troops there was at Boston, I verily thought there was not a call for us to muster on the Sabbath, and rush down from this distance. I spoke my mind. But it would have been better, I apprehend, if I had not."[28]

Smalley misread community opinion. No sooner had he appealed for calm during a public emergency than his parishioners suggested that he was actually scheming to undermine the American cause. They recounted sermons he had delivered in recent months that smacked of a pernicious political doctrine known as passive obedience or nonresistance. The theory had been employed during the seventeenth century to buttress support for Stuart monarchs who had no love for representative government. Indeed, John Locke wrote his famous *Two Treatises of Government* to counter despotic arguments of this sort. Those who accepted this doctrine counseled the people—no matter how justified their grievances against their civil rulers may have been—to obey authorities who were responsible ultimately only to God.

The minister's apparent efforts to obstruct mobilization in New Britain served to persuade townsmen that he did in fact harbor such obnoxious political ideas. A local committee, whose own authority in these matters rested on little more than suppositious claims to represent the will of the people, began to call witnesses who testified to what they heard Smalley say on the crucial Sunday when the alarm arrived. These records capture as well as any documents that have survived from the period the political culture of the American insurgency. Those giving testimony were ordinary colonists speaking at the moment that the imperial crisis swept through their community. Moses Andruss, for example, remembered that during the morning, Smalley had argued in public that the community did not have enough evidence "to make such a stir upon the Sabbath." When Andruss countered with the observation that it seemed to him that everyone was obliged to help the victims of British aggression in Boston, Smalley exclaimed, "What! Will you fight against your King?" Lemuel Hotchkiss provided an even more damning statement. The interruption of the church service had deeply offended Smalley, and in an unguarded moment the minister had said "he thought it very strange the people should think of fighting in this cause, for that he thought they had not a call or right to do it—that they could not go by any authority, but must be considered as a mob, which

Mr. Smalley repeated several times." One after another the people of New Britain came forward to denounce their own minister.[29]

A month after the residents of New Britain learned that the British Army had not in fact destroyed Boston, they were still squabbling about the political soundness of their minister. In mid-October, Smalley felt compelled to publish a defense of his actions, and although the apology did not satisfy many parishioners, it revealed what he thought the men who followed Putnam wanted to hear. In other words, even if Smalley's words were somewhat disingenuous, he understood the central political tenets driving the local insurgency. Smalley admitted that he feared the consequences of social unrest. But however much he feared anarchy, he rejected out of hand the doctrine of passive obedience and non-obedience to rulers. He then listed his own core political beliefs: the end of civil government is the good of the people, all laws should promote the common good, the legitimacy of civil government is based on a mutual compact between the governors and the governed, and taxation without representation is unacceptable in the American context.

The soldiers who mustered in early September would have found none of these points objectionable. Smalley added something more, however, and this final tenet revealed not only how swiftly the insurgency was spreading, but also how effectively moderates were being squeezed out of the debate over the political future of the American people. "I am not for suffering the chains of slavery to be fastened on our necks," the minister explained, "[or] on the necks of unborn posterity, without resistance and opposition." Nonimportation of British manufactures offered one way to stand up to despotism. But a pressing question remained. How should the people react to violence sanctioned by king and Parliament? "If we are driven to it by dire necessity," Smalley concluded, "and there is a rational prospect of being able to defend ourselves in this, and in no other way, we must have recourse to arms."[30] While their minister had been a little slow off the mark, Moses Andruss, Lemuel Hotchkiss, David Lusk, Ladwick Hotchkiss, Elihu Andruss, Giles Cooper, and Stephen Lee—some of the men who marched from New Britain to save Boston—had already come to accept the rationale for armed resistance.

A similar controversy broke out in Saybrook, a small town at the mouth of the Connecticut River. As in many other communities in the region, the people learned of the Boston tragedy on a Sunday morning.

Everyone sprang into action. It was as if the able-bodied men of Say-brook had simply been waiting for a reason to mobilize their forces. As a newspaper observed a few days later, "A large body of men voluntarily appeared to enroll themselves to march forthwith for the relief of their distressed brethren, and were all properly equipped for battle and on their march before noon." The day would have gone much more smoothly, however, if an outspoken individual had not decided to make a fuss. "When the soldiers were there enlisting," reported a journal, "Hezekiah Whittlesey, Esq . . . used every method in his power to prevent any aid being forwarded for the relief of the country and uttered many disagreeable and opprobrious expressions concerning the people of Boston—the country and [the Connecticut] General Assembly, of which he has very frequently been and is now a member, which gave great offense." A substantial group calling itself "the real friends of American liberty" immediately confronted the man and initiated a process of political reeducation. The members of this unofficial body—containing "many aged, [and] substantial persons"—visited Whittlesey and, in the understated rhetoric of the day, employed "proper application" to persuade him to make a full confession and recantation.

Whittlesey's stunning disgrace revealed that no one—not even a person who had long represented the town in the colonial legislature—could stand against the insurgency. Forced to speak to the people from a humiliating position on "a high horse-block," he stated before "an audience of sundry true sons of American liberty" that he indeed had uttered insulting opinions. It is amazing that he then repeated the exact words that had originally angered his neighbors. One might have thought he would simply apologize without reviewing the details. No doubt the educational value of so simple an apology was deemed insufficient. Instead, he admitted to having declared that "Boston was in a state of open rebellion, and that the measures taken by the parliament were good enough for them, and whoever went to their relief were as bad as they, and if they were taken [they] would all be hanged; and that I saw the same spirit at the General Assembly and did all I could to oppose it." To hold such ideas at all was a matter of public concern, but showing a remarkably inept sense of timing, Whittlesey had spoken out just as "the minds of the good people of this town were struck with horror and just resentment, upon the news of the town of Boston being cannonaded by his Majesty's forces and fleet." His expression of contrition must have satisfied the real friends of American liberty as genuine, for no sooner had he finished his painful recantation than he joined the people "in three huzzas," after which "they all dispersed and returned to their several places of abode."[31]

Israel Putnam, who of course knew nothing of these local quarrels, had not traveled very far on his journey to Massachusetts when he learned the truth of the matter. After calling out the militia captains of Connecticut, he had ridden his horse as far as Douglas—only a few miles from Worcester—where he encountered an officer in the local militia. That man had just returned from the outskirts of Boston, and he assured Putnam that the whole business had been a false alarm. There was no emergency. The British Army and Royal Navy had not bombarded or burned the city, nor had they killed innocent Americans. Units of the Sutton and Worcester militias had turned back, as did Putnam and the Connecticut soldiers.

Putnam later pieced together the source of the rumor. "I believe," he explained, "the alarm was first occasioned by Mr. Benjamin Hallowell, who, going into Boston in a great fright, informed the Army that he had killed one man and wounded another, while they were pursuing him from Cambridge." Putnam learned that as a result of Hallowell's exaggerations—one is tempted to label them outright lies—the British troops were thrown "into great consternation; and they quickly were paraded and put into the most convenient posture of defense." In the midst of this confusion someone dispatched an alarm. Putnam tried to discover exactly who made the decision, but his inquiries came to nothing. He was left only with rhetorical questions. Who had sent the original message? What purpose had he had in mind when he did so? Whatever the answers, "what took place in consequence of it is evident."[32]

For Putnam the story of the destruction of Boston had one additional, and quite irritating, chapter. No sooner did the Tories learn of the massive mobilization in response to a false alarm than they began to call Putnam's judgment into doubt. If this was the ablest military leader the Americans could count on, they certainly had no chance at all against well-drilled redcoats. One dismissed the entire episode as "Putnam's blundering story."[33] Hugh Gaine, publisher of the *New York Mercury*, ran a particularly patronizing account. An author who styled himself "A New-York Freeholder" asserted that Putnam lacked the calm, deliberative temperament expected of professional officers. In fact, it was fortunate that Putnam's intemperate actions had not triggered a bloody civil war.

One might have expected the aging general from Connecticut to ignore provocations of this sort. After all, during this period the loyalists tried to stake out the rhetorical high ground. By their own lights, they were informed, reasonable, and fair-minded. These characteristics distinguished them from ordinary farmers—the American insurgents— who allowed passion to cloud their political judgment. But even though Putnam understood that newspapers spun news for partisan purposes, he still regarded the charges as a personal assault. Only someone who had not been present that Sunday when word of the British assault on Boston first arrived, he insisted, could seriously entertain the notion that he had overreacted. The people had demanded immediate revenge. And who could blame them? After all, as Putnam explained, he was dealing with men and women "drove to a state of desperation by the oppressive hand of tyranny and the lawless violence of arbitrary power." He turned the Tory appeal to reason on its head. "What people on earth would not be justified," he asked, "in the eye of right reason and common sense, for the resistance even to the shedding of blood, if the preservation of their liberties demanded it?"

Addressing his Tory critic, Putnam inquired "whether he does not betray a total want of the blessings of humanity, if he supposes, in the midst of confusion, when the passions are agitated with a real belief of thousands of their fellow-countrymen being slain, and the inhabitants of a whole City just upon the eve of being made a sacrifice by the rapine and fury of a merciless Soldiery, and their City laid in ashes by the fire of the Ships of War, he or any one else could set down under the possession of a calmness of soul becoming a Roman Senator." Genuine compassion in these circumstances translated into action. Violence against innocent people—imagined here as "fellow-countrymen"—justified an armed response.[34] Indeed, he argued that he had had no alternative when the alarm reached Pomfret but to write "to one of the militia captains . . . when I really believed the story to be true."[35] Putnam's appeal yielded the result that he most desired. His honor remained intact. And eight months later, when British troops really did kill Americans at Lexington, the old soldier once again rode north to save his countrymen.

## III

The ordinary people of southern New England most emphatically did not regard their response to the false alarm as an embarrassing blunder. The entire episode—particularly the spontaneous mobilization of so many men—generated an exhilarating sense of pride. They congratulated themselves on having participated in a genuinely significant event. Their reflexive willingness to assist other Americans had given meaning to their corporate lives; they had suddenly been caught up in the flow of history. Various witnesses marveled that such a large number of soldiers had been involved in the defense of Boston.

The figures were entirely impressionistic. But accuracy was not the point. The sheer size of an imagined insurgent force became the measure of success. An observer from western Connecticut confessed that his count amounted to little more than a guess. Still, he declared, "'tis highly probable there were not less than ten thousand men [who] actually marched, and as many more ready to march from this colony." A Windham report agreed: "By the most moderate computation, in the colony of Connecticut alone, there were not less than twenty thousand men completely armed actually on their march for Boston." Others thought that fifteen thousand might be closer to the mark. As the original story of Hallowell's ride had taken on a life of its own as it spread through New England, the numbers of colonial troops inflated with each telling. A man living in Boston asserted on good authority that nearly a hundred thousand Americans "were equipped with arms and moving toward us from different parts of the country."[36]

The Reverend Ezra Stiles tried his best to verify these figures. Asking anyone who seemed to possess reliable information about the September rising, he reconstructed "the spreading of the Wave of the Report." His informants told Stiles that the news of armed confrontation had traveled from Cambridge swiftly in three separate directions. Riders carried the story north into New Hampshire and Vermont, others alerted those who lived in the far western part of Massachusetts, and the third path brought the news south into Connecticut. But as Stiles soon discovered, the direction the intelligence moved did not have much effect on the number of soldiers who immediately took up arms. "For about fifty miles each way round," Stiles observed, "there was an almost universal Ferment, Rising, seizing Arms & actual March into Cambridge." About two thousand men from Bennington, Vermont, prepared to join the colonial forces. Another two thousand soldiers from Berkshire County in far western Massachusetts responded to the alarm. Stiles gathered even more useful information from Connecticut. Men set off to revenge the destruction of Boston from scores of towns. An entry into his diary reveals how seriously Stiles took his research.

> East Guilford 83 armed, with Mr. Todd their pastor.
> Pachauge 38 out of 60 — marched to Rope Ferry.
> Chester — as forward — doubly equipt — 2lb. powder apiece.
> Haddam — 100 armed — animated by Rev. Mr. May.
> Saybrook [and]
> Lyme, & c. 200 marched almost to New London.
> Lebanon — 100 Marched.
> Chatham — 100 Marched with Rev. Mr. Boardman Pastor.

After he had tabulated the local returns, Stiles concluded that Connecticut alone had supplied "20,000 men in arms." Moreover, "from the best Accounts I judge 30,000, or near perhaps more than one Third of the effective Men in all New England took Arms & were on actual March for Boston."[37]

Whatever the precise numbers may have been, the mobilization of an irregular army sparked a powerful feeling of confidence. For New Englanders at least, the lesson learned from the march on Boston was that they could in fact hold their own against British soldiers — indeed, could drive them from the colonies. The newspaper stories that analyzed the massive insurgent rising of early September were not intended to intimidate General Gage or to persuade the leaders of Parliament of the impossibility of ever taxing Americans without their consent. In this instance, the colonists were communicating a message of strength and commitment to other colonists. No one had known in advance whether scattered communities from New Hampshire to Connecticut would volunteer to sacrifice — even accepting the possibility of death itself —

for a common cause. Now they knew. Throughout the entire region, Americans acting without a clear chain of military command had demonstrated courage and resolve. "The unshaken fortitude and determined resolution to conquer or die, which appeared in all ranks on the arrival of the news, would do honor to veteran troops," concluded a witness from New London.

The author of a piece in the *Connecticut Gazette* bragged that the combined forces from Connecticut and Rhode Island composed a more "formidable army than ever appeared in America, and perhaps even in Europe itself, in the present age." It did not require "the penetration of a Newton" to discern what would have happened had this insurgent army met with a genuine emergency. The soldiers would have taken their vengeance on those colonists who had betrayed the cause of freedom. Venting his full rage, the man who called himself HARMONIUS & ARISTOGITON explained exactly how the insurgents would have dealt with their political enemies: "You would have fallen the first sacrifice."[38]

The alarm did something more than simply give a boost to the colonists' military confidence. News of the destruction of Boston reached separate communities where men and women with few personal ties to the great port made the most important decision of their lives. Without deep reflection, without prolonged debate about the justification for their acts, they rushed to help strangers who were victims of aggression. But on the roads that led north they encountered others like themselves. It was in these adventitious circumstances that the insurgents of America initially became conscious of their membership in larger communities built upon shared identities. Crisis encouraged political imagination on the ground. No one could have seen it coming, but Hallowell's crazed ride from Cambridge helped weave local experiences into a larger and much more compelling narrative of a united cause. Without bothering to consult with a single Founding Father, the people took up arms en masse against the empire.

## *IV*

Paul Revere galloped into Philadelphia on September 16, carrying among other items a copy of the Suffolk Resolves. The radical declaration, which sanctioned a defensive war against the British, would seem to have placed the delegates to the Continental Congress in an impossible dilemma. By voicing support for the Resolves, they threatened to alienate moderate representatives such as Joseph Galloway, who still thought that the parliamentary leaders might listen to courteous appeals from the colonists. But that is not what happened. Although the members of the various delegations pledged not to reveal to outsiders the substance of the debates that occurred in Carpenters' Hall, they did note in private correspondence that the Suffolk Resolves received near unanimous approval on the seventeenth.[39]

The explanation for this unexpected decision lay in the unsettling reports from New England that the delegates had been discussing for at least a week before Revere rode into town. When the representatives learned that the British had not in fact leveled Boston, they also discovered that the people had taken the initiative in resisting the empire. This was staggering news. It did not matter whether the American forces numbered fifteen thousand or a hundred thousand. The challenge for Congress was how best to gain control over a huge irregular army that had spontaneously taken the field and on the slightest provocation might engage Gage's troops in pitched battle. The leaders of a nation that had not yet declared independence found themselves in the extremely awkward position of becoming followers—perhaps even irrelevant spectators—while ordinary people in communities like New Britain and Windham assumed the lead in defining the character of resistance against Great Britain.

Private letters written during this period help us to understand how reports of the spreading insurgency in New England affected political judgment. Joseph Reed, a respected lawyer in Philadelphia, ardently hoped that British policy makers might head off violent confrontation with the colonists. He also firmly believed that Parliament had violated the constitutional rights of all Americans. On September 25, in an effort to keep up the conversation, he warned Dartmouth of the anger that was poisoning colonial public opinion. Reed cited the case of the Boston emergency. "A few days ago we were alarmed," he recounted, "with a report that General Gage had cannonaded the town of Boston. So general a resentment, amounting even to fury, appeared everywhere, that I firmly believe, if it had not been contradicted, thousands would have gone at their own expense, to have joined in the revenge." Reed adopted the vocabulary of insurgency. The people of Philadelphia were driven by fury, resentment, and a desire for revenge.

The chaotic scene—one that the members of the Continental Congress would also have witnessed—unnerved Reed. "Those who served in the last war in the Provincial troops, others discharged from the regulars, and many who have seen service in Germany, and migrated to this country, with such others as would have joined them, would have formed from the best accounts a considerable body." He estimated that an irregular army of forty thousand men from Pennsylvania would have marched to support the New Englanders had the volunteers not learned at the last moment that Boston was safe. And then, as the logic of the situation carried Reed forward, he informed Dartmouth that Congress had just approved the Suffolk Resolves. The decision to take a radical course reflected a rising spirit of resistance that could in time lead to "continued violence." Reed urged Dartmouth to pay particular attention to the actual vote in Congress, where the "unanimity of provinces . . . [and] of individual members" manifested "a spirit leading to desperation."[40]

On September 19 Caesar Rodney, the congressional delegate from Delaware whom John Adams described as the "oldest looking man in the world," disclosed how much the unexpected creation of a large American army had transformed the political environment in Philadelphia. In a letter to his younger brother Thomas, Rodney reviewed the familiar story of the destruction of Boston. Everyone now knew that the muffled bells in Philadelphia had signaled a false alarm. What most interested Rodney—and he was writing only a day after acceptance of the Suffolk Resolves—was the time lag of "about 3 days between this report passing thro' the Mass. & Conn. govts. & its being contradicted." In this short period of time, ignorance and fear yielded amazing results. The people had taken charge. As Rodney explained, when messengers finally informed the people of southern New England that no bombardment had occurred, they "found in those 2 govts. in different parties upward of 50,000 men well-armed, actually on their march to Boston for the relief of the inhabitants."

In Rodney's rendering of the tale, the mobilization touched everyone. Even farmers whose physical condition precluded participation in actual combat had formed supply lines, loading their carts "with provisions, ammunition, baggage &c." More impressive were reports claiming that "vast numbers more were preparing to march." To this heroic narrative Rodney added a new detail, a plausible explanation of popular insurgency based on conspiracy. He had heard that the entire episode had been staged "by some of the friends to the ministerial plan [Tory supporters of North] in order to try whether there was that true valor in the people." The scheme backfired. If probing the American resolve had been the intention of the Tories, Rodney assured his brother, then the colonists should see Putnam's blunder as a magnificent success, for after the march on Boston, no one any longer could credibly question the people's will to resist.[41]

Richard Henry Lee, the most outspoken defender of American rights on the Virginia delegation, also believed that the stories of violence and destruction coming out of New England had had a bracing impact on the members of Congress. In a letter sent to his brother William on September 20, Lee reviewed what had occurred in Philadelphia in only three weeks. Like Rodney, he seized on the false alarm. "Since we came to this place," he explained, "a universal alarm has been occasioned by a report that Boston had just been Cannonaded. This proves not true, and took its rise from a night maneuver of the Generals to seize some Provincial Powder that had been stored by law for Militia uses."

Of course, everyone was happy to learn the truth of the matter. Lee realized, however, that something much more important was at stake than correcting misinformation. He assured William that the Boston report had served "to sow the spirit and situation of the people in that part of America, for we have good intelligence that 50,000 Men were in Arms in the Massachusetts Government and Connecticut, and that 30,000 were on march, well armed and provided, to Boston." Lee understood immediately the power of the insurgency. "Does not this show," he asked rhetorically, "that no small difficulty will attend forcing a submission from these people, and they are most firmly resolved to die rather than submit to the change of their Government?" And then Lee made a direct connection between the indisputable evidence that the people had taken charge of their revolution and the congressional passage of the Suffolk Resolves. He declared that as an expression of the delegates' support of the people, they had approved "in strong terms the resolves of the County of Suffolk." Lee sensed that this moment signaled the birth of a united movement to resist oppression. He told William, who was living in London, that it would be a serious mistake for the members of North's cabinet to ignore the news from America, for they "may be certain of a full, complete, and steady opposition from all North America."[42]

John Adams provided additional insight into the mysterious ratification of the Suffolk Revolves. In a letter to Abigail written only a day after Congress approved the document, Adams returned to the moment when the bells had tolled for Boston. "When the horrid News was brought here of the Bombardment of Boston," he told his wife, "[it] made us completely miserable for two days." What most pleased Adams was that even during the darkest hour, the representatives of the other colonies had declared their unqualified support for the people of Massachusetts. An imagined assault had brought forth unity. "WAR! WAR! WAR! Was the Cry," he announced, "and it was pronounced in a Tone, which would have done Honour to the Oratory of a Briton or a Roman. If it had proved true, you would have heard the Thunder of an American Congress." What exactly had the other delegates done to turn Adams's depression into "one of the happiest Days of my Life"?[43] The answer was, of course, acceptance of the Suffolk Resolves. Although he did not bother to calculate the size of the army of revenge, he well understood that the people were out in front of their representatives. It had been a great mass of country soldiers throughout New England—many without proper shoes and socks—who on this occasion forced the leaders of America to catch up with the American people.

The crisis sparked by a false alarm ended without further incident. The thousands of soldiers who had marched toward Boston returned home, no doubt pleased with themselves and happy not to have taken on Gage's well-trained soldiers. Congress turned to other business. The delegates surely breathed a sigh of relief that during their first three weeks in Philadelphia they had not found themselves managing a war for which they were not prepared.

But it would be a misreading of the evidence to dismiss the entire incident as merely a curious anomaly that—however interesting it may have been—cannot be easily made to fit into traditional narratives of revolution. The point is not that we should discount the contributions of leading political figures such as Adams and Lee to the overthrow of British authority. Rather, by restoring the people to the history of their own resistance, we rediscover a complex interplay between the deliberations that took place in Carpenters' Hall and what was happening on the ground. Once the people had demonstrated their resolve, there was no turning back. Some congressmen may have wished that they could have disavowed the Suffolk Resolves and concentrated on producing learned legal appeals to king and Parliament for colonial rights. Whatever their hopes for restoring the empire may have been, they could never erase the memory of an insurgent army.

This is precisely the message that some members of the colonial elite dispatched to Dartmouth. "I cannot dissemble with your lordship," exclaimed Joseph Reed in late September 1774, "that it appears to me we are on the verge of a civil war not to be equaled in history for its importance and fatal consequences."[44] John Penn, the governor of Pennsylvania and no radical in political matters, wrote much the same thing. North and his allies were not facing a few disgruntled provincial gentlemen. "The resolution of opposing," observed Penn, ". . . is in great measure universal throughout the colonies and possesses all ranks and conditions of people."[45] How exactly Dartmouth read such letters is not known. Not wanting to hear what he did not want to hear, he pushed forward with policies guaranteed to enrage all ranks and conditions of Americans.

## *V*

For his part, General Thomas Gage closely monitored the activities of the American insurgents. Unlike those Tories who had ridiculed Putnam for his allegedly precipitate response to the Boston alarm, Gage recognized immediately the seriousness of the threat to his forces. He tried to warn Dartmouth that the colonists had developed the ability not only to mobilize large numbers of armed men, but also to ferret out those few "friends of government" who remained in the countryside. "Upon a rumor propagated with uncommon dispatch through the country that the soldiers had killed six people and that the ships and troops were firing upon Boston," he explained to Dartmouth on September 25, "the whole country was in arms and in motion and numerous bodies of the Connecticut people had made some marches before the report was contradicted." People loyal to the Crown now streamed into the city, desperate for protection. Beyond the main garrison, the British Army could not even pretend to offer them help, for as Gage concluded, "From present appearance there is no prospect of putting the late Acts [the Coercive Acts] in force but by first making a conquest of the New England provinces."[46]

The people's astonishing response to the alarm effectively reduced Gage's military options and set off a remarkable exchange between the general and the newly created provisional government of Massachusetts. Sensing his vulnerability, Gage authorized construction of several fortified positions on the road connecting Boston to the mainland. From the perspective of military engineers, the order presented no serious challenge. The highway ran along a narrow stretch of land known as the "Neck," and within a few days the British had thrown up fresh earthworks and gun emplacements. The American reaction to this move— which after all was a visible reminder of how successfully the insurgents had managed to confine several thousand British soldiers in the city— surprised the general. They demanded that the new fortifications be demolished "lest the inhabitants of the town should be enslaved and made hostages of, to force the country to comply with the late Acts."[47] The British dismissed such demands without second thought. If Gage would not take down the forts, spokesmen for the people declared, then he must allow anyone who wanted to leave Boston to do so without punitive sanctions.

The plan caught the members of the Continental Congress totally off guard. Once again the ordinary colonists were getting ahead of their leaders. John Adams reported that someone—he was not sure who— had floated a suggestion "of removing the Inhabitants out of Boston." He could not conceive of such an exodus. "This would be the grandest Movement, imaginable, if it is practicable," he wrote to his friend William Tudor. "But how all their Effects can be removed—how 20,000 People can go out—where they can find Support, I know not." Still, whatever the logistics, Adams gave the idea guarded backing. "It has always been my opinion, that it was best for every Man, Woman, and Child who had an Inclination to go, to find a Place, to leave the Town."[48]

Richard Henry Lee expressed greater enthusiasm. He even drafted a motion, which he presented to the full Congress, "for quitting the town of Boston." The wording of his statement serves as a salutary reminder that many people sympathetic to the insurgency viewed Boston as an occupied city. As Lee declared, "The Congress are of opinion that it is inconsistent with the honor and safety of a free people to live within the Control and exposed to the injuries of a Military force not under government of the Civil Power."[49]

Lee's congressional colleagues refused to support his motion. They understandably reasoned that such a huge relocation project would not only overstrain the limited resources of the provisional government, it would also provoke the British to adopt even more objectionable policies. But the prudence of the Congress should not obscure for us the implications of the proposal. The entire population of Boston in 1774 probably numbered about eighteen thousand. One can only guess how many people would have accepted the invitation to become political refugees. Like Adams, however, we can imagine the roads clogged with desperate men and women hauling their possessions to small communities throughout Massachusetts, where these refugees would have been compelled to beg for proper food and lodging. It is an image we do not generally associate with the American Revolution. In any case, the colonial irregulars who surveyed Gage's fortifications were not impressed. "The new erected Fortifications on the Neck are laughed at by our old Louisbourg Soldiers [veterans of the Seven Years' War]," one man reported, "as mud-walls in comparison with what they have subdued; and, were it necessary, they would regard them no more than a beaver dam."[50]

Gage kept up a steady stream of letters to Dartmouth, reminding him repeatedly that the three thousand troops stationed in Boston could not possibly pacify the countryside. He urged the government to dispatch a much larger force, for as Gage reasoned from his headquarters in the fortified city, only a surge of military strength could achieve the goals of the current ministry. He thought that an additional twenty thousand British troops might be able to reestablish the authority of the Crown beyond the Neck.

Dartmouth concluded that Gage had made a terrible mistake. Surely, he responded, Gage must have overestimated the threat posed by scattered, undertrained American soldiers. Dartmouth explained, in the condescending manner of bureaucrats who have no direct knowledge of the situation on the ground, that he had not seen documentation "to show that the outrages which had been committed were other than merely the acts of a tumultuous rabble without any appearance of general concert or without any head to advise or leader to conduct that could render them formidable to a regular force led forth in support of law and government." Gage was left to solve the problem with the army he had.[51]

For his part, North stayed the course. His supporters in Parliament thought Dartmouth's assessment of the American crisis made a lot of sense. Only a few dissenters wondered where a policy designed to punish the colonists might lead. David Hartley, a member of Parliament who did not blindly follow North, recorded his impressions of the government's arguments for the application of overwhelming military force. In his *Letters on the American War*, Hartley remembered "the highest authority of government was made use of, to inculcate opinions, which when put to the test, have proved totally unfounded." What had the ministers who had read Gage's dispatches from Boston reported to the House of Commons? They were assured "that the disturbances in America, were only the tumults of a deluded mob, misled by a few designing persons; that the appearance of a slight military force, to sustain the civil power, would soon quell all disturbance, and that as soon as the King's standard was set up in America, the whole country would flock to it." Hartley suspected that the insurgents were more formidable than he had been told. The willingness of North's party to manipulate information, however, had muted opposition. "All this was confidently asserted, in the declarations of Ministers in Parliament, who were in possession of the most authentic correspondences with the several provinces in America."[52]

In mid-November the Massachusetts delegation to the First Continental Congress returned to Boston. Their arrival sparked a huge celebration. Nathaniel Appleton, a stout defender of universal rights, noted, "The bells rang the whole evening."[53]

SIX

# The Association:
# The Second Stage of Insurgency

Successful revolutions require more than popular anger. Americans learned this lesson during the autumn of 1774. The spontaneous fielding of a huge insurgent force both constrained Congress's choices and lent credibility to ordinary Americans determined to resist king and Parliament. Instead of causing the revolution to dissipate or run amok, creative tensions between local militants and continental leaders produced a brilliant structure that at once legitimated Congress's leadership and authorized the people to sustain, define, and channel the insurgency within their own communities.

The critical moment came unexpectedly, in response to Congress's endorsement of a general boycott on British manufactured goods—a declaration known as the Association. This bold act allowed ordinary people to project the raw passion that had energized Israel Putnam's army into the work of local committees. In fact, months before General Gage's troops attacked Lexington and Concord, huge numbers of Americans had already participated in the establishment of a massive committee system, putting into place the vital infrastructure of resistance and extending support for the cause far beyond the boundaries of New England. Throughout America these committees enforced their revolutionary agenda on entire communities, punishing dissenters and organizing military training. Without dampening popular zeal, the committees took opposition to Great Britain to a second stage, less spontaneous, perhaps, but ultimately more effective.

Appreciation of the centrality of committees in the story of the revolution revises our understanding of how popular mobilization worked. After all, questions about sustaining commitment on the local level do not occur if we want only to chronicle the beliefs or accomplishments of the members of the Continental Congress. However, once we focus attention on the ordinary people—those who supported the insurgency over the two years before the Declaration of Independence—the problem of maintaining revolutionary momentum becomes a pressing concern.

A familiar explanation for the rising of the American people gives major credit to a bundle of shared political notions about liberty and virtue that allegedly drove the movement forward.[1] Without discounting the significance of ideas in energizing insurgency, we would do well to examine the processes and procedures that, on the community level, served to stiffen resistance. This shift in interpretive goals raises compelling new questions. Where, in fact, did revolution occur for most Americans? Where precisely was it initially experienced? Or, put in different terms, in what circumstances did ordinary people feel compelled to declare openly before friends and neighbors whether or not they supported the American cause?

John Adams inadvertently made the task of answering these questions a lot harder. In a letter written in 1813, he famously claimed that only a third of the American people enthusiastically supported resistance to the British Empire. He estimated that another third were trimmers who attempted to stay uninvolved until one side or the other emerged victorious. And the third part, he believed, had remained loyal to George III. We should view Adams's impressionistic numbers with a grain of salt. He did not offer up these figures until long after the colonists had won the war. In any event, more recent historians have not done a much better job in gauging with confidence how many Americans fell into these fluid categories. Nor does it make much difference. Such calculations serve only to deflect attention from a much more significant issue. Even if the insurgents represented a minority of the colonial population on the eve of independence, they still managed to control the political agenda in all but those few regions where the British Army offered the loyalists reliable military support.

For the overwhelming majority of colonists, the decision to join the insurgency took place in small communities where, during the last

months of 1774, extralegal committees seized control of local government. Some individuals who served on these committees had held office before the final imperial crisis. But many others were *new* men who
found themselves thrust into positions of authority by a wave of popular
resistance to the policies of Great Britain.

Although they possessed no constitutional legitimacy, the members
of the local committees literally enforced the Revolution. When pressed
to justify their proceedings, they claimed to be acting in the name of the
people, or the public, or a vaguely defined American cause. The committees of safety—or, as they were sometimes called, committees of observation or committees of inspection—made key decisions on the local
level about ideology and resistance, about accommodation and violence, which in this highly unstable political environment carried the
force of law. And with increasing rigor they took it upon themselves to
identify and punish persons deemed enemies of the country; they encouraged denunciations, often based on no more than personal animus
and hearsay evidence. Moreover, these revolutionary bodies showed
little patience for dissent.

In communities throughout America the committees determined
the progress of revolution. They quickly seized the political initiative,
and before those who harbored doubts about the wisdom or legality of
taking up arms against the king could organize effective countermea-
sures, they found themselves marginalized by extralegal bodies fully
prepared to intimidate, even terrorize those who dared to criticize the
American cause. It is not that the loyalists were kinder or more open-
minded than their opponents. When they had the opportunity, they
engaged in practices as vicious as any sanctioned by the insurgents. It is
simply that in case after case, they were slow off the mark, and as popular
resistance to British authority evolved into a full-scale war, the committee structure kept them on the defensive, so that whatever their numbers may have been at the end of 1774 or the beginning of 1775, loyalists
seldom mounted a serious threat to the revolutionary movement.

The American committees of safety provoke another consideration.
Whatever prerogatives they may have assumed, they seldom allowed
the policing of popular ideology to get out of hand. The contrast with the
experiences of other revolutions throughout the world is striking. The
French Revolution, for example, conjures up deeply disturbing images

of mass executions and destruction of private property.[2] Similar events in Russia and China could be added to the list. In these countries popular violence spun out of control, and groups who had called for radical change one day often fell out of favor and found their followers labeled enemies of the people the next.

That kind of bloodletting did not occur in the British colonies. The reason is not that the Americans were exceptional.[3] They surely would have burned houses and murdered neighbors if the situation had invited a continuous purging of ideological dissenters. Rather, the explanation for the containment of violence from late 1774 through 1775 rests on the recognition that the social context in which these committees operated was quite different from that of other nations. Some elements are obvious. Unlike revolutionaries in France, the colonists did not face an entrenched aristocracy or rentier class that might have fought hard to maintain privileged status. Wealthy Americans—great planters in the South or leading merchants in northern ports, for example—certainly harbored doubts about resistance to British rule, but when push came to shove, they depended more upon the goodwill of their neighbors than upon representatives of an imperial establishment. Southern planters additionally feared that total social upheaval would encourage slaves to turn on their masters. Britain's leaders might have found ways to co-opt the members of the colonial elite with special titles and timely favors, but they never bothered to do so. Moreover, many American loyalists emigrated at the first sign of trouble—fleeing to Britain or, after 1775, to the region around New York City—thus denying large areas of the countryside an effective counterrevolutionary force. And of course, the committees could make a plausible argument that they did in fact represent the people on the local level.

It is important to remember that there was a fundamental agreement between the insurgents and the Congress on revolutionary goals. Americans were not attacking the need for central government, nor, for that matter, the need for taxes. They rejected a corrupt government that denied them a voice in legislation and failed to protect their God-given rights and property. Broad agreement on basic grievances helped the colonists to avoid the kind of vicious factionalism that would have compromised the Revolution from the very start. Differences arose not over a shared revolutionary agenda, but over strategy. As so many ordinary people throughout America aggressively pushed to achieve common ends, they often got ahead of Congress.

These conditions — the mix varied from region to region — mandated that the committees generally sought a tactical balance between meting out harsh punishment and reeducating potential enemies of the revolution before they had a chance to organize large-scale counterinsurgency. These extralegal bodies came down hard on marginal persons who stood apart from the community or aggressively proclaimed their loyalty to the Crown. Resident Scots, Anglican ministers, and small-time merchants were especially vulnerable.

Instead of executing enemies wholesale, however, the committees tried to shame them into giving public confessions. These proceedings took on a ritual quality in which terror and humiliation were aimed at converting dissenters. The bark was generally worse than the bite. More to the point, local show trials served to remind frightened and uncertain moderates that authority, at least within their immediate communities, rested firmly in the hands of those who supported resistance to the British Empire. Not surprisingly, most of these moderates chose silence over confrontation. By following a pragmatic course during a crisis that threatened to degenerate into anarchy, the committees of safety spoke the language of revolution while at the same time maintaining social order.

The story of the insurgent committees raises an even more significant point. These bodies played a central role in the development of a republican form of government in the United States. Theorists had long debated how such a polity might actually work. Drawing upon abstract models and ancient histories, many concluded that a republic based on the will of the people was inherently unstable. In the American context, however, the theorists need not have worried.

## I

By mid-September 1774, the members of the Continental Congress felt reasonably certain that tensions in New England would not immediately trigger full-scale war. The British had not in fact destroyed Boston, and the insurgent forces that had spontaneously responded to the rumor of atrocity returned peaceably to their homes. But the core issues driving the imperial conflict remained. The delegates knew that they had to find a way to persuade king and Parliament to negotiate a settlement that Americans would accept without thereby exacerbating enmity to the point of no return. Of course, the hour was late. The Philadelphia gathering in itself signaled to Lord North's government that the colonists were not prepared to back down. Within the structure of the imperial constitution, the Americans had absolutely no right to hold such a meeting.

Although the delegates divided over how to deal with Parliament, they agreed that Congress had to devise quickly a plan capable of sustaining and strengthening American resistance to parliamentary oppression. A coordinated boycott of British commerce presented an obvious answer. Beginning roughly in the 1740s, the colonial market for goods manufactured in the mother country had taken off. Eager to participate in an Atlantic economy that transformed the character of everyday material life, American consumers purchased an ever-larger share of British exports. It did not require great insight to realize the political implications of this commercial relationship. To be sure, colonial buyers depended on Britain for a wide range of imported goods—especially cloth—that added comfort and color to even modest households. But by the same token, British manufacturers depended on American consumers for their own prosperity.[4]

So long as the imperial commercial system satisfied all parties, no one complained too vociferously. During the 1760s, however, Americans gradually came to appreciate that through an interruption of the flow of goods—by making goods from the mother country the objects of political protest—they could force Parliament to reconsider the more obnoxious features of colonial policy. The plan had undeniable appeal. A general boycott, the Americans argued, would soon create massive unemployment in Britain, and as wage laborers identified the true source of their suffering—legislation designed to crush the liberties of colonial Americans—they would organize public protests that few members of Parliament could ignore. A stoppage of American trade with Britain's Caribbean colonies would soon bring the sugar economy to its knees. In this broad context, nonconsumption gave otherwise vulnerable colonists a voice in imperial affairs without having to resort to violence.

Disruption of imperial commerce had other virtues. First, an effective boycott required personal sacrifice by almost every family from New Hampshire to Georgia. The politicization of consumer products offered a means to mobilize huge numbers of unhappy Americans. Second, since the purchase of highly visible imported items could easily be monitored, boycotts forced people literally to display their political ideology on their bodies or in their homes. Public appearance and behavior thus became badges of support for resistance to imperial policies.

The challenge was enforcement. The problem had a contentious history. Colonists had initially called for a boycott of British manufactures during the Stamp Act crisis of 1765. The strategy yielded disappointing results. Protest groups in major ports such as Boston and New York expected leading merchants to curtail orders for imported goods. Americans placed the burden of responsibility on the business community, not on the people themselves. The merchants remained unenthusiastic, complaining that their income suffered while competitors in other cities engaged in normal trade. The loosely organized boycott had little impact on Parliament's decision to rescind the Stamp Act. Between 1768 and 1770, in response to a new round of parliamentary taxes known as the Townshend program, Americans tried again to use consumption as a political weapon. The results were only marginally more encouraging. Instead of depending on the merchants to halt trade with Great Britain, the colonists relied on town meetings to police local commerce. These groups drew up long lists of prohibited items. Many communities, especially outside New England, simply ignored the effort, and although a greater number of ordinary people than in 1765 participated in the disruption of imperial commerce, regional suspicions remained. The Coercive Acts revived enthusiasm for boycotts. Several colonies—Massachusetts, Maryland, and Virginia—advocated a complete stoppage of British imports, but so long as Americans in other areas refused to cooperate, these actions did not seriously threaten the prosperity of the mother country.

These experiences informed debates in the Continental Congress. Over several weeks of spirited discussion marked by special pleading and timely compromise, the delegates hammered out a workable plan for putting economic pressure on Great Britain. Unlike previous colonial efforts, this scheme not only demanded the support of all Americans, it also advocated serious penalties for those who refused to cooperate. On October 20 Congress endorsed the Association. The document established a precise schedule for when various aspects of the program—nonimportation, nonconsumption, and nonexportation—were to go into effect. As the representatives announced in the preamble of the Articles of Association, "To obtain redress of [the] grievances which threaten destruction to the lives, liberty, and property of his majesty's subjects in North America, we are of opinion, that a non importation, non consumption, and non exportation agreement, faithfully adhered to will prove the most speedy, effectual, and peaceable measure."

Fourteen separate articles followed this opening statement. Several spelled out the specific dates when each part of the Association became the law "of our country." Other sections sounded almost puritanical in their insistence that Americans forgo entertainments such as "horse racing . . . all kinds of gaming, cock fighting, exhibitions of shows, plays, and other expensive diversions." In addition, Congress forbade extravagant funerals in which men appeared with "a black crepe or ribbon on the arm or hat" and women with "a black ribbon and necklace." The members of Congress may have sensed that if the wealthiest families in America failed to sacrifice pleasures associated with privilege, they could not persuasively ask ordinary Americans to adopt more frugal habits. And finally, anticipating that a boycott of British woolens would compromise the colonists' ability to clothe themselves, the Association encouraged Americans to protect sheep.

What made the Association one of the more significant documents in American history—what made it a truly radical declaration—was Article Eleven. This section addressed the perplexing problem of enforcement. Congress clearly did not have the resources needed to oversee commercial transactions on the community level. It had to transfer that responsibility—and the power that went with it—to people actually able to police the movement of imports and exports. The delegates came up with a brilliant solution that had far-reaching consequences for revolutionary government. They ordered "that a committee be chosen in every county, city, and town, by those who are qualified to vote for representatives in the legislature, whose business it shall be attentively to observe the conduct of all persons touching this association."

When a majority of the members of a local committee witnessed a violation, they were empowered "forthwith [to] cause the truth of the case to be published in the gazette; to the end, that all such foes to the rights of British America may be publicly known, and universally contemned [*sic*] as the enemies of American liberty; and thenceforth we respectively will break off all dealings with him or her."[5]

Records of the First Continental Congress do not reveal why the representatives from the various colonies placed so much trust in locally elected committees. They may have decided that they had no other viable option. It is more likely, however, that they assumed that such groups would adopt a narrow view of their responsibilities and concentrate on trade. There was nothing strikingly innovative about using committees to achieve political goals. They had played an important part in the protest against parliamentary policy for more than a decade. Most of the colonial legislatures had created committees of correspondence, which authorized small groups of elite representatives to transmit news and declarations of mutual support to their peers in other regions. Many New England communities formed committees—usually accountable to town meetings—that exchanged intelligence with a Boston committee, but before 1773 it would not have been accurate to label these groups radical cells or expressions of a genuinely revolutionary infrastructure.[6] That is what Congress achieved on October 20 without fully realizing what it had done. The Association created what had been missing during the initial burst of spontaneous rage. It provided a framework for sustaining and strengthening the insurgency.

What is especially striking about the Association is the extraordinary vagueness of Article Eleven. Congress offered no guidelines about the size of the committees. A small working group, of course, might have been able to monitor the flow of commerce without too much trouble, but the wording included no prohibition against turning the committees into a kind of posse comitatus—groups of citizens charged with maintaining law and order—composed of scores of ordinary people. Article Eleven was no clearer about the selection process. Congressional delegates must have known that limiting the franchise only to Americans normally allowed to vote for representatives hardly amounted to a meaningful restriction on popular participation. A great majority of adult white males was eligible to vote in colonial elections, and although it might be a stretch to describe the system as democratic, contests for public office often brought large numbers of ordinary people to the ballot box. Moreover, the enforcement provision said nothing about how the committees should actually deal with offenders. The Association gave no advice on matters of due process or standards of evidence, which any court at the time would have observed.

Congress, in fact, threw the problem of organizing committees and policing commercial violations back onto the local communities. It was entirely up to them to decide how best to proceed. And not surprisingly, the size, character, and composition of the committees varied immensely. Rather than adopt a general model, insurgents responded to local political and social conditions. No committee, however, showed the slightest reluctance to expand its prerogatives. For several months following the announcement of the Association, the committees did in fact focus on alleged commercial violations, and in terms of the immediate impact on imperial trade, the Association more than achieved its stated goal. The value of British imports fell from almost 3,000,000 pounds in 1774 to just over 220,000 pounds in 1775. Soon, however, these committees accrued additional powers. Although no one seems to have planned such an expansion, it was probably inevitable. Following the disintegration of effective British authority—especially in the countryside—the committees filled the vacuum and soon began to punish ideological crimes.

Although the Association might appear to represent a top-down measure allowing the members of Congress to contain the rising of the people, it did not in fact do so. Of course, many Americans seemed relieved that the country's most respected leaders had devised a coordinated plan of economic resistance. As one newspaper reported, "It appears the inhabitants of Maryland are all in Motion, forming County Meetings, choosing *Committees of Observation* to carry into effectual Execution, without Fear, Favor or Partiality, the Measures recommended by the Grand Continental Congress."[7] Other communities throughout America adopted similar rhetoric. We should not be misled, however. Sustaining resistance to Great Britain is more accurately described as an interactive process in which the localities took their cues from Congress and then worked out the details of organization and enforcement in hundreds of different ways, each reflecting the particular conditions of the people on the ground. The call to establish oversight committees provoked debates within communities—among friends and neighbors—not only about how best to proceed but also about how a general political crisis affected the lives of ordinary colonists. Thus, at the same time that many Americans voiced support for Congress's boycott of British manufactured goods, they also worked out the administrative details of enforcement within the context of their own experience.

In local communities, the committees accepted an invitation from the Continental Congress to advance resistance to Great Britain. Committees acquired legitimacy in part from this central body, at the same time boldly experimenting with participatory forms of government at the local level. Long before the Declaration of Independence, they served as laboratories for republican rule. By carrying out the mandates of Congress within communities, they provided ordinary people throughout America with the experience of republican rule. Although no one envisioned it in precisely these terms, the Association effectively became a working constitution, a revolutionary framework in which a central governing body interacted productively with local units. The insurgents never questioned the need for central government. What they condemned were the policies of a corrupt king and Parliament. Even the smallest, most isolated committee, however, had no difficulty imagining itself as operating within a grand continental structure.

The records of one Massachusetts community reveal just what could happen when ordinary people set their minds to translating the will of Congress into local regulations. Sutton was a small farming community south of Worcester. In January 1775 the residents called for a discussion "to see if the Town will choose a Committee of Inspection to see that said Association is duly observed and to choose such Committee." When the hour arrived to consider the proposition, the assembly approved of Congress's trade restrictions, and without opposition Sutton elected seven men to serve on the committee. The villagers then reviewed Article Eleven of the Association, noting carefully the obligation "to break off all Dealings with any one convicted of violating said Association."

At this point the people of Sutton demonstrated why it is so hard to identify a typical committee of safety. When it came to working out administrative procedures, they seem to have been overcome by a wave of scrupulosity rooted perhaps in their strong Calvinistic heritage. They noted that the Association recommended shaming violators by publishing their names in local newspapers and, after that, by ceasing to have any dealings with the person so accused. The townsmen wondered whether punishment of this sort might be too harsh. What would happen, they asked, "if there should appear any symptoms of sorrow and hopes of Repentance?" Men or women who publicly apologized deserved to be restored "to Fellowship" without having their names broadcast throughout the province as enemies of America.

That was only the start of Sutton's painstaking analysis. Someone noted that if a neighbor ignored the penalties issued by the committee and continued to have relations with an offender, then that person was just as guilty of undermining the Association as was the original violator. That logic did not strike some townsmen as fair. After all, what if the offender begged for help because of sudden illness or because "a Building or the Life of some person or creature was in danger of immediately perishing?" Did insurgency mean that a revolutionary had to turn his back on a neighbor's sick cow or burning barn? What if a person accused of drinking tea asked "about the Things of the Eternal World"? And suppose, they continued, that Sutton's hypothetical Good Samaritan gave only a short answer, perhaps a casual reply, forgetting temporarily the injunction to cut off all contact with a violator. Surely such a slip would not implicate the helper in counterrevolutionary activities.

The residents of Sutton then turned to enforcement. On this subject they showed themselves committed insurgents. To ignore the committee's demand for information or knowingly to give false testimony was a crime. Moreover, "it is the Duty of every Head of a Family, in this Town, to use his or her Parental Authority in obliging all under them strictly to observe said Association."[8] What we encounter in Sutton's revolutionary moment is a community turning a general recommendation from the Continental Congress into a set of specific rules that made sense to local inhabitants. An interactive process of working out these regulations—even the strictures on religious or animal emergencies—reinforced the general commitment to resist imperial oppression. Following this public debate, it would have been very hard and very dangerous for someone in Sutton to call the Association into question.

The Association had another, highly significant aspect that has largely gone unnoticed. The creation of hundreds of committees throughout America during the fall of 1774 and spring of 1775 represented a key chapter in the constitutional history of this country. Although towns such as Sutton acted independently, they were all in effect ratifying the Association, which they chose at a moment of political crisis to interpret not simply as a strategic plan to disrupt imperial trade, but as a foundational document. Perhaps because of the commercial character of the Association, modern historians have ignored its larger importance in creating a national framework in which local communities claimed to derive authority from an elected national congress. By setting up committees—however different the final results may have been—they affirmed their support for a central ruling body whose power flowed up from the people. In later times this type of relationship was worked out in much greater detail, and political theorists developed innovative arguments for a federal system of government. The Association was, of course, a far cry from the Constitution of 1787. Nevertheless, we should appreciate that many months before the signing of the Declaration of Independence, it provided American insurgents with a pragmatic scheme for sharing power.

Many committees perceived their mandate in precisely these terms. A group enforcing the Association in Charleston, South Carolina, for example, informed its counterpart in New York City on March 1, 1775, "We have the pleasure to inform you that in this colony the Association takes place as effectively as law itself."[9] Another committee, operating in Philadelphia, came to a similar conclusion about the foundational character of the Association. The members of the Pennsylvania group explained in the *Pennsylvania Journal*, that "In the present unnatural struggle, where the child is obliged to defend itself against the violence of the parent, an attempt on our liberty is made, under the form of law." When such a breakdown of authority occurred, "we were obliged to recur to the first principles of the Constitution, and to delegate to men, chosen for the purpose, powers to suspend the former laws and customs of our Country, so far as was necessary for the preservations of our privileges, and to establish others of a temporary nature, to answer the present exigencies." What exactly did such rhetoric mean in the present crisis? In the vacuum left by Parliament's betrayal, who could secure basic constitutional principles? "This our honorable Congress performed: and that their laws might fully answer the purposes for which they were made, they recommended to their constituents to choose in our several

Towns and Counties, Committees to take care that those laws were complied with. On the conduct of these Committees depends the whole success of our measures; for however good the laws of the Congress may be, if they are not faithfully executed, they answer no valuable purpose."[10]

Other testimony suggests that contemporaries saw the Association as providing legitimacy for the insurgency. In November 1775 the Reverend Isaac Mansfield, Jr., reviewed the recent rising of the people for the American troops stationed at Roxbury, Massachusetts. Mansfield served as their chaplain, and although his account of the coming of the Revolution has gone missing from most scholarly accounts, it did in fact provide a splendid account of the events that had brought these soldiers to the battlefield. What drew Mansfield's curiosity—indeed, a major theme of this study—was the ability of so many separate communities to come together in a common cause. "The union," he pointed out, "is remarkable, and beyond the reasonable expectation of any that were acquainted with the complicated views and various tempers of mankind." Assuming the perspective of a political philosopher, he analyzed "the means" by which ordinary Americans managed to reach out effectively to distant strangers. For Mansfield, the committees held the answer. "District Committees," he explained, "were appointed in most of the towns of this province, and through the continent for the management of special matters, particularly such as were of a commercial nature." These bodies not only were impressively large, but also were "composed of persons that had not before been honored with the confidence of the public."

The committees became training grounds for revolutionary leadership. Mansfield declared, "The public eye stimulated them to exertion in their department; they naturally improved others, that were still their inferiors; each one acquired a degree of importance, which was new to him; and by this means, whole communities and societies were cemented together." The insurgency brought new men to positions of authority. It did so, however, within particular communities. What transformed local resistance into a broad popular mobilization was the willingness of local groups to imagine themselves as part of a larger movement from which they derived legitimacy. "These Committees," Mansfield observed, "early corresponded with similar Committees, far and wide. Those of the same county consulted, and appointed County Congresses . . . Provincial Congresses committed the concerns of the whole to a Continental Congress, the most grand and august Assembly that ever existed in America."[11]

Unlike histories of the American Revolution that focus only on the major figures who served in Congress, Mansfield's account turned on the dynamic interaction between Congress and the committees. He also understood—as did the soldiers who listened to him—that revolution depended ultimately upon events at the community level, indeed, on the political commitment of the people themselves.[12]

# II

The reaction of resident British administrators to the Association was equally telling. From the beginning of the controversy, figures such as General Gage appreciated the growing threat of a colonial insurgency. He drew mainly from his experiences in New England. But the Association took popular resistance to imperial rule to an entirely new level. Gage had faced the unorganized rage of the people. Without a clear chain of command, angry militiamen from more than a hundred miles around Boston took up arms. But the committees provided structure to the rising. Even more significant to the story of insurgency, the Association drew colonists who had only the dimmest notion of what had happened in Massachusetts during the last months of 1774 into a larger, genuinely continental movement.

The most astute observations on the danger posed by the committees came from John Murray, the fourth Earl of Dunmore. This ambitious Scottish nobleman had come to America in 1770 to repair his personal finances. Like many persons of privilege, he had lived beyond his means—having his portrait painted by the celebrated artist Sir Joshua Reynolds was an obvious example—and when concerned patrons finagled the governorship of New York for Dunmore, he jumped at the opportunity. Much to his chagrin, however, within a few months his friends in high places negotiated his transfer to Virginia. Since Dunmore had already found ways to enrich himself through land deals in New York, the news came as an unwelcome surprise. Still, he sailed off to Williamsburg intent on securing a reputation as a capable, aggressive administrator who could bring the colonists to their political senses.

The early days in Virginia went well for Dunmore. He was an urbane person who entertained the great planters. What was more, he sparked a war against the Native Americans on the colony's western borders, a popular move since so many well-placed Virginians hoped to acquire frontier land for themselves. But however energetically Dunmore threw himself into his duties, his aggressive efforts to enforce British policy eroded initial feelings of goodwill. He soon found that he could not quash the insurgency. Almost without fully comprehending what was happening, he suddenly discovered that the committees charged with enforcing the Association had become revolutionary cells. They stood between the royal governor and the ordinary people of Virginia.

On Christmas Eve 1774—only two months after Congress had endorsed the Association—Dunmore informed Lord Dartmouth in London how swiftly conditions had changed for the worse in Virginia. Throughout the colony the governor encountered local committees enforcing nonimportation "with the greatest rigor." Dunmore stressed that no area was immune to the spreading insurgency. "A Committee," he reported, "has been chosen in every County, whose business it is to carry the Association of Congress into execution." Extralegal officials selected to enforce the prohibitions against British goods assumed they had a right "to inspect the books, invoices, and all other secrets of the trade and correspondence of Merchants."

But illegal searches represented only part of the threat. Dunmore informed his superior in London that the committees had taken it upon themselves "to watch the conduct of every inhabitant, without distinction, and to send for all such as come under their suspicion into their presence; to interrogate them respecting all matters which, at their pleasure, they think fit objects of their inquiry; and to stigmatize, as they term it, such as they find transgressing what they are now hardy enough to call the Laws of the Congress." As we have seen, the colonists were treating the Association as a kind of constitution; it legitimated acts on the community level that Dunmore regarded as treason. Moreover, the committees encouraged individuals to adopt cruder, more violent means to silence opposition. As the governor explained, the new structure invited "the vengeance of an outrageous and lawless mob to be exercised upon the unhappy victims."

The various counties had also recruited companies of armed men—insurgents by another name—who had responsibility for "protecting their Committees, and to be employed against Government, if occasion require." What had happened in Massachusetts during the violent summer of 1774 was now taking place in Virginia. More than a year and a half before the signing of the Declaration of Independence, British authority in this province hung by a thread. Although Dartmouth's capacity for denial seemed extraordinary, he might have digested the news from the ground more fully. As Dunmore warned, "The Committee of one County has proceeded so far as to swear the men of their Independent Company to execute all orders which shall be given them from the Committee of their County." The governor had nowhere to turn: "There is not a Justice of the Peace in Virginia that acts, except as a Committeeman."[13] Even allowing for exaggeration, Dunmore revealed for those in London prepared to listen that the resistance movement was no longer simply a New England problem.

The loyalist press in America—admittedly a dwindling number of newspapers by the end of 1774—also sensed that the Association posed unprecedented dangers for continued British rule. *Rivington's Gazette*, published in New York City, sounded the alarm. A writer who took the pen name of "Massachusettensis" recognized that the creation of formal revolutionary cells had taken the insurgency to a new level. In January 1775 he warned readers of the sudden creation of so many committees. Friends of Parliament should be on guard. These committees could not claim any standing in law, the author observed. But legality was not the real issue. These committees frequently organized "themselves into a tribunal, where the same persons are at once legislators, accusers, witnesses, judges and jurors, and the mob [of] executioners." Massachusettensis explained that "the accused has no day in court, and the execution of sentence is the first notice he receives. This is the channel through which liberty matters have been chiefly conducted the summer and fall past." And there was no question in the mind of this loyalist that the network of committees had had a major impact on the political landscape of colonial America. "It is chiefly owing to these committees that so many respectable persons have been abused and forced to sign recantations and resignations: That so many persons, to avoid such reiterated insults as are more to be deprecated by a man of sentiment than death itself, have been obliged to quit their houses, families and businesses, and fly to the army for protection."[14]

British newspapers likewise broadcast warnings of a surge of popular resistance in the colonies. Early in 1775, readers of the *Gazetteer and New Daily Advertiser* encountered a letter that the editor claimed to have just received from a Boston correspondent. It confirmed what Dunmore and others had reported. "Our insurgents," it announced, "are making great preparations for opening their rebellion in the Spring with a numerous body of troops." In response to anyone in London who inquired whether there was anything the British could do to save the situation, the writer stated, "You may send as many troops and ships as you please, and enforce a submission; but, as I have often repeated to you, this country never will be quiet till these vermin our Committeemen are seized and brought to trial." They were the ones pushing "their deluded countrymen to rebellion."[15]

# *III*

Dunmore had no direct knowledge about the resistance movement in eastern Connecticut. If he had, he would have immediately recognized that the committees in this area—as they had in Virginia—were running the show. By transferring so much authority to the people, the Association had given birth to a committee culture that energized insurgency.

Ebenezer Punderson witnessed this transition firsthand. An irascible supporter of Great Britain, he provided a highly emotional account of a revolutionary society in which spontaneous rage against the imperial state had been channeled through local committees. In his narrative published originally in London, Punderson claimed to have provided an accurate—and extremely disturbing—report of the contagion of terror that spread across the countryside in late 1774 and early 1775. It was, admittedly, a self-serving exercise, since the obvious goal was winning special favor from North's government, perhaps even a highly coveted commission in the British Army. Punderson had every reason to exaggerate his suffering, and on almost every page he seems to have done so. Nevertheless, he provides a valuable historical perspective. We know that he traced his genealogy in America back several generations. He was also unquestionably a loyalist. Although the veracity of every detail of his account is beyond our ability to ascertain, that he was run out of Connecticut, forced to abandon trade, home, and family, is certain. Punderson's tale suggests just how quickly the Association transformed the political landscape.[16]

His ordeal began sometime in 1774 when he announced—a little too loudly, a little too publicly—that he had had enough of "American Rebels," and in a striking case of ill-timed rectitude, he took it upon himself to confront those "poor, well-meaning, deluded wretches" who seemed intent on destroying the British Empire in America.

Punderson's neighbors in Norwich, Connecticut—a country town located about a dozen miles north of New London—were probably not surprised that this otherwise unprepossessing figure made a stand for political beliefs that they deemed thoroughly obnoxious. His father had done much the same thing a generation earlier. That man—also named Ebenezer—accepted ordination as a Congregational minister, but he soon expressed second thoughts about his decision. In a move that raised hackles, the Reverend Punderson announced his conversion to the Church of England, an institution that descendants of the original Puritan settlers still associated with intolerance and superstition. To add to his unpopularity, the senior Punderson openly pointed out to the local Congregationalists their alleged theological errors.

What the son learned from his father's uncompromising defense of principle remains unclear. We do know that he graduated without distinction from Yale College in 1755, and although one might predict that a young man enjoying such an education would have a successful career, the younger Ebenezer drifted, unwilling apparently to commit himself to one calling over another. He studied for the ministry, but after eight years he turned to schoolteaching and agriculture. He also tried his luck as a small-time merchant. It was while he was traveling through eastern Connecticut on business that he found himself at odds with the newly established revolutionary committees.

In 1774, while New Englanders were devising commercial strategies to resist the Coercive Acts, Punderson went about his community lecturing whoever bothered to listen about the wrongheadedness of the

American cause. He regarded the colonial newspapers as the main source of popular misunderstanding. In his estimation the weekly journals published "untruths against the King, Earl Bute, Lord North, and the majority in parliament." In this uneasy environment he insisted on giving political tutorials to "many well-meaning people, ignorant as to the true characteristics of those personages."[17] It is significant that Punderson never mentioned selling imported British goods prohibited by the Association. Perhaps he did not do so. For him, the animosity of the local committees could be traced solely to his political opinions.

Reports of Punderson's seditious activities spread rapidly throughout eastern Connecticut. The first sign of trouble came in July 1774—several months before the First Continental Congress met in Philadelphia—when a mysterious group in nearby Stonington bluntly informed him that unless he repudiated statements supporting the sovereignty of Parliament, he would be tarred and feathered. Punderson dismissed the message as an idle threat. He claimed that many of his neighbors in Poquetanuck Cove, a district of Norwich, told him not to worry about Stonington's blustering Sons of Liberty. They were wrong. They too had misjudged the surge of popular anger.

In September, Punderson had criticized as foolish those who wanted to take their revenge on General Gage for what they imagined to have been the destruction of Boston. For this he was forced to appear "before an inquisitive mob in Preston." Whether these people had formed a revolutionary committee is not clear from Punderson's account. He seems to have had difficulty distinguishing between mobs and committees. Whatever the group's standing in Preston, "they passed a decree that no man should trade or deal with me." In other words, this extra-legal body that anticipated the Association stigmatized him as an enemy of the people. No sooner had Punderson escaped these tormentors than he fell "into the hands of a mob about fifty miles from home, who only abused me with provoking words and threatenings."

Punderson somehow survived the winter without further incident. The countryside was alive with political activity. Scattered communities throughout the region were electing men to serve on local enforcement committees now officially sanctioned by Congress. During the spring of 1775, however, Punderson managed to antagonize the newly empowered committees that no longer restricted themselves solely to violations of the boycott. They had turned to the problem of rooting out political dissent. In early April, a body that Punderson described as "the mob's committee at Norwich" demanded that he come before it to justify his support of parliamentary policies. Although he refused the invitation to self-incrimination, the members of the committee proceeded to convict him of ideological crimes. As he complained, they publicly forbade "all people to have 'any intercourse or commerce whatever with me' because 'I denied their authority and had drank tea since March 1st and had said—the Congress was an illegal body, and that their petition to the king was haughty, insolent, and rascally.'"

A few days later the inhabitants of Stonington renewed the attack. Why Punderson risked doing business in a hostile community, especially in the wake of reports that British forces had attacked Lexington and Concord, is not clear. When he arrived, "a mob instantly gathered and were very fierce." These people soon alerted the local militia company that a dreaded enemy was in town. The soldiers swore an oath "that I should be instantly drawn in quarters before the Liberty Pole." His fate hung in the balance for more than three hours. The emotional toll must have been immense. His wife and children were overcome with fear. Only the belated intervention of several local justices of the peace "kept them from violence." Time was running out for Punderson. No sooner had he returned home than he learned from three separate informants that his "life was in imminent danger."

The death threats persuaded the beleaguered merchant to ask the governor of Connecticut for help. As it happened, Jonathan Trumbull lived in Lebanon, only a few miles from Norwich. Punderson explained to the governor that he now believed the people were planning to murder him. The personal appeal came to nothing. Trumbull had no intention of condemning the actions of the various committees acting in the name of the Continental Congress, and instead of asking how he might best protect Punderson from further persecution, he demanded to know whether in fact the man "had acted inimical to America." Punderson protested that he had done nothing of the sort. Indeed, the worst that could be said of him was that he "had constantly endeavored to convince people that Great Britain had given America no just cause of complaint."

No doubt such self-congratulatory statements played well before a British audience convinced that the ungrateful colonists had promoted anarchy. But Trumbull did not even bother to argue the point. He summarily informed Punderson that he could not provide "any kind of protection whatever." The governor also turned a deaf ear to Punderson's request for safe passage to New York City, where the terrified merchant assumed he would be able to preserve his life. Without an official pass from Trumbull, Punderson determined that the wisest course would be to seek sanctuary immediately in New York. He took "a road not much traveled." He was a man on the run. Everyone in eastern Connecticut now knew his story. Vulnerable and alone, he soon discovered the perils of being an outcast in a revolutionary society.

Punderson's attempted escape ended very quickly. On April 22, as he neared Colchester, "a mob of three or four hundred people" intercepted the fugitive. Even if he exaggerated the numbers, this was a huge crowd. Perhaps a quarter of the town's population had turned out to humiliate the traveler. Exactly how so many people learned that Punderson would be taking a little-used back road is not clear. Intelligence of this sort probably passed quickly from community to community. His captors escorted Punderson to the village center, where it happened that "the committee of safety were [*sic*] sitting." John Watrous acted as chairman for the group.

The members of the Colchester committee closely cross-examined their prisoner. While this was taking place, local soldiers had appeared on the scene. Perhaps playing to the crowd, Watrous demanded to know whether Punderson "would take arms and go to Boston." Punderson's answers infuriated those "armed soldiers [who] had just then joined the mob." The committee did nothing to defuse the tensions. The Connecticut troops who were on their way to fight the British forces occupying Boston "begged" Watrous that Punderson "might be delivered up to them." His courage at that moment was extraordinary. "I told them that I would suffer any death rather than take up arms against my king." For one soldier who was willing to fight for American rights, Punderson's defiance was too much. He declared that if Punderson would just move "four rods" away from the people—thus providing a clear target—"I will soon put it out of his power to hurt our cause." Another insurgent added, "Ay, let us take the charge of him."

Courting political martyrdom, Punderson threw himself on the committee's mercy. His plea for protection elicited a demand that he sign something called "the continental covenant." It was a pledge "to take up arms against the king's troops." Punderson refused. At this point more local "soldiers were called in," and "their ferocious looks" convinced the prisoner that his only hope of survival was endorsing some sort of moderate confession. He wanted a clause in the document explaining that his acceptance had come as the result of coercion. After nine hours the Colchester committee finally accepted his terms, but it declined to let him go free. "I was sent to the Norwich Committee of Inspection," Punderson recounted, "under a guard, with the paper I had signed." Insurgents in the town had been forewarned. They roused the members of the Norwich committee from their beds. "I showed them my confession," Punderson observed, "which they altered a little and I again signed it." But his tormentors were not done with the hapless traveler. They would not allow him to return to his family for eight days, the time required to publish Punderson's most recent confession "in the News Papers."

For the man who defied the Association, the darkest moment occurred on the eighth night. Walking home alone, Punderson confronted a menacing figure identified as "Bebee," who "had his gun, sword, and other accoutrements with him." Bebee apparently had taken it upon himself to administer the people's justice. He followed his prey along the deserted road to Poquetanuck Cove. Somehow Bebee managed to lose his sword. But before we judge him simply an extraordinarily incompetent assassin, we should acknowledge that he was certainly successful at instilling mortal fear in a despised Tory.

Punderson sensed that his only hope was to stay so close to Bebee that the assailant would not have enough room to raise his gun. The two men kept up this curious dance for some time. At one point they separated momentarily, and sure enough, Bebee "had put his gun in a proper position for charging and had his powder horn in his hand." Punderson stared the man down. Bebee eventually "shouldered his gun." It took several more intricate maneuvers on Punderson's part finally to elude the bumbling killer. According to Punderson, "I got home, where I kept close for the space of thirty nights, and upon my guard in the day, during which time my aged mother was frightened almost into fits, and my wife and children in perpetual fears."

In late May, Punderson received more death threats from local soldiers who "had sworn to take my life before they went to Boston, and they expected to march the next day." On the twenty-eighth, certain that the moment of reckoning had truly arrived, Punderson rowed a small boat at midnight about six leagues out into Long Island Sound, where a British warship picked him up. He eventually made his way to London, at last finding a safe haven. Driven into exile, he wrote a letter to his wife reflecting on how their comfortable provincial world had come tumbling down. He insisted that a small group of "smuggling traders" and "Calvinistic preachers" had systematically misled "the giddy rabble."

Punderson reminded her—as if she needed the lesson—that the American insurgency in eastern Connecticut contained elements of malice, revenge, oppression, manipulation, violence, and cruelty. One can appreciate Punderson's negative assessment. Nevertheless, it would be shortsighted not to recognize that his vocabulary of revolution failed to include more positive words such as "liberation," "justice," and "responsibility." These terms resonated powerfully with ordinary soldiers preparing to fight the British. They represented a face of colonial insurgency that Punderson never understood. Moreover, because of his own sense of having been wronged, he did not appreciate how the committee system established by the Association had successfully sustained and strengthened popular resistance.

We might pause to reconsider the nature of Punderson's crimes. Several communities declared him a pariah for behavior that one might expect of a stubborn, imprudent figure. But he was no secret agent. At no time did he send military intelligence to the British. There is no record that he even contemplated such betrayal. Nor had he attempted to organize an armed band of loyalists. Punderson offended the people of eastern Connecticut by stating openly that colonial subjects had no right to resist the Crown. For this indiscretion—for the expression of personal political opinion—he endured psychological torment. But we should also note that the committees never physically harmed him. They strove to exact a public confession of his ideological errors. In that way they channeled—indeed, constrained—popular violence. However menacing their behavior may have seemed to Punderson, it occurred within an elaborate committee framework that marked the second stage of revolutionary resistance.

By demonizing Punderson—driving him from community to community—the committees also opened the door for the likes of Bebee, an overzealous man who entered the political sphere as an angry individual rather than as a member of a collective body. He acted without authorization. Perhaps Bebee reasoned that he was carrying out the will of the local committees. If so, he made a major mistake. Like Punderson, he misread the evolving character of revolutionary politics. In fact, his actions represented as great a threat to the American cause as did Punderson's, for if Punderson encouraged ordinary people to obey king and Parliament, Bebee invited them to take the law into their own hands. It was precisely this kind of spontaneous violence that the Association discouraged.

# SEVEN

# Schools of Revolution

During the months following the announcement of the Association, in October 1774, the insurgency gathered momentum. Indeed, no sooner had the Continental Congress authorized this infrastructure for enforcing a commercial boycott than hundreds of committees throughout America seized control of local government, quickly becoming the face of revolution. For ordinary people, they were community forums where personal loyalties were revealed, tested, and occasionally punished.

The proliferation of local committees represented a development of paramount importance in the achievement of independence.[1] Before this time, colonial resistance to imperial rule lacked a formal structure capable not only of policing the revolution on the ground but also of solidifying ties with other committees. These networks amplified and reinforced a shared sense of purpose. Long before Congress declared independence, committees spoke to Americans of an imagined collectivity—a country of the mind—and so, by aggressively monitoring popular allegiance to a common cause, they laid the foundation for a shared identity that later generations would celebrate as nationalism.

Committee members initially focused their activities on curtailing the importation of British manufactured goods.[2] Within a short period, however, they began to assume greater powers. As they took control of the resistance movement, they often devised the rules as they went along. Success in this uncertain environment required an exquisite sense of political balance. By moving too fast, committees risked triggering a formidable counterinsurgency, which in some areas would have been hard to contain. However, the situation also required a firm hand. Serving on committees of safety—or, as they were sometimes called, committees of observation—was certainly not an activity for the faint of heart. The members of these groups exposed ideological dissenters, usually people well-known in the communities in which they lived. Although the committees attempted as best they could to avoid physical violence, they administered revolutionary justice as they alone defined it. They worked out their own investigative procedures, interrogated people suspected of undermining the American cause, and meted out punishments they deemed appropriate to the crimes.

By mid-1775 the committees increasingly busied themselves with identifying, denouncing, and shunning political offenders. By demanding that enemies receive "civil excommunication"—the chilling words of a North Carolina committee—these groups silenced critics without sparking the kind of bloodbath that has characterized so many other insurgencies throughout the world.[3]

More was at stake on the community level, however, than intimidation. The committees served as powerful schools of revolution. By exposing enemies, they unmistakably communicated to spectators—to those who might have preferred to remain uncommitted—what it meant at a time of crisis to be an American.

## *I*

The records of very few committees of safety have survived.[4] This is not surprising. Throughout history, radical political groups have found record keeping dangerous. Had events turned out differently and the British reasserted the Crown's authority over the restive colonists, those who had served on the committees would have found themselves in a perilous situation. No doubt, when it came to documenting their decisions, they elected to downplay the more unsavory aspects of local enforcement. What we know about the activities of the committees, therefore, comes to us largely through such indirect sources as the newspapers. In most cases, published warnings and official resolutions in the weekly journals reveal how the insurgency organized itself on the ground.

The Wilmington, North Carolina, Committee of Safety was an exception. Formed in the autumn of 1774, it had no scruples about record keeping. The official entries read like the minutes of a fraternal society. The members noted dates and times; the names of those attending meetings were always listed. But however transparent the source may appear, using it to understand the surge of insurgency requires a certain amount of skepticism. It is the curiously businesslike character of the Wilmington material that should put us on guard. With the exception of one incident in which the committee threw an incorrigible loyalist into jail, the committee seems to have avoided documenting the messy details of day-to-day enforcement.[5]

What fills the bureaucratic silences of the Wilmington records is a remarkable journal in which a young woman recorded the terror she and her friends experienced living under the authority of a revolutionary committee. To this day, Janet Schaw remains a mysterious figure. Between 1774 and 1776 she accompanied members of her Edinburgh family on an adventurous journey that took them to Antigua, the Cape Fear region of North Carolina, and Portugal. Her brother held a minor post in the royal government. Other than what we encounter in the journal, however, we know surprisingly little about Schaw's life.[6] Like many well-to-do women of the eighteenth century, she knew how to hold her own in polite society. Witty and charming, she must have been a marvelous companion.

Yet despite her impressive accomplishments, Schaw disappeared from the records altogether soon after returning to Scotland. For us, fortunately, obscurity is not a serious concern. For a brief moment she found herself in the eye of the revolutionary storm. Her trenchant remarks about the collapse of Crown authority in Wilmington reveal her to have been a bright, playful, and energetic person who without qualification defended the British Empire. She made no effort to provide a balanced account of the events in North Carolina. After all, it was her immediate friends who suffered at the hands of the local insurgents, and with each unpleasant encounter, her anger increased. Moreover, she had a whimsical streak. "As every subject will be guided by my own immediate feelings," Schaw confessed, "my opinions and descriptions will depend on the health and humor of the moment in which I write; from which cause my sentiments will often appear to differ on the same subject."[7]

What we have, therefore, are two quite different historical sources. Each witness provides us with a partial, obviously self-serving account of a community caught up in revolutionary ferment. The committee chronicled its decisions in the frustratingly laconic rhetoric of formal bodies that have something to hide. By contrast, Schaw brought emotion to the story. She documented incidents that went missing from the committee minutes. Of course, she was no more objective. Schaw was looking for crimes against the empire. It is only by playing one record off against the other—treating them as complementary voices—that we begin to comprehend more clearly how one local committee managed to endorse violence against the Revolution's ideological enemies, at the same time keeping that violence from destroying the social fabric of the community.

The proceedings of the Wilmington Committee of Safety began on the afternoon of November 23, 1774—the time was amazingly precise— with the announcement of an election. The "Freeholders" of the town gathered at the courthouse to select persons "to carry more effectually into Execution the resolves of the late congress held at Philadelphia." It was not in the true sense a contest. The townsmen proposed nine names, and with almost no discussion, the nominees were "universally assented to."[8] This formulaic report should not deflect attention from an extraordinarily significant element in this account. The members of the committee derived authority from an act of Congress. From that perspective, we can say that power flowed down from a central governing body. Of course, the status of Congress at that moment may have been insecure. But that is not the point. The members of the Wilmington committee situated themselves from the very start within a web of power relations that insulated them from charges that their own actions could be construed as arbitrary. They were carrying out orders.

At the same time, the committee owed its initial existence to the freeholders who chose the members and who presumably held them accountable for their decisions. After only a few months, it ordered a new election—this time expanding the franchise to include "all the inhabitants qualified to vote for members of the Assembly"—because it believed it was important that "the people may have an opportunity of confirming or annulling their former choice."[9] What we witness in Wilmington more than a year before the Declaration of Independence is the creation of a rough republican structure in which the sources of power remained elusive. The voters might well have viewed the members of the committees as their representatives, but at the same time, the members of the committee had complete discretion in interpreting the meaning of the key articles of the Association, a document that functioned as a constitution for a nation before it was a nation. Over the course of the next two years, the Wilmington committee never in fact asked Congress for clarification on the exact character of its duties; nor, for that matter, did it refer complex enforcement issues to the local voters.

During the early months of operation the Wilmington Committee of Safety hardly seemed to qualify as a genuine revolutionary body. It moved slowly, a little uncertain perhaps of its ability to back up its own claims to authority, and even when confronted with merchants who appeared to have violated the Association, the members treated suspicious individuals with surprising generosity and compassion. Committeemen were feeling their way forward, testing the political waters, and avoiding confrontations that had the potential to spark organized opposition. On January 5, 1775, for example, the committee addressed a letter "To the Merchants of the town," which seemed less like an order from insurgents than an invitation to old friends to attend a special event. The members, the notice stated, "earnestly request of you, as well wishers to the common cause of America, in which we are all embarked, to signify to them, by the bearers of this, if you have any gunpowder on hand, and what quantity, that this committee, may in consequence of that information, take the most prudent steps, to guard against the melancholy effects, which may result from this part of the Province, being left in a state totally deficient from want of ammunition."[10] The gentlemanly language conveniently ignored the fact that the military supplies in question were intended to protect the citizens of Wilmington from their own royal governor, Josiah Martin. Martin, for one, was not fooled. The committee's high-minded rhetoric, he insisted, was simply a ruse employed by "the Mob" or "the Multitude"—Martin saw these terms as interchangeable—intent upon "usurping dominion and giving Law."[11]

The official records of the committee provide not the slightest indication that such a radical confrontation was in the offing. The members calmly set prices for certain trade goods, monitored the movement of slaves, communicated with other committees in the area, and, on one occasion, discouraged a group of local gentlemen from staging a horse race, an extravagant activity that seemed inappropriate at a time when Congress was urging ordinary people to forgo the purchase of British imports. "As a friend to your country," the members explained in the most solicitous manner, "we have no doubt but you will readily relinquish an amusement that however laudable in other respects, is certainly attended with considerable expense, and even destruction to many individuals; and may very justly be condemned at a time when frugality should be one of our leading virtues."[12]

The local insurgency took a dramatic turn on the morning of March 6, 1775. It is not clear why at this precise moment the Wilmington committee moved so aggressively to identify enemies of the American cause. News of the gathering storm in New England—coupled with Governor Martin's persistent efforts to raise a force prepared to defend the king's authority in North Carolina—may have contributed to the committee's energetic efforts to expose ideological dissent.

The crackdown began with the drafting of an oath of revolutionary allegiance termed the "Association." The wording of the statement merits close attention, for among other things, it assumed the existence of "our Country" long before the creation of an independent republic. And this country—at that moment no more than a shared vision or a projection of hope—demanded patriotic sacrifice.

At the same time, without betraying any sense of contradiction, the agreement spoke of a negotiated settlement with the Crown. It was as if the committee wanted to mask its own actions, which, of course, had made a settlement with king and Parliament highly unlikely.

We the Subscribers, in Testimony of our Sincere approbation of the proceedings of the late Continental Congress . . . have hereunto set our hands & we do most solemnly engage by the most Sacred ties of Honor, Virtue & Love of our Country, that we will ourselves Strictly Observe every part of the Association recommended by the Continental Congress as the most probable means to bring about a Reconciliation between Great Britain & her Colonies & we will use every Method in Our power to endeavor to Influence others to the Observation [observance] of it by persuasion & such other Methods as Shall be consistent with the peace & Good Order & the Laws of this Province &

we do hereby intend to Express our Utter detestation of all such as shall endeavor to defeat the purpose of the Said Congress & will Concur to hold forth such Characters to Public Contempt.[13]

At three o'clock the same day, the committee reconvened. Those favoring firm opposition to imperial control were determined to put teeth into the loyalty oath. Membership on the committee had increased to twenty-five, more than doubling the size of the original group. This move may have reflected a commitment to a more inclusive revolutionary body. The Wilmington committee had recently merged with the nearby New Hanover County committee. A better guess is that as relations with the royal governor deteriorated, Wilmington insurgents wanted to demonstrate the broad popularity of their position. Moreover, if the king's friends in North Carolina did manage to mount a serious counterthreat, the revolutionaries could take a measure of comfort from the knowledge not only that their numbers were growing but also that those who had seized control of the local government were willing to have their names made public. This greatly expanded body resolved "that all Members of the Committee now present go in a body & wait on all Housekeepers in Town with the Association before mentioned & request their signing it, or declare their reasons for refusing, [so] that such Enemies to their Country may be set forth to public View & treated with the Contempt they merit."[14]

This was an extraordinary decision. One can imagine the shock when local householders came to the doors of their homes and encountered twenty-five earnest men—the entire committee—demanding a signature on a document that pledged full and informed support for the Association. These must have been tense moments. A person who took the occasion to insist on privacy or on the importance of tolerating diverse political opinions would surely not have won favor with the visitors. And so, with little concern for due process, the committee exposed friends and enemies. Most householders signed the oath, but a few individuals held out. The official records provide no explanation for their decision.

By March 7 a great majority of the people living in the region had been canvassed. The committee reported that it had encountered eleven men who had "refused or declined under various pretenses to sign the Association of the Continental Congress."[15] These "Enemies to their Country" received what we might call today psychological punishment. To be sure, they did not suffer incarceration or physical abuse, but in some ways the actual penalty may have been harder to bear. Stigmatized, shunned, made outcasts of the local community, they became nonpersons. Without explaining their interrogation procedures—after all, the committee was now acting in a judicial capacity—the members announced to their constituents that "we will have no trade, Commerce, dealings or Intercourse whatsoever with the above mentioned persons or any others . . . who shall hereafter violate the said Association, or refuse to Subscribe thereto; but will hold them as unworthy of the rights of freemen & as Inimical to the Liberties of their country & we recommend it to the people of this Colony in particular & to the Americans in General, to pursue the Same Conduct."[16]

The committee had already demonstrated its capacity for invention. When the Continental Congress drafted the Association, it specifically recommended that the names of those people found to be "foes to the rights of British America" should be made known to the public. Congress assumed that the committees would disseminate this information through local newspapers. But Wilmington had a problem. It had no journal, so in anticipation of the need to denounce ideological dissenters, the committee endorsed Adam Boyd's proposal to establish a proper gazette.

The prospects must have seemed unpromising. Boyd's earlier printing ventures had failed. Still, the committee pushed forward with a joint enterprise that may have been the only American newspaper sponsored by an extralegal revolutionary body. On January 30, 1775, the Wilmington committee had resolved that "so far as their Influence extended, [they] would support him [Boyd] on the following terms—That he, Mr. Boyd, should weekly continue a News-paper denominated the *Cape Fear Mercury*, of 21 Inches wide, 17 Inches long, 3 Columns on a page & of the small pica or long primer letter & in return receive his payments at the following periods, viz. 10 shillings at the delivery of the first Number, 10 shillings at the Expiration of a Year & to be paid 10 shillings at the end of every succeeding 6 Months thereafter."[17]

The committee treated public denunciation with obvious trepidation. In this intimate world in which everyone knew one another, shunning cut ideological offenders adrift. They lost face before their neighbors and, if they were engaged in commerce, were deprived thereby of the means to support their families. Just at the moment the committee moved energetically to enforce the Association, it backed off, allowing those who refused to sign the document a brief period to reconsider their decision. The committee understood that this was a critical moment. For all parties involved, there would be no turning back, no pretending that insurgents had not filled the political vacuum left behind by an ineffectual royal establishment. "Resolved Unanimously," the members announced, "that as the measures which this Committee must be under an Absolute necessity to adopt, in case any person should mark themselves as Objects of distinction in Opposition to the General American cause, it must be greatly detrimental in their present Operation & future consequence to them." Holdouts had one last chance. They had six days to reconsider. Those who changed their minds could ask "the Chairman, Deputy Chairman or Secretary of this Committee" for permission to "set his name to the Said Association" and, by so doing, avoid "the dangerous consequence that may ensue from a longer Neglect."[18] Monday arrived. Almost all of the men who had originally rejected the Association remained obdurate. And for their resistance, they suffered the full pain of public exposure.[19]

If our only window into insurgent mobilization in Wilmington was the committee's official record, we might conclude that it had acted in a tough, although fair manner. After all, it did try to reason with dissenters. Only after they had failed twice to sign the Association—something that the great majority of the community had done without apparent coercion—did the body reluctantly denounce its opponents by name. But there was another side to the story. Janet Schaw saw the same events from a completely different perspective. For her, the enforcement of revolution on the local level was a nightmare for the king's supporters in North Carolina, and as she insisted in her journal, the committee's businesslike rhetoric simply disguised the terror she and her friends had endured.

One day in March 1775 Schaw decided to travel into the center of Wilmington from the outlying plantation where she had taken up temporary residence. What she witnessed was deeply disturbing. When she arrived, she found the main street "closed up by a detachment of the soldiers." Since the committee records covering this period make no mention of soldiers, we must conclude that local militiamen played an active role in policing dissent. Whatever their responsibilities, Schaw negotiated her way through the checkpoint, and to her amazement, she soon encountered a number of her closest social friends standing as a group in the middle of the road. Although the men seemed nervous, she was slow to appreciate the gravity of the situation. "I stopped to speak to them," she recounted, "but they with one voice begged me for heaven's sake to get off the street, making me observe they were prisoners, adding that every avenue of the town was shut up, and that in all human probability some scene would be acted very unfit for me to witness."

What exactly these men feared is hard to discern. The royal governor—a person prone to hyperbole—claimed that local soldiers under the command of John Ashe threatened the prisoners "with military execution, if they did not immediately sign the Association dictated by the committee."[20] We would conclude from this report that this group of "the first people in town" wanted to spare Schaw from witnessing a bloody atrocity. That seems a little over the top. Her acquaintances may have worried that enduring insults from those who did not rank as "first" in Wilmington would unhinge the woman. Whatever Ashe's insurgents had in mind, Schaw almost swooned. "I could not take the friendly advice [to leave the scene immediately]," she recalled, "for I became unable to move and [was] absolutely petrified with horror."[21]

Schaw quickly rallied. Confronting an officer whom she recognized from a recent dinner party, she demanded an explanation for the rude treatment her friends had received. He politely took a copy of the Association out of his pocket and informed her that if she would persuade the prisoners to sign, they would be set at liberty immediately. Overhearing the conversation, one man who had been detained responded, "And we will suffer every thing before we abjure our king, our country, and our principles." He informed Schaw that the public humiliation was "what they [the insurgents] call their Test, but by what authority this Gentleman forces it on us, we are yet to learn." The officer shrugged off the complaint. The loyalists could whine all they liked, but the source of his authority was never in doubt. "'There is my Authority,' [he said] pointing to the Soldiers with the most insolent air, 'dispute it, if you can.'" The committee probably would not have stated the point quite so bluntly, but then, the soldiers did have the guns. Schaw later confided to her journal, "Oh Britannia, what are you doing, while your true obedient sons are thus insulted by their unlawful brethren?"[22]

The standoff came to an end, although not quite in the manner one might conclude from reading the committee records. The prisoners refused to back down, and "tho' every threatening was used to make them comply," they remained in the street "till past two in the morning." According to Schaw, the insurgents received reports that a force of armed men might attempt to rescue the loyalists. Faced with the possibility of organized resistance, Wilmington's "ragamuffins"—the word is Schaw's—allowed the men to return to their homes on parole. She interpreted the whole episode in explicit class terms. It pitted proper "Gentlemen" against the "ragamuffins," and at the end of the day, wealth apparently bred good politics. She praised Wilmington in a backhand manner. "To the credit of the town . . . ," she confessed, "there are not five men of property and credit in it that are infected by this unfortunate disease."[23]

Another incident greatly agitated Schaw. Even though she was well aware that Wilmington had become an insurgent center, she accepted an invitation in town to watch the "rebels" acquire the rudiments of military discipline. The day was oppressively hot. Without strong drink, the American militiamen might have wilted. Under these conditions, they did the best they could, but their fumbling maneuvers struck Schaw and her circle as bizarre. "Their exercise was that of bush-fighting," she noted, "but it appeared so confused and so perfectly different from any thing I ever saw, I can not say whether they performed it well or not."

Standing on the balcony of Dr. Thomas Cobham's house—one of the committee's "enemies" who refused twice to sign the Association—Schaw watched another clumsy exercise. "I must really laugh while I recollect their figures," she explained, "2000 men in their shirts and trousers, preceded by a very ill-beat drum and a fiddler, who was also in his shirt with a long sword and a cue [pigtail] at his hair, who played with all his might. They made indeed a most unmartial appearance." Schaw's ridicule rang a little hollow. She sensed—however dimly—a fundamental truth about insurgency. The ill-clad colonists were not practicing for the show of it. They attended training day to learn how to resist the might of the empire. And she realized—as so many British commanders did not—"the worst figure there [Wilmington] can shoot from behind a bush and kill even a General Wolfe."[24]

The outing soon took an ugly turn. The local troops had been drinking too heavily. "This I know," Schaw informed her journal, ". . . they were heated with rum till capable of committing the most shocking outrages." Someone shouted "a cry of tar and feather." Again Schaw almost fainted. She assumed that the victim must be one of her friends, and although the target of the popular anger in fact worked as a groom for a loyalist family—a person "in a humble station"—she watched in horror as the revolutionary drama played itself out. "You can hardly conceive what I felt when I saw him dragged forward," she exclaimed, "poor devil, frightened out of his wits." Just when it seemed that the ordinary soldiers of Wilmington would carry out their threat, an officer intervened and persuaded the men to accept a lesser punishment. The groom was forced to stand on a table and beg their "pardon for having smiled at the regiment. He was then drummed and fiddled out of the town, with a strict prohibition of ever being seen in it again."[25] Whether the committee sanctioned this ritual humiliation is not known. The records are silent on such matters. But without additional evidence one could safely speculate that the groom was a surrogate for a person of wealth in the community, and his moment of terror no doubt sent a sobering message to those who had rejected the Association.

A few days later a leader of the insurgency visited Schaw's house. For her it was the occasion to obtain a measure of revenge. She cleverly staged the conversation so that he was forced to read lines spoken by Shakespeare's Henry IV in which bumbling rank-and-file soldiers are the objects of derision. The visitor was no fool. He too had witnessed the recent training session in Wilmington. He mouthed the words, "he coloured like Scarlet," and when he finished, he whispered to Schaw, "You will certainly get yourself tarred and feathered; shall I apply to be executioner?"[26]

The committee's records and Schaw's journal provide conflicting perceptions of a society mobilizing to resist imperial rule. The committee filled a vacuum left by the collapse of Crown authority. Some members of the enlarged committee may have felt an exhilarating sense of empowerment as they went door-to-door demanding prominent loyalists to sign the Association. To be sure, the group had little patience for dissent. Considering that a royal governor was busy trying to raise an army capable of crushing the insurgents, the committee not only protected the ordinary people of Wilmington, it also showed restraint when dealing with ideological "enemies." It made its points through intimidation and threat rather than outright physical violence.

Schaw interpreted the same developments as evidence of the destruction of a traditional order. She was correct. Her friends no longer received the deference they had come to take for granted. For the remaining representatives of a crumbling colonial establishment, Schaw chronicled a tragedy. But there was another side to her story. Perhaps unwittingly she reminds us that in one small community, many months before the Declaration of Independence, some two thousand American ragamuffins had already rejected the political principles that she held dear.

## II

The obvious question to ask at this point is whether the Wilmington Committee of Safety was typical of the hundreds of other committees formed throughout America during the second half of 1774. The Wilmington group stands out mainly because of the amount of evidence it generated. By contrast, the day-to-day operations of most committees remain opaque. We learn about their activities largely through fragments of information—chiefly from announcements in local newspapers and irregular entries found in town records. Cumulatively, however, these scattered pieces of intelligence allow the reconstruction of how angry colonists formed new collectivities that became the infrastructure of revolution.

Even before the meeting of the First Continental Congress, committees had played a central role in articulating American grievances against taxation without representation. These efforts were only the start. Throughout America, the revolutionary character of the committees changed swiftly as more and more ordinary people were drawn into the protest against the Coercive Acts. To claim that the local committees were recruited from the general public would be an exaggeration. There is no doubt, however, that the insurgency thrust thousands of new men into positions of political responsibility.[27]

How people actually became members of committees of safety and observation varied so greatly from colony to colony that the process al-most defies intelligent generalization. In some areas—Maryland, New Jersey, and Massachusetts, for example—conventions organized at the county level established a hierarchical order, and these conventions tried to instruct the local units how to go about their business. Perhaps not surprisingly, most local communities seem to have responded to calls to enforce the Association as they alone saw fit.[28] Some towns ap-pointed members. In the majority of cases, however, communities held elections open to freeholders—those who owned property—as well as to inhabitants.[29]

Whatever procedures were adopted, the towns and counties throughout America encouraged expanding the traditional pool of people involved in local political affairs.[30] On this point, the general committee of Charleston, South Carolina, waxed euphoric. Rural and urban districts now communicated more effectively, thereby creating "one compact regularly organized body." Reforming traditional pro-cesses strengthened the general will to resist imperial oppression. "The enemies of American freedom . . . endeavor to prevent it," the Charles-ton group exclaimed, "well knowing that while the different districts of a colony are kept apart, they do not all receive the same information and are exposed to the baneful effects of jealousy and division, espe-cially when any considerable part supposes itself neglected by not being called in to give its voice." But even more important, the insurgency in South Carolina had opened the revolutionary forum to people who de-served to be heard. "And we find," reported the general committee, "that the larger this representation is, the less danger of corruption and influence, the more is sly deceit deterred from venturing its efforts, and the more weight goes with every determination."[31]

In other areas, the Association invited increased popular participa-tion. In Essex County, New Jersey, committees were open to "All the inhabitants" who were "friends to the Constitution, the Liberties, and Properties of America." The ruling probably excluded very few from participation in extralegal government. In nearby Middlesex, a gather-ing had to be moved from the courthouse to the larger Presbyterian church to accommodate the crowd of people who wanted to be involved in committee business. It is no wonder that the royal governor of New Jersey, William Franklin—Benjamin Franklin's estranged and loyalist

son—complained to Lord Dartmouth that he could not prevent meetings of this sort "where the chief Part of the Inhabitants incline to attend
them."[32] On April 19, 1775, the committee for Baltimore insisted, "Our
meetings have been held in public, nor has any person who thought fit
to attend ever been excluded; our records are free and open for inspection. From the public we received our authority, not by personal solici-
tation, but a free and voluntary choice; to that tribunal we submit our
actions."[33]

Perhaps because so many ordinary people were suddenly coming
forward, some communities protested that only "respectable" freeholders or inhabitants had been allowed to vote in committee elections.[34]
They feared that critics of the revolution would claim that the committees were open to anyone who wanted to participate, the hoi polloi.
Their defensive tone reminds us that many Americans who supported
resistance to British policy feared the radical possibilities of revolutionary democracy. From this perspective, it stood to reason that if the insurgents could in fact pass as respectable gentlemen, then the overthrow of
the imperial government seemed less threatening. There was always a
danger that angry colonists would take matters into their own hands,
introducing lawlessness and inviting anarchy. This danger seems to
have haunted those attending a convention of delegates "appointed by
the several counties of the province of Maryland" held in early December. Among other things, the representatives resolved "that it is earnestly
recommended, by this Convention, to the people of this province, that
the determination of the several county committees be observed and
acquiesced in: That no persons, except members of the committees,
undertake to meddle with or determine any question respecting the
construction of the association by the Continental Congress: And that
the peace and good order be inviolably maintained throughout this
province."[35]

Wherever they lived, colonists who supported active resistance to
Great Britain do not seem to have been troubled that the extralegal
committees would become authoritarian cells acting against the common good. The initial instructions to the committees were usually so
vague that the members might have felt justified in condoning almost
any act that purported to uphold the spirit of the Association. The freeholders of Somerset County, New Jersey, for example, recommended

that all local committees "be vigilant and active in the discharge of their duty, in taking cognizance of every person of whatsoever rank or condition, who shall, either by word or deed, endeavor to destroy our unanimity in opposing the arbitrary and cruel measures of the British Ministry." The inhabitants of Woodbridge Township, New Jersey, simply urged committee members to "follow the directions of the Association, as much as if it was a law of this Province." The inhabitants of Portsmouth, New Hampshire, were a little more explicit in their instructions, resolving on December 16, 1774, "That a COMMITTEE of 25 Persons be appointed . . . in Behalf of this Town, whose Business it shall be attentively to observe the Conduct of all Persons touching the Association, that every Person within the Limits of their Appointment conform to the same, and if any should be hardy enough to violate it . . . the Committee shall forthwith cause the Truth of the Case to be published in the Gazette according to the Recommendation of the Congress."[36]

Size mattered for committees of safety and observation. From the very beginning the question of numbers fell to the local communities. No one knows why they were given such power. When it drafted the Association, Congress had failed to stipulate how many people should serve on the enforcement committees. Nor did it recommend a mandatory quorum. Left to their own devices, those most eager to resist the empire encouraged broad participation.

Committees established in port cities such as New York and Philadelphia listed as many as 50 or 60 names. But curiously, in frontier villages where monitoring the import trade could not have been a serious challenge, the committees of inspection sometimes had more than 150 members. A review of all Virginia committees shows that they averaged about 21 members. In Maryland the size of the committees was substantially larger, ranging from 20 to 200. A rough calculation of Americans serving on these enforcement committees in 1774 and 1775—the records are incomplete and the figures fluid—suggests an impressive total of about ten thousand.

Over time, local committees continued to expand. In November 1774, for example, insurgent leaders in Prince Georges County, Maryland, constituted a committee of 84 people. Just two months later that figure had risen to 171. We have no evidence to indicate that these huge committees went door-to-door demanding signatures on the Association as the Wilmington committee had done. Still, meetings of these extra-legal committees in many communities must have involved a very large percentage of the population of adult males, and their visible solidarity must have intimidated many of the king's remaining friends in America.

And that was precisely the point. The committees served to politicize daily life throughout the colonies. They functioned as schools for revolution. They shaped public opinion and discouraged dissent. To be sure, committees may have claimed that their members were "respectable" gentlemen, but in fact they were opening the gates to almost anyone prepared actively to participate in resistance to Great Britain. If the insurgency had involved only scattered cells—small groups of individuals willing to employ violence against the empire—it would never have succeeded. By openly recruiting and identifying so many supporters, however, the movement gained strength. Perhaps some men whose names appeared on committee lists would have preferred to remain neutral. Perhaps a few of them secretly hoped that the old order could be restored. But once they agreed to join a committee, they made a political declaration whether they wanted to or not, and they knew that other committee members were ready to denounce neighbors who failed to show proper enthusiasm for the American cause. One Baltimore man confessed that while the town's original committee had contained "no less than 70" names, it kept growing, for insurgent leaders believed that "it would engage the Country People more warmly if gratified in a more Numerous Appointment amongst them." A Philadelphia writer championed the creation of new committees in rural districts because "by interesting people in most remote townships, the enforcement will be more effective."[37]

During the late fall of 1774 and early winter of 1775, committees of safety and observation throughout America seemed content to interpret strictly the articles of the Association that related to the importation of consumer goods from Great Britain, the curtailment of extravagant entertainment, and the protection of sheep so that during an ongoing political crisis Americans would have an adequate supply of wool. As in Wilmington, local committees looked into charges that merchants were selling prohibited items such as East Indian tea. Although they were energetic in the execution of their official duties, the committees generally treated violations of the Association more as minor lapses of judgment than as serious crimes. They certainly tried to avoid situations that could turn stubborn or ignorant neighbors into irreconcilable enemies.

Several cases show how the process worked. In New Jersey, the Cumberland County Committee discovered that one of its own members, Silas Newcomb, had secretly been sipping tea, which of course was "in open violation of the Third Article of the aforesaid Association." Newcomb's colleagues spent many hours trying to correct his erroneous views. After several unproductive conversations, they reluctantly concluded "that it is the duty of this Committee, agreeable to the Eleventh Article of the above-mentioned compact, to break off all dealings with him and in this manner publish the truth of the case, that he may be distinguished from the friends of American liberty."[38] The committee for the upper part of Frederick, Maryland, encountered a similar problem. On November 26, 1774, John Parks was supposed to surrender a "chest of tea," but instead of doing so, he tried to fool the committee into believing that the chest it demanded was now located in another place. After showing remarkable patience with Parks, the committee finally decided, "after mature deliberation . . . that John Parks should go with his hat off, and lighted torches in his hands, and set fire to the tea, which he accordingly did, and the same was consumed to ashes, amongst the acclamations of a numerous body of people." Some people apparently concluded that the committee had shown too much consideration for Parks, and the investigative report noted, "The populace thought the measures adopted by the committee were inadequate to the transgression, and satisfied themselves by breaking his door and windows."[39]

The committee for Prince Georges County, Maryland, demanded that John Baynes appear to answer charges that he had slaughtered a lamb. Baynes "acknowledged that he had killed a lamb." In his defense, he argued that "he had not thereby violated the continental association." The committee set him straight. Even though he insisted that he supported the Association, the committee still felt obliged to remind him that killing lambs "may be of mischievous consequence, as tending to create a disregard to public regulation, formed for preserving the liberties of America."[40]

In late November 1774 a committee in Philadelphia schooled Martha Washington in revolutionary etiquette. The challenge presented itself in the form of a ball that had been scheduled for the night of the twenty-fourth. The ordinary people thought the assembly was a very bad idea. After all, the Continental Congress had recently urged everyone to cut back on expensive entertainment. They cited Article Eight of the Association. On the eve of the party, one witness reported hearing "some threats thrown out, that if the ball [was] assembled this night, as it was proposed, they presumed that the New Tavern would cut but a poor figure tomorrow morning." The real problem was that Mrs. Washington had been invited to attend. No one wanted to insult the wife of the newly appointed commander of the American army. The full Committee refused to back down. It formally resolved that "there should be no such meeting held, not only this evening, but in future, while these troublesome times continued." Finally it dispatched four representatives to speak with "Lady Washington." The assignment required considerable social skills. The messengers told her of the "Committee's great regard and affection to her, requesting her to accept of their grateful acknowledgement and respect, due to her on account of her near connection with our worthy and brave General, now exposed in the field of battle in defense of our rights and liberties, and request and desire her not to grace that company, to which, we are informed she has an invitation." Mrs. Washington was a good sport. After a polite exchange, she "thanked the Committee for their kind care and regard in giving such timely notice, requesting her best compliments to be returned to them for their care and regard, and to assure them that their sentiments on this occasion, were perfectly agreeable unto her own." The next day, having saved the committee considerable embarrassment, she left Philadelphia for Massachusetts, "attended by the troop of horse, two companies of light infantry, &c. &c."[41]

The key moment in the history of the American insurgency—and, by extension, in the popular mobilization for national independence— occurred on the local level after the committees had been in place for several months. Everywhere these bodies expanded their police powers. No longer concerned chiefly with commercial violations, more aggressive committees turned to ferreting out ideological enemies—in other words, to activities involving denunciation, censorship, and punishment.

The transformation took place in different places at different times. The committees followed no mandate from Congress. Acting on their own authority roughly between December 1774 and May 1775, extralegal groups—several hundred of them—no longer interpreted the Association as simply an "instrument of peaceful economic coercion." As British troops poured into occupied Boston and as the king's ministers persuaded themselves that overwhelming military force would solve the colonial problem, Americans came to view a document that Congress had drafted in October 1774 to promote nonimportation of consumer goods as "the political charter of the insurrection."[42]

Loyalists throughout America immediately sensed the profound implications of this shift when it came to their own well-being. The polite tone of earlier exchanges gave way to tough commands. In this more menacing climate, committees in such towns as Woburn, Massachusetts (May 24, 1775), assumed that they had a mandate "to examine into the principles and conduct of any person suspected of being inimical to the liberties of this country." Formal protest against annoying parliamentary legislation had evolved into a people's revolution.

It was this dramatic development that caused a leading New Jersey loyalist in April 1775 to condemn the "Tyranny of the People," which he believed reflected "the progress of human passions inflamed in a popular cause uncontrolled by Power or Unawed by Authority."[43] Observing the same phenomenon, another loyalist railed against "the prevailing rage of the present times for people of all ranks, orders, and professions to form Associations [committees]." These groups, he claimed, passed arbitrary resolves that resulted in "many peaceable and well disposed persons, who have declined joining in such illegal Associations, [in being] insulted, persecuted, proscribed, and oppressed, and have suffered all the cruelty and torture that brutal, cowardly rage could devise; and, as in obedience to the orders of such Congresses and Committees, much private property has been destroyed, the most daring piracies and robberies have been perpetrated in the face of open day, and death and destruction denounced [i.e., broadcast] against all who dare oppose their lawless banditti."[44] Of course, complaints from loyalists about alleged atrocities are not necessarily more reliable than are uncritical celebrations of American patriotism. What they do indicate is that the insurgency had suddenly become a much more serious threat to those who feared that without the stabilizing anchor of monarchy, colonial society would dissolve into anarchy.

What caught the attention of local committees were words—written and spoken—that seemed to indicate that a member of the community had attempted to undermine the American cause. The vagueness of the charge invited interpretation. In some cases, committees acted on reports of people who had openly affirmed their allegiance to king and Parliament. Strong drink encouraged such loose talk. On these occasions, men—they were almost always male—ran their mouths, forgetting that tavern companions might come forward as witnesses against them. Abiel Wood learned the danger of speaking his mind in public. A committee of inspection in Pownalborough, New York, found that Wood "declared the Acts of Parliament for raising a revenue in America were not grievances, but ought to be submitted to; and that the Act for blocking up the Port of Boston was a just punishment; and said that John Hancock, Esquire, Samuel Adams, and Josiah Quincy, were the cause of all the disturbances and difficulties we are involved in." Moreover, Wood swore that Hancock had persuaded ordinary people to participate in the Tea Party with promises that "one of them should be a King, another a Governor, and that they should be in some great places of honor and profit." Although Wood was a wealthy merchant in the town, the members of the committee could not tolerate such loose talk. "To deprive a man of the benefits of society, by holding him up to the world as an enemy to his Country," the Pownalborough committee declared, "is a task that must be disagreeable to humanity; but the duty incumbent on every person who is entrusted with power, to prevent the violation of the American Association" made it necessary to punish Wood for his words.[45]

Other suspects complained a bit too publicly of the actions of the committees, suggesting in one form or another that in their zeal to protect liberty, the committees had denied the Crown's loyal subjects *their* liberty. Dr. Fallon, who ran afoul of the Wilmington committee, put such unwelcome ideas on paper. A friend, William Green, made a copy of Fallon's two-page statement, entitled "A Lawyer" and addressed "To those who have a true sense of distributive justice and untrammeled liberty." To make matters worse, someone—probably Green—displayed the document at the courthouse for the public to read. Under interrogation, Green confessed he had duplicated a text borrowed from Fallon. That was all the evidence the committee needed. On January 15, 1776, it resolved "the said paper contains many false and scandalous reflections on this committee, tending to inflame the minds of the people; to create division and dissention amongst us by destroying that unanimity

so essentially necessary to our mutual defense." Fallon further antago-
nized the Wilmington committee by leveling "an illiberal and groundless charge against a respectable gentleman deservedly high in office in
this colony." It placed the doctor under arrest, demanded a huge bond,
intercepted his mail, and recorded the names of all his visitors. None of
this apparently discouraged Fallon, who schemed to convert the guards
to his own political thinking. When the committee learned that Fallon
had become "an insinuating and dangerous person among the soldiers,"
it threw him into "the common jail . . . there to remain until he make a
full concession for his offenses to the public and asks pardon of the
Committee for the repeated insults he has in person offered."[46]

The Wilmington experience is instructive. As schools of revolution,
committees of safety rapidly transformed an entire political culture. In
towns and counties throughout America they enforced the Association.
They could not have succeeded without broad popular support. This is
the key to effective mobilization. In every community a large number of
people observed the committees as they dispensed revolutionary justice.
The people were not, however, neutral spectators. The committees
drew them into the revolutionary process. On the local level, they educated friends and neighbors about the new rules of commerce, about
the need for self-censorship in public exchanges, and, perhaps most
important, about political responsibilities to other Americans — ordinary
people like themselves — who sustained the insurgency.

# EIGHT

# *Insurgents in Power*

Janet Schaw, John Parks, and Dr. Fallon, who experienced the dark side of revolution, remind us of an unpleasant truth. Popular resistance to the British Empire before independence could well have been a dreary tale of mass murder and destruction of property. The absence of repeated waves of terror should not encourage us to celebrate our good fortune in avoiding the massive purges and human suffering that characterized other revolutions over the last two centuries. Rather, the possibility that political passions could have raged out of control compels us to ask an unfamiliar question. How did American insurgents manage to restrain their own anger and desire for revenge and turn a loose network of extralegal committees into a vehicle for national unity and political moderation?[1]

Many loyalists might well have found this proposition absurd. They complained bitterly during the last two years of imperial rule that committees of safety had made a mockery of the rule of law. But they overstated their grievance. However intimidating these bodies may have appeared to those who spoke out forcefully in support of the Crown, they were not in fact eighteenth-century equivalents of modern kangaroo courts, dispensing summary punishment to anyone brave or foolish enough to challenge the insurgency. It is true that some local committees could have become vehicles for overmighty citizens to harass rivals in the name of the American cause. During the period we are examining, however, evidence of such abuse of power is very thin.

What in fact occurred was that even when they felt most vulnerable, those Americans who served on the extralegal governing committees tried hard to avoid the appearance of arbitrary practice. They did not always succeed. Yet unpleasant exceptions should not obscure the major accomplishment of these revolutionary bodies. The ordinary people who energized the Revolution seldom sanctioned the use of physical violence as a political tool. They seem to have adopted a pragmatic perspective on dealing with ideological opponents.

As the insurgency took on institutional form, it stressed repeatedly the need for unity and the desirability of reincorporating outspoken opponents into the life of the community. But another element was at work. Although the committee may have had no proper legal standing—claims that the Association was in fact a kind of constitution did not always do the trick—they operated in a society that had a deep, almost unquestioned commitment to a rule of law. However messy the enforcement of revolutionary mandates was on the ground, the committees struggled to observe rough forms of due process and judicial procedure. To be sure, some of them failed some of the time. If we focus on the rough music of revolution, however, we will overlook the processes that brought solidarity to a colonial rebellion that appeared to have no chance of success.

## I

Considering the extraordinary popular rage generated by the imperial controversy, it is striking that committees throughout America strove so hard to mobilize resistance within familiar legal and administrative frameworks. Consider the instructive example of Worcester, Massachusetts. What occurred in this New England town reveals not only how ordinary men and women pushed their spokesmen to take ever more radical positions, but also how a committee that shared their political concerns studiously avoided actions that might have resulted in violent rampage against real and imagined opponents. Like many other committees, this body refocused the raw and personal emotions of the insurgents into less disruptive bureaucratic channels.

In Worcester, constraint was quite an achievement. Those people who supported the Crown—many of them belonging to the wealthiest families in the town—mounted an aggressive campaign to undermine the legitimacy of the local committee of correspondence. If any group might have provoked retaliatory violence, this was it. And yet instead of butchering neighbors, the militants of Worcester launched a war of petitions and counterpetitions, engaging in a process that reaffirmed their own demands for resistance to imperial authority without thereby driving moderate or undecided neighbors into opposition.

During the last years of empire, Worcester was a deeply divided community.[2] A number of its leading families identified with the British Empire. Some men bearing respected surnames—the Chandlers, Paines, and Putnams, for example—had accepted appointments from Thomas Hutchinson, the despised royal governor of Massachusetts. Most people in the town wanted no part of the imperial establishment, and much to the annoyance of the members of the dominant families, they supported positions that served to escalate the imperial crisis. They celebrated the destruction of the tea in Boston Harbor, and after learning of the Coercive Acts, they gave enthusiastic support to a plan to halt the importation of British manufactured goods into the American colonies. On May 20, 1774, a committee impaneled by the town meeting informed their representative to the Massachusetts legislature, "As English America is in a general alarm, in consequence of some late unconstitutional stretches of power, we are sensible this is the most difficult period that hath ever yet commenced since the arrival of our ancestors into this unexplored, uncultivated wilderness." They instructed the man to resist the Coercive Acts, encourage "a strict union of the colonists," and stand vigilant against the "wanton exercise of power."[3]

During the summer of 1774, simmering political differences came to a boil. The king's friends in Worcester decided that the moment had come for "the sober judicious people of the town" to teach local troublemakers a lesson. Adopting some dodgy procedural moves in the town meeting, they issued a thundering proclamation that, among other things, condemned the town's committee of correspondence. It was a high-risk maneuver. The leaders of the self-styled "respectable Inhabitants" of Worcester entered into the official town records a chronicle of objectionable militant activities that deserved public condemnation. And on June 30, as part of a campaign to generate additional backing throughout the Massachusetts countryside, they published an inflammatory proclamation in the *Boston News-Letter*. The following week the piece appeared in the *Massachusetts Gazette*.

The whole performance smacked of condescension. The authors blamed the insurgency in Massachusetts on irresponsible agitators who had played on the emotions of ordinary men and women. These activities had produced near anarchy. Everywhere one could see the destructive results of "riotous, disorderly and seditious practices." According to Worcester's loyalists, the ordinary people had no business engaging in political matters beyond their comprehension. Like poor beasts of the field, they had listened to "evil-minded and ill-disposed persons" who "under the disguise of patriotism, and falsely styling themselves the friends of liberty, some of them neglecting their own proper business and occupation, in which they ought to be employed for the support of their families, spending their time in discoursing of matters they do not understand, raising and propagating falsehoods and calumnies of those men they look up to with envy, and on whose fall and ruin they wish to rise, intend to reduce all things to a state of tumult, discord and confusion." In modern parlance, the loyalists played the class card. As the crescendo of criticism reached a peak, it became clear that the real culprits were "the persons styling themselves the Committee of Correspondence."

The king's friends in Worcester saw no hope of reconciliation with Great Britain unless the respectable people of Massachusetts challenged the rule of the extralegal committees. After all, these obnoxious bodies could claim no legitimacy. Fifty-two men of loyalist persuasion declared that "it is our firm opinion, that the Committees of Correspondence in the several towns in this Province, being creatures of modern invention, and constituted as they be, are a legal grievance, having no legal foundation, contrived by a junto to serve particular designs and purposes of their own."

However unwelcome these observations may have been to the insurgents, the Worcester loyalists made an astute political observation. The committees were, in fact, a modern invention. They represented an expanding revolutionary infrastructure that posed a major problem for those who wanted to restore the old order. And although the members of these extralegal groups have over the centuries achieved almost mythic status as patriots, they seemed more like dangerous insurgents to the signers of this strident attack. "And we fear," the signers of the protest declared, "it is in a great measure owing to the baneful influence of such committees, that . . . enormous acts of violence and oppression have been perpetrated, whereby the lives of many honest worthy persons have been endangered and their property destroyed."

For the loyalists, the time had come to draw the line, to stand up for the empire in America. The militants were gaining strength. Respectable people in Massachusetts had to be made aware that these committees were circulating radical propaganda "inviting and wickedly tempting all persons to join them, fully implying, if not expressly denouncing the destruction of all that refuse to subscribe to those unlawful combinations, tending directly to sedition, civil war, and rebellion."

The protesters threw down the glove. And if the insurgents who supported the committees had been as violent as the loyalists claimed, they would have responded by destroying property and endangering the lives of "many honest worthy persons." Nothing of the sort occurred. Joshua Bigelow, the town's representative in the Massachusetts Assembly and an advocate of resistance to Great Britain, issued a warrant calling for a special town meeting. Like a formal legal document written by an attorney for the defense, Bigelow and his allies in Worcester responded to the specific charges their opponents had made. The complaints the king's friends had chronicled for the newspapers amounted to no more than malicious slander. Particularly groundless were claims that "Committees of Correspondence in the Several Towns, of this Province are a grievance, and that they as they have been and now are managed, in this Town are a Nuisance." This amounted to calumny. The enemies of militancy had "Invidiously and falsely" attacked "the charactors [sic] of those very worthy Gent., of which our committee is Composed." In any case, as Bigelow reminded the other party, the town had every right to choose a committee—modern invention or not—and to ask the members to distribute forms asking the ordinary people of Worcester to show their contempt for the Coercive Acts by not purchasing British imports.

When the inhabitants of the town did gather on August 22, 1774, they were more than prepared to follow Bigelow's lead. The suggestion that their committee was composed of "a Parcell of unprincipolled knaves" annoyed everyone. But the major objection was that a group of

loyalists had sullied the official town records with the text of their protest. That insult could not be allowed to stand. The townsmen demanded that the clerk who had actually entered the loyalist slander in
the book remove the execrable words. Clark Chandler tried to strike out
the insulting passages with a pen. That was not good enough. One
could still make out some words. The town then forced Chandler to
dip his fingers in the inkwell and rub them across the town records
so that the attack on the committee would be "utterly illegible and
unintelligeable."[4]

The whole episode reflected ingrained assumptions of a legal culture. No one imagined that a dispute over the composition of a committee would spark violence in the streets. It was one thing to take firm
action against a British army of occupation, quite another to threaten
obnoxious neighbors with force of arms. On September 5 a group of
loyalists issued a formal apology to the town. Published in two Boston
newspapers, the recantation, signed by forty-three men, confessed their
political errors and begged to be reunited "to the people." "We acknowledge," they declared, "we have cast cruel aspersions upon the town of
Worcester and upon the Committee of Correspondence for said town,
and upon all Committees of Correspondence throughout the Province,
for which we are sorry."[5] The Worcester crisis played itself out through
a series of protests and rejoinders, arguments and motions, and pronouncements about the sanctity of official records. Bigelow and his colleagues were not less radical for arguing their case before the town
meeting. They mobilized the ordinary farmers of Worcester and affirmed the central place of committees in the revolutionary process.
The major casualty of the affair was Chandler's dirty fingers.

# II

Throughout America the committees of enforcement seldom acted on
the basis of a single denunciation. When they learned of a possible violation—usually a report about someone who seemed intent on undermining American resistance—they called for witnesses. Although it is
not certain whether these people were required to swear an oath to the
truth of their testimony, they provided the committees with what might

be loosely called depositions. If the case seemed particularly complex, local committees sometimes asked provincial committees of safety to review the matter and render a verdict. However problematic their own legal status, the committees felt an obligation to provide at least the rudiments of due process. They wanted not only to preserve justice in a revolutionary environment but also to persuade enemies that the committees had not become drumhead courts.

One committee has left us an excellent account of its procedures. Early in 1775 the members of a general committee of inspection for New Haven County, Connecticut, announced, "We will vigilantly discharge our duty as Committees of Observation, and will use our utmost influence to prevent any Violation of the Associations in our several Districts, but if any Person, contrary to our hopes and wishes, shall be accused of any willful breach of said Association in any particular, we do agree, that the Process against him, shall be carried on in an open, candid and deliberate manner." They then spelled out exactly what transparency involved. First, when local district committees learned of possible infractions, they issued an official summons "signed by one of the Committee of Observation for that town." Someone representing the committee served the document upon the accused person. It spelled out the specific elements of the charge and invited him "if he see cause to appear before the Committee of Observation in that Town in which he resides, at a certain day and place to exculpate himself, if he be able." The rules made no explicit provision for counsel for the defense. The hearing had to take place at least six days after the original summons had been served. The committees pledged that "the Person accused and his Answer shall be openly, fairly, and fully heard, Witnesses and Proof." After the evidence had been presented, and only then, did the town committees proceed "deliberately and coolly to determine the Question, whether the Person accused hath violated said Association or not."

The New Haven County committee recognized that one of its own members might possibly find himself either "an Accuser or Witness." If that happened, he was advised not to cast a vote except "upon the fullest, clearest and most convincing Proof." At the end of the process, "any Person found guilty of willful and deliberate violation of said Association, in the calm and regular manner aforesaid, may assuredly expect that we will hold him up to the public View as an Enemy to the Liberties of his Country."[6] We note in the New Haven protocol loud silences about several traditional legal safeguards. The committee not only ignored representation by counsel, it also failed to mention any basis for appeal or the rules governing cross-examination. No doubt it was more concerned at that moment with persuading the public—which in the New Haven region contained many people who were skeptical of the insurgency—that the committees were in fact prepared to act in a cool and deliberate manner.

Other committees did not bother to sketch out procedural guidelines in such detail. Nevertheless, it is apparent that in their judicial business they strove to avoid even the suggestion of arbitrary practice. A few examples show how the general process worked. Like the New Haven committee, Maryland's Eastern Shore Council of Safety demanded solid evidence before it punished alleged enemies of the resistance. On November 17, 1775, it summoned Isaac Atkinson to appear. He had already been interrogated by the committee of observation for Somerset County, and that body submitted a report as well as several depositions, all of which indicated that Atkinson had indeed "been raising a Company in Somerset County to oppose the measures of the Continental Congress and the Convention of this Province, and of his having declared he would protect any set of men who would not sign the Association." The Eastern Shore council gave the accused more than two weeks to gather witnesses. The council itself collected depositions, all of them demonstrating that Atkinson had been busy organizing and arming counterinsurgents. One man claimed that these volunteers "all huzzaed for the king, and pulled off their hats."

Atkinson mounted an inspired defense. He insisted that he had no problem with the Continental Congress. It was the local Presbyterians he despised. When the members of the Somerset committee learned of Atkinson's claim, they reminded the Eastern Shore council that he had never mentioned Presbyterians during the initial hearing. Moreover, the committee had shown him compassion at every stage. "In the course of our proceedings against this unhappy man," wrote the Somerset committee, ". . . he had every indulgence that the nature of his offence could entitle him to. His trial was put off from day to day, and an opportunity always given of confronting the evidences against him, in hopes that he might be able to exculpate himself to the satisfaction of the public." The local committee admitted that many members of the Church of England believed that "the Presbyterians are enemies to their present establishment, greedy of power, and oppressive in executing it, which makes them jealous of every measure, however laudable, that the Presbyterians engage in."[7] At this point both committees seem to have washed their hands of the matter. As long as Atkinson was not a threat to the American cause, he could be excused for insulting Presbyterians. The temptation to reach a speedy resolution must have been great. But if the committees had done so, they would have become entangled in a religious controversy of which they wanted no part.

When confronted with potentially dangerous situations, the committees tried to drag out the investigations as long as possible. Even when there seemed little doubt about the guilt of the accused, these extralegal bodies endeavored to resolve the contest through negotiation. They wanted to give neighbors whose acts or words suggested that they represented a real threat to the security of the community an opportunity to rethink their position. Official judgment terminated such conversations and turned former friends into implacable foes. When committees did reluctantly move against their enemies, they made a point of mentioning how hard they had worked to resolve the matter in other, more productive ways. Early in 1775 the committee for Petersham, Massachusetts, discovered that fourteen "inhabitants of this town" had pledged that "we will not acknowledge or submit to the pretended authority of any congresses, committees of correspondence or other unconstitutional assemblies of men, but will at the risque of our lives, if need be, oppose the forcible exercise of all such authority." The committee assembled evidence against the group, taking care that "each of such persons should be served with a copy of such intelligence and complaint, that they might have [an] opportunity at this present meeting to clear up their characters." The conspirators refused to appear. Only after all efforts to reach out to the members of the group had failed did the committee conclude, "it appears that those persons still remain incorrigible enemies of America, and have a disposition to cast their influence into the scale against us, in order to enslave their brethren and posterity forever. And, after all the friendly expostulations and entreaties which we have been able to make use of, we are with great reluctance constrained to pronounce those, some of which have here-tofore been our agreeable neighbors, traitorous patricides to the cause of freedom."[8]

A second major reason why the American insurgency did not gener-ally become a vehicle for physically punishing ideological opponents is that the committees did not have authorization to hear cases involving life and limb. Nor did they desire such power. However obnoxious the words and deeds of their enemies may have been, the committees aimed in the first instance not at destroying the accused, but rather at rein-corporating the person into the community. From this perspective, for-mal hearings before local committees should be seen as a kind of political theater. When the parties followed the proper script, the indi-vidual charged with a crime against the Association admitted he had made a serious error. The explanation for the change of heart did not matter much so long as the villain sounded sincere. The perfect sce-nario featured a public confession that in turn generated forgiveness. If all these elements were in place, the members of the committee as well as the defendant could maintain that the spirit of unity had trumped partisan dissent.

Only on those occasions when the accused stubbornly or bravely resisted political reeducation did discussion turn to punishment. This involved the publication of names in newspapers and a strong recom-mendation to the inhabitants of the local community that they sever all commercial connection with those who "have by their conduct in vari-ous instances manifested a disposition inimical to the rights and privi-leges of their countrymen." When confronted with such hardened enemies, the committee of Hardwick, Massachusetts, advised the sup-porters of the Association to treat those convicted of political crimes as nonpersons, "to shun their causes and persons, and treat them with that contempt and neglect they deserve."[9]

It would reveal a high degree of insensitivity to make light of rituals of shunning and humiliation. Finding oneself cut off from the human links that defined community life must have been a frightening pros-pect. Those who would argue that real insurgents must be prepared to take more drastic measures to realize their political goals fail to appreci-ate fully the context in which ordinary people made revolutionary deci-sions. Within this society the terrifying prospect of public shunning was often sufficient to stifle political dissent.[10]

Whatever the psychological pressures may have been, reconciliation was the primary goal. Such an effort to restore local relations played itself out in a small Delaware community. On August 7, 1775, the committee for White Clay Creek interrogated the Reverend Morgan Edwards. Before the question of punishment had even been raised, Edwards offered an abject recantation. He informed the committee, "I have for some time since frequently made use of rash and imprudent expressions with respect to the conduct of my fellow countrymen, who are now engaged in a noble and patriotic struggle for the liberties of America, against the arbitrary measures of the British Ministry." He begged the committee's compassion. "I now confess that I have spoken wrong," he said, "for which I am sorry, and ask forgiveness of the public; and I do promise, that for the future I will conduct myself in such a manner as to avoid giving offense, and, at the same time, in justice to myself, declare, that I am a friend to the present measures pursued by the friends to American liberty." Edwards's performance apparently satisfied the insurgents of White Clay Creek, for they immediately readmitted him to the fellowship of the community.[11]

The committee of safety of Bucks County, Pennsylvania, demonstrated remarkable patience for people who insulted Congress and the American cause. No sooner had Thomas Meredith been called before the committee than he confessed to a serious lapse of judgment. He had disparaged the people of Boston. Since the committee had just collected an impressive donation "for the sufferers" of that city, it probably was in no mood to overlook Meredith's performance. Perhaps sensing that he had gone too far, he acknowledged, "I have spoken injuriously of the distressed people of the town of Boston, and disrespectfully of the Measures prosecuting for the redress of American Grievances; I do hereby declare, that I am heartily sorry for what I have done, voluntarily renouncing my former principles, and promise for the future to render my Conduct inexceptionable [*sic*] to my Countrymen." His sincerity seems to have impressed the committeemen, for they quickly voted to accept his confession.

Thomas Smith presented the Bucks County committee with a much harder case. On the same day it forgave Meredith, the committee announced that it possessed "incontestable evidence" that Smith had uttered a number of politically offensive expressions. He told whoever would listen in Upper Makefield that the Continental Congress "had already enslaved America and done more Damage than all the Acts of Parliament ever intended to lay upon us." And why had it acted in this irresponsible way? According to Smith, "the whole was nothing but a scheme of a parcel of hot-headed Presbyterians and that he believed the Devil was at the Bottom of the whole." Four months after Gage's troops had murdered Americans at Lexington, Smith still declared "the taking up Arms was the most scandalous thing a man could be guilty of, and more heinous than an hundred grossest offenses against the moral law, &c., &c., &c."

If anyone deserved tough treatment, it was Smith. In short order, the committee condemned him for dishonoring Congress and raising "invidious Distinctions between different denominations." His ill-considered words revealed him "an Enemy to the Rights of British America." The committee ordered "all persons [to] break off every kind of dealing with him until he shall make proper satisfaction to this Committee for his misconduct." The committee took almost three weeks to prepare a statement about Smith for the local press. On September 11, just as it was about to publish the public condemnation, Smith had second thoughts. He communicated a sudden desire to express "remorse and penitence." He then came before the committee, where he offered an abject apology and confession. That was good enough. The committee decided that forgiveness made more sense than did driving Smith from the community.[12]

Rituals of reconciliation occurred throughout New England. Acceptance depended on demonstration that the confession had been made voluntarily. Evidence of coercion would only have called the sincerity of the apology into question. Moreover, once the accused came to his ideological senses, he had to broadcast his remorse to the public. Private statements of sorrow did nothing to advance the common cause. As with the confessions that eighteenth-century criminals made moments before execution, these statements were intended to instruct ordinary people about correct politics; the contrite dissenter reminded them of core political principles that sustained the insurgency.[13]

On October 24, 1775, after a local committee in Williamstown, Massachusetts, had expressed suspicion about his "principles and conduct in regard to our public affairs," David Noble decided to issue a voluntary confession. He admitted that as recently as 1773 he had acted "in opposition to the measures pursued for the defense of our common rights and privileges." He had even trusted the despised Thomas Hutchinson. But Noble had experienced a new political birth. "Impressed with a sense of my duty to myself and the public," he now insisted that he had been wrong to support that "arch traitor to his country." He insisted that whatever his errors, he had been a friend to the liberties of America. Noble followed the script. A full public town meeting voted to forgive him.[14]

An even more curious case came before the Accomack County, Virginia, committee. In June 1775 an informer charged James Arbuckle, a member of the committee, with aiding and abetting the enemy, which in this setting meant giving logistic support to Virginia's royal governor, Lord Dunmore. Arbuckle had drawn a detailed map of the Eastern Shore. When his colleagues on the committee observed that the British could use such a map if they invaded the region, Arbuckle ridiculed the idea. As he pointed out, he had copied the material from an old map that contained no intelligence not already in Dunmore's hands. The committee accepted his explanation. The complaint did not merit branding Arbuckle an enemy to his country.

Another man in Accomack seemed determined to annoy the local committee. John Sherlock did not know when to keep his mouth shut. An informer denounced him for expressing "himself in such a manner as to prove him an enemy to the liberties of this Country." When the members of the committee requested that he respond, he "wrote them an abusive and insulting letter." Witnesses came forward. One person in particular offered what seemed damning evidence. In conversation, this man heard Sherlock state that "such people as oppose the Ministerial measures with America are rebels, that he shall be employed hereafter in hanging them, and that if no hemp can be got, he has plenty of flax growing."

The next day the Accomack committee decided that it could not ignore such abusive behavior. Announcing publicly that it had proceeded against Sherlock "agreeable to the rules of the Association," it dispatched a company of local soldiers to the culprit's house and literally carried him to the courthouse. The arrest almost turned violent, for at the last moment Sherlock grabbed "two loaded guns" and "took shelter in an upper room." Fortunately, he decided to surrender before shots were fired. After "a solemn trial" before the committee, local insurgents led him to "the Liberty Pole," and before an assembly of ordinary people he delivered a "recantation." He confessed to saying that he would one day hang his neighbors as rebels. He also admitted "calling the Independent Company of this County an unlawful mob, and many other idle and foolish words." About the treasonous language, Sherlock whined, "I did not mean as much as I said."

At the last moment Sherlock recanted his political errors. The independent company was actually "a very respectable body of men." And on proper reflection, he most heartily wished "success to this my native Country in her present honest struggle for liberty with the Mother Country, and do here promise to do all in my power to retrieve my character with my countrymen." The confession appeared in the local newspaper. Sherlock was lucky to have been "a native." A Scottish merchant might not have gotten off so lightly. Sherlock, however, served another purpose. His ritual "recantation" before the local soldiers and the members of the community helped reinforce their commitment to the American cause.[15]

The Chesapeake colonies had no monopoly on stubborn or obnoxious people. The small town of East Haddam, Connecticut, dealt with a man—really an entire family—who voiced political opinions so provocative that one wonders how he managed to avoid a beating or worse. But as in the Maryland cases, the person who brazenly insulted the local committee of inspection managed not only to survive the insurgency but also to be forgiven his political sins.

The confrontation with Jonathan Bebee began on September 12, 1775. After the committee had received a number of complaints about Bebee's behavior, it asked him to participate in a formal hearing of the matter. Bebee initially ignored the request. His failure to appear did not stop the investigation. The committee called witnesses who testified in writing that they had heard Bebee "justifying and approving all the late tyrannical Acts of the British Parliament, &c. and that he hoped Gage and his Men would have Success, and prevail, for they were in the Right, &c."

The committee adjourned its regular meetings while members gathered additional evidence. Then, on October 3, in a move so audacious that even his opponents were shocked, Bebee appeared, accompanied by two relatives whom he introduced as legal counsel. The committee dismissed one of them—Dr. Abner Bebee—immediately, noting in the records that he was "well known to be an Enemy to his Country, and had been advertised in the Publick Papers as such." If anything, the explanation understated the awkwardness of the moment. Only a few months earlier Abner had come before the committee accused of expressing political opinions even more heinous than those of his brother Jonathan. The committee had indeed declared Abner an enemy and ordered the inhabitants of East Haddam to shun him. But according to one account, the people found Abner's political view so repellent that they took the law into their own hands. Acting without the Committee's approval, a group described as a "Mob" had assaulted him. After he had been "stripped naked, & hot Pitch was poured upon him, which blistered his Skin, he was then carried to an Hog Sty & rubbed over with Hog's Dung; They threw the Hog's Dung in his Face, & rammed some of it down his Throat; & in that Condition exposed him to a Company of Women. His House was attacked, his Windows broke, when one of his Children was sick, & a mill was broke, & Persons prevented from grinding at it, & from having any Connections with him." One might take this alarming report with at least a few grains of salt, since it comes from a partisan history of the Revolution written by Peter Oliver, an arch-loyalist and friend of Governor Hutchinson's.[16] No other accounts of Abner's torture in the pigsty have surfaced. In any case, it must have surprised the members of the committee when he declared his intention to represent his brother before the insurgent panel. Jonathan protested Abner's exclusion and withdrew from the proceedings "in an angry and contemptuous manner."

The committee then got down to business. The evidence denouncing Jonathan indicated at the very least that his pronouncements had strained his neighbors' patience. Witnesses claimed that he had openly declared that the Americans had no justification for opposing "the late tyrannical Acts of Parliament." He had also insisted that "those that opposed them [the Coercive Acts] would have their Bowels taken out, and quartered, and be hung up in the public corners of the Streets." On another occasion, Jonathan warned local militants against "taking up Arms, even if an Act should be passed to take the Bible from us." Depositions revealed finally that he hoped John Hancock's "Head . . . would be cut off; and that the [British] Regulars had a Right to fire on our People, if they would not deliver up their Ammunition; and calling the Congress a parcel of Mob Men, and that they were chose by Tom, Dick, and Harry, etc." Jonathan had at once insulted local insurgents—some who had undoubtedly fought against General Gage's troops after Lexington and Concord—and arrogantly dismissed the ordinary people who viewed Congress as a proper representative body.

Confronted with such a record, the committee might well have condemned the entire Bebee clan. But, eager to avoid another episode with the hogs of East Haddam, and committed to a rule of law as set forth by the Association, the committee reviewed the testimony and unanimously declared, "The said Jonathan Bebee is Guilty, as set forth in said Complaint." Henceforth this abrasive man was to be treated "as an Enemy to his Country, that all Persons may break off Dealings and Commerce with him." The committee then sent the entire record of Jonathan's trial to a local newspaper.

The chances of restoring Jonathan to the good graces of the community would have seemed slim. But in fact a few months later he was back before the committee, announcing that he had experienced a political conversion. On April 12, 1776, it was reported in the newspaper that he had "discovered that I was then in an Error in particularly holding that the King and Parliament had [the] Right to bind us in all Cases whatever, and being desirous to be restored to my former situation, I applied to the Committee of Inspection . . . for relief, upon this my new Sentiments." He and the members of the East Haddam committee negotiated the precise wording of his public confession. "[I] desire," he explained, "wherein I have offended, the Forgiveness of all good People, &c. and desire to be restored to the Friendship of all my Neighbours and Acquaintances, and of all the good People of these Colonies, hoping that the glorious Struggle for the Liberties and Privileges, both Civil and Sacred of these United Colonies, may be crowned with Success, and vindicate us and ours from the Hands of Tyranny to the latest Posterity." Jonathan's performance was good enough for the committee. If the members questioned his sincerity, they kept their doubts to themselves. They voted to approve the confession and to restore Bebee to "Favor." It apparently made more sense to reincorporate him into the community than to keep unpleasant memories alive.[17]

These troublesome cases do not reveal that American insurgents were more tolerant of dissent than we might have anticipated. The members of the East Haddam committee probably despised the Bebees. But as militants in communities throughout the colonies aggressively came forward to resist the imperial power, the committees strove for balance. If they had ignored the provocations of a Jonathan Bebee, the people might have taken matters into their own hands, driving the Revolution in directions that could have permanently fractured local society. They did just that when they tormented Abner in the pigsty. Failure to respond, therefore, was not an option. But when neighbors with long histories in the community mouthed obnoxious opinions, the committees had to keep an eye on dangers of counterinsurgency. Ritual confessions and formal votes of forgiveness preserved a veneer of unity on the ground.

## *III*

Not all cases ended with a mutually acceptable confession. When this occurred, the committees still did their best to preserve ideological unity within the community. The records contain a number of controversies that did not follow the preferred script in which charges sparked a sincere apology before the public. Of these cases—and we can review only a few of them here—most seem to have involved a person or persons only marginally connected to the community before the imperial crisis began. They were outsiders. Of course, considering the problematic character of surviving documents, it is impossible to state with statistical authority how many complaints of this type came before the committees. It does not seem mere chance, however, that many difficult cases in which the accused received full punishment involved men—they were almost always men—who had held posts in the royal government, traveled to America from Scotland as merchants, were Anglican ministers, or worked as peddlers or itinerant tradesmen.[18]

The committees in New Hampshire appear to have been particularly wary of this last group. In January 1775 the Newmarket committee warned that "every Innkeeper or other Inhabitant that shall harbor or entertain any Hawker, Pedlar [*sic*], or Petty-Chapman, offering as such, to purchase or sell any Goods, Wares, or Merchandise, shall be esteemed and treated by us as an Enemy of his Country."[19] The committee in Epsom, New Hampshire, declared, "We view the Scotch Merchants and Traders in general to be no Friends to our Country."[20] In the Chesapeake colonies, Scottish merchants and schoolteachers often found themselves the objects of committee investigations. It would seem that by punishing transient figures who had never been accepted as members of the local community, the committees reaffirmed the core values of the insurgency. These were show trials. By marginalizing itinerants, the committees could credibly maintain the fiction that everyone else in the neighborhood supported the American cause. In this highly politicized environment, hard cases may have made good militants.

The committee for Orange County, Virginia, had its hands full with the Reverend Mr. John Wingate. An informer had revealed that the Anglican minister had in his possession a number of pamphlets that contained "very obnoxious reflections on the Continental Congress and their proceedings, and calculated to impose on the unwary." On March 27, 1775, the committee held a hearing at the county courthouse, where it demanded that Wingate explain his reading habits. Leaders of the local resistance took the matter extremely seriously. They had received a number of reports that pamphlets deemed a threat to the insurgency circulated freely throughout the county. Indeed, it seemed that ordinary Virginians were able to purchase these materials at a printer's shop in nearby Williamsburg. The committee feared that this loyalist propaganda had made an unfavorable impression "on some people's minds by the confident assertions of falsehoods and insidious misrepresentations of facts contained in them."

But when Wingate was asked about the dangerous titles, he refused to cooperate. He insisted that the writings in his library belonged to a Mr. Henry Mitchell of Fredericksburg, and without that man's permission, the minister had nothing to say. The committee argued with Wingate. It assured him that Mitchell would not object to the proceedings. Still, Wingate remained unforthcoming. According to an account that ran in a local newspaper, "At length the Committee, finding there was no prospect of working on Mr. Wingate by arguments and entreaties, peremptorily demanded the pamphlets with a determination not to be defeated in their intentions."

What the members encountered in the pages of five pamphlets shocked them. They immediately resolved "that as a collection of the most audacious insults on that August body (the grand Continental Congress) and their proceedings, and also on the several Colonies from which they were deputed . . . of the most slavish doctrines of Provincial Government, the most imprudent falsehoods and malicious artifices to excite divisions among the friends of America, they deserved to be publicly burnt, as a testimony of the Committee's detestation and abhorrence of the writers and their principles." The committee was as good as its word. In the "presence of the Independent Company [local soldiers] and other respectable inhabitants of the said County," the publications went up in flames. Wingate neither confessed his errors nor was reconciled to the community. The whole episode had the effect, however, of reaffirming popular support for resistance to Great Britain. It was reported that all the spectators "joined in expressing a noble indignation against such execrable publications, and their ardent wishes for an opportunity of inflicting on the authors, publishers, and their abettors, the punishment due to their insufferable arrogance and atrocious crimes."[21]

In August 1775 a particularly thorny dispute came before the Prince George's County committee. The case involved the honor and veracity of a well-respected man who lived in Bladensburg, Maryland. As Richard Henderson insisted throughout the controversy, he enthusiastically supported the insurgency. Not only had he been selected to serve as an officer in the local militia, but he also produced a letter in evidence, written in 1774, in which he effusively praised the political judgment of ordinary Americans. "They are a well-informed, reasoning commonality," he stated, ". . . perhaps the most of any on earth, because of the free intercourse between man and man." These were not the sort of people who would "stand in awe of rank and station." The strength of this marvelous civil society, Henderson believed, was the openness of the courts of law, where the colonists "hear the rights of the subject nobly debated; their frequent and free elections, which give occasion for candidates to scan each other's principles and conduct before the tribunal of the people, together with the freedom and general circulation of newspapers, and the eagerness and leisure of the people to read them, or listen to those who do." In a word, Henderson seemed precisely the sort of individual most apt to receive from neighbors and soldiers what he most desired, "general esteem."

Whatever his virtues, Henderson did not anticipate the problems that George Munro would create. Munro was a young Scot who worked as a clerk in a store operated by Henderson. Like Henderson, Munro wrote letters commenting on a society in the throes of insurgency. He did not like what he saw. In a chatty note mailed to the Scottish firm that supplied the store with consumer goods, Munro observed in passing, "There are so many d___d lies going about the country, and in the newspapers, that it is not worth while mentioning any of them." He and his employer must have had spirited conversations about the value of a free press. When his opinions became common knowledge in Bladenburg, Henderson's militiamen demanded Munro's immediate arrest, "unless some person would be answerable for his appearance before the Committee on the next day." Henderson was the obvious candidate. By hiring a suspicious outsider, he suddenly found himself on the defensive before the very people he drilled in arms.

Munro initially agreed to testify before the committee, but as the moment for his scheduled appearance arrived, the young man let fear get the best of him. He believed his life was in danger. And he may have been correct. The ordinary people of Bladenburg seemed intent on taking the law into their own hands. According to Henderson, "When I was sent for by the Committee & asked to bring Mr. Munro, I went, but about noon a great number of men, with loaded Arms, having come to Town, & declared their determination to Tar & Feather him, & having brought an old, lean, sore backed, dull horse, whereon to set him & drum him through the Town, whatever might be the sentiments of the Committee." The records of the proceedings indicate—in wonderfully expressive language—"the youth was struck with an agony of fear." Munro rode off as fast as he could, and even though townsmen gave chase, no one could catch him. It was rumored that he made a desperate attempt to board a ship bound for Scotland.

Not surprisingly, suspicion soon fell on Henderson. Perhaps he had warned the boy that a mob was on its way to punish him. People may have wondered whether Henderson secretly shared notions deemed subversive to the American cause. Whatever they may have thought, neighbors threatened to destroy Henderson's property. Jasper Wirt even contemplated pulling Henderson's entire house down. As popular anger increased, Henderson begged the committee for help. In turn, it asked the Maryland Convention, the provisional legislature, to rule on the matter.

This body made two interesting decisions. First, it ordered the committee for observation for Prince George's County "to determine and certify . . . whether the said Richard Henderson did collude with, or in any manner promote the said George Munro in his said Escape." Second, instead of condemning the people for behaving like vigilantes—in essence, undermining the authority of the extralegal committee that had taken control of the insurgency—the provisional authorities in Annapolis declared "this Convention [being] strongly impressed with an idea of the confusion and disorder which . . . must necessarily follow, from the people at large being collected and inflicting punishments before a cool and temperate investigation of the case; and consequently the injury which may be thereby done to the common cause of Liberty, confide, that the Virtue of the people, and their attachment to the liberties of America, will guard them against a commission of the Excess apprehended." This amounted to arguing that a people genuinely committed to liberty will constrain violence and champion due process simply because they are a people committed to liberty. One might pardon Munro for questioning such safeguards.

At the end of the day, Munro did not leave Maryland. At least not immediately. The Prince George's Committee examined him closely and voted unanimously that he was in fact "inimical to American liberty." For him, the possibility of reconciliation was not on offer. Henderson, however, fared much better. The investigation cleared him of "aiding, assisting, or even [being] privy to the said George Munro's escape." Moreover, after being dramatically reminded that the people had their own ideas about "the common cause of Liberty," the committee once again returned to the other business of revolution.[22]

The Baltimore County committee also had to deal with a person who had never been fully accepted into the community. James Christie, a Scots merchant living in America, became involved in a controversy that might be called the Affair of the Intercepted Letter. It was not unusual for committees in other colonies to examine the contents of private correspondence. In this case, Christie penned a particularly incriminating piece of evidence that the Maryland committee could not have ignored. According to the prosecution, Christie raised the possibility that he planned to organize and arm a group of counterinsurgents.

What initially sparked the investigation was a letter that Christie sent to his cousin in late February 1775. How exactly it reached the committee was never made clear, but since the addressee was a lieutenant colonel stationed with British forces on Antigua, its contents seemed particularly disturbing. In one passage Christie claimed, "We have some violent Fanatical Spirits among us, who do every thing in their power to run things to the utmost extremity, and they have gone so far that we moderate people are under a necessity of uniting for our own defense, after being threatened with expulsion, loss of life &c., for not acceding to what we deem treason and Rebellion." There was still time to save the day. If the Crown dispatched "a number of soldiers" to Baltimore, he was certain it "would keep them [the Baltimore militants] very quiet." It should be noted that the letter was the final straw. Earlier in the year, a rumor had circulated on the city streets that "he with some of his friends were to be made a publick example of."

The Baltimore committee immediately ordered Christie to appear. The members apparently had concluded that the letter provided sufficient evidence to convict, but since people wondered whether Christie had acted alone or had conspired with others, it pursued the investigation. Just who, the committee wanted to know, were these "moderate" individuals with whom Christie had spoken about uniting for "their [own] defense"? At first Christie argued that ill health kept him from attending the formal hearings. But he could not hide for long. A delegation of committee members who interviewed him at his house reported that he "declared there never was any association between him and his friends for the purpose alluded to, or for any other purpose." It was true that the people had made threats against him, but Christie dismissed these as bluster. After that, neither he nor his colleagues again mentioned the matter. However, Christie did point out that he penned the intercepted letter at the time when he felt most uneasy about his personal safety. In other words, what he told his cousin did not reflect his current political views. The committee, he thought, should take the context of the correspondence into account before it condemned him.

The committee dismissed Christie's defense. Mitigating circumstances could not possibly exonerate the accused for telling an officer of the British Army that the people of Baltimore were a bunch of traitors and rebels. It made no difference, of course, that these claims were probably not far off the mark. Even though the committee was an extra-legal body, it did not think a Scottish merchant should be allowed to label them militants. And it was not about to tolerate calls for an army of occupation in Maryland. The committee declared Christie "an enemy to this Country." All persons were advised "to break off all connection and intercourse with him." For good measure, the committee searched his house. To its disappointment, it found only "two Guns and a Pair of Pistols and no ammunition." However ill considered his words may have been, Christie obviously did not possess enough arms to challenge the new rulers.

As it became clear that Christie had no remaining options, he issued a confession and apology. It was too late. No one expressed the slightest desire to reincorporate an outspoken Scottish merchant into the community. Christie insisted that whatever he had said in the letter was a purely private matter. In any case, he asked rhetorically, why would a man who had a wife and family in Baltimore, who had built up a commercial enterprise, ever welcome an army of occupation? The intensity of the popular response to his letter made no sense to Christie. "In the most solemn manner," he explained, "your memorialist avers, that he never harbored a wish to introduce a military force into this Province for the purpose of enslaving the inhabitants therefore." The Maryland Convention heard an appeal, and then, adding to Christie's woes, it resolved that "the said James Christie be Expelled and banished [from] this Province forever, and that he depart this Province before the first Day of September."[23]

David Wardrobe seems to have been a quiet, self-effacing man who one day found himself called before the committee for Westmoreland County, Virginia. Like Christie, Wardrobe had written a private letter that in a curiously roundabout way became the basis for his prosecution as an enemy of his country. Wardrobe may strike us today as an entirely sympathetic figure. Like many Scots during this period, he migrated to America looking for employment opportunities. He had the good fortune to obtain a position as a schoolteacher in Virginia. The local vestry provided a room for his classes. But however positively the move to the colonies may have affected his pocketbook, it did not alter Wardrobe's political principles. Like Janet Schaw, he lamented the erosion of the Crown's authority in America. And on June 30, 1774, Wardrobe recorded his impressions in a long, reflective letter that if nothing else revealed him to have been an astute observer. He mailed the piece back to Glasgow, and since it represented a private exchange between two Scots, he probably did not give the matter another thought.

Wardrobe misjudged the political climate of his former home. People in Scotland were hungry for news from America. Somehow on August 18 his letter appeared in the pages of the Glasgow Journal, and as luck would have it, a ship originally carrying tobacco from Virginia for the European market carried the newspaper back to Westmoreland, where it came to the attention of the local committee of safety. Wardrobe reported that many Virginians supported the people of Boston. Indeed, the Coercive Acts had stirred up a hornet's nest of protest. On a trip to nearby Richmond County, Wardrobe had witnessed a vast concourse of ordinary people burn "an elegant effigy of Lord North." "I was particularly attentive," he explained, "to the countenances of the spectators, and was really pleased to see so very few express any outward signs of approbation on the occasion." The whole episode struck Wardrobe as somehow being artificial, as if the protest had been staged rather than the result of an outpouring of popular anger. Later, he encountered a similar event in Westmoreland. The meeting lacked spontaneity, and the schoolteacher wondered whether a few hotheads had manipulated the people.

It is hard to appreciate why this commentary aroused such hostility. After all, some cases in other localities had involved talk of hanging American rebels. But Wardrobe was an outsider. For the members of the Westmoreland County committee the letter in the Glasgow Journal required a swift and tough response. On November 8, 1774—about a month after Congress announced the Association—it interviewed Wardrobe, and he immediately confessed that he was indeed the author of the piece in question. In short order, the committee informed him that political reports of this character compromised the American cause. It had to seriously consider "the fatal consequences that will infallibly be derived to the dearest rights and just liberties of America if such enemies are suffered to proceed in this manner of giving false and mischievous accounts to Great Britain." Just what claims in the letter impressed the committee as dishonest were not made clear in the official records of the incident. Wardrobe's punishments included the loss of a room to teach students, a demand that parents take their children out of his school, and an order that he publish in the *Virginia Gazette* (Williamsburg) a full confession "expressing to the world his remorse." And if these actions were not sufficient, the committee ordered the Scottish teacher to appear before it a second time.

At a key moment in the proceedings, Wardrobe hesitated. Like others who found themselves in his situation, he feared what might happen as the community closed ranks against him. He ignored a summons from the committee. On a second occasion he did come forward, and, perhaps in the belief that an abject confession would save the day, he apologized to the members of the Westmoreland committee. Because he had committed a "gross" offense, he announced "most heartily and willingly, on my knees, [I] implore the forgiveness of the country for so ungrateful a return made for the advantages I have received from it, and the bread I have earned in it, and hope, from this contrition for my offense, I shall be at least admitted to subsist amongst the people I greatly esteem." He even urged the committee to send his statement to the editors of the *Virginia Gazette*.[24] As with others who did not have personal ties in the community, Wardrobe was not forgiven.

## *IV*

During the dark months of 1775, as colonial protest against imperial policy blossomed into a massive armed rising of the people against the British Army in New England, local committees of safety and observation increasingly functioned as a revolutionary government. To be sure, they still enforced the main articles of the Association and remained vigilant for expressions of ideological dissent within their communities. But the pressure of events forced committees to take on other responsibilities. This was a moment of great significance in the development of the American insurgency, for as protest became a genuine war of colonial liberation, the committees demanded more of ordinary people. Some of their activities may make us uncomfortable, for increasingly in the name of national unity—the American cause—they compromised individual rights that we now take for granted. They had no scruples, for example, about censoring the press and monitoring the flow of information in ways that effectively silenced those who opposed the insurgency. The committees circulated loyalty oaths, which made it hard for a person to maintain ideological neutrality. At some point these groups concluded that if a person did not openly endorse resistance, he or she must be an enemy. And finally, as the British military attacked American towns and as some loyalists contemplated recruiting colonists to fight for the king, the committees disarmed those who seemed to represent a threat.

The American press overwhelmingly supported resistance to the Crown. Editors in colonial towns not occupied by British troops regularly published resolutions passed by local committees of safety and observation. They also ran shrill, incendiary essays that put the king and Parliament in the worst possible light. But however many newspapers advocated militancy, a few took the opposite position. One produced in New York City and distributed to some thirty-six hundred subscribers throughout New Jersey and southern New England posed a real threat to mobilization. If James Rivington's *New York Gazetteer* had merely counseled a moderate response to imperial taxation and regulation, it would have probably amounted to little more than an annoyance. This was not, however, a struggling country paper. Rivington operated a large, highly professional shop, and he turned out not only an appealing journal but also several well-written, extremely persuasive pamphlets. Rivington's struggle to preserve his business reminds us that in a time of political turmoil, American insurgents abandoned the whole notion of a free press.

What we know of Rivington suggests that he was a talented editor whose penchant for gambling forced him to leave England for the colonies. After working in several different American cities, he successfully established himself in New York as a leading printer. Although he insisted that he favored a balanced coverage of the news, his critics accused him of blatant partisanship. Even more than the content of the newspaper, the pamphlets he sold encouraged obedience to the Crown. Because they were so well argued, they had the capacity to persuade the skeptics and moderates. As a Boston paper thundered, "For sometime past we have observed a number of dirty, malicious paragraphs and extracts of letters in Rivington's paper, published in New York, greatly misrepresenting the proceedings of this town." This journal assured readers, "It is now well known, and we have ground to assert, that these paragraphs, extracts, &c. are the offspring of a little junto of hireling prostitutes placed under the command of an unsavory, high flying, Jacobite priest, who sometime since came to this town in order, to settle a plan with his brethren here, for dividing the colonies."[25] How many people believed that Rivington was actually an agent for a Papist plot is impossible to discern, but the over-the-top response indicates how irritating the militants found his paper.

Perhaps because they did not trust their ability to counter the appeal of Rivington's publications, committees throughout the area moved to keep this material out of the hands of the people. Just as punishment for violating the Association had played itself out within a framework of confession and reconciliation, censorship often occurred within ritual performances involving the entire community. Crowds turned out to condemn texts they deemed too dangerous to read. On March 6, 1775, the committee of observation and inspection for Freehold, New Jersey, closely examined *Free Thoughts on the Resolves of the Congress* printed by Rivington. "Said pamphlet was . . . read," the members reported, "and upon mature deliberation unanimously declared to be a performance of the most pernicious and malignant tendency." The committee returned the essay "to the people," who already made clear their contempt for Rivington. They "immediately bestowed upon it a suit of tar and turkey-buzzard's feathers [which had been] plucked from the most stinking fowl in the creation." But the gathering decided that the buzzard treatment did not fully reflect the true odiousness of *Free Thoughts*. The loathsome pamphlet was then "in its gorgeous attire, nailed up firmly to the pillory-post, there to remain as a monument of the indignation of a free and loyal people against the author and vender of [the] publication." Indeed, the committee ordered the people of Freehold to treat Rivington's title as "a noxious" weed "incapable either of cultivation or improvement in this soil of freedom, and only fit to be transported."[26]

Although other communities showed less imagination in dealing with Rivington's work, the results of their actions effectively cut readers off from arguments critical of the insurgency. Public rituals enforcing censorship served to warn ordinary people that such titles were best avoided. In Essex County, New Jersey, for example, two pamphlets traced to the Rivington press were condemned "as containing many notorious falsehoods, evidently calculated to sow seeds of disunion among the good people of America." Local insurgents ordered the offending pages "committed to the flames, before the Court House." The destruction of these materials received "the universal approbation of a numerous concourse of people."[27] In Middlesex, New Jersey, committees of observation and inspection pledged to expose "those insidious scribblers . . . [who] persist in retailing the rotten, exploded, and ten thousand times confuted doctrines of a passive acquiescence in the measures of [the British] Government, however distempered and tyrannical."[28] Committees in nearby Morris County simply denounced Rivington as an enemy and promised, "we will discountenance any Post-Rider, Stage-Driver, or Carrier, who shall bring his Pamphlets or Papers into this County."[29]

The committee of observation in Elizabethtown, New Jersey, developed a different strategy. On December 19, 1774, the members not only canceled their subscriptions to the *New York Gazetteer* but also voted no longer to send paid announcements to the newspaper. They strongly urged local militants to find another journal for personal advertisements.[30] Committees in New York showed a similar determination in curtailing Rivington's ability to confuse public opinion. The committee of observation for New Windsor ordered a pamphlet bearing his imprint publicly burned, since it is "artfully designed to impose on the illiterate and unthinking part of mankind" political principles that, however "plausible," were judged to be "notoriously false."[31]

Committees occasionally felt compelled to state why they were cutting off the free flow of political information, which they, of course, regarded as dangerous propaganda. Even though they found themselves confronting a serious crisis and needed to arm and train soldiers, they put forward arguments explaining why the people had to be protected from Rivington's publications. In January 1775, for example, a committee in Newark, New Jersey, drew up a four-point statement in defense of censorship entitled "Queries and Resolves." It was not a balanced performance. The group had no sympathy for Rivington. That the committee members even bothered to explain their position is significant, since it suggests that some people in Newark really did still need persuading. The rhetorical exercise, therefore, took on the character of an official prosecution. The committee wondered "whether a Press, which weekly throws out pamphlets and other public pieces, replete with the most bitter invectives, scandalous and criminal reflections on the reputable body, the Continental Congress, and their constituents; and all, with a manifest design to blind the eyes of the less judicious; sow the seeds of faction and discord . . . prejudicing the honest, unthinking against their real interest; whether such a press is not inimical to the country where it is, and does not forfeit its support?" The committee did not explain exactly who fell into the category of the less judicious, but whatever its reasoning may have been, it clearly did not endorse the notion that the public on its own could be trusted to resist Rivington's appeals. The other arguments put forward by the Newark committee reiterated the claim that the loyalist editor was no more than a "Ministerial hireling," and to protect the community from his calumnies, it resolved "henceforth [to] take no more of his papers, pamphlets, or any other public performance of his press." The ordinary people were warned to follow the committee's example.[32]

The call for censorship did not sit well with the members of the Newport, Rhode Island, Committee for Inspection. They appreciated, of course, the threat that opposition propaganda presented to the insurgency. Still, in theory, they insisted on endorsing the freedom of the press. It was essential to maintaining a healthy "civil society." Without open access to information, they asked, how could a citizen begin to comprehend "the advancement of truth, science, morality and arts in general"? Even more important, they declared that the "ready communication of thoughts between subjects, and its consequential promotion of union among them" was the means by which "oppressive officers are shamed or intimidated into more honorable and just models of conducting affairs." Without doubt, it was the responsibility of "every friend of Civil Government to protect and preserve from violation that invaluable right, that noble pillar, and great support of Public Liberty . . . so long as it shall be employed in promoting those beneficial purposes."

And there was the rub. During a political crisis, the free press functioned properly only so long as it supported fundamental political values. Rivington compromised open communication by publishing what the militants defined as lies. Why he engaged in such dishonest journalism was clear enough to the members of the Newport committee. The New York editor had allowed greed and arrogance to pervert honest reporting. The record spoke for itself. Rivington "hath, for a long time, in the dirty *Gazetteer*, and in pamphlets, if possible still more dirty, uniformly persist[ed] in publishing every falsehood which his own wicked imagination or the imaginations of others of the same stamp . . . could suggest and fabricate, that had a tendency to spread jealousies, fear, discord, and disunion through this country." The committee recommended to all people who subscribed to Rivington's newspaper "immediately to drop the same." What one read became a measure of loyalty to the American cause. It was without a sense of irony that the committee voted to announce the condemnation of Rivington's journal in "the next *Newport Mercury*," a publication that American insurgents could trust.[33]

Rivington mounted a spirited defense of the freedom of the press. His rhetoric drew upon traditional liberal theories of political right. One can sense his bewilderment as community after community prohibited the distribution of his newspaper. Sometime in May 1775 he formally appealed to the Continental Congress for protection from those who sought to close down his press. The men who served in that body, he reasoned, were without question "gentlemen of eminent rank and distinction." Unlike the ordinary people who endangered his life and property, the members of Congress possessed "enlarged and liberal sentiments." Such attributes surely made them aware that "as a printer," Rivington had "always been conformable to the ideas which he entertained of English liberty, warranted by the practice of all printers in Great Britain and Ireland, for a century past, under every administration; authorized, as he conceives, by the laws of England, and countenanced by the declarations of the late Congress." Anyone who read the pages of his journal, Rivington argued, would immediately see that he had tried to promote an open and fair debate about the most sensitive political issues of the day. And yet the reward for balanced discussion was hostility. To preserve his business, he had even issued a public apology and promised that he would in the future avoid "giving any further offense." Rivington added a purely pragmatic argument as well. He pointed out that he employed sixteen workmen "at near one thousand pounds annually." A free press was obviously good for a struggling colonial economy.[34]

Unhappily for Rivington, American gentlemen of rank and distinction did not control the revolution on the ground. The local committees had branded him an enemy of the people. There was no clearing his name. In late November 1775 a party of about one hundred "light horse from Connecticut" rode into New York City and on their own authority took up positions around Rivington's shop. They affixed bayonets and posted a guard at each door. At that moment a small group of the insurgents stormed the building. They demanded that the workers surrender all the type. No one resisted, and within minutes the militants had packed the lead into bags. They then "destroyed the whole apparatus of the press." By this time the Connecticut troops had attracted the attention of a crowd of more than fifteen hundred people. They "signified their approbation by three huzzas." The horsemen galloped toward home, carrying "their booty." According to a newspaper report, throughout their visit to New York City they offered not the slightest "insult on any of the inhabitants."[35]

By the middle of 1775, local committees devised yet another way to force opponents into the open. They drafted oaths, which they then presented to community inhabitants for signature. In New Hampshire every inhabitant had to promise to uphold the Association. The number of people coming forward was impressive.[36] Of course, failure to cooperate amounted to a declaration that one supported king and Parliament and thus stood exposed as an enemy to the country. We must remind ourselves that the country deserving allegiance existed only in the hopes and the imaginations of countless insurgents from Portsmouth to Savannah. The wording of surviving loyalty oaths reveals how much significance committees placed on reaffirming a strong sense of national identity. In other words, while these groups enforced the insurgency among immediate friends and neighbors—on the ground, as it were—they drew inspiration and conviction from a larger political cause of which they were only parts.

The committee for inspection for the town of Fairfield, Connecticut, provided a particularly good example of how a local group mobilized popular resistance through an appeal to a broader movement of political liberation. On August 15, 1775, it directed the inhabitants of the community to pledge their support for the Association. Signatures were required. The exercise was designed "to show that they are friends to the liberties and privileges of their Country, and that the enemies of it may be known." The wording of the Fairfield oath invited ordinary people of the town to ratify the proposition that "the British Administration have long been plotting against the liberties of America, and finally stept [*sic*] forth and openly avowed their wicked system, and are now pursuing measures, which, if successful, will terminate in the total destruction of American liberty." After bloody battles had taken place in Massachusetts, it was clear that halting the tide of tyranny required the unqualified support of all people, not only in opposing "force to force" but also in defending rights that all Americans claim "as men, Christians, and freemen." By coming forward, the inhabitants of Fairfield demonstrated that they did indeed "agree and associate with each other, and with all friends of liberty throughout this land." The very act of signing this pledge separated militants from loyalists, friends from enemies. But it did more. It defined how the insurgents defined true Americans; it placed personal sacrifice—abstract notions of suffering for a political cause—within a larger national context. The Fairfield committee acted out of necessity. The towns of western Connecticut witnessed the development of a determined counterinsurgency that unsettled the region throughout the entire war. But on August 15 the prospects for the American militants seemed promising. Eight hundred and fifty-five males over the age of sixteen took the pledge. Some seventy others refused. There was no turning back once the lines of political identity had been drawn.[37]

In Maryland the process of formally proclaiming allegiance to the insurgency followed a similar course. In July 1775, committees of observation throughout the colony required all freemen to sign a pledge specifically supporting armed resistance against Great Britain. In a statement that came close to proclaiming independence, the Marylanders chronicled how king and Parliament had systematically assaulted American liberty, provocations so serious that they now justified repelling "force by force." Legitimization of organized violence against the imperial state was a major step in the evolution of the American insurgency. The freemen of Maryland—like so many other ordinary Americans from New Hampshire to Georgia—swore to "unite and associate as one band, and firmly and solemnly engage and pledge ourselves to each other, and to America, that we will, to the utmost of our power, promote and support the present opposition." The possibility that the people might not restrain their passions remained a real threat. Insurgency could easily lapse into anarchy and present as great a menace to liberty as did despotism. To avoid such a result at a time when "the energy of Government may be greatly impaired," the Maryland committees of observation called upon militants to "unite, associate and solemnly engage in maintenance of good order and the public peace, to support the civil power in the due execution of the laws, so far as may be consistent with the present plan of opposition."[38]

To identify a person as an enemy did little good, of course, if he then took up arms against the insurgents. The committees recognized — especially after the battles of Lexington and Concord—that good order and security depended on disarming Americans who refused to support the resistance. In May 1775 the Provincial Congress of Massachusetts explained to the members of the various local colonial committees the need to act swiftly. Even as American soldiers prepared to take on General Gage's troops in Boston, a few people who had "discovered themselves to be enemies to the rights of mankind and the interests of America" remained at large. Prudence demanded that these troublesome individuals not be allowed to form what today we might call guerrilla units. As the Provincial Congress stated, the committees should carefully examine "the principles and conduct of such suspected persons; and that they cause all such to be disarmed, who do not give them full and ample assurances, in which they can with safety confide, of their readiness to join their countrymen on all occasions in defense of the rights and liberties of America."[39] In Massachusetts the local committees did as they had been instructed. In Worcester, "the Tories in this town were notified to appear with their arms and ammunition." The loyalists obeyed. "They accordingly appeared," the Worcester militants reported, "and after surrendering their arms to the Committee of Correspondence, and being strictly ordered not to leave the town or to meet together, without a permit, were dismissed."[40]

And that was that. No one advocated harsh physical punishment; no moves were made to throw the enemies of America into prison. At a later time, as the war for independence dragged on and as Tories formed military companies, these people suffered serious penalties, including the loss of property and incarceration. When resistance to the empire began, however, violence and terror of this sort were rare. It is true that the country's enemies found it hard to publish their opinions in the press. They refused to sign documents in support of the Association. They surrendered their weapons. But even after the British Army had killed ordinary American farmers such as Isaac Davis, no one advocated— especially not the men who served on the local committees—the wholesale slaughter of those who had abetted "the cursed plans of a tyrannical ruler and an abandoned ministry."[41] Considering the atrocities that have occurred in other revolutions over the last two centuries, we might wonder at such restraint.

# NINE

# An Appeal to Heaven:
# Religion and Rights

Ordinary Americans understood why they were fighting. They put forward a compelling justification for insurgency. The personal risks involved in organizing resistance to Great Britain were great, and as protest turned violent, as it rapidly did after mid-1775, the people were able to explain quite clearly why it was necessary for them to sacrifice for the country's cause. And yet the ideas that energized popular resistance before independence have not received much attention. Instead, we are encouraged to regard well-known figures such as John Adams and Thomas Jefferson as surrogates for the ordinary men and women who participated in the insurgency. From this top-down perspective, it becomes an article of faith that whatever the leading planters and lawyers wrote about the abuse of power reflected the core beliefs of the general political culture.

This assumption is unwarranted. There is no question that insurgents—the men who actually served on committees of safety and who turned out in huge numbers following the attack on Lexington, for example—shared many notions about rights and liberty with privileged Americans who read widely in classical history and British political theory. But the people's ideas were neither identical to those encountered in the learned pamphlets nor watered-down versions of the principles found in those formal productions.

Rather, ordinary Americans stressed distinct elements within a shared bundle of ideas. Like different organists playing a familiar piece of music, they pulled particular stops that resonated convincingly within the realm of their own experience. This meant that on the community level, they found ways to channel their own anger through a rhetoric that spoke to a common cause. And unlike the more acclaimed figures of the period, they often expressed their aspirations within a self-consciously religious framework.[1] This bundle of popular assumptions and beliefs explained to the people the personal sacrifice they had to make. It translated abstract principles into action.

The Reverend Zabdiel Adams understood what was at stake. In early January 1775—more than eighteen months before the signing of the Declaration of Independence—he told the members of a militia company in Lunenburg, Massachusetts, "We fervently pray, that you may never be called . . . to fight with, or shed the blood of British soldiers, *who are bone of our bone, and flesh of our flesh.*" But the prospects were dark. If "our invaluable liberties cannot be preserved, but by the sword, you will not shrink from danger, nor desert the cause, but be of good courage and play the men valiantly for your people, and the cities of your God." Should they die, Adams assured them, "you will die in the bed of your honor."[2]

The ideas that gave meaning to the American insurgency possess a simple elegance. The central element in popular political thought was a set of rights that God gave every man and woman long before they established civil government. These rights were universal; every human being could claim them. But rights carried responsibilities. God expected the people to preserve their rights. However burdensome this duty may have been in theory, it served to empower ordinary people in the contest against tyranny. As vigilant defenders of rights, they became judges of those who held authority, and in the imagined compact that bound rulers to subjects, it was the subjects who determined whether their magistrates were in fact working for the common good.

In general terms, the Americans were all children of the great seventeenth-century philosopher John Locke. But one should not exaggerate his influence. Many Americans had never read Locke's work; quite a few would not have even recognized his name. They are probably best described as popular Lockeans. They subscribed to his rights-based philosophy without much caring about intellectual genealogies. We encounter this perspective on state power in humble statements. Early in 1773 the inhabitants of Hubbardston, a small farming community in Massachusetts, worked out for themselves the ligaments of this system of thought. In the language of the folk, they announced, "We are of opinion that Rulers first Derive their Power from the Ruled by Certain Laws and Rules agreed upon by Ruler and Ruled, and when a Ruler Breaks over Such Laws and Rules as agreed to by Ruler and Ruled, and makes new ones that then the Ruled have a Right to Refuse Such new Laws and that the Ruled have a right to Judge for themselves when Rulers Transgress."[3]

We should remember as we reconstruct insurgent beliefs that the goal is not to understand better arguments for national independence or, still less, the rationale for adopting a republican form of government. Those issues came to the fore at a later date. The major challenge in 1775 was persuading ordinary people of the legitimacy of using violence against a constitutional government that no longer protected their rights. The most pressing decision in the lives of such men as Isaac Davis and Samuel Thompson turned on precisely this issue. How much, they asked, should a God-fearing person endure before taking up arms against the state?

For the Reverend John Cleaveland, the minister in the small village of Chebacco, Massachusetts, the moment came in the days following the British attack on Lexington and Concord. Writing in a local journal, Cleaveland declared, "King George the third adieu! No more shall we cry to you for protection! No more shall we bleed in defense of your person, — your breach of covenant! Your violation of faith! Your turning a deaf ear to our cries for justice, for covenanted protection and salvation from the oppressive, tyrannical and bloody measures of the British parliament, and putting a sanction upon all their measures to enslave and butcher us, have DISSOLVED OUR ALLEGIANCE to your crown and government!"[4]

# I

A curious incident that occurred on or about six o'clock on the morning of July 18, 1775, reveals the centrality of rights thinking in justifying insurgency against the British Empire. The event opens a window for us onto the popular political culture of the day. Only a few weeks earlier, militia units—one of them Isaac Davis's from Acton—had engaged British regulars at Lexington and Concord, and then later at Bunker Hill. In the intoxicating wake of these encounters, colonial troops from communities throughout New England rushed to the suburbs of Boston. As we have seen, Matthew Patten's son and his friends marched from New Hampshire to participate in the action. George Washington had not yet arrived to take command of the American forces; a formal declaration of independence would not be issued for almost a year.

During those exhilarating days when protest turned to armed resistance, rhetoric to violence, the main units of the Continental Line serving under General Israel Putnam—the man who rushed from Connecticut in 1774 to revenge the destruction of Boston—unfurled for the first time the standard they intended to carry into battle. The flag possessed immense significance for the insurgents, who before this time had trained within their own communities. It was emblematic of a larger cause; it provided a symbolic awareness of American unity.

Several accounts of the dawn ceremony survive. The fullest explained that the largely untested colonial soldiers assembled "on Prospect-Hill, when the Declaration of the Continental Congress [calling on Americans to take up arms] was read; after which an animated and pathetic [expressing tenderness] Address to the Army was made by the Rev. Mr. Leonard, Chaplain to General Putnam's Regiment, and succeeded by a pertinent Prayer."[5] Leonard begged the Lord to preserve the "people of this land . . . [who] have been reduced to the dreadful alternative of submitting to arbitrary laws and despotic government; or taking up arms in defense of those rights and privileges, which thou, in thy goodness, hast conferred upon them as men and as Christians."[6]

At that moment Putnam gave a prearranged signal. "The whole Army shouted their loud Amen by three Cheers, immediately upon which a Cannon was fired from the Fort, and the Standard lately sent to General Putnam was exhibited [,] flourishing in the Air, bearing . . . this Motto, 'AN APPEAL TO HEAVEN.'"[7] A loyalist spy confirmed the news. He reported to General Thomas Gage in Boston that "our people [have] got a famous New large Standard," and when it was raised, "all of us huzzahed at once, then the Indeans [sic] gave the war hoop and to conclud[e], of[f] went [the] Cannon," a grand ceremony "that was worth you seeing."[8]

If Gage had in fact ventured outside the occupied city that July morning, he would have observed a single pine tree framed against a white background. Underneath the evergreen ran the words APPEAL TO HEAVEN. The inclusion of the tree in the design of the flag poses no mystery. It had a long, iconic history in New England. As a symbol of the region, the tree made its first appearance on coins minted in Massachusetts in the mid-seventeenth century. The three-word phrase, however, raises more complex issues. The insurgents surely hoped that the Lord would protect them in battle, but that was not all they were doing. Confronting General Gage's army, they appealed to God to bless the entire insurgency.

About the source of the soldiers' chosen motto, there can be little doubt. Ordinary Americans had encountered the phrase in the pages of John Locke's *Second Treatise*, where "Appeal to Heaven" appears numerous times.[9] When Locke originally penned these words on the eve of England's Glorious Revolution in 1688, he associated them specifically with the biblical story of Jephthah in the eleventh chapter of Judges. When the Israelites begged Jephthah, "a mighty warrior," to take up their cause against the Ammonites, he in turn asked God to decide the controversy. In other words, he made an appeal to heaven. "Let the LORD, who is judge, decide today for the Israelites or for the Ammonites."

Locke was skating on thin ice. References to the Old Testament hardly disguised the radical implications of his argument, the fact of which he was uncomfortably aware.[10] At a moment when his own countrymen had grown weary of Stuart tyranny, Locke counseled that in extreme cases, when a ruler forfeited the trust of the people and those people seeking justice found that the very judges entrusted to hear their cause had compromised their integrity by siding with the tyrant, the people had a right to take their political grievance to the Lord. Like Jephthah, they could make an appeal to heaven.

In Locke's interpretation of the biblical story the people had no assurance that God would in fact favor them over their enemies. He might even brand them rebels against lawful authority. In the penultimate paragraph of the final chapter of the *Second Treatise*, entitled significantly "Dissolution of Government," Locke explains the insurgents' dilemma:

If a Controversie arise betwixt a Prince and some of the People, in a matter where the Law is silent, or doubtful, and the thing be of great Consequence, I should think the proper *Umpire*, in such a Case, should be the Body of the *People*. For in Cases where the Prince hath a Trust reposed in him, and is dispensed from the common ordinary Rules of the Law; there, if any Men find themselves aggrieved, and Think the Prince acts contrary to, or beyond that Trust, who so proper to *Judge* as the Body of the *People* . . . how far they meant it should extend? But if the Prince, or whoever they be in the Administration, decline that way of Determination, the Appeal then lies no where but to Heaven.[11]

Much of what Locke had to say about political rights in the *Second Treatise* pertains to individuals, but in this crucial section he specifically described the appeal as an act of desperation by an entire community, which, after much suffering and deliberation, feels itself betrayed by rulers who claim constitutional authority. It is hard to imagine who during the dark days of mid-1775 would not have made a direct connection between Locke's counsel and the Americans' controversy—a thing obviously of "great Consequence"—with Great Britain. The language echoed out through the Massachusetts countryside, even to the smallest communities such as Hubbardston.

The Continental soldiers who justified their own political resistance through an "Appeal to Heaven" did not have to rummage through musty libraries to read Locke's words. Nor did they have to rely on ministers such as the Reverend Leonard or educated lawyers to tell them what the seventeenth-century theorist had written. A popular edition of the *Second Treatise* had just been issued by a Boston publisher who, in a newspaper announcement, assured Americans, "Perhaps there never was a Time since the Discovery of this new World, when the People of all Ranks every where show'd so eager a Spirit of Inquiry into the Nature of their Rights and Privileges, as at this Day." The printer declared that in these troubled times "it has therefore been judged very seasonable and proper to put it in the Power of every free Man on this Continent to furnish himself at so easy a Rate with the noble Essay just now republished."

During much of the eighteenth century, Americans had not paid much attention to Locke's writing, especially not to his theory of government.[12] But after 1773 the imperial crisis thrust his work into the center of colonial political thought. The confrontation with traditional constitutional authority gave Locke new relevance; better than other sources then available to the people, he explained why in the name of fundamental rights they must resist. It was in this climate that the advertisement for the *Second Treatise* guaranteed that "this Essay alone, well studied and attended to, will give to every intelligent Reader a better View of the Rights of Men and of Englishmen." Women as well as men were invited to study Locke's arguments. The American printer also noted that he completely dropped Locke's *First Treatise*, a market decision that not only lowered the price of the new popular edition but also saved "all Lovers of Liberty" the nuisance of having to slog their way through a "prolix Confutation of [Sir Robert] Filmer and his Disciples, few of which are yet to be found in this Country."[13]

To comprehend the significance of an appeal to heaven, however, one did not have to read the *Second Treatise*. Several years earlier the members of the Massachusetts House of Representatives had engaged in a hot debate with the colony's lieutenant governor about the implications of Locke's political theories for the doctrine of parliamentary sovereignty. The lieutenant governor happened to be Thomas Hutchinson, and there can be no doubt that when the elected representatives of the people spoke about rights, they lectured Hutchinson on the writings of "the great Mr. Locke." In an exchange followed closely throughout the colony, they quoted from the *Second Treatise*, arguing that in certain constitutional disputes between the people and their rulers, "the people have no other remedy . . . but to appeal to heaven."[14]

British contemporaries were perhaps the first to point out how aggressively Americans mouthed notions about rights. Dean Josiah Tucker, an English religious figure who wrote thoughtfully about the imperial economy, found it almost impossible to take the colonists seriously in this regard, and in *The Respective Pleas and Arguments of the Mother Country, and of the Colonies, Distinctly Set Forth*, published in 1775, he weighed the solid "Facts and Precedents" advanced by the leaders of Parliament against the Americans' airy rhetoric about "what they call immutable Truths—the abstract Reasonings, and the eternal

Fitness of Things—and in short to such Rights of Human Nature which they suppose to be unalienable and indefeasible." Even at this early date, Tucker labeled the colonists "the Disciples of Mr. Locke," a description that suggested they—like the Irish of an earlier generation—had succumbed to a kind of ideological madness. To this characterization, Tucker's spirited adversary Richard Price responded, "Glorious title!"

In 1782 Tucker was still grumbling about the fuzzy-thinking Americans, and in a pamphlet entitled *Cui Bono?* he imagined what would happen should the provincial insurgents actually emerge from the war victorious. "When that happy Day should come," the dean observed with bitter sarcasm, "all Grievances, and all Complaints would cease for ever. The People of *America* were to be blessed with a *Lockean* Government, the only just one, the only free one upon Earth." Other English writers took up the chorus, announcing as early as 1775 that the colonists had foolishly appointed Locke "their political Apostle" and "their professed Director." John Roebuck, a London pamphleteer, added more soberly in 1776 that the "present revolt has arisen solely from speculative notions" about natural rights.[15]

One can appreciate why English commentators such as Tucker might have greeted the colonists' rights talk as an intellectual muddle.[16] Yet his criticism missed a key point about the relation between ideas and mobilization. The ordinary Americans whom he found so objectionable were advancing a positive case for the defense of their own God-given rights. Although their arguments may have lacked sophistication, they successfully translated abstract concepts about rights into a persuasive justification for resistance and sacrifice. It is within this popular context that we should try to understand why a writer in the *Pennsylvania Packet* would announce on April 19, 1775, as a matter of fact, "The venerable name of LOCKE carries so much weight and authority, that on every subject relative to politics or government, his arguments seem irresistibly persuasive."[17] Such claims certainly made sense to the young American soldiers who volunteered for the Continental Army in Massachusetts in April 1775. Anticipating that they might soon participate in real combat, they took an oath to protect "the free exercise of all those civil and religious rights and liberties, for which many of our forefathers fought, bled, and died."[18]

## II

Popular political thought in insurgent America began with an imagined contract. At some moment long before recorded history, people had lived in a state of nature. Commentators disagreed about whether living in such a society had been a pleasant experience. To be sure, everyone possessed valuable rights, mostly associated with the free possession of property. In the state of nature, people could do pretty much as they pleased. That was the problem. Freedom without constraint promoted a kind of thuggery. The strong preyed on their weaker neighbors and seized property to which they had no claim other than the irresponsible exercise of physical power. As the Reverend Samuel Williams explained in 1775, the state of nature gave license to "lawless, desperate, and designing men, [who] joined together for the purposes of fraud, rapine, and oppression."[19]

However nasty such a society might have been in the natural state, ordinary people refused to give it up without powerful assurance that the establishment of government and society would not compromise their God-given rights to property. In order to secure fundamental rights from violent assault, they transferred to rulers the responsibility to judge and punish those who threatened the peace of civil society. According to the Reverend Samuel Lockwood, a Connecticut minister, "no people, who have tasted the sweets of liberty and enjoyed the happiness of freedom" would ever subject themselves to a ruler "but from a rational prospect of benefit to the whole, and to each individual." The goal of government was "not to loose, but . . . to secure and perpetuate their personal liberties and properties, unmolested; as well as to enjoy the pleasures of social life, to be found in society only."[20] In these terms, therefore, good government was a rational bargain; it protected basic rights without encroaching on the inviolability of property.

About the ultimate source of their rights, the people had no doubts. God gave them to men and women; rights were a fundamental aspect of the human condition. This religious element in popular political thought provided an irrefutable foundation for rights claims. The celebrated leaders of the day—such men as John Adams and George Washington—tended to place less emphasis on the spiritual essence of rights talk than did ordinary Americans. Which is precisely why it is important to keep this aspect of popular thinking in mind: religious conviction infused arguments about rights with an energy not often encountered in more academic writings. In this political culture, one writer affirmed what the readers of the *Connecticut Courant* (May 1775) already believed. "The rights of mankind," he observed, "viz. to personal security, liberty, and private property, are derived from the great first cause—are holden by a divine tenure, the great Charter of him that made us, and are natural to our very existence."[21] The reflexive connection that ordinary people made between God and rights helps explain why they frequently equated the defense of rights and liberties with moral behavior. It seemed a matter of common sense that those who cherished their political rights would also be good Christians.[22]

On the popular level, insistence on the sanctity of rights seldom generated much precision about exactly what those rights were. At the time, no one seems to have seen a need to list various rights in order of importance. Such an ordering of rights would have to wait until Americans passed a formal Bill of Rights. For the people caught up in the insurgency, rights talk generally focused on property. Their arguments possessed both a negative and positive aspect. In the state of nature, individuals had a positive right to the property they had developed through their own labor. By the same token, no one else had a right to seize the property of another person. Moreover, when people entered a contract to form government, they did not give up their original right to property. As the Reverend Foster told his parishioners, a "man and his family, when considered with reference to mankind, have an absolute and individual right to, and property in, all they have earned by their labors, industry and frugality."[23] Ordinary Americans had no doubt that Foster was correct. In local assemblies people who had had no exposure to formal political philosophy complained bitterly about parliamentary taxation not because the sums involved threatened them with financial hardship, but because taking property without due process represented a clear violation of their God-given rights. It was wrong; it was theft. And if ordinary people did not stand up for what was their own, they lost their liberty and became slaves.

In town meetings, abstract ideas about property rights fueled genuine passion, even anger. They legitimated resistance. In hardscrabble communities such as Gorham, Massachusetts (Maine), for example, inhabitants resolved early in 1774 "that our small possessions, dearly purchased by the hand of labor, and the industry of ourselves, and our dear ancestors, with the loss of many lives, by a barbarous and cruel enemy, are, by the laws of God, nature and the British Constitution, *our own*, exclusive of any other claim under heaven." When a government violated private property, it engaged in "State robbery." As the residents of Gorham concluded, "the Parliament of Great Britain have no more right to take money from us without our consent than they have to take money . . . from the inhabitants of France or Spain."[24] A town meeting in Newport, Rhode Island, agreed. It declared in no uncertain terms "that the disposal of their own property is the inherent right of freemen; that there can be no property in that which another can, of right, take from us, without our consent."[25]

The notion that God expected the people to resist tyrants had a very long history. In this uncertain political environment, however, the idea sparked a new sense of empowerment, an exhilarating sense of self-confidence. As the inhabitants of Pittsfield, a small community in far western Massachusetts, announced early in 1776, "We beg leave . . . to represent that we have always been persuaded that the people are the fountain of power."[26] This was not a call for popular democracy. What the Pittsfield farmers meant was that the people had an obligation to judge for themselves when government abused their rights. The imperial crisis gave them warrant to scrutinize policies and to voice fears that those in authority no longer served the interests of the people. In February 1776 the provisional government of Massachusetts reminded a population already at war with Great Britain, "The happiness of the people is the sole end of government." It followed therefore that "the consent of the people is the only foundation of it, in reason, morality, and the natural fitness of things." Unless it enjoyed popular assent, the exercise of power yielded only "injustice, usurpation and tyranny." The provisional government told the insurgents what they already knew: "It is a maxim that in every government, there must exist somewhere, a supreme, sovereign, absolute, and uncontrollable power: But this power resides always in the body of the people; and it never was, or can be delegated to one man, or a few; the great Creator having never given to men a right to vest others with authority over them, unlimited either in duration or degree."[27]

Possession of fundamental rights—even the right to hold property—made no sense to insurgent Americans in the absence of other people. As they repeatedly declared, man is a sociable animal. It was in his nature to reach out to others to form families, communities, and associations held together by a sense of mutual obligation. Hermits deserved no respect precisely because their isolation cut them off from proper social exchange. According to the Reverend Samuel Lockwood, God made man "a sociable creature, capable of the delights and advantages of social life; to be enjoyed in pursuing his own good, with that of others at the same time; consequently, his happiness in degree must consist, in the exercise of those social virtues essential to his nature."[28] Other commentators praised "the social state" while condemning the "solitary state."[29] Within popular political thought, insistence on cooperation meant that revolutionary rights theory avoided the kind of aggressive, often selfish individualism that modern critics sometimes associate with liberalism.[30] Living in society not only made men and women more fully human, it also provided them with an opportunity to work together to fulfill God's expectations.

Belief in man's natural sociability led logically to the conclusion that private grievances had no legitimacy in organized protest. Individual interests or the demands of a noisy faction served only to fragment communities, to spawn civil war, and, when pushed to excess, to invite anarchy. The Reverend John Zubly made precisely this point at the opening of the Georgia Provisional Congress in July 1775. "There was a time when there was no King in Israel, and every man did what was good in his own eyes," he noted. "The consequence was a civil war in the nation, issuing in the ruin of one of the tribes, and a considerable loss to all the rest."[31]

However much the loyalists protested that popular resistance to Great Britain had degenerated into mob action and mindless violence, the insurgents could always respond that they were looking out for the common good, not the self-serving interests of a small body of troublemakers. They specifically rejected the notion that a group of people were justified in overthrowing a ruler simply because they did not like him or because he supported policies that made some subjects unhappy. A challenge to constitutional government based on no more than self-interest could never win God's approval. Indeed, according to the Reverend Nathaniel Niles, "The true spirit of a mob consists in unconstitutional violence, done with a design to bring about some private end."[32]

In July 1774 the Reverend Nathan Fiske expanded on this idea before a congregation in Massachusetts: "When people oppose the authority of their rulers, it is generally called insurrection and rebellion. And when a mob assumes the government into their own hands, they are in danger of committing such violence and outrage as are many degrees beyond the guilt and mischief of bare opposition." For Fiske, resisting "arbitrary rulers" was one thing, while engaging in "lawless riots" that had the capacity to become "tyrannical, imperious, and oppressive" was quite another.[33] This is an important point. American insurgents provide no comfort to those in our own time who claim that a single cause or narrow agenda justifies armed violence against neighbors or the state. Those who resisted the British Empire spoke for the common good; they reached out to distant strangers, creating broad political solidarities. They would have regarded those who are prepared to employ violence in the name of a particular vision of the truth not only as self-serving but also as threats to the larger goals of a just society.

During the anxious months before publication of the Declaration of Independence, the most pressing challenge for unhappy Americans was deciding precisely when in fact a ruler had gone too far. As the Reverend Peter Whitney explained, "In these cases the people must be judge of the good or ill conduct of their rulers; to the people they are accountable."[34] Resistance was a serious undertaking. Within the popular political culture, each person had an obligation to define the tipping point that separated incompetence from despotism, frivolous complaint from a lawful appeal to heaven. Insurgents walked a fine line. A mistaken judgment on their part might encourage anarchy. By the same token, accommodating a genuinely corrupt regime threatened the security of the people's fundamental rights.

The responsibility for making a correct judgment fell to ordinary Americans. As one minister informed the members of the Georgia Provincial Congress, "When a people think themselves oppressed and in danger, nothing can be more natural than that they should inquire into the real state of things, trace their grievances to their source, and endeavor to apply the remedies which are most likely to procure relief."[35]

The Reverend Andrew Eliot, a respected New England minister, laid out the challenge as clearly as did any of his contemporaries: "It is exceedingly difficult to determine exactly where submission ends, and resistance may lawfully take place, so as to leave no room for men of bad minds unreasonably to oppose government, and destroy the peace of society."[36]

In small communities throughout America, insurgents carefully weighed the evidence of misrule, looking for signs that British authorities had in fact systematically and irrevocably betrayed fundamental rights. They had some help in this matter. Educated pamphleteers who drew upon the lessons of more than a century of English history provided them with a list of symptoms that indicated when tyranny was on the rise. According to this literature, one sounded the alarm if the king and his counselors tried to censor the free press, raised standing armies, or incurred huge national debts. These actions informed vigilant subjects that the famed balanced constitution was in grave danger.

How much attention ordinary people paid to these writings is not clear. They generally assessed the danger to their rights in less historical, often more religious language, which while lacking specificity had the advantage of provoking a highly passionate response. The Reverend Eliot advised, for example, "where rulers pervert their power to tyrannical purposes; when they evidently encroach on natural and constitutional rights; when they trample on those laws which were made to limit the regal power, and defend the people, submission, if it can be avoided, is so far from being a duty, that it is a crime . . . It is an offense against God, who is good to all, and who has appointed government for the welfare and happiness, and not for the destruction of his creatures."[37]

Ministers such as Eliot laid out for insurgents a practical justification for resistance. To be sure, ordinary people should always remember that governments can and should do things that may be unpopular. They have authority to levy taxes, raise troops, and enforce regulatory policies. Such matters may be annoying, but they are not in themselves legitimate causes for armed rebellion. At issue, therefore, was not the actual burden of supporting government, but rather the conviction based on observation that it had imposed taxes and raised troops through procedures that any reasonable person would describe as arbitrary. One did not have to review the long and contentious history of English liberty to appreciate when an allegedly lawful government started acting in an unlawful way. People could interpret the political evidence for themselves. Parliament endorsed the Coercive Acts as a punishment; the army of occupation in Boston had no interest in preserving basic rights. Personal experience revealed the tipping point. "When punishments are mediated and inflicted to gratify revenge, or merely to show power and superiority; or when they greatly exceed the demerit of the crime; or involve a whole community in distress for the offenses of a few; when acts are made and continued, yea, and enforced by military power, which, in general, are considered as unconstitutional and grievous; all these are instances of oppression."[38]

Within a political culture so profoundly influenced by religion, it seemed logical to assume that arbitrary rulers would most likely be men lacking righteousness. As the Reverend Nathan Fiske observed, "If a king does not rule in righteousness, his subjects will, in many instances, have their rights and liberties, and perhaps their lives endangered, if not destroyed."[39] In 1774 the Reverend Samuel Lockwood preached a similar message in Connecticut. "No one can pretend that civil government, as an ordinance of GOD, was ever designed to advance men to seats of dignity and rule, to plume themselves with the gilded feathers of state; in order to indulge sloth—luxury—and avarice, at publick expense, much less wantonly to exercise the power with which they are invested, in acting the tyrant. Nor yet, to improve fawning dependents and parricides, to oppress the subjects with unconstitutional decrees, and unrighteous measures, which they will greedily execute, for a low title, and a piece of bread. *Surely no.*"[40]

This rhetoric—at least before 1776—rarely condemned monarchy as a form of government. It was still possible for ordinary colonists to imagine righteous kings who ruled in the fear of God and who saw arbitrary acts as an assault on the people's rights. Almost no one who participated in resistance on the ground advocated the creation of a new republic. But within a theoretical framework in which the people claimed the right to judge the ruler's fitness to rule—and in which despotic and unrighteous acts by a king eroded his legitimacy—it did not take much to persuade Americans that monarchy itself worked against the true interests of the people. As a writer in the *Norwich Packet* (Connecticut) observed, "Whenever any man declares that Englishmen have no other title to their liberty than the will of the Prince, he may be said most severely to touch the people, and deserves to be severely reproved for his impudence. Blessed be God, we do not hold our liberties by the precarious tenor of any man's will. They are defended by the impregnable bulwarks of law, and guaranteed by the most awful sanctions; and whoever asserts to the contrary is a liar, and the truth is not in him."[41]

What distinguished popular rights thinking—indeed, what made it resonate so powerfully among American insurgents—was its unmistakable call for resistance. Unlike the more abstract political theories put forward by constitutional lawyers and enlightened thinkers at the time, this bundle of ideas encouraged action rather than reflection. It spoke directly to questions of individual responsibility and personal sacrifice. From the people's perspective, if their rulers had become tyrants who ignored normal channels of complaint, the ordinary subject had no choice but to take up arms against the state. God specifically rejected neutrality or passive resistance. Within such a religious mind-set, resistance became an obligation. Arguments of this sort had a long history, going back to the earliest years of the Protestant Reformation. But in this atmosphere the rhetoric acquired renewed persuasiveness. Readers of the *Connecticut Gazette* (New London), for example, learned just after passage of the Coercive Acts that "the man who refuses to assert his right to liberty—property—and life—is guilty of the worst kind of rebellion. He commits high treason against GOD."[42] In 1774 the Reverend Jonathan Parsons repeated what most ordinary Americans viewed as common sense. "As Christians," he observed, "we may not give up those rights and privileges that Christ has purchased for and bestowed upon us; for giving them up, would not only reflect great dishonor upon Christ, but would be inconsistent with the peace and welfare of the people and therefore be quite intolerable."[43]

About the character of the resistance sanctioned by God, the people had no doubts. The moment for petitions had passed. For more than a decade, colonial assemblies had urged Parliament to reconsider policies that the people deemed oppressive. These supplications had failed to bring relief. It is not surprising, therefore, that after British forces closed Boston Harbor, the people's resolve stiffened. Religious obligation came to be associated with armed violence. Again, we should remind ourselves that the Massachusetts farmers who purged the countryside of Crown officials and the Connecticut militiamen who spontaneously marched with Israel Putnam to revenge the alleged destruction of Boston thought about their political responsibilities as deeply as did the gentlemen who served in the Continental Congress. They did so, however, on intellectual grounds that made sense to them. While their leaders fretted about proceeding too fast or appearing too radical, by the summer of 1774 many ordinary people had accepted the notion that the defense of rights required armed opposition. The Reverend John Allen joined a chorus of ministers who taught New Englanders that it was their duty to do whatever was necessary to preserve "the Rights of the People." What other choice did they have? "Shall a man be deemed a rebel that supports his own Rights?" Allen asked, and then asserted, "It is no more rebellion for the people to stand up for, and maintain their rights than it is to breathe in the free air."[44]

Such ideas echoed throughout the popular political culture. In his *Freedom from Civil and Ecclesiastical Slavery*, Jonathan Parsons translated a general discussion of duty into a passionate demand for militant response. What, he wondered, should a person do who finds that an arbitrary ruler has turned a deaf ear to the people's cries for justice? Parsons gave a tough-minded answer. Oppressed subjects must fight. "Christian benevolence," he preached, "will inspire us to secure our rights, and repair our injuries at the point of the sword; for if one man may defend himself and his rights against an assailant, much more may a whole country defend themselves when their rights are invaded." The prospect of a mass rising was unnerving. "In such case, the spirit of Christian benevolence would animate us to fill our streets with blood, rather than suffer others to rob us of our rights."

Parsons sensed that many Americans were reluctant to inflict injury on the British. Sentimental attachment to the colonial power, however, could never justify arguments for appeasement. "If former friends are now resolved to entangle us with a yoke of bondage, God forbid that we should suffer them to cut off our limbs and mangle our whole body to gratify their injurious demands. Such terms of peace are no better than what *Nahath* the *Ammonite* proposed to the men of *JabeshGilead* [1 Samuel 11], that they would let him thrust out their right eyes, and bring reproach upon all Israel, leaving them one eye to serve him in some mean and servile drudgery." Only people of little faith could possibly accept humiliating terms. "If it should be so that our natural and constitutional liberties cannot be recovered and maintained without repelling force by force, who could hesitate for a moment, about the propriety of taking up arms!" Who indeed? Insurgents who understood that religious duty and political obligation were inseparable would have confidence that "if we go forth in the name and strength of Christ, he will be our sun to guide and animate us, and our shield to defend and give us salvation."[45]

Many Americans, of course, regarded talk about an appeal to heaven as nonsense. This group included Tories who supported imperial rule as well as neutrals who simply wished that the entire controversy would be resolved without forcing them openly to take sides. Most of these people also agreed with the insurgents on the key points of a rights-based theory of politics. If this was indeed the case, how did such broadly shared ideas about rights and liberties motivate some colonists to take up arms while persuading others to uphold the monarchical regime? One answer might be to abandon analysis of political theory altogether and search instead for factors, such as personal wealth and social standing, that might better elucidate patterns of political allegiance.

There is no need to do so. The discovery that insurgents and their opponents agreed on fundamentals should come as no surprise. In almost every revolution in modern history, people who assumed that they shared a general ideology have come to blows over seemingly small points related to strategy or implementation. One thinks of the lethal hostilities that separated Girondins and Jacobins in revolutionary France or Leninists and Trotskyites in Russia. In America one encounters similar conditions. Most God-fearing loyalists celebrated rights and condemned tyranny as fervently as did the insurgents. What divided them—what made all the difference—was how they applied common beliefs to the specific demands of a developing political crisis. The Tories were convinced that the insurgents had overreacted. The militants, they insisted, mistook passion for reason and as a result cried out like Henny Penny that their rights were in danger, when any fair-minded person could see that the liberties of the king's subjects were perfectly secure.

In A *Friendly Address to All Reasonable Americans* (1774), Myles Cooper, an Anglican priest and president of King's College (later Columbia University), advised unhappy colonists to remember that "if the supreme power of any kingdom or state, through want of due information or attention, should adopt measures that are wrong or oppressive, the subjects may complain and remonstrate against them in a respectful manner, but they are bound, by the laws of Heaven and Earth, not to behave undutifully, much more not to behave insolently and rebelliously." Like others of Tory persuasion, Cooper worried that the insurgents had opened a Pandora's box that would inevitably lead to the dissolution of "the bands of society" and confound "the harmony of the world." He could see no justification for armed resistance to the constitutional government of Great Britain when so many other possibilities for resolution presented themselves. Cooper even employed scriptural language to deprecate insurgent claims. "No tyrant was ever more despotic and cruel than Nero, and no Court ever more corrupted than his, and yet to the government of this cruel and despotic tyrant and his corrupt ministry, peaceable submission was enjoined by an Apostle, who had a due regard for the rights and liberties of mankind." Cooper asserted that even if the Americans should find themselves subjects of "the Grand Turk," they would be guilty of "an unpardonable crime" if they promoted "popular insurrections."[46]

Arguments of this sort infuriated insurgents. They never likened George III to the Grand Turk, but they were certain that they could not hang the defense of rights and liberties on the reed of peaceable submission. In any case, as the Reverend Peter Whitney countered, the popular "zeal for liberty" resulted not from the people's licentiousness, but from "grievous, oppressive, and unconstitutional acts of government."[47]

People of Cooper's temperament do not seem to have fully appreciated the role of fear in shaping how insurgents interpreted political events. As the imperial crisis developed into a full-scale colonial rebellion, militant rhetoric took on a desperate quality, often bordering on outright panic. In this environment, fear served to amplify everyday ideas about rights. Indeed, for the ordinary Americans who served on local committees of safety and sent their sons and husbands to fight British troops, the threat to basic values appeared very real. Their anxiety derived not simply from a love of liberty or conviction that God expected the Americans to resist tyranny, but also from an unshakable belief that a group of evil plotters who controlled the British government were conspiring to crush American freedom.

The insurgents could find no other plausible way to explain their recent experience within the empire. For a very long time the government of Great Britain had brought British subjects throughout the world commercial prosperity, a rule of law, and a bulwark against the ambitions of Catholic France. At some moment around 1760, however, the whole system had suddenly imploded. George III gave ear to advisers jealous of popular liberty. These scheming courtiers corrupted Parliament. And with each passing year, the plan to enslave Americans wrapped its tentacles more tightly around the instruments of power. Time was growing short for those who cherished rights. The evidence for the spreading rot could be seen everywhere—most disturbingly in a series of taxes passed by the House of Commons without American representation and in the occupation of Boston by British troops.[48]

As with most conspiracy theories, it is not necessary for us to demonstrate the existence of such a plot. No evidence survives showing that the king or his ministers contemplated a complex plan to destroy American rights. Although they may have struck contemporary critics as being incompetent, stubborn, and vindictive, they possessed neither the will nor the ability to carry out this ambitious design. Nevertheless, when conspiratorial thinking comes into play, truth is not the issue. To insurgents trying to interpret the political situation after the summer of 1774, it seemed entirely plausible that the British government was consciously working to turn them into slaves.

Tales of the conspiracy echoed through American newspapers; preachers warned parishioners to be vigilant. Fear fueled the reception of the story, turning wild conjecture into fact. In 1775 the Reverend Joseph Perry expressed not a shred of doubt when he informed a congregation of "a determined *plan* already pushed on, to the astonishment of all true Englishmen, calculated in its natural tendency to subvert the British constitution . . . and to substitute in the room thereof, *absolute despotism*, and as the certain consequence, *cruel tyranny*, and the *total slavery*, of all America."[49] At about the same time, the Provincial Congress of Massachusetts issued a proclamation reminding a society already in arms against Great Britain that "the British Administration have formed, and have been for several years executing a plan to enslave this and other American Colonies, is a proposition so evident, that it would be an affront to the understanding of mankind to adduce proofs in support of it."[50]

Of the many renderings of this plot, one particularly shrill account shows how insurgents wove it into an appeal for the defense of American rights. To a potent blend of popular ideas about rights and responsibility, this essay added the spark of conspiracy. It was as if knowledge of an insidious plot—like the introduction of a chemical catalyst—could transform popular discontent into revolutionary resistance. On March 6, 1775, the *Boston Evening-Post* carried an alarming statement entitled "May Truth's Bright Beams and Freedom's Rage, Confound the Villains of the Age." The author admonished readers that "the enemies to Freedom" were calling for the subjection of the colonists by force. At stake were the rights of all Americans. Although the contest would be demanding, "I believe they CAN and WILL defend them [their rights]; and if the Sword should be drawn against them, they may strike such a Blow as will shake Britain to the Center." This was the final test. "A tyrannical Ministry," the writer claimed, "encouraged by the Tories in both Countries, are now pushing their destructive Plans with such rapidity and violence that we must look forward to the last grand step for defense." The argument made no reference to a genealogy of political thought reaching back many centuries. It aimed at the heart, not the mind. It inserted passion into the revolutionary equation. "THIS IS THE DERNIER RESORT—and this, O AMERICANS! YOU CAN DO—and THIS YOU MUST DO." The piece not only called for resistance but also helped demonize the enemy. For a very long time Americans had felt an affinity for "their Brethren in Britain." Those days had passed. Former friends now conspired "to invade your Liberties."[51]

Thinking of this sort—about responsibility to God, about rights, about fighting for an imagined country—surely went through the mind of Israel Shreve, an ordinary soldier who wrote to his wife in June 1776, "I shall soon Experience the feeling of Battle . . . God only knows whose fate it will be to fall." He wanted to return home, to be with her. "But knowing I owe my service to my Country, [I] am Determined to Defend our Rights and privileges so just, with all my [p]owers."[52]

# III

At one time or another, almost everyone has had the experience of reading something—perhaps a newspaper essay or a popular novel—and discovering suddenly and powerfully that the contents strike a responsive chord. The author has expressed in clear, persuasive prose exactly what one has been thinking. The moment yields a certain satisfaction, since it is always good to know that someone else shares one's perspective on the current state of affairs. The piece reaffirms a point of view, which perhaps before that time had not been worked out fully. Thomas Paine's *Common Sense* (1776) provides a good example of a text that crystallized ideas and assumptions about monarchy that many Americans had not been able to articulate so convincingly, even to themselves. Paine did not convert readers. Rather, he legitimated inchoate notions about the abuse of power. Harriet Beecher Stowe's *Uncle Tom's Cabin* (1852) did much the same thing for Northern readers on the eve of the Civil War. Her novel focused public opinion, turning a vague sense of uneasiness about slavery into angry rejection of a practice that the nation had accepted for much too long.

In 1775, *The Crisis* expressed better than any other title then available the concerns of ordinary Americans about the threat to their rights and the need to resist the country's enemies with force of arms. *The Crisis* consisted of a series of essays, some of which ran in newspapers and others as separate pieces. By any measure, it was an extraordinary success. It reached more readers than had any other publication—except, of course, the Bible—before the release of Paine's *Common Sense*. *The Crisis* spoke to insurgents in the language of resistance, weaving themes of violence and betrayal with exposures of conspiracy and corruption at the heart of the empire. And yet, unlike *Common Sense*, *The Crisis* is now forgotten, erased from our shared memory of the period immediately preceding independence.

The publication—often described as a "periodic paper"—first appeared on the streets of London on January 20, 1775. The initial essay bore the provocative heading "The Altar of Despotism Is Erected in America, and We Shall Be the Next Victims of Its Lawless Power."[53] From the beginning, *The Crisis* adopted an unusual format, possessing some characteristics of a pamphlet, some of a newspaper. It was released weekly in small folio, four to eight pages, and although each issue contained a discrete essay on some political topic, the continuing numbers were paginated consecutively like a book. Its low price indicated that the printer, T. W. Shaw of Fleet Street—an obscure figure—aspired to reach a large readership. About the author or authors of The Crisis we know almost nothing. Many investigators have taken up the challenge. The identity of the writer eluded British authorities. One name tentatively put forward is Philip Thicknesse, an individual so disagreeable and so reviled by contemporaries that his only biographer—a modern scholar with no obvious ax to grind—entitled his study simply *Dr. Viper*. While his mean-spirited attacks on alleged enemies—including his own son—make plausible a claim for Thicknesse's participation in *The Crisis*, the source of its shrill voice will probably remain a mystery.[54]

The first issue of *The Crisis* set the tone for the entire run of ninety-one segments. Strident, intemperate, and adversarial, it sounded an alarm. It informed English people that the survival of the British Empire hung in the balance. Time was running out; the end of political freedom was at hand. "It is in your defense," proclaimed *The Crisis*, "I now stand forth to oppose, the most sanguinary, and despotic court that ever disgraced a free country." Like a frantic coach attempting to rally a losing team, the author pledged to stand up "with a firmness and resolution becoming an Englishman determined to be free, to oppose every arbitrary and every unconstitutional act, of a venal and corrupt majority, smuggled into the present new fangled court parliament, through the villainy of Lord North, and purchased with the public money to betray their trust, enslave the people, subvert the Protestant religion, and destroy the glory, honor, interest, and commerce . . . of England and America."[55] *The Crisis* could not claim genuine literary merit. Its descriptions of contemporary political figures were vulgar and heavy-handed. Indeed, the publication made its mark through the force of rhetoric. It did not worry a lot about evidence or, in fact, about the logic of argumentation. Instead, *The Crisis* cried out against a vast and evil conspiracy.

After only a few weeks the paper had a marvelous piece of luck. Parliamentary leaders declared the third number—entitled "To the King" and dated February 4, 1775—so insulting to George III that in both the House of Commons and the House of Lords they proposed prosecuting *The Crisis* for high treason, a capital offense. The government's decision probably saved the publication. If the authorities had considered the situation with greater care, they would have probably ignored *The Crisis*. But, like so many other tetchy officials who over the centuries have mistaken a tough response for political wisdom, British lawmakers apparently reasoned that they might silence harsh and unwelcome expressions of dissent through intimidation. After a short debate, the members of the House of Commons concluded "that the said Paper is a false, scandalous, and seditious libel, highly and unjustly reflecting on his Majesty's sacred person, and tending to alienate the affections, and inflame the minds of his Majesty's subjects against his person and Government."⁵⁶

Official condemnation failed to achieve the desired results. However much the king's supporters in Parliament reviled *The Crisis*, they could not demonstrate to the satisfaction of the government's lawyers that the paper had actually committed treason, at least not according to the language of the statute. In the House of Lords, speakers chafed at such technical constraints. As one reporter noted of a certain "noble Duke," he "bestowed almost every Opprobrious epithet his memory could furnish him with on the Paper, but was clearly of opinion that it did not contain a single word of treason."⁵⁷

Unable to bend the law, the question now was how best the government should move forward. Capital offense or not, *The Crisis* had flagrantly pressed the limits of acceptable political dissent. The troublesome third issue brought the matter to a head. It recounted fourteen years of the king's "shameful and inglorious reign." The monarch had systematically encouraged corruption; he had appointed petty despots to positions of power. And during the long night of misrule, the people had suffered patiently, waiting for relief and liberation. The moment of reckoning had arrived. In words that seemed to suggest the possibility of regicide, *The Crisis* announced that the king might not be able to save himself from the "vengeance, of a brave and mighty people, with law, justice, heaven, and all its sacred truths on their side." The political slate must be cleaned. And so, in the last days before judgment, George should know that "the people" will "treat you, Sir, with as little ceremony, as little respect, and as little mercy, as you and your minions have treated them; for, Sir, whenever the state is convoluted by civil commotions, and the constitution totters to its center, the throne of England must shake with it; a crown will then be no security, and at ONE STROKE *all the gaudy trappings of royalty may be laid in the dust.*"

Parliament settled for a bizarre punishment that served only to increase the offending paper's celebrity. Authorities instructed the common hangman to burn the third issue of *The Crisis* at New Palace Yard,
Westminster, on March 6, 1775. The following day the entire procedure
was to be repeated before the Royal Exchange. Whatever the official
plans may have been, the event quickly turned into a fiasco. When the
hangman and two high sheriffs arrived at the place where the publication was to be executed, they encountered people handing out broad-
sheets entitled "The Last Dying Speech of the Crisis." Whether the
mysterious author himself was trying to profit from the publicity generated by the mock execution is not known. A primitive illustration on the
broadsheet depicts four men on a London street hawking print materials and crying out, "No. 3. *The Crisis*."[58]

As the crowd swelled, the hangman went about his business as best
he could, laying down dry wood and arranging *The Crisis* for destruction. As he prepared to light the fire, the street people dramatically intervened to save a publication that they thought had spoken truth to
power. According to the *Gentleman's Magazine*, "There was a prodi-
gious concourse of people, some of whom were at first very riotous; they
seized and threw about the first brush and faggots which were brought,
and treated the city marshal and the hangman very ill; but more faggots
being sent, which were dipped in turpentine, they immediately took
fire." The flames failed to discourage the friends of *The Crisis*. The
*Kentish Gazette* reported that a wild scene ensued. "As soon as the fire
was lighted . . . it was immediately put out," the provincial paper observed, "and dead dogs and cats thrown at the officers." Another source,
taking note of a more diverse supply of ammunition, explained that the
London protesters pelted Crown officers "with dead cats, raw hides, po-
tatoes, rotten cabbage, and other filth."[59]

The execution of *The Crisis* soon turned violent. One journal
claimed, "Sheriff Hart was wounded in the wrist, and Sheriff Ploner in
the breast with a brick-bat; Mr. Gates, the City Marshal, was dismounted,
and with much difficulty saved his life. Three of the ringleaders were
taken into custody, but soon after rescued by the mob." Gates apparently gave as good as he got during these exchanges. One witness saw
him "riding round and knocking down such as he thought came too
forward, (among whom was one of the Printer's journeymen, whose

head he broke with his mace)."[60] Only after the authorities had restored order did they manage to burn the paper. And so it must be said, like so many outspoken figures throughout history who have mocked state officials, *The Crisis* achieved martyrdom in death. But it did not die in the flames. The publishers continued to produce new numbers, more popular than ever and showing not the slightest sign of moderating its incendiary rhetoric.

Had the story ended with a shower of dead dogs and cats, *The Crisis* would merit little more than a footnote in the chronicles of the radical London press. But it did not do so. No one could have possibly anticipated the next chapter in the publication's adventitious history. Ships quickly transported it across the Atlantic Ocean, where it found a market far larger and more receptive than anything it had enjoyed in Britain. The voyage to America took between ten and twelve weeks. The first indications of a spectacular reception in the colonies were not evident until the last days of April 1775, about two and a half months after Parliament had originally announced its intention to have the common hangman publicly execute *The Crisis*.

American printers distributed the London sheet in two different forms. In eight cities—New York, Philadelphia, Hartford, New Bern, Williamsburg, Norwich, Newport, and New London—*The Crisis* appeared exactly as it had in England, as a periodic paper or series of independent essays released on a weekly schedule.[61] These American publications carry no date, making it impossible to establish precisely when the periodic papers first went on sale. We know that demand must have been substantial, for in at least two cities—New York and Norwich (Connecticut)—colonial printers produced multiple editions of certain early numbers.

In the colonies, this level of commercial print activity was without precedent. For the sake of comparison, we might note that the formal political pamphlets that have received so much scholarly attention usually had only a single printing, a total pressrun seldom amounting to more than a thousand copies.[62] A few titles such as John Dickinson's *Letters from a Farmer* enjoyed substantially wider circulation. The figures for *The Crisis*, however, during some weeks between April and July 1775 must have reached as many as eight to ten thousand, and although we do not know what the relationship may have been between the number of copies printed and their ultimate readership, we would be safe to conclude that *The Crisis* had the potential as a separate paper of reaching a huge American audience.

But that is only part of the publication's amazing story. Its claim to have been the country's first bestseller rests on additional evidence. At least fourteen American printers ran selected numbers of *The Crisis* as newspaper articles. They appeared in almost every major city, a sure sign that publishers recognized that the newly imported material might increase sales. The polemical pieces could be found as far south as Charleston, South Carolina, and as far north as Portsmouth, New Hampshire. Most New England journals reproduced at least eight numbers in their columns. The pieces seem also to have enjoyed wide popularity in New York, Philadelphia, and Baltimore. Since the printers were savvy businessmen working on tight budgets, they were eager to provide subscribers with timely materials. *The Crisis* owed its mass appeal, however, to more than profit margins. It was politically sensitive, a hot item that needed to be put before Americans as swiftly as possible. The editor of the *New London Gazette* (Connecticut) explained the situation to his own readers. "We have obtained eight Numbers of this valuable Paper," observed Thomas Green, "and published Seven of them in a Pamphlet." The people demanded more. "Several of our Customers choose to have them continued in this Method; but as we conceive they would be more generally read if published in a News-Paper, and better serve the cause of LIBERTY, we propose the succeeding Numbers (as they may come to Hand) in the Gazette."[63]

With this additional information about patterns of distribution, we might reconsider how many copies of those newspapers containing *The Crisis* may have actually reached American readers during the late spring and early summer of 1775. An advertisement that ran in the *Virginia Gazette* provides a clue. In that announcement the editor for a new Baltimore journal claimed that he could not successfully launch his enterprise—the *Maryland Gazette and the Baltimore Advertiser*—unless he had a guaranteed list of one thousand subscribers.[64] If we take this figure as a rough guide to a printer's break-even point, we can account for another seven to eight thousand copies of *The Crisis*. These are conservative estimates. Even so, if we calculate total circulation—both as a separate publication and as a newspaper column—

we begin to realize that by any measure, *The Crisis* reached a very large readership.

The timing of its arrival goes a long way toward explaining its extraordinary popularity throughout British America. The imported essays began to appear in the newspapers just as the colonists learned of the bloody battles that had occurred at Lexington and Concord.[65] These engagements in Massachusetts transformed—almost overnight—the character of the entire imperial controversy. For almost a decade before the events of April 1775, Americans had hoped that the British government would come to its senses and back down from legislative policies that seemed to the colonists to jeopardize not only the constitution itself but also a commercial empire that had generated widespread prosperity. Americans had been angry before this moment, of course—so angry that they had rioted, torn down the houses of hated imperial officials, and thrown a small fortune in East Indian tea into the Boston Harbor.

The killing of ordinary people by an army of occupation raised the stakes. Lexington and Concord forced the members of communities throughout America to think more seriously about the burden of resistance than they had ever done before. But now the issue was violence. The escalation of the contest compelled families to make hard decisions—about husbands and sons taking up arms, about local militia units drilling in earnest, about pledging full support to the provisional governments that had seized political authority in so many colonies. The deaths of Americans incited insurgency.

Within this highly unstable political environment *The Crisis* spoke the language of the ordinary people. Newspaper editors throughout America recognized immediately that these essays—more than any other publication then available—explained to colonial readers not only who was to blame in Britain for the oppressive imperial policies but also what they must now do to save their country. It helped that Parliament had ordered a common hangman to execute *The Crisis*. Stories about how a London mob had pelted officials with dead cats and dogs appeared in American gazettes that also carried the actual essays. Knowledge of the martyrdom of the publication served to legitimate its political message. After all, a paper held in such contempt by a Parliament that had only recently passed the Coercive Acts and sent an army to Boston surely had something worthwhile to say to Americans who were anxious lest the violence of Lexington and Concord visit their own towns.

*The Crisis* itself thus became news. The editor of the *New London Gazette* introduced the first appearance of *The Crisis*, noting, "The Tyranny of the King and Parliament of Great-Britain, hath been lately exposed in a periodical Paper called 'the CRISIS' in very bold and explicit Terms; which has given such great Offense as to produce an Order of the House of Lords for burning the same by the Hands of the common Hangman."[66] The *Pennsylvania Evening Post* was even more explicit, announcing, "This DAY is PUBLISHED, and SOLD, by the Printer hereof, THE CRISIS EXTRAORDINARY, Proving unanswerably, that there is a faction against the laws and constitution, and that AMERICANS are not REBELS."[67] They were not rebels—troublemakers with a private cause—because they had made an appeal to heaven; a corrupt ministry had ignored their real grievances. The *Massachusetts Spy* declared in its May 17 issue, "We have received six numbers of a periodical paper, published in London, entitled the CRISIS:—Because they contained too great truths—truths that the ministry would conceal from the people, the Printer, in England, was prosecuted, and the production burnt by the hands of common hangman by order of the House of Lords."[68]

For at least one editor, *The Crisis* dramatically brought home just how swiftly the character of political resistance had changed in America. On May 23, 1775, the publisher of the *South Carolina Gazette and Country Journal* decided to run what was in fact the fourth issue of *The Crisis*. The piece opened with a polemical declaration: "The steady and uniform perseverance in a regular plan of despotism, since the commencement of this reign, makes it evident to the meanest capacity, that a design was formed . . . for subverting the religion, laws, and constitution of this kingdom, and to establish upon the ruins of public liberty, an arbitrary system of government." Such incendiary rhetoric shocked Charles Crouch, who managed this Charleston journal. "There was a Time," he reflected only a month after Lexington and Concord, "and that not very far back, when the Editor would have thought the following Paper gross and licentious, too violent for the Public." But the public had changed. Terror of an army of occupation in America had altered political sensibilities. Writing in the third person, Crouch explained,

"The Adoption of the late iniquitous ministerial Measures has convinced him, that this is not a Season to lisp, and whisper, to cog [to
cheat], and frown, and flatter; when plain truths are to be argued, plain
direct Language is absolutely necessary; therefore without further Introduction or Apology, he inserts the ensuing Extract." *The Crisis* issued
a call to action. A letter submitted to the *South Carolina Gazette*
two weeks later described *The Crisis* as a "fiery piece . . . wrote pro-
fessedly in favor of Liberty and America, and which, from its freedom,
has suffered martyrdom at Westminster . . . by order of a prostituted
Parliament."[69]

The words of *The Crisis* resonated just as persuasively in northern
New England. In late October, for example, the editor of the *New-
Hampshire Gazette*, a newspaper published in Portsmouth, decided to
print *The Crisis* number 22, entitled "BLOOD calls for BLOOD." The
essay offered a grim and gory description of Americans suffering at the
hands of a British administration that had lost control over imperial
policy and in its floundering incompetence had come to rely on state-
sponsored violence against its own subjects. "Consider the gloomy, the
dreadful Prospect before you," urged *The Crisis*, "the Plains of America
are running with the BLOOD of her Inhabitants, the Essence of the
English Constitution destroyed, and nothing but the Form, the mere
Shadow of it remains." The New Hampshire editor could not resist adding for local readers, " 'Tis worthy of Observation that this CRISIS was
printed in London, the Day of the Battle of Bunker Hill." It was as if *The
Crisis* knew in advance what was going to happen in America. It could
predict that pervasive executive and legislative corruption in the imperial capital would inevitably bring violence and death to the distant
colonists.[70]

*The Crisis* spewed forth across the American political landscape an
uncompromising message.[71] It informed colonists that the current king
of Britain and his leading advisers had—from the start of George's reign,
in 1760—conspired to undermine the famed English constitution and
to deprive the British people of their God-given rights and liberties. The
actors in this diabolical plan were the king's ministers, flagitious, incompetent officials who abused the public trust by taking and giving bribes,
by encouraging dangerous Catholic practices, and by using armed force
against ordinary subjects as a means to achieve their corrupt and self-

serving goals. As *The Crisis* mockingly informed the monarch, "Men, Sir, at three thousand miles distance, must think it extremely hard to work, toil, and run hazards; only to support the infamous luxury of high pampered Lords, a rotten Court, and your Tribe of venal Senators, Minions, Pimps, and Parasites, the Pest of Society."[72]

Months before many Americans abandoned the king, *The Crisis* aggressively criticized the monarchy. American insurgents learned from the pages of *The Crisis* that the king had compromised the people's rights and liberty too many times; he had supported persons in power who had betrayed the nation. Raising the specter of Charles I, who had been beheaded during the seventeenth century for his authoritarian acts, *The Crisis* observed, "The present sovereign, not wishing to make a figure in history without a head . . . has improved upon the plan, and is now tearing up the constitution by the roots, under the form of law; this method of proceeding is certainly much safer, and more judicious, as well as just; for what right can an Englishman have to complain, when he is legally made a slave by act of parliament." The people may out of the generosity of their hearts have been willing to overlook the king's faults during the first years of his reign, but as the conspirators had chipped away at liberty, bribed elected officials, corrupted Anglican bishops, intimidated the free press, and used the military for partisan purposes, the king's venality became clearer. "It no longer remained to determine," *The Crisis* concluded, "who is now the greatest CRIMINAL in England."[73]

Americans who read these essays during the troubled summer of 1775 may not have been prepared to advocate a genuine republican government—that bit of persuading required the brilliance of Paine's *Common Sense*—but they did endure a steady, relentless diminishment of the Crown, a process that would prove fatally corrosive to the bonds of empire. Within an insurgent political culture, the publication made several significant contributions. In at least three ways *The Crisis* not only encouraged but also legitimated popular resistance to the abuse of power.

First, in unmistakable language, the essays reminded Americans that the people themselves were the true source of government authority. The king and Parliament ruled the British Empire not as God's special agents, nor as the representatives of landed privilege, but as the servants of the people who had raised them up and who could cast them down. They held this authority because government was a contract that the people—and the people alone—could dissolve. "When the rage is burning in the breasts of Englishmen," *The Crisis* declared, "provoked by wrongs not to be borne by men; all distinctions must cease, the common safety and rights of mankind, will be the only objects in view; while the King and the peasant, must share one and the same fate, and perhaps fall undistinguished together." Another number in the series lectured General Thomas Gage, who then commanded an army of occupation in Boston, that he should never call the Americans "incendiaries"—as he had done in one of his recent public pronouncements—since it was the king and parliament who had revealed themselves as "traitors to the people." Colonial grievances, *The Crisis* insisted, must be resolved "by the collective body of the people, in whom all power virtually resides, from whom it originates, and to whom it must perhaps shortly dissolve again. What the General calls treason, this collective body (an awful tribunal) will pronounce constitutional resistance."74

Second, *The Crisis* imagined a grand union—a vast, unofficial solidarity—of oppressed and angry people throughout the British Empire. From this revolutionary perspective, the political interests of ordinary subjects in Britain could not be separated from those of the Americans, who were so valiantly defending their rights against armed tyranny. As *The Crisis* explained, "In England and America . . . the field of glory is open before us; let us rouse from a state of apathy, and exert ourselves in a manner becoming Englishmen, worthy of men who love liberty, and deserve to be free. Let us show to the world, we are not to be enslaved by one, nor by five thousand tyrants: for the sons of cruelty, corruption and despotism, will pursue their bloody designs, with greater vigor, and with all the unrelenting malice of barbarians, against our fellow subjects in America, in proportion as we are tame and acquiescing."75 Although *The Crisis* did not articulate as clearly as would Thomas Paine in *The Rights of Man* a belief in an international brotherhood of people joined together in resistance against arbitrary power, it encouraged American insurgents—frightened people confronting the British Army—to imagine that they were not alone.

And finally, *The Crisis* sanctioned violence against a state that suddenly seemed intent on stripping the people of their God-given and constitutional rights. This element—so easy to take for granted—was crucial in the publication's mass appeal in the colonies; it assured Americans trying to make sense of the bloody confrontations at Lexington and Concord, and a few weeks later at Bunker Hill, that the time had come to mount an armed defense of liberty. The taking up of weapons in a political cause is an act that modern historians have generally evaded. Perhaps the assumption has been that farm boys rushed to the scenes of military conflict during the spring and summer of 1775 without too much deliberation. But that is clearly wrong. Mobilization on this scale proceeds from conversations within families and communities—worried discussions about whether there might be some other means to defend rights—and it was in this fragile political environment that *The Crisis* announced it was "High Time you should be roused and awakened to a sense of your danger, and by an appeal to heaven, by a glorious resistance, provide for your common safety."[76]

About the character of popular resistance *The Crisis* left no doubt. It advocated an appeal to heaven. "When the humble supplications of an oppressed people are treated with contempt, and a deaf ear turned to their complaints; when their rights are daily invaded, their property unlawfully wrested from them, and their blood inhumanly shed, it is incumbent on them, it is a duty they owe to God and their country, to take the field and resist their oppressors, to show themselves brave." If English history taught nothing else, *The Crisis* declared, it revealed that the Americans were justified "in taking up arms, and resisting the present arbitrary, cruel, and bloody measures now carrying on against them, by an infatuated, obstinate, perverse King, his infernal ministers, and their agents." The essays insisted that April 19 was not a date that should live in infamy. Rather, it deserved to be celebrated by freedom-loving men and women everywhere. What American insurgents achieved that day "ought to stand forever recorded in the calendar, to the eternal honor of America, who that day not only disappointed, but bravely resisted [a] considerable party of the King's military assassins."[77]

Like the threatening clouds of a summer storm, *The Crisis* had no sooner dispensed its rhetorical thunder than it disappeared from view. For a few key months these essays had dominated public attention, instructing Americans from South Carolina to New Hampshire about the horrific state of affairs at the center of the empire, assuring them that ordinary British people would support the colonists in their fight for liberty, and legitimating armed violence in the name of basic rights. One printer in New York City, John Anderson, continued releasing *The Crisis* long after other publishers had turned their attention to more current news and commentary. Although the title circulated in London until the end of 1776, it did not do so in America. The last appearance of *The Crisis* in the colonies was in the October 10 issue of the *New Hampshire Gazette*.

The reasons why this extraordinary publication faded so quickly are not difficult to discern. The major themes that *The Crisis* had advanced in such forceful language seemed after the fall of 1775 less relevant to American insurgents than they had in the wake of battle reports from Lexington and Concord. The king and Parliament had not come to their senses; the conspiracy against American rights continued with even greater intensity. Moreover, as negotiations gave way to traditional warfare, it became increasingly clear that ordinary British men and women would not support the American cause. The colonists were on their own. And finally, after Bunker Hill—after the ill-fated attack on British positions in Canada—Americans no longer needed to justify violence as a means of political resistance.

By that time, frightened, angry people who felt betrayed and abused by the agents of imperial rule had persuaded themselves that they would defend their communities with force of arms against an encroaching power. What we must remember is that before ordinary Americans could address national independence, before they could contemplate seriously the formation of a new republican government, they had to accept the legitimacy of insurgent violence. For that, they owed much to *The Crisis*. Put another way, the road to *Common Sense* led through *The Crisis*, and it is perhaps no surprise that when Thomas Paine wrote his own brilliantly motivational essays in late 1776, he called them *The American Crisis*, a gesture that recalled an earlier *Crisis* we have chosen to forget.

# TEN

# Endgames of Empire

The end of empire elicits two strikingly different though complementary stories. One features ordinary Americans who made the decision to
sever the ties of allegiance with Great Britain many months before
Congress issued a formal declaration. In this scenario, the key date is
April 19, 1775, not July 4, 1776. Reports that British troops murdered
farmers in Lexington and Concord cut the bonds of political identity
and affection that had held the empire together for so many generations. Indeed, the killing of militiamen by an army of occupation permanently transformed the American political landscape.

Like a shock wave, news of Lexington and Concord spread from
Massachusetts north to New Hampshire and south to Georgia and
South Carolina. The nightmare predicted by *The Crisis* had come to
pass. Everywhere one encountered a burst of furious activity. In small
communities the people took resistance into their own hands: arming,
training, and mobilizing resources. This was the time when they discovered that they were no longer British subjects, no longer colonists, but
something splendidly different—Americans allied with other Americans in a truly American cause.

A second story of the imperial endgame can be told from the perspective of the last Crown officials left in America. Burdened with an
impossible assignment and lacking the manpower necessary to reassert
British authority, they witnessed firsthand ordinary people surging forward. The final moments of British rule did not occur in all the colonies

at the same time. When the collapse came, however, royal governors fled to safety, usually to a British warship anchored off the coast. Known as the governors who "took to the waters," they desperately tried to restore the old order, knowing in advance that they had almost no chance of success.[1] Like imperial bureaucrats throughout history who have raced to escape local insurgents, these men witnessed a powerfully spontaneous expression of independence as angry Americans not only seized the last outposts of empire but also attempted in a final spasm of fury to erase evidence of the old regime from the face of the earth.

## *I*

The attack on Lexington and Concord did not come as a surprise to the people who lived in the New England countryside.[2] For many weeks before the clash, insurgents in local committees throughout Massachusetts had been preparing for the possibility of such an event. Because General Gage dispatched two trusted soldiers—Captain John Brown and Ensign Henry De Berniere—to gather intelligence about roads and bridges, he had a good sense of what was happening on the ground. The men kept a detailed journal that reveals the dynamics of insurgency through hostile eyes. The mission was dangerous, far more so than the spies realized when they volunteered for the assignment. Had Gage been less concerned about planning possible lines of march and more about the willingness of the militants to resist, he might well have paid closer attention to what his agents reported about the Americans' state of mind. The two men encountered people prepared for violence, fearful that their rights as well as their homes were in peril, and confident that God expected them to make a stand.

Brown and De Berniere tried to pass themselves off as common laborers. Wearing "brown cloaths and reddish handkerchiefs," they set off toward Watertown. The disguise fooled no one, and they would surely have been arrested had they not been mistaken for two of the large number of British deserters who traveled the same country roads. When they reached the town, the spies entered a tavern in search of dinner. "A black woman" served the meal. At first she betrayed no sign of suspicion. But soon the two men noticed she was inspecting them closely. Striking up an innocuous conversation, one soldier observed, "It [is] a very fine country." She responded that indeed Watertown possessed great appeal and then added gratuitously, "We have got brave fellows to defend it." Taking her words as a warning, they left the tavern immediately. Once outside, a servant who traveled with them explained that the woman "knew our errand was to take a plan of the country." The clumsy soldiers had foolishly let her catch a glimpse of their drawing of the "river and road through Charlestown." She told the servant that the group should turn back, since if they went farther into the country, they "should meet with very bad usage."[3]

Ignoring her advice, the two soldiers took the road to Worcester, exercising greater care this time to seek out inns owned by the king's friends. After making a number of sketches, they reached Mr. Jones's tavern late in the afternoon on a Saturday. As they were refreshing themselves, locals appeared who recounted disturbing stories about how the "rebels" were disarming Tories in nearby Petersham. The spies then moved to another tavern, where, to their surprise, they discovered a company of insurgents "exercising near the house." The Americans did not appear to take notice of Brown and De Berniere. This allowed them to witness the enemy in action. Huddled close to the window of their room, the British overheard the local commander encouraging the militants. He assured them that they would emerge victorious over Gage's forces if they just remembered to have patience and courage. He recommended them "to charge us coolly, and wait for our fire, and everything would succeed with them." The American officer quoted the wisdom of famous Roman generals, reminded them of the experience of General Israel Putnam, and recalled how, during earlier imperial wars against the French in Canada, the colonists had outperformed their British allies. At the conclusion of his spirited talk—this occurred only seven weeks before Lexington and Concord—"the whole company came into the house and drank until nine o'clock."

The two British agents wisely sent their servant back to Boston with the incriminating sketchbook. Although they now knew that their cover had been blown, they pushed ahead to Barnes's tavern in Marlborough. A friendly source tipped them off that a "party of liberty people" were hot on their trail. Brown and De Berniere turned to Barnes for advice. "We asked Mr. Barnes if they did get us into their hands, what they would do to us." It was a hard question. Barnes hesitated. "We asked him again," and only then did he say, "he knew the people very well, [and] that we might expect the worst of treatment from them."

A crowd began to gather outside the inn. Even though it was snowing, Barnes told the two men they were no longer safe in town. In the dark of night they fled across woods and fields, and after walking more than thirty miles in the intense cold, they finally made it back to Boston. A few days later the two soldiers learned that the insurgents had come very close to capturing them. "Mr. Barnes came to town from Marlborough," they recounted, "and told us, immediately on our quitting the town [Marlborough], the committee of correspondence came to his house and demanded us; he told them we were gone . . . and when they found we were gone, they told him if they had caught us in his house, they would have pulled it [down] about his ears." Later in March the spies carried out a second mission—this time to Concord—and during this trip into the heart of the insurgency they met a woman who "came in crying, and told us they [the militants] swore if she did not leave the town, they would tar and feather her for directing Tories on their Road."

Since Gage was under pressure from his superiors in London to show progress in putting down the rebellion, he pressed ahead with a plan to seize military supplies, which he believed had been stored in Concord. The story of the British misadventure is a well-told tale. It usually turns on whether the Lexington militiamen provoked British troops by firing first, or whether the British, frustrated by the insurgents' resistance, shot down innocent farmers. Whatever happened on Lexington Green on the morning of April 19, the British expedition stirred up a hornet's nest. By the end of the day, ill-organized Americans drove the redcoats back to Boston.

Accounts of the battle—many of them inaccurate and exaggerated—triggered an outpouring of popular anger. From the perspective of the insurgency, the events at Lexington and Concord provided a major boost. It was not that ordinary people throughout America welcomed the deaths of the militiamen. Rather, the incident powerfully confirmed popular assumptions about the cruelty and insensitivity of a corrupt imperial power. As a writer in a Connecticut newspaper exclaimed on May 29, the attack revealed "this pretended mother [Great Britain] is a vile imposter—an old, abandoned prostitute—a robber, a murderer—crimsoned over with every abominable crime, shocking to humanity!"[4] Within days of the event, Thomas Jefferson recognized how dramatically the political situation had changed. Writing on May 7, he observed, "This accident has cut off our last hope of reconciliation, and a phrenzy [sic] of revenge seems to have seized all ranks of people."[5]

Even more significant in the realm of public opinion was the belief that the men who died at Lexington did so not to defend their own small Massachusetts communities or a distinct New England way of life, but for an American cause. People interpreted the event within a framework of revolutionary solidarity. The process of rethinking the empire had begun during the summer of 1774. It drew upon the networks of communication that William Goddard had encouraged, upon thousands of charitable donations for the poor, unemployed laborers of Boston, and upon newspapers that disseminated reports of local committees having punished ideological enemies. These marvelously creative links established effective political bonds of affinity between distant strangers, and so, when Americans learned that the insurgency had sparked a fatal military confrontation, they drew almost instinctively upon what had become a shared revolutionary identity.

Within this expanding framework, one could sympathize with the fallen colonists who in other circumstances might have been seen as intolerant Puritans or sharp-dealing Yankees. As the Reverend Jonas Clark explained to a Lexington congregation, "Instead of awing the people into submission, by those measures of violence and cruelty, with which they [the British] commenced hostilities against us, as they undoubtedly expected, their spirits have been roused and awakened thereby, beyond what any other means could have ever effected: and with a union and firmness, exceeding the most sanguine expectations, they [the Americans] have armed to defend themselves and their country, and to revenge the injuries received and the innocent blood of their brethren slain."[6]

A report that appeared in the *Connecticut Courant* a few days after the battle made the same point in much shriller language: "AMERICANS! Forever bear in mind the BATTLE OF LEXINGTON:—where British troops, unmolested and unprovoked, wantonly, and in a most inhuman manner fired upon and killed a number of our countrymen."[7]

The point is not that the death of innocent militiamen suddenly brought forth a binding sense of country. A common identity had already been established, the product of almost two years' of popular resistance. News of the sacrifice at Lexington merely served to transform inchoate assumptions about an imagined solidarity—a country of the mind—into a force that we might call nationalism.

Contemporaries expressed surprise that the news of Lexington spread so quickly. "Nothing could exceed the celerity with which the intelligence flew everywhere that blood had been shed by the British troops," one man in Connecticut observed. "The country, in motion, exhibited but one scene, of hurry, preparation and revenge."[8] Sir Henry Clinton, a leading British general who reflected on the causes of the Revolution after the Americans had won, marveled, "It is . . . astonishing with what rapidity the news of them [Lexington and Concord] spread from one end of the continent to the other, and what influence they had in diffusing the spirit of revolt through the provinces."[9]

Express riders alerted the communities to the north. A garbled report reached Newburyport, Massachusetts, on the day of the battle. People in New Hampshire learned the next day that "the sword is now drawn."[10] Messengers carried the account southward into Connecticut and Rhode Island, and from New England as swiftly as fresh horses could gallop into the Middle Colonies and the Chesapeake. Riders noted the time of their arrival in various towns along the route. Israel Bissel, for example, an experienced post rider at the age of only twenty-three, carried the initial story along the Boston Post Road, pushing his mounts so hard that one died of exhaustion. Although his courageous ride does not enjoy the same heroic standing as does Revere's, he may have played a more important role in mobilizing popular support for the American cause. He traveled from one Connecticut community to another, reaching New York City on the afternoon of April 23. Other riders then took over. The first alarm arrived in Philadelphia in the morning of the twenty-fourth and was published within hours under the title "To all Friends of American Liberty." In this form, readers were assured that they could put their faith in the accuracy of the story, in part because it had been "attested and forwarded by the Committees of Brookline, Norwich, New London, Lyme, Saybrook, Killingsworth, E. Guilford, Guilford, Branford, [and] New Haven." On the twenty-sixth, the people of Baltimore learned the rough outlines of what had happened. Riders made it to Williamsburg on the twenty-eighth. Not until May 3 did the alarm reach North Carolina. The news broke in Charleston, South Carolina, on May 9.[11]

Whether the people received an accurate account of the events of April 19 is not of great significance in understanding the widening insurgency. They believed that innocent Americans had died at Lexington and Concord. That knowledge alone served to convert skeptics and cowards. One could almost feel the growing support for resistance. As Dr. Joseph Warren, a leading Boston militant, noted, "The people never seemed in earnest about the matter until after the engagement of the 19th . . . and I verily believe, that the night preceding that barbarous outrage committed by the soldiery at Lexington, Concord, &c., there were not fifty people in the whole colony [Massachusetts] that expected any blood would be shed in the contest between us and Great Britain."[12]

Although Warren exaggerated, he had a point. As one New England minister explained, "This ever memorable day [April 19] is full of importance to all around—to this whole land and nation; and big with the fate of Great Britain and America.—From this remarkable day will an important era begin for both America and Britain. And from the nineteenth of April, 1775, we may venture to predict, will be dated, in future history, THE LIBERTY or SLAVERY of the AMERICAN WORLD, according as a sovereign God shall see fit to smile, or frown upon the interesting cause, in which we are engaged."[13]

In town after town from New Hampshire to Georgia, the news of Lexington triggered a swell of popular outrage. At this critical moment—as they had been when they thought the British destroyed Boston in September 1774—the people took charge of their own revolution, demanding revenge for the imagined atrocities that had occurred in Massachusetts. Without encouragement from congressional leaders, they managed to inflame the controversy with Great Britain. The popular reaction to the events of April 19 blended spontaneous fury about the killing of innocent colonists with a commitment to a defense of rights and a sense that God had sanctioned their cause. It was a volatile mixture. The demand for retribution served to amplify deeply held political beliefs. On April 24, 1775, the *Newport Mercury* announced, "Through the sanguinary Measures of a wicked Ministry, and the Readiness of a standing Army to execute their Mandates, has commenced the *American Civil War*, which will hereafter fill an important Page in History."[14] On the twenty-fifth, the *Essex Gazette* praised the "vast army of our brave countrymen" who had rushed to assist their counterparts in Massachusetts. A few days later the major New Hampshire journal observed in a piece that ran under the black banner of mourning, "The Public most sincerely sympathize with the Friends and Relations of our deceased Brethren, who gloriously sacrificed their Lives in fighting for the Liberties of their Country. By their noble, intrepid Conduct, in helping to defeat the Forces of an ungrateful Tyrant, they have endeared their Memories to the present Generation, who will transmit their Names to Posterity with the highest Honor."[15]

The abrupt rising of the people paralyzed royal government in New York. Cadwallader Colden, the colony's lieutenant governor and a person of extensive political experience, feared that anarchy had spread to the streets. Even before the news of Lexington and Concord had reached the city, the situation had been tense. "Several incidents," he explained, "combined to depress all legal authority and to increase the terror of the inhabitants, which seemed to vanquish every thought of resistance to popular rage." Whatever the people's previous state of mind may have been, the killing of ordinary colonists by British soldiers seemed to accelerate the breakdown of normal authority. "In this unfortunate situation . . . the first accounts of an action between the King's troops and people near Boston was published with horrid and aggravating circumstances. The moment of consternation and anxiety was seized. The people were assembled and that scene of disorder and violence begun, which has entirely prostrated the powers of government."[16]

Colden—a man of aristocratic temperament—probably overstated the immediate threat. Nevertheless, there is no question that the killings in Massachusetts had spurred the people to act on their own behalf. One account claimed, "The news of the attack at Boston reached New York on Sunday the 23rd, and that very day the populace seized the city arms, and unloaded two provision vessels bound for the Troops at Boston. In the course of the week, they formed themselves into companies under Officers of their own choosing, distributed the arms . . . convened the Citizens by beat of drum, drew the cannon into the interior country, and formed an association of defense . . . which is signed by all ranks."[17]

In New Jersey the news of Lexington had an equally stunning impact on the attitude of the ordinary people toward Great Britain. The royal governor, William Franklin, sensed that the stand the Massachusetts farmers had made represented a major turning point in the imperial controversy. Like Colden, he feared that the insurgents now controlled what passed for government in the colony. In a painful letter sent to Dartmouth on May 6, Franklin explained, "The Accounts we have from Massachusetts Bay respecting the Proceedings of the King's Troops, and the late Engagement between them and the Inhabitants of that Province, have occasioned such an Alarm and excited so much Uneasiness among the People throughout this and the other Colonies, that there is Danger of their committing some outrageous Violences before the present Heats can subside." Everywhere men were arming, creating new companies, and practicing exacting military drills. Almost overnight the situation in New Jersey had assumed a menacing character. "Every Day new Alarms are spread," Franklin wrote, "which have a Tendency to keep the Minds of the People in a continual Ferment, make them suspicious, and prevent their paying any Attention to the Dictates of sober Reason and common Sense."

Of course, like so many other figures who have represented empires in distant places over the centuries, William Franklin equated popular political resistance with madness, as if a passionate commitment to a political agenda in itself indicated mental instability. American leaders who enjoyed the privileges of wealth sometimes spoke in such terms. The people knew better. And in point of fact, as Franklin must have realized, the insurgency did not advocate random violence. Its energies were clearly funneled through recognized groups within a complex revolutionary infrastructure. As he observed of New Jersey, "All legal Authority and Government seems to be drawing to an End here, and that of Congresses, Conventions, and Committees establishing in their Place." Franklin confided—somewhat ungraciously—that he thought Gage had made a major strategic mistake. What did he have in mind when he sent troops to Lexington? The whole expedition had been doomed to failure. Franklin concluded that whatever Gage's thinking may have been, he was responsible for "one of the most unlucky Incidents that could have occurred in the present Situation of Affairs."[18]

South of New Jersey, the news of Lexington sparked unprecedented levels of support for the American insurgency. George Cuthbert, the provost marshal of Jamaica, was traveling through Philadelphia at the time and described the situation. "When the Account of the affair of Lexington arrived," he claimed, "all ranks of Men were exasperated and the different Wards of the City met to form a Militia out of themselves, electing their own Officers, etc.; in short, from the 1st April, when they only viewed things at a distance, they now seemed to enter into all the Violence that some time before possessed the Northern Colonies!" The officer had also learned that "immediately after the Account of Lexington in the Southern Colonies, the rage for taking up Arms was general. Philadelphia being the seat of the [congressional] Delegates, all Men who were willing to enter into Measures of the most Violent sort, resorted to this City."[19]

Evidence from Virginia corroborates Cuthbert's intelligence. When the Fincastle committee met on July 10, the members recorded their distress upon learning of the killings in Massachusetts. In their opinion the news fully justified calling "upon all, even the most distant and interior parts of the colonies, to prepare for the extreme event, to avert ministerial cruelty, in defense of our just and reasonable rights and liberties."[20] And on June 30 the *Cape Fear Mercury* of Wilmington, North Carolina, published "A CIRCULAR LETTER" originally directed to all the committees of South Carolina. After recounting what they thought had occurred at Lexington and Concord, the Charleston insurgents concluded, "Let it be delivered down to posterity, that the American civil war broke out on the 19th day of April, 1775.—An epoch that, in all probability, will mark the declension of the British empire!"[21]

The whirlwind of fury that drew increasingly large numbers of ordinary people into the resistance movement left moderates with no place to hide. The irony is that Parliament's show of force—the occupation of Boston and a surge in troop strength—had been intended to give the "Friends of Government" greater confidence. The members of Lord North's cabinet reasoned that if the Crown's supporters in America felt safe, they would take the lead in restoring order. The debacle at Lexington and Concord put an end to such talk. Only two weeks after an insurgent army had driven British soldiers back to Boston, Gage sent Dartmouth a candid assessment of the situation on the ground. The occupying forces had lost the contest for the hearts and minds of the Americans. "From what can be learned," the general explained, "it is not found that one province is in a better situation than another, the people called friends of government are few in all . . . [as are] those moderate men who abhor violent proceedings and wish for peace and quiet; the opposition party [is] numerous, active and violent."[22]

However much the report undermined his own credibility in London, Gage provided accurate intelligence. John Dickinson, the highly respected Pennsylvania author of *Letters from a Farmer*, observed only a few days after Lexington and Concord that the battle had effectively silenced political dissent. "A Tory," Dickinson explained in a letter to Arthur Lee, "dare not open his mouth against the cause of America, even at New York." Indeed, it was clear that "the Continent is preparing, most assiduously for a vigorous resistance; and that freedom, or an honorable death, are the only objects on which their [ordinary Americans] souls are at present employed."[23]

Although congressional leaders still hoped to negotiate a settlement with Great Britain, the people showed no hesitation in taking action that they knew would transform an insurgency into a full-scale war. As the Reverend William Stearns asked in a sermon delivered in the wake of the events of April 19, "And what is now our duty? Must we now sit still and maintain peace with the butchers of our friends? Shall we maintain it 'at the expense of property, liberty and life, and all that's dear'? God forbid! If ever there was a call in providence to take the sword, there now is—Therefore to arms!—To arms!—lest that curse fall upon us, which fell upon the dastardly inhabitants of Meroz (Judges 5:23)." The scriptural reference was to the Israelites who after enduring humiliating oppression belatedly rose up against Jabin, king of Canaan. Stearns echoed the rhetoric of the Old Testament. "May we now put on the whole armor of God, and acquit ourselves like men and be strong, and having done all, make a vigorous stand—May we all enlist in this spiritual warfare."[24]

Although determining the impact of these entreaties on the ordinary people is bound to be imprecise, one case speaks quite clearly. A letter sent from Weathersfield, Connecticut, only four days after Lexington observed, "We are all in motion here . . . one hundred young men who cheerfully offered their service . . . are all well armed, and in high spirits . . . We shall, by night, have several thousands from this colony on their march." Mobilization took on the character of a crusade. "We fix on our Standards and Drums, the Colony Arms, with the motto, '*qui transtulit sustinet*,' round it in letters of gold, which we construe thus, 'God, who transplanted us hither, will support us.'"[25]

The news took much longer to reach London. Much to the embarrassment of the North government, accounts from the American press arrived almost two weeks before Gage's official report. Since the colonial newspapers described Lexington and Concord in terms of a stunning victory for the insurgents, British officials dismissed the intelligence as rebel propaganda. The king mused that perhaps "some detachment sent by Lieut. General Gage may have not been strong enough to disperse the provincials assembled at Concord." In the absence of reliable information, officials in charge of colonial affairs went about their business as if nothing unusual had occurred. They had not taken American resistance seriously before this moment, and they saw no reason to do so now. As one commentator noted at the time, "Your American news seemed for almost two days to draw some attention, but people are returned to that happy tranquility of mind, which cannot, I fancy, be much interrupted, unless the Regatta day should prove wet and cold."[26]

Finally, on June 10, Gage's statement arrived. The administration realized immediately that the insurgents had defeated a sizable British force. It was perhaps too much to expect that the setback would provoke a serious review of colonial policy. According to George III, the lesson to be learned was that the occupying troops had been too small and too timid. The only way to discourage colonial militants was to hit them hard and to demonstrate through overwhelming firepower that they had no chance whatsoever of gaining a favorable political settlement. The king saw the matter in apocalyptic terms. Either the British Army crushed the insurgency, or the empire would lose face throughout the world. "I cannot help being of opinion," he explained, "that with firmness and perseverance America will be brought to submission: if not, old England will perhaps not appear so formidable in the eye of Europe as at other periods." There could be no compromise. "America must be a colony of England or treated as an enemy. Distant possessions standing upon an equality with the superior state is more ruinous than being deprived of such connections." The ministry quickly reorganized itself as a war cabinet. With the king's blessing, it recommended raising an additional twenty thousand soldiers to be deployed in America no later than April 1776. Colonial resistance mandated imperial resolve. "I am clear as to one point," George declared, "that we must persist and not be dismayed by any difficulties that may arise on either side of the Atlantic; I know I am doing my Duty, and I can never wish to retract."[27]

Leaders who think they know better than their own military advisers about conditions on the ground seldom listen to intelligence that suggests the need for a different approach. This was certainly the case during the summer of 1775. However much Gage welcomed promised troop reinforcements, he sensed that the British were in over their heads. The ministry simply did not understand the character of the colonial insurgency. The men who flocked to Massachusetts in defense of their rights and liberty, and justified resistance in the language of the Old Testament, were not likely to be discouraged by ill-coordinated displays of toughness. Writing to Dartmouth soon after the Battle of Bunker Hill, Gage confessed, "The trials we have had [in America] show the rebels are not the despicable rabble too many have supposed them to be, and I find it owing to a military spirit, encouraged among them for a few years past, joined with an uncommon degree of zeal and enthusiasm, that they are otherwise."[28]

The spontaneous rising of the ordinary people in support of other Americans marked the end of an imperial order that the colonists had known for more than a century. We should be clear on this point: popular resistance to Great Britain compelled the members of Congress to accept independence. Without doubt, many were strongly so inclined. After two years of resistance that witnessed the mobilization of tens of thousands of Americans, however, the size, pace, and logic of insurgency meant that they had no other choice. A person writing in a newspaper on December 1, 1775, under the name "A FREEMAN," fully appreciated where the political cart stood in relation to the horse. Addressing "the WORTHY OFFICERS AND SOLDIERS IN THE AMERICAN ARMY," he announced as a matter of fact, "we expect soon to break off all kind of connection with Britain, and form into a GRAND REPUBLIC of the AMERICAN UNITED COLONIES." He offered a wonderful vision. The new nation "will, by the blessing of heaven, soon work out our salvation and perpetuate the liberties, increase the wealth, and the power and the glory of this Western world." A FREEMAN assured the soldiers, stirred originally by outrage but sustained by a commitment to rights, "the farther we enter into the field of independence, our prospect will expand and brighten, and a COMPLETE REPUBLIC will soon complete our happiness."[29]

## *II*

There is another way of looking at the insurgency. This story draws upon the painful reflections of the last British officials to abandon their colonial posts. At a moment of crisis, these beleaguered figures offered valuable insights into the character of popular militancy. By viewing the insurgents as British officials did, we discover that the Americans were not unlike so many oppressed people throughout the world who have taken up arms in defense of what they regard as their just rights. In more recent times, we have come to adopt the point of view of the imperial officials—sometimes even as we watch in horror as the representatives of our government flee from the last secure compound—but at such moments we might reflect that once, long ago, at the beginning of our national history, Americans challenged the legitimacy of the occupying regime.

Like the characters one encounters in the writings of V. S. Naipaul, colonial officials dispatched to distant American outposts were able to date the collapse of the British Empire with precision. For them, the experience of large-scale popular resistance was real, very frightening, a phenomenon they had not been trained to handle. It is not surprising, therefore, that the Crown's representatives could pinpoint the moment— often within the span of only a few months—when effective British rule crumbled, a traumatic event in their lives that revealed colonial government in America to be little more than a house of cards. Cabinet members in London may have claimed that they had seen the crisis coming all along or that the final debacle reflected complex factors, commercial and demographic, military and religious. But customs collectors, naval officers, and royal governors—middle-level appointees who actually served the king on the ground—took a different perspective. For them the end came dramatically, often violently, and when confronted with colonial insurgency, these harried bureaucrats bore witness to the birth of a new political culture.

British officials produced a number of accounts of imperial collapse, most of which, as one would expect, were self-serving in character.[30] For our purposes, however, some accounts of the last days of British authority in America are more valuable than others. A case in point are the records of two mediocre royal governors whose fumbling attempts to restore the old order centered on derelict forts—physical expressions of colonial power—to which before the final moment of political crisis no one had paid more than passing attention. The governors served their king in the sleepy backwaters of empire—in North Carolina and New Hampshire—where they believed that however unrewarding their posts may have been in monetary terms, they were secure from the kinds of organized resistance to parliamentary legislation that had plagued port cities such as New York and Boston.

They were wrong. In 1775—many months before the signing of the Declaration of Independence—British authority broke down along the entire Atlantic Coast. Governor Josiah Martin of North Carolina and Governor John Wentworth of New Hampshire tried their best to make sense of a massive insurgent movement, which for them had no precedent, and as the waves of violence rolled over colonial America, they placed their hopes on two crumbling forts—Fort Johnson, which guarded the mouth of the Cape Fear River in North Carolina, and Fort William and Mary, which greeted ships entering Portsmouth harbor in New Hampshire. When tested by American militants, these structures revealed themselves to be hollow shells, physical expressions of an empire that had lost legitimacy.

As their worlds fell apart, Martin and Wentworth chronicled a revolution that was unfolding. Their correspondence with Lord Dartmouth, who in 1772 had taken over as secretary of state for the colonies, is housed in the archives of the British Colonial Office, where, it is safe to say, it has not generated much interest since Parliament originally decided to dispatch a large army to put down an American rebellion. Dartmouth was a somewhat phlegmatic administrator who seemed at times more interested in evangelical religion than in the business of empire. The letters of Martin and Wentworth have a desperate quality, simpering, obsequious, and uncertain; this is the testimony of frontline bureaucrats who dared not call insurgency by its name and who sensed that even if they had had the courage to do so, imperial officials in

Whitehall would have denigrated reports from the field that failed to confirm what they already had declared to be the truth of the matter. The two governors tell how they were literally driven from their posts and forced in the final days to seek safety on board British warships, where they issued impotent edicts.[31]

Josiah Martin was a child of the Atlantic World. Born in Dublin in 1737, he grew up on Antigua, the son of a prosperous sugar planter. Martin's father does not seem to have held the boy in high regard, calling him "mulish" and criticizing his chronic "indolence." Perhaps to escape a dysfunctional family, Martin joined the British Army, an institution that rewarded lack of military talent with steady promotion. In 1770, after marrying his cousin, he accepted an appointment as the governor of North Carolina, grumbling all the while that he would have preferred a more lucrative assignment. Before Martin arrived, his predecessor, Governor William Tryon, had put down a rebellion of Piedmont farmers known as Regulators. For the new governor, therefore, the danger of making a hash of his new job must have seemed small. The only suggestion that he may not have been up to the challenge came when a well-dressed woman claiming to be the queen's sister appeared in New Bern, then the capital of North Carolina. She promised her admirers major posts in the army, navy, and treasury. Although no one had written from London to announce a royal visit, Martin interpreted an extravagant display of expensive jewelry as proof of her authenticity. He organized a grand ball in the Governor's Palace in North Carolina to honor the royal traveler. It was only later, in Charleston, South Carolina, that skeptics exposed the woman as a fraud—indeed, as a thief who had liberated some of the queen's most valuable possessions and then fled to America.[32]

As the political storm clouds swept across the northern colonies, Martin appraised his own situation as best he could. Early in 1774—probably before news of the destruction of the tea in Boston Harbor reached North Carolina—he assured Dartmouth that he was fully prepared to thwart the demands of local protesters, who he insisted comprised only a few of the more irascible members of the colonial assembly. But Martin misjudged the character of popular resistance. During the autumn of 1774 the counties and major towns of eastern North Carolina had formed extralegal committees. One of them, in Wilmington, had harassed Janet Schaw's friends. "In this province as in all others to the northward," Martin informed Dartmouth, "Committees have been chosen by the people to carry into execution the measures of the General Congress."[33]

At first these local groups publicly shamed neighbors who had purchased British goods in violation of a continental nonimportation agreement. They soon expanded their powers. They denounced "enemies of the country," encouraged inhabitants to take up arms, and effectively silenced those who might have been Martin's allies. He labeled these agitators "motley mobs" and "promoters of sedition." In August the governor issued a proclamation "to discourage as much as possible proceedings so illegal and unwarrantable in their nature, and in their effect so obviously injurious to the welfare of this Country."[34] Martin's words had no impact on the people of the region, except perhaps to encourage those serving as members of the committees to act more aggressively.

Although Martin did not yet comprehend the depth of popular resistance to royal authority, he sensed rightly that the committees represented the revolutionary core of rebellion. No group presented him with a more serious threat than did the Wilmington Committee of Safety.[35] In March 1775 it drafted an oath that it strongly advised every white male in the immediate area to affirm. "We do most solemnly engage by the most Sacred ties of Honor, Virtue & Love of our Country," declared the Wilmington insurgents, "that we will ourselves Strictly Observe every part of the Association . . . & we will use every Method in Our power to endeavor to Influence others to the Observation of it by persuasion & such other Methods as Shall be consistent with the peace & Good Order & the Laws of this Province."[36]

For Martin, the endgame of imperial rule played itself out during the spring and early summer of 1775. In March he still thought there was a chance to save the situation. Writing to General Thomas Gage, the head of British military forces in America and a man confronting an even stronger insurgency, Martin insisted, "The people in some parts of this Country begin to open their eyes and to see through the artifices and delusions by which they have been misled, and they discover good dispositions to renounce the power and authority of the committees."[37] He felt confident that the Scottish Highlanders who had recently migrated to central North Carolina would defend the king's authority.

Martin was clinging to a slender reed, but he desperately wanted—even at the last—to show that he had the situation under control.

There was a problem. Fort Johnson was "totally unprovided with powder." By April, Martin had changed his tune. He informed Dartmouth, "I am bound in conscience and duty to add, My Lord, that Government is here absolutely prostrate . . . and that nothing but the shadow of it is left." Unless London acted swiftly and with appropriate "British Spirit," "there will not long remain a trace of Britain's dominion over these Colonies."[38] What Dartmouth made of this intelligence is not clear. It was certainly not the kind of report that he welcomed from officers on the ground. In any case, neither Gage nor Dartmouth attempted to supply Fort Johnson with gunpowder.

News that a British expeditionary force had killed colonists in Lexington and Concord served to strengthen the local insurgency. In May a fearful Martin retreated to the apparent safety of Fort Johnson. In a letter to Dartmouth dated June 30, he explained that reports from New England had "like all first impressions, taken deep root in the minds of the vulgar here . . . and wrought a great change in the face of things." Not surprisingly, the leaders of the North Carolina resistance discovered that it had suddenly become easier to recruit "the fickle, wavering and unsteady multitude to their party." Martin may have blamed the collapse of royal authority on a few agitators, but he could not deny that he was now confronted with a massive rising of the ordinary people of the colony. He explained to Dartmouth that the people—a large and threatening body he never described in detail—"freely talk of Hostility towards Britain in the language of Aliens and avowed Enemies." When a delegation of committeemen from Wilmington demanded an interview with the governor to discuss the condition of the cannons at Fort Johnson, Martin panicked. He ordered the guns taken off their carriages, and then on July 18, learning of a possible attack on the fort, he fled to the *Cruizer*, a heavily armed British frigate anchored offshore.[39]

Martin's decision to take to the waters came not a moment too soon. He left Fort Johnson under the command of Captain John Collet. As this officer must have known, the situation was untenable. Rumors that Martin and his few remaining supporters had disabled the cannons and seized the last gunpowder spread through the region. Stories circulated that the governor intended to kidnap the leaders of the North Carolina assembly and take them back to London, presumably to face charges for rebellion. It was reported that Collet "was preparing the said fort . . . for the reception of a promised reinforcement, which was to be employed in reducing the good people of this province to a slavish submission to the will of a wicked and tyrannic [sic] minister, and for this diabolic purpose, had collected several abandoned profligates, whose crimes had rendered them unworthy of civil society." Martin fueled the fire by announcing that he might have to arm the local slaves to defend the interests of the empire.[40]

How many colonists participated in the final assault on Fort Johnson is not clear. Witnesses judged the number to have been between five hundred and two thousand. Many came from Wilmington, but in the words of one observer, others "marched down [from] the country." As this huge, irregular force approached, Collet and the rear guard escaped, joining the governor on the *Cruizer*. The initial victory did not mollify the insurgents. They literally razed Fort Johnson. They set fire to all the buildings within the compound, tore down the back wall of the fortification, and, as one militant announced with reference to Martin, "effectively dislodged that atrocious freebooter." The frenzy spread. Leaving the smoldering ruins of Fort Johnson, the Americans "wantonly destroyed the corn and burnt the houses of several planters, who had at times been useful to those aboard the frigate."[41]

Martin apparently did not see anything ridiculous about attempting to govern North Carolina—a huge colony in terms of territory—from the cramped quarters of a British warship. Indeed, secure in the knowledge that the insurgents did not have the means to attack the *Cruizer*, he issued thundering proclamations calling for the return of law and order. He sent the local newspaper—the *Cape Fear Mercury*—a statement condemning the members of the colony's "seditious Committees" who had employed "evil, pernicious, and traitorous" tactics to mobilize popular resistance. Martin reasoned that he could address the people over the heads of their irresponsible leaders. It was a doomed effort. But he soldiered on, reminding those "deluded" Americans who might have cheered the storming of Fort Johnson that the attack was really an example of "wanton barbarity that would disgrace human nature in the most savage state." No one paid the slightest attention to the governor's pathetic fulminations. In his idle moments he urged Dartmouth to get tough with the insurgents. If the British would only transport a small army to North Carolina, they would in a short time take back the southern colonies and silence those nettlesome committees. It was an irresponsible fantasy, and although Dartmouth briefly considered the prospect of moving troops from Ireland to the Cape Fear region, he found no way to return Martin to his palace or rebuild the ruins of Fort Johnson.[42]

## III

New Hampshire provides another, somewhat earlier example of the people taking charge of their own revolution. The political history of this colony is a chronicle of one Wentworth following another to the governorship. Some complained about the dominance of this "clan," but they did not do so within hearing distance of a member of this powerful provincial family. The first Wentworth received his appointment from the Crown in 1717. Nothing suggests that the ruling group engaged in practices that might be described as flagrantly corrupt. They understood the privileges of office—when to reward a follower, when to make a timely land grant—and so when, in 1767, John Wentworth replaced his uncle Benning as the governor of the province, no one thought anything amiss.[43]

Wentworth dreamed of continuing this cozy status quo for as long as possible. Unhappily for him, no sooner had he acceded to office than many people living in New Hampshire turned their attention south to Massachusetts, where resistance to parliamentary acts had taken a violent turn. Late in 1774 a false report triggered a series of events that brought the king's government in New Hampshire to its knees. Governor Wentworth may well have seen this as the moment when imperial authority in New Hampshire collapsed. It made no difference that the alarming intelligence had almost no basis in fact. During the final days of December 1774 the story spread rapidly from community to community that General Gage intended to send two regiments of redcoats from Boston to secure Fort William and Mary, an unimpressive structure constructed more than a century earlier to guard Portsmouth harbor. However unremarkable the building may have been, it housed the colony's supply of gunpowder, and the insurgents rightly concluded that Gage's preemptive move might leave them defenseless.

On December 14, 1774, the people of New Hampshire openly defied the British Empire. In Portsmouth a drumbeat summoned a curious band—local militiamen, armed strangers, committeemen from neighboring towns—for a march on the fort. No one made the slightest effort to maintain secrecy. The entire action took on a festive air. The initial group numbered about 200. Along the way another 150 armed men joined the insurgency. Captain John Cochran, the British officer in charge of the fort, watched the proceedings. He found himself in command of an inadequate force of five invalids, all of whom had been retired from regular military service. The Americans ordered Cochran to surrender. He refused and then foolishly allowed the pensioners to fire. Although they failed to hit a single attacker, the shots enraged the insurgents, who now swarmed over the walls of Fort William and Mary. They briefly took Cochran and his men prisoner, and seized almost a hundred barrels of powder, several small cannons, and an impressive supply of small arms. According to one report, they "triumphantly gave three huzzas and hauled down the King's colors."[44]

The desecration of the royal standard seemed to loyalists in other colonies more worrisome than did the theft of cannons and small arms. "No history," announced James Rivington's journal in New York City, "I believe will furnish us with an instance of a King's Fort being taken and his colors struck by his own subjects in a time of peace, and without any cause or provocation."[45] Some of the New Hampshire men carted the gunpowder to Exeter, a difficult winter trip of fifteen miles. Others returned to Portsmouth. A depressed and frightened Wentworth watched from his home as they celebrated in the streets a victory over their own government. All of this occurred more than six months before the battles of Lexington and Concord.

The governor's ordeal had only just begun. The people of New Hampshire still had unfinished business at Fort William and Mary. During the day following the first attack, December 15, men from throughout the colony arrived in Portsmouth. They represented scattered communities; they had no official commander. One witness reported, "This morning about 60 horsemen accoutred [fully equipped for military duty], came into town, and gave out that 700 more were on their march to Portsmouth from Exeter, Greenland, Newmarket, &c. and would be in that town by eleven o'clock; their intentions, it is suspected, is to dismantle the Fort."[46] Within a few hours, the number of armed colonists had reached almost two thousand.

This is a truly impressive figure. It indicated that even at this early date in the imperial conflict, about one out of every six adult males in New Hampshire was prepared to halt normal farmwork, travel scores of miles over icy roads, and assault the king's property. Within the context of the experience of these men, the episode was not a lark or a harmless show of force. They marched to the fort a second time, stripping it of small arms and gunpowder that the first insurgents had overlooked. A few large cannons they could not transport to secure hiding places were simply thrown into the water. As had been the case with Fort Johnson in North Carolina, the Americans not only plundered the site, they also tried to erase it from the provincial memory. On the margins of empire, raw anger energized repeated waves of destruction. It was not until the seventeenth that two British warships arrived from Boston, but by then the damage had been done.

On December 20, 1774, Governor Wentworth drafted the most difficult letter of his career. He was obliged to inform Dartmouth of what had happened in New Hampshire. Wentworth opened the report with the kind of explanation that made a lot of sense to those who never understood the wellsprings of insurgency. Wentworth assured Dartmouth that on their own, the ordinary people could never have organized an attack on Fort William and Mary. "Factious leaders in Boston" and troublemakers in Portsmouth had manipulated the common folk, and "though it may appear strange that people of that stamp should succeed in such attempts, yet true it is that a person even below the middling class by setting up a cry about liberty will captivate and bear away with the populace, who carry all before them at present in this country." To compound the difficulties, the "better sort" had remained "inactive through fear of subjecting themselves to the resentment and rage of the ruling multitude."

The governor then chronicled the sack of the fort. In the process he undermined his own argument that a few incendiaries had duped the people. The numbers had been too large, the enthusiasm for political violence too widespread. "The country is so much inflamed," he confessed, ". . . that many magistrates and militia officers who ought to have given their aid and assistance in restraining and suppressing this uproar were active to promote and encourage it." Wentworth protested that he had not in fact lost control. After all, he concluded, "Upon the whole, my Lord, I can only say that I have done everything in my power to prevent the military stores from being taken away and to quell this tumult."[47]

The governor did not flee New Hampshire, at least not immediately. Like Martin, Wentworth attempted to mask his own loss of power by issuing fierce proclamations. No doubt General Gage's willingness to post a company of regular troops in a building at Fort William and Mary left undisturbed by the local insurgents restored the governor's hope, if not his courage. Wentworth had been forced to beg British authorities even for this modest military assistance. "The People do not support the Magistrates, who thence are unable to do their duty," he told Gage, who was having problems of his own in Massachusetts. "And if any Person should be taken up, He wou'd be either immediately rescued or the Jail would be broke open directly, as experience proves the Militia will not Act."[48]

In January 1775, despite a widespread belief that no one was listening, Wentworth called for the arrest of the colonists who had allegedly masterminded the December attack. These militants had, in fact, committed serious crimes. They had "in the most daring and rebellious Manner [conspired to] invest, attack, and forcibly enter into His Majesty's Castle William & Mary." These "several Bodies of Men" had not only overpowered the captain and his tiny garrison, they were also responsible for "many treasonable Insults, & Outrages . . . in open Hostility and direct Oppugnation [opposition] of His Majesty's Government."[49] He ordered the colony's attorney general, Samuel Livermore, to bring the guilty parties to justice.

To his credit, Livermore recognized that the political horse was long out of the barn. In a letter addressed to Wentworth that found its way to Dartmouth, the Crown's chief legal officer in New Hampshire explained, "I beg leave to offer to your Excellency my opinion that such a prosecution at this time would be altogether useless both for the impossibility of apprehending and securing the offenders and for the getting them convicted in case they could be brought to a trial." An investigation into the Fort William and Mary incident had yielded not a single name. The entire population seemed to suffer from amnesia. Any attempt to press the issue, Livermore concluded, might backfire, for as the governor should know, "whenever civil power attempts things hazardous and fails in the execution it becomes a miserable example of its own weakness and lessens its usefulness in other matters."[50]

And finally, unlike Wentworth, Livermore had developed a more realistic appreciation of insurgency. The people did not regard the plundering of the fort as a treasonous breaking and entering. Quite to the contrary, they classified the sack of the castle as a "political" crime, an ideologically acceptable response to the abuse of imperial authority, and so Livermore wondered whether the governor might ask, "is there not the greatest reason to suppose the populace would totally interrupt the administration of justice rather than suffer their champions of liberty to be brought to a trial."[51]

From the British point of view, conditions in New Hampshire swiftly deteriorated. In May 1775 news arrived of the killings at Lexington and Concord. Like so many officials over the centuries who have watched helplessly as the people surged forward in the name of rights and liberty, Wentworth could only whine that without more troops he was unable to do the king's business. "It is difficult," he informed Dartmouth, "to describe how exceedingly this part of the country has been agitated and disturbed since the unhappy affair happened between the troops and country people near Boston." His report mentioned not a single leader. The people had taken over. "I am satisfied," he observed, "if the country people should come in with a determination to do mischief, as is daily threatened, it will not be in the power of the town to restrain them." New Hampshire was experiencing independence some fifteen months before the Declaration of Independence. "This is the dismal situation we are now reduced to," Wentworth concluded, "without any government power of remedy and without any place of strength or security in the province for any person to take shelter in, there being only one frigate near the entrance of the harbor to cover the fort."[52]

Wentworth hung on until August, but the threat of another round of violence persuaded him to take to the waters. On the twenty-third, he and the members of his family sailed from New Hampshire aboard the *Scarborough*. Soon after their departure, insurgents returned to demolish what was left of Fort William and Mary.[53]

Other royal governors followed Wentworth and Martin. Governor William Tryon of New York boarded the *Halifax* in October 1775. Governor William Franklin of New Jersey made a desperate attempt to reach a British ship, but local insurgents arrested him in June 1776. The Earl of Dunmore, Virginia's royal governor, was driven from Williamsburg and took refuge on the *Fowley* in June 1775. For several months he employed the vessel as a floating base from which to launch raids on exposed riverfront plantations. Such tactics failed to win supporters. Dunmore never returned to Williamsburg. Lord William Campbell, governor of South Carolina, sought the security of the *Tamer* in September 1775. Governor James Wright of Georgia managed to hold off the insurgents a few months longer than Campbell had, but at the end of the year, even he had to admit the game was over. He sailed away on the *Scarborough*.

## IV

The ordeal of two mediocre governors and two insubstantial forts adds a new dimension to the traditional narrative of the coming of the American Revolution. The celebrated events familiar to nearly all of us — the long debate among members of the Continental Congress over the wisdom of declaring independence, for example — suggest that most Americans were mere spectators in the initial confrontation with the British Empire. But this historical perspective is surely inadequate. As Martin and Wentworth discovered, the people of North Carolina and New Hampshire were fully mobilized more than a year before the delegates to the Continental Congress summoned the will to proclaim national independence. Long before there was a nation, there was a country of the imagination. As early as 1774, insurgents operating in the backwaters of empire were prepared to employ violence against the king's representatives and, perhaps more significant, against the king's forts. The irregular troops who hauled down the royal standard at Fort William and Mary in December 1774 engaged in a revolutionary act. And they knew it.

The governors did what most beleaguered imperial officers have done in such situations. They blamed the unpleasantness on a few troublemakers. A few arrests, a timely show of military force, and the deluded people would give up the insurgency. It never occurred to Wentworth and Martin that they faced a new kind of popular resistance. They had no vocabulary with which to describe what they were witnessing. And in any case, to inform Dartmouth that they had lost control of the situation was something they could not bring themselves to do. It was easier to beg for additional military support. Even as they took to the waters, they were calling for additional troops. Gage himself joined the chorus. Several thousand additional redcoats, well armed and well trained, could restore the empire to its former glory.

The ruined forts bore witness to an extraordinary achievement. Angered initially in late 1773 by the special privileges Parliament had granted to a corrupt London corporation, a small group of Boston militants destroyed property owned by the East India Company. This provocation persuaded the leaders of the British government to punish an entire city for the actions of a few residents. The patent unfairness of such a blanket response caused ordinary people throughout Massachusetts— many of them young, reasonably prosperous, and highly religious—to drive the agents of an oppressive empire from the countryside.

Within a few months, however, insurgents discovered innovative ways to communicate their discontent to other Americans who happened to live many hundreds of miles away. Newspapers reported the activities of distant strangers; a charity for the unemployed workers of Boston created a common bond of sympathy for those who had sacrificed for an American cause. Gradually the resistance movement gained momentum. In every town and county, committees made up of local people—many of them new to political office—channeled spontaneous rage into an elaborate committee system that drew legitimacy from the participation of the people as well as from the Continental Congress.

The people who laid waste to the two forts—like many other American insurgents we have encountered—imagined the creation of a new, more equitable national government that would work for the common good. They challenged the British Empire. Through the crucible of confrontation that stretched from years of resistance to Britain's eventual capitulation, American insurgents emerged as American patriots. And now, as so many other people throughout the world demand their rights and justice, they challenge modern Americans to remember their own revolutionary origins.

# Notes

## Introduction: The Revolutionary World of Matthew Patten

1. This book owes a great deal to a number of historians who have tried to restore the ordinary people to the story of their own revolution. Without question, the most important and inspiring source was Peter Force, *American Archives*. Force (1790–1868) was trained as a printer. But for reasons that are not altogether clear, he developed a passion for the American Revolution. After a successful career as an army officer, a publisher, and mayor of Washington, D.C., he decided to collect every surviving document related to this event. He paid copyists from Georgia to New Hampshire to transcribe materials for a penny a word. The results flooded into his offices, thousands of pages documenting daily resistance to Great Britain on the local level. The task overwhelmed Force. But he did manage to produce nine huge volumes. Since he organized the reports chronologically, he provides readers with a dynamic sense of the Revolution. On any given day, people in New England as well as in the South were organizing; they did not know what other colonists were doing. Communication was slow and unreliable. Force managed to capture hundreds of different stories happening simultaneously, and without paying much attention to the Founding Fathers, he reminds us that in communities throughout America the people took charge of the Revolution.

   Several modern historians have helped me rethink the traditional narratives of national independence. I can list here only a few of the more provocative and original works: Alfred F. Young, *The Shoemaker and the Tea Party: Memory and the American Revolution* (Boston, 1999); Gary B. Nash, *The Urban Crucible: The Northern Seaports and the Origins of the American Revolution* (Cambridge, MA, 1986); Woody Holton, *Forced Founders: Indians, Debtors, Slaves, and the Making of the American Revolution in Virginia* (Chapel Hill, NC, 1999); Charles Royster, *A Revolutionary People at War: The Continental Army and the American Character, 1775–1783* (Chapel Hill, NC, 1996); Hermann Wellenreuther, *The Revolution of the People:*

*Thoughts and Documents on the Revolutionary Process in North America, 1774–1776* (Gottingen, Ger., 2006); Pauline Maier, *American Scripture: Making the Declaration of Independence* (New York, 1998); and David Ammerman, *In the Common Cause: American Response to the Coercive Acts of 1774* (Charlottesville, VA, 1974).

2. For example see, Officer of the Army, *The History of the Civil War in America* (London, 1780), 69, 72. See also Michael Rose, *Washington's War: From Independence to Iraq* (London, 2007).

3. Edward L. Parker, *History of Londonderry, Comprising the Towns of Derry and Londonderry, N.H.* (Boston, 1851), 68.

4. The fullest account of the Patten family can be found in Kerby A. Miller et al., eds., *Irish Immigrants in the Land of Canaan: Letters and Memoirs from Colonial and Revolutionary America, 1675–1815* (Oxford, UK, 2003), 547–50. Miller places the history of such families as the Pattens in the larger social context in *Emigrants and Exiles: Ireland and the Irish Exodus to North America* (Oxford, UK, 1985), chap. 4. Also T. H. Breen, "Ireland's 18th-Century Revolution on New England's Northern Frontier" (Lecture, Keough-Naughton Institute for Irish Studies, Notre Dame University, November 20, 2009).

5. Cited in James G. Leyburn, *The Scotch-Irish: A Social History* (Chapel Hill, NC, 1962), 331.

6. Matthew Patten, *The Diary of Matthew Patten of Bedford, N.H.: From 1754 to 1788* (Concord, NH, 1903).

7. See Patrick Griffin, *The People with No Name: Ireland's Ulster Scots, America's Scots Irish, and the Creation of a British Atlantic World, 1689–1764* (Princeton, NJ, 2001).

8. *Virginia Gazette* (Pinkney), May 18, 1775.

9. Cited in David Doyle, *Ireland, Irishmen and Revolutionary America, 1760–1820* (Dublin, 1981), 110.

10. T. H. Breen, "An Irish Revolution in Eighteenth-Century America?" *Field Day Review* (Dublin) 2 (2006): 275–84. Also, Kevin Whelan, "The Green Atlantic: Radical Reciprocities Between Ireland and America in the Long Eighteenth Century," in *A New Imperial History: Culture, Identity, and Modernity in Britain and the Empire, 1660–1840*, ed. Kathleen Wilson (Cambridge, UK, 2004), 216–38.

11. An account of this ongoing dispute can be found in Miller, *Irish Immigrants*, 549. Also, Kenneth Scott, "John Houston, Tory Minister of Bedford," *Journal of the Presbyterian Historical Society* 22 (December 1944): 172–97.

12. Patten, *Diary*, 329–30.

13. Ibid., 330.

14. *New-Hampshire Gazette*, September 30, 1774.

15. Patten, *Diary*, 342.

16. Ibid.

17. Ibid., 342, 345.

18. Ibid., 361.

19. Nathan Fiske, *The Importance of Righteousness to the Happiness and the Tendency of Oppression to the Misery of the People* . . . (Boston, 1774), 24–25. Fiske originally delivered the sermon on July 14, 1774. Steve Pincus provides a valuable comparative perspective on revolution in *1688: The First Modern Revolution* (New Haven, CT, 2009).

20. Thomas Paine, *Common Sense*, in *Complete Writings*, ed. Philip Foner, 2 vols. (New York, 1945), 1:22–23.
21. Charles Lane Hanson, ed., *A Journal for the Years 1739–1803 by Samuel Lane of Stratham, New Hampshire* (Camden, ME, 1993), 44–45.
22. *Massachusetts Spy*, June 21, 1775.
23. I want to thank Professor Randolph Roth, department of history, Ohio State University, for his generosity in sharing this material from his current research.
24. Abner Sanger, *Very Poor and of a Lo Make: The Journal of Abner Sanger*, ed. Lois Stabler (Portsmouth, NH, 1987), 6.
25. Peter Force, ed., *American Archives: Consisting of a Collection of Authentik [sic] Records, State Papers, Debates and Letters . . .* , 4th Series, 6 vols. (Washington, D.C., 1837–53), 1:1262.

## 1: The Face of Colonial Society

1. Hannah's deposition can be found in Josiah Adams, *An Address Delivered at Acton, July 21, 1835 . . .* (Boston, 1835), 47. See also the correspondence concerning Hannah's later appeal for a widow's pension from the United States government in *The Life of John J. Crittenden*, ed. Chapman Coleman (Philadelphia, 1873), 1:133–34. For the other quotations and the description of the fighting at Concord, I have relied upon David Hackett Fisher, *Paul Revere's Ride* (New York, 1994); Allen French, *The Day of Concord and Lexington: The Nineteenth of April, 1775* (Boston, 1925); Harold R. Phalen, *History of the Town of Acton* (Cambridge, MA, 1954), 66–94; Lemuel Shattuck, *A History of the Town of Concord . . .* (Boston, 1835); and Robert A. Gross, *The Minutemen and Their World* (New York, 2001).
2. Force, *American Archives*, 2:369. See also Christopher M. Jedrey, *The World of John Cleaveland: Family and Community in Eighteenth-Century New England* (New York, 1979).
3. Jonas Clark, *The Fate of Blood-Thirsty Oppressors . . . A Sermon, preached at Lexington, April 19, 1776* (Boston, 1776), 27–28.
4. *Pennsylvania Journal*, March 25, 1756. The ablest general introduction to mid-eighteenth-century provincial society is Richard Hofstadter, *America at 1750: A Social Portrait* (New York, 1973). Also, Jon Butler, *Becoming America: The Revolution Before 1776* (Cambridge, MA, 2001).
5. The problem of projecting present-day values onto the past is discussed in Brendan McConville, *The King's Three Faces: The Rise & Fall of Royal America, 1688–1776* (Chapel Hill, NC, 2006), 1–14.
6. Joseph Plumb Martin, *A Narrative of a Revolutionary Soldier: Some of the Adventures, Dangers, and Sufferings of Joseph Plumb Martin* (New York, 2001), 6–7.
7. John J. McCusker and Russell R. Menard, *The Economy of British America, 1607–1789* (Chapel Hill, NC, 1985), 301. See also Carole Shammas, "How Self-Sufficient Was Early America?" *Journal of Interdisciplinary History* 8 (1982): 263–68; Jan de Vries, "Between Purchasing Power and the World of Goods: Understanding the Household Economy in Early Modern Europe," in *Consumption and the World of Goods*, ed. John Brewer and Roy Porter (London, 1993), 85–132; Ann Smart Martin, *Buying into the World of Goods: Early Consumers in Backcountry Virginia* (Baltimore, 2008); T. H. Breen, *Marketplace of Revolution: How Consumer Politics Shaped*

*American Independence* (New York, 2004); and David Hancock, *Oceans of Wine: Madeira and the Emergence of American Trade and Taste* (New Haven, 2009).

8.  T. H. Breen, *Tobacco Culture: The Mentality of the Great Tidewater Planters on the Eve of Revolution* (Princeton, NJ, 1985).

9.  Kenneth A. Lockridge, *Literacy in Colonial New England: An Enquiry into the Social Context of Literacy in the Early Modern West* (New York, 1974); and Richard D. Brown, *Knowledge Is Power: The Diffusion of Information in Early America, 1700–1865* (New York, 1989).

10. This story can be found in Edmund S. Morgan, *American Slavery—American Freedom: The Ordeal of Colonial Virginia* (New York, 1975), 378–79. Michael A. McDonnell provides similar examples in *The Politics of War: Race, Class, and Conflict in Revolutionary Virginia* (Chapel Hill, NC, 2007).

11. Morgan, *American Slavery–American Freedom*. See also Rhys Isaac, *The Transformation of Virginia, 1740–1790* (Chapel Hill, NC, 1982) and A. G. Roeber, *Faithful Magistrates and Republican Lawyers: Creators of Virginia Legal Culture, 1680–1810* (Chapel Hill, NC, 1981).

12. Harry J. Carman, ed., *American Husbandry* (New York, 1939), 124. Jack P. Greene discusses these issues in *The Intellectual Construction of America* (Chapel Hill, NC, 1993), chap. 4.

13. Alexis de Tocqueville, *The Old Regime and the Revolution*, ed. François Furet and Françoise Melonio, trans. Alan S. Kahan (Chicago, 1998), 206.

14. Quoted in Stephen A. Marini, *Radical Sects of Revolutionary New England* (Cambridge, MA, 1982), 14. See also John L. Brooke, *The Refiner's Fire: The Making of Mormon Cosmology, 1644–1844* (Cambridge, UK, 1996).

15. See Frank Lambert, *Pedlar in Divinity: George Whitefield and the Transatlantic Revivals, 1737–1770* (Princeton, NJ, 1994); and Timothy D. Hall, *Contested Boundaries: Itinerancy and the Reshaping of the Colonial Religious World* (Durham, NC, 1994).

16. Quoted in Frank Lambert, *Inventing the "Great Awakening"* (Princeton, NJ, 1999), 119.

17. Patricia U. Bonomi, *Under the Cope of Heaven: Religion, Society, and Politics in Colonial America* (New York, 2003); and Christine Leigh Heyrman, *Southern Cross: The Beginnings of the Bible Belt* (New York, 1997).

18. Peter Oliver, *Origin and Progress of the American Revolution*, ed. Douglass Adair and John A. Schutz (Stanford, CA, 1961), 149.

19. Lambert, *Great Awakening*; Mark A. Noll, *America's God: From Jonathan Edwards to Abraham Lincoln* (New York, 2002), chaps. 2–4; Marini, *Radical Sects of Revolutionary New England*; and Heyrman, *Southern Cross*.

20. Mary Cooper, *The Diary of Mary Cooper: Life on a Long Island Farm, 1768–1773*, ed. Field Horne (Oyster Bay, NY, 1981), 13–24; see also Hall, *Contested Boundaries*.

21. This essay was reprinted in the *Connecticut Gazette and the Universal Intelligencer* [New London], May 27, 1774.

22. Gray's letter is reproduced in Ellen D. Larned, *History of Windham County*, 2 vols. (Worcester, MA, 1874–80), 2:154–55. See also Ruth Bloch, "Religion, Literary Sentimentalism, and Popular Revolutionary Ideology," in *Gender and Morality in Anglo-American Culture, 1650–1800*, ed. Ruth Bloch (Berkeley, 2003), 128–29, and Susan Juster, *Disorderly Women: Sexual Politics and Evangelicalism in Revolutionary New England* (Ithaca, NY, 1996).

23. David Armitage, *The Ideological Origins of the British Empire* (Cambridge, UK, 2000).

24. Bernard Bailyn, *The Origins of American Politics* (New York, 1968).

25. See Tim Harris, *Revolution: The Great Crisis of the British Monarchy, 1685–1720* (London, 2006); Peter Laslett, *The World We Lost* (New York, 1965); and Linda Colley, *Britons: Forging the Nation, 1707–1737* (New Haven, CT, 1992).

26. Owen Stanwood, "Creating the Common Enemy: Catholics, Indians, and the Politics of Fear in Imperial North America, 1678–1700," unpublished dissertation, Northwestern University, 2005. Also, Nathan O. Hatch, *Sacred Cause of Liberty: Republican Thought and the Millennium in Revolutionary New England* (New Haven, CT, 1977).

27. Cited in Charles W. Akers, *Called unto Liberty: A Life of Jonathan Mayhew, 1720–1766* (Cambridge, MA, 1964), 195.

28. Breen, *Marketplace*; and Jan de Vries, *The Industrious Revolution: Consumer Behavior and the Household Economy, 1650 to the Present* (Cambridge, UK, 2008).

29. *New-Hampshire Gazette*, July 13, 1764. Also, T. H. Breen, "Interpreting New World Nationalism," in *Nationalism in the New World*, ed. Don H. Doyle and Marco Antonio Pamplona (Athens, GA, 2006), 41–60.

30. "The Autobiography of the Rev. John Barnard," *Massachusetts Historical Society Collections* 5 (1836): 200.

31. McConville, *King's Three Faces*, 1–8; Gordon Wood, *The Radicalism of the American Revolution* (New York, 1992), 11–92.

32. Edmund S. Morgan, *Puritan Political Ideas* (Indianapolis, 1965).

33. *Connecticut Gazette and Universal Intelligencer* (New London), September 30, 1774.

34. Andrew Burnaby, *Travels Through the Middle Settlements in North America* (Ithaca, NY, 1963), 113.

35. *Cape-Fear Mercury* [North Carolina], July 28, 1775.

36. Samuel Lane, *A Journal for the Years 1739–1803 by Samuel Lane of Stratham, New Hampshire*, ed. Charles Lane Hanson (Concord, NH, 1937), 11, 45.

37. John Allen, *An Oration on the Beauties of Liberty, or the Essential Rights of the Americans* . . . (Hartford, CT, 1774), 25–26.

38. Merrill Jensen, *The Founding of a Nation: A History of the American Revolution, 1763–1776* (New York, 1968), 512.

39. Force, eds., *American Archives*, 2:229.

40. Oliver, *Origin and Progress*, 65.

41. Force, *American Archives*, 1:343.

42. Alexander Graydon, *Memoirs of His Own Time*, ed. John Stockton Littell (New York, 1969) 134–35.

43. Michael A. McDonnell, "Popular Mobilization and Political Culture in Revolutionary Virginia: The Failure of the Minutemen and the Revolution from Below," *Journal of American History* 85 (1998): 946–81.

44. Griffin McRee, *Life and Correspondence of James Iredell, One of the Associate Justices of the Supreme Court of the United States*, 2 vols. (New York, 1857–58), 1:335–36.

45. Nathan Perkins, *A Sermon Preached to the Soldiers, Who Went from West-Hartford, in Defence of Their Country. Delivered the 2d of June, 1775* . . . (Hartford, CT, 1775), 13–14.

46. Nathaniel Niles, *Two Discourses on Liberty; Delivered . . . in Newbury-port on Lord's Day, June 5th, 1774* (Newburyport, MA, 1774), 35.

47. Donald A. Yerxa, *The Burning of Falmouth: A Case Study in British Imperial Pacification* (Portland, ME, 1975), 130.

48. Cited in Jack P. Greene, *Imperatives, Behaviors, and Identities: Essays in Early American Cultural History* (Charlottesville, VA, 1992), 236.

49. James S. Leamon, *Revolution Downeast: The War for American Independence in Maine* (Amherst, MA, 1993), 62–63. Contemporary opinions are cited in Nathan Goold, "General Samuel Thompson of Brunswick and Topsham, Maine," Maine Historical Society *Collections* 1 (1904): 423, 427.

50. George Augustus Wheeler and Henry Warren Wheeler, *History of Brunswick, Topsham, and Harpswell, Maine, Including the Ancient Territory Known as Pejepscot* (Boston, 1878), 812–13.

51. Ibid., 813; Goold, "General Samuel Thompson," 427.

52. Cited in Leamon, *Revolution Downeast*, 63. Also, William Southgate, "History of Scarborough," Maine Historical Society *Collections* 3 (1853), 189–90; and Charles Edwin Allen, *History of Dresden, Maine . . .* (Augusta, ME, 1931), 387–92.

53. Cited in Goold, "General Samuel Thompson," 435.

54. Cited in ibid., 437–39.

55. Cited in Leamon, *Revolution Downeast*, 66.

56. Ibid., 67.

57. *New-England Chronicle*, November 23, 1775.

58. *Boston Gazette*, March 17, 1777.

59. John P. Kaminski and George J. Saladino, eds., *The Documentary History of the Ratification of the Constitution*, 22 vols. (Madison, WI, 2000), 4:1291, 1354.

60. Goold, "General Samuel Thompson," 424–25.

## 2: *Ghost Stories in a Time of Political Crisis*

1. THE WONDERFUL APPEARANCE . . . (Boston, 1774), 1–31.

2. *Massachusetts Spy*, December 8, 1774. Also, *Boston Evening-Post*, January 9, 1775; and *Essex Journal*, January 25, 1775.

3. Cited in Jensen, *The Founding of a Nation*, 577. Also, Bernard Donoughue, *British Politics and the American Revolution: The Path to War, 1773–1775* (London, 1964), 16–41, 67.

4. Donoughue, *British Politics*, 53; and H. T. Dickinson, "Britain's Imperial Sovereignty: The Ideological Case Against the American Colonies," in *Britain and the American Revolution*, ed. H. T. Dickinson (London, 1998), 64–96; and H. T. Dickinson, *Liberty and Property: Political Ideology in Eighteenth-Century Britain* (London, 1979).

5. Force, *American Archives*, 1:5, 223.

6. Ibid., 1:5.

7. This extraordinary correspondence can be found in K. G. Davies, ed., *Documents of the American Revolution, 1770–1783*, Colonial Office Series, Transcripts 1774, 21 vols. (Dublin, 1972–81), vol. 8.

8. Cited in Donoughue, *British Politics*, 53. Bernard Bailyn provides the fullest account of Thomas Hutchinson's efforts to straddle two political worlds in Bernard Bailyn, *The Ordeal of Thomas Hutchinson* (Cambridge, MA, 1974).

9. Officer of the Army, *The History of the Civil War in America*, 1.
10. Cited in Donoughue, *British Politics*, 59, 61–62. Also, Davies, ed., *Documents*, 61.
11. Force, *American Archives*, 1:37–39.
12. Ibid., 45.
13. Ibid., 66.
14. Ibid., 42–46. Also, Peter D. G. Thomas, *Lord North* (London, 1976), 32–76; and Donoughue, *British Politics*, 63–86.
15. Force, *American Archives*, 1:40–41, 49, 54.
16. Ibid., 50–51.
17. Ibid., 51.
18. Donoughue, *British Politics*, 132.
19. Cited in R.T.H. Halsey, *The Boston Port Bill as Pictured by a Contemporary London Cartoonist* (New York, 1904), 145–46; Paul Langford, "British Correspondence in the Colonial Press, 1763–1775: A Study in Anglo-American Misunderstanding Before the American Revolution," in *The Press & the American Revolution*, eds. Bernard Bailyn and John B. Hench (Worcester, MA, 1980); Kathleen Wilson, *The Sense of the People: Politics, Culture and Imperialism in England, 1715–1785* (Cambridge, UK, and New York, 1995), chaps. 3–5; John Brewer, *Party Ideology and Popular Politics at the Accession of George III* (Cambridge, UK, and New York, 1976), chaps. 8–10; G. A. Cranfield, *The Development of the Provincial Newspaper, 1700–1760* (Oxford, UK, 1962); and Bob Harris, *Politics and the Rise of the Press: Britain and France, 1620–1800* (London and New York, 1996), 29–52.
20. Force, *American Archives*, 1:42–43.
21. David Hartley, *Letters on the American War* (London, 1778), 3.
22. Donoughue, *British Politics*, 49.
23. On the responsibility of royal governors during this period, see Leonard Labaree, *Royal Government in America: A Study of the British Colonial System Before 1783* (New York, 1958).
24. *Connecticut Courant*, May 17–24, 1774. Also, *Essex Gazette*, May 31–June 7, 1774; and *Connecticut Gazette and the Universal Intelligencer* (New London), June 10, 1774.
25. *Connecticut Courant*, May 17–24, 1774.
26. Davies, *Documents*, 8:116.
27. Ibid., 87.
28. Ibid., 124.
29. Ibid., 137.
30. Force, *American Archives*, 1:332.
31. *Essex Gazette*, May 31, 1774.
32. *Connecticut Gazette and the Universal Intelligencer* (New London), April 15, 1774.
33. Ibid., June 3, 1774.
34. NEW-YORK. *The Following DIALOGUE being conceived, in Some Measure, calculated to advance the Cause of FREEDOM . . . [May 21, 1774]* (New York, 1774).

## *3: Revenge of the Countryside*

1. *Essex Gazette*, May 24–31, 1774. Also, Force, *American Archives*, 1:336. News of Farmington appeared in various newspapers, so that even if the report itself was exaggerated, other New Englanders learned of it through trusted journals. Note that the Boston town meeting may have circulated a call to protest, but the specific

response was designed by Farmington. For the Boston town debate, see *Report of the Record Commissioners of the City of Boston Containing the Boston Town Records, 1770 through 1777* (Boston, 1887), 175–77.

2. *Connecticut Gazette and the Universal Intelligencer* (New London), June 3, 1774.
3. Ellen D. Larned, *History of Windham County, Connecticut*, 2 vols. (Worcester, MA, 1880), 1:122–23; For a description of protest in neighboring Lebanon, Connecticut, see *Essex Gazette*, June 14–21, 1774.
4. L. Kinvin Wroth, ed., *Province in Rebellion: A Documentary History of the Founding of the Commonwealth of Massachusetts, 1774–1775* (Cambridge, MA, 1975), doc. 128.
5. Josiah Pierce, A *History of the Town of Gorham, Maine* (Portland, ME, 1862), 115–17.
6. For example, see Frantz Fanon, *The Wretched of the Earth*, trans. Constance Farrington (New York, 1963).
7. "Letter to the Inhabitants of Massachusetts Bay," *Essex Gazette*, January 31–February 7, 1775.
8. Samuel Williams, A *Discourse on the Love of Our Country; Delivered on a Day of Thanksgiving, December 15, 1774* (Salem, MA, 1775), 18–20; and "Samuel Williams," *Sibley's Harvard Graduates*, ed. John Langford Sibley and Clifford K. Shipton, 17 vols. (Boston, 1970), 15 (1761–65): 134–46. On the problem of colonial nationalism, see Breen, "Interpreting New World Nationalism," 41–60.
9. See, for example, Roger D. Petersen, *Resistance and Rebellion: Lessons from Eastern Europe* (Cambridge, UK, 2001).
10. Force, *American Archives*, 1:397–98, 434–35, 489–91. Also, Jensen, *Founding of a Nation*, 461–70.
11. George Fulsom, *History of Saco and Biddeford* (Saco, ME, 1830), 277–78. Also, for the use of boycotts as a political weapon see Breen, *Marketplace of Revolution*.
12. *Connecticut Gazette and the Universal Intelligencer* (New London), July 8, 1774.
13. *Essex Gazette*, September 6–13, 1774. See also *Connecticut Gazette*, September 23, 1774; and Lemuel Shattuck, A *History of the Town of Concord* (Boston, 1835), 82–85.
14. Force, *American Archives*, 1:769–70.
15. *Essex Gazette*, August 30–September 6, 1774.
16. Force, *American Archives*, 1:951.
17. Ibid., 1:796. See also Shattuck, *Concord*, 85–87.
18. *Connecticut Gazette*, July 8, 1774; also Jonathan Parsons, *Freedom from Civil and Ecclesiastical Slavery* (Newburyport, MA, 1774), 16.
19. Force, *American Archives*, 1:767–69.
20. *Connecticut Gazette*, September 2, 1774.
21. *Pennsylvania Packet* ["extra" for No. 152], September 19, 1774. See also Force, *American Archives*, 1:724, 745, 1261–63.
22. Force, *American Archives*, 1:747–49; *Boston Evening-Post*, September 5, 1774, and *Essex Gazette*, September 6–13, 1774.
23. *Essex Gazette*, July 5–12, 1774.
24. Force, *American Archives*, 1:669–70.
25. Davies, *Documents*, 8:122–24.
26. Ibid., 8:164–66; and Jensen, *Founding of a Nation*, 550–67.
27. *Essex Gazette*, August 23–30, 1774.
28. Ibid.

29. Davies, *Documents*, 8:166–68; also Force, *American Archives*, 1:745; Wroth, *Province in Rebellion*, doc. 154; *Connecticut Gazette*, September 2, 1774; *Essex Gazette*, August 23–30 and August 30–September 6, 1774; Sibley and Shipton, eds., *Sibley's Harvard Graduates* (Boston, 1962), 12 (1746–50): 292–97. William Browne of Salem also accepted a position on the council. He took refuge in Boston, refusing to resign, but he never was allowed to return. *Essex Gazette*, September 13–20 and 20–27, 1774.
30. Wroth, *Province in Rebellion*, doc. 160; Davies, *Documents*, 8:169–70.
31. Sibley and Shipton, *Sibley's Harvard Graduates*, 13 (1751–55): 336–44; *Essex Gazette*, September 6–13, 1774, and Davies, *Documents*, 8:182–84.
32. *Essex Gazette*, August 23–30, 1774; and Wroth, *Province in Rebellion*, doc. 158.
33. On the fate of Ruggles, see *Essex Gazette*, August 23–30, 1774. For Danforth and Lee, see *Essex Gazette*, August 30–September 6, 1774; *Pennsylvania Packet*, September 19, 1774; Sibley and Shipton, *Sibley's Harvard Graduates*, 8:593–95. For Watson, see *Essex Gazette*, August 23–30, 1774; *Pennsylvania Packet*, September 5, 1774.
34. Davies, *Documents*, 180; Force, *American Archives*, 1:731–32; *Connecticut Gazette*, September 2, 1774; and Larned, *History of Windham County*, 130.
35. *Connecticut Gazette*, June 3, June 10, and July 8, 1774; *Essex Gazette*, June 14–21, 1774.
36. Force, *American Archives*, 1:629–33.
37. William Southgate, "History of Scarborough," Maine Historical Society *Collections* 3 (1853): 189–92; also Leamon, *Revolution Downeast*, 62–80, 157–62.
38. Force, *American Archives*, 1:447–48.

## 4: Reaching Out to Others

1. Isaiah Thomas, *The History of Printing in America: With a Biography of Printers and an Account of Newspapers*, ed. Marcus A. McCorison (1810; reprint, Barre, MA, 1970), 267.
2. Several works have helped me think—or more aptly, rethink—the challenge of how to establish effective networks of communication in late colonial society: Joel Mokyr, *Gifts of Athena: Historical Origins of the Knowledge Economy* (Princeton, NJ, 2002); Michael Ignatieff, *Needs of Strangers* (London, 1984); Benedict Anderson, *Imagined Communities: Reflections on the Origin and Spread of Nationalism* (London, 1983); C. A. Bayly, *Empire and Information: Intelligence Gathering and Social Communication in India, 1780–1870* (Cambridge, UK, and New York, 1996); Richard D. Brown, *Knowledge Is Power: The Diffusion of Information in Early America, 1700–1865* (New York, 1992); and Richard R. John, *Spreading the News: The American Postal System from Franklin to Morse* (Cambridge, MA, 1998).
3. Nathaniel Bouton et al., eds., *Documents and Records Relating to New Hampshire, 1623–1800*, 40 vols. (Concord, NH, 1873), 7:413.
4. Joel Mokyr, "The Intellectual Origins of Modern Economic Growth," *Journal of Economic History* 65 (2005): 295.
5. Cited in Robert M. Wier, "The Role of the Newspaper Press in the Southern Colonies on the Eve of the Revolution: An Interpretation," in *The Press and the American Revolution*, ed. Bernard Bailyn and John B. Hench (Worcester, MA, 1980), 100.

6. *Boston Evening-Post*, October 12, 1767.
7. *Morning Chronicle and London Advertiser*, March 30, 1775, in *Letters on the American Revolution, 1774–1776*, ed. Margaret Wheeler Willard (Port Washington, NY, 1968), 67.
8. *Connecticut Gazette and the Universal Intelligencer*, March 11, 1774.
9. *Essex Gazette*, July 5–12, 1774.
10. Hugh Finlay, *Journal Kept by Hugh Finlay, Surveyor of the Post Roads, On the Continent of North America* (Brooklyn, NY, 1867), 32, 67, 68–69.
11. Ward L. Miner, *William Goddard: Newspaperman* (Durham, NC, 1962); and Richard F. Hixson, "Goddard, William," *American National Biography Online*, Feb. 2000 (www.anb.org.turing.library.northwestern.edu/articles/01/01-00326.html, Access Date: Mon. May 18, 2009).
12. William Goddard, *The Partnership: or, the History of the Rise and Progress of the Pennsylvania Chronicle* (Philadelphia, 1770).
13. *Maryland Journal and the Baltimore Advertiser*, August 20, 1773.
14. William Goddard, *The Plan for Establishing a New American Post-Office* (Boston, 1774).
15. William B. Reed, *Life and Correspondence of Joseph Reed*, 2 vols. (Philadelphia, 1847), 1:56–57.
16. Force, *American Archives*, 1:501–504.
17. Ibid., 500–501.
18. *Connecticut Gazette*, April 1, 1774.
19. Force, *American Archives*, 1:500–501.
20. Ibid., 502.
21. *Essex Gazette*, March 15–22, 1774.
22. Force, *American Archives*, 1:502, 503.
23. Ibid., 503–504.
24. Cited in Miner, *Goddard*, 124.
25. *Boston Gazette*, August 1, 1774.
26. "Boston Committee Reply to Worcester County, Maryland (October 10, 1774)" in Massachusetts Historical Society [MHS] *Collections* 4 (1858): 81. I want to thank Andrew Wehrman for his help in interpreting the committee's records.
27. *Essex Gazette*, June 27, 1774, quoted in MHS *Collections* 4 (1858): 38–39; and *Boston Gazette*, June 27, 1774.
28. "Correspondence in 1774 and 1775, Between a Committee of the Town of Boston and Contributors of Donations for the Relief of the Sufferers by the Boston Port Bill," MHS *Collections* 4 (1858), 1–2.
29. *Boston Gazette*, September 26, 1774.
30. Ibid., "Reply to New Castle," MHS *Collections* 4 (1858): 34–35.
31. T. H. Breen, *Marketplace of Revolution*, chap. 7.
32. *Boston Gazette*, September 26, 1774.
33. Broadside, *The Committee . . . Appointed by the Town of Boston to Receive Donations . . .* (Boston, 1774).
34. Force, *American Archives*, 1:485.
35. *Connecticut Courant*, June 14, 1774.
36. *Boston Gazette*, July 4, 1774; "Letter from Windham," MHS *Collections* 4 (1858): 4–7.

37. Cited Larned, *History of Windham County*, 1:126.

38. *Connecticut Courant*, June 26, 1775.

39. *Connecticut Gazette*, August 5, 1774.

40. *Boston Gazette*, September 5, 1774, *Essex Gazette*, July 19, 1774, MHS *Collections* 4 (1858): 64, 110.

41. Ibid., April 10, 1775.

42. Ibid., July 11, 1774.

43. "Minutes of the Committee of Safety of Bucks County, Pennsylvania, 1774–1776," *Pennsylvania Magazine of History and Biography* 15 (1891), 262.

44. *Boston Gazette*, December 12, 1774.

45. Ibid.

46. *Essex Gazette*, June 21–28, 1774.

47. *Connecticut Gazette*, July 29, 1774.

48. William L. Saunders, ed., *The Colonial Records of North Carolina*, 10 vols. (Raleigh, NC, 1886–90), 9:1034; James Sullivan, ed., *Minutes of the Albany Committee of Correspondence 1775–1778*, 2 vols. (Albany, NY, 1923), 1:9–10.

49. "Committee of Safety of Bucks County," *Pennsylvania Magazine*, 265.

50. *New-Hampshire Gazette and Historical Chronicle*, December 30, 1774, and January 20, 1775.

51. *Minutes of the Committee and of the First Commission for Detecting and Defeating Conspiracies in the State of New York, December 11, 1776–September 23, 1778*, 2 vols. (New York, 1924–25), 1:99.

52. "Letter from Durham to the Boston Committee," MHS *Collections* 4 (1858), 144–45.

53. *Connecticut Gazette*, July 29, 1774.

54. Cited in Alfred Moore Waddell, *A History of New Hanover County and the Lower Cape Fear Region* (Wilmington, NC, 1909), 77–78.

55. "Letter from Durham," 144–46.

56. *Connecticut Gazette*, June 3, 1774.

57. Cited in Larned, *History of Windham County*, II:127–28.

58. Ibid., 128. Also, *Connecticut Courant*, June 21, 1774.

59. Davies, *Documents*, 8:150–51. For a similar report from Governor Wentworth of New Hampshire see page 169 in Davies.

60. *New-Hampshire Gazette*, July 22, 1774.

61. *Pennsylvania Packet*, February 6, 1775.

62. *Pennsylvania Packet or General Advertiser*, June 6, 1774.

63. "Letter from Brooklyn, [Connecticut]," MHS *Collections* 4 (1858), 51–52.

## 5: *The Power of Rumor: The Day the British Destroyed Boston*

1. See Chapter 2. Also, "Joseph Galloway on the First Continental Congress," in *English Historical Documents: American Colonial Documents to 1776*, ed. Merrill Jensen, 12 vols. (New York, 1969), 9:801–3; Edmund Cody Burnett, *The Continental Congress* (New York, 1964), 42–47; and Worthington Chauncey Ford, ed., *Journals of the Continental Congress*, 34 vols. (Washington, D.C., 1904–37), 1:32–40, 63–73.

2. Cited in John Chester Miller, *Sam Adams: Pioneer in Propaganda* (Boston, 1936), 324; and Jensen, *The Founding of a Nation*, 495.

3.  Myles Cooper, *A Friendly Address to All Reasonable Americans* . . . (New York, 1774), 31–33.
4.  *Essex Gazette*, January 31–February 7, 1775.
5.  The fullest and most subtle analysis of the deliberations of the Continental Congress during this period is Jack N. Rakove, "The Decision for American Independence: A Reconstruction," *Perspectives in American History* 10 (1976): 217–75.
6.  "Joseph Galloway," *English Historical Documents*, 9:801.
7.  Christopher Marshall, *Extracts from the Diary of Christopher Marshall Kept in Philadelphia and Lancaster During the American Revolution, 1774–1781*, ed. William Duane (Albany, NY, 1877), 9.
8.  Paul H. Smith, ed., *Letters of Delegates to Congress, 1774–1789*, 26 vols. (Washington, D.C., 1976), 1:29, 32, 34, 85–86.
9.  Ibid., 49.
10. Ibid., 34.
11. Broadside, *TO THE PUBLIC. BOSTON, SEPTEMBER 2, 1774* (Boston, 1774), 1.
12. *New-Hampshire Gazette*, September 9, 1774; Clark, *The Fate of Blood-Thirsty Oppressors*, 25. See Chapter 3 for an account of the Oliver resignation.
13. Davies, *Documents*, 8:187.
14. Force, *American Archives*, 1:763–84; *Pennsylvania Packet*, September 19, 1774; *Boston Post-Boy*, September 12, 1774; and Davies, *Documents*, 8:188–89.
15. *Pennsylvania Packet*, September 19, 1774; *New-York Gazette, and Weekly Mercury*, September 12, 1774.
16. Davies, *Documents*, 8:190.
17. *Connecticut Gazette and the Universal Intelligencer*, September 9, 1774.
18. Ibid.
19. Ibid.
20. Ibid.
21. *Boston Gazette*, October 4–11, 1774.
22. The notes from Stiles's research can be found in *The Literary Diary of Ezra Stiles*, ed. Franklin Bowditch Dexter, 4 vols. (New York, 1901), 1:476–84.
23. *Pennsylvania Packet* ["extra" for No. 152], September 19, 1774.
24. *Maryland Journal and the Baltimore Advertiser*, September 21, 1774.
25. *Connecticut Gazette*, October 7, 1774. Also, William Farrand Livingston, *Israel Putnam: Pioneer, Ranger, and Major-General, 1718–1790* (New York, 1905), 187–89.
26. Livingston, *Israel Putnam*, 183–85; Winthrop Sargent, ed., "Letters of John Andrews, Esq., of Boston, 1772–1776," *Massachusetts Historical Society Proceedings* 8 (1865): 355; and David Humphreys, *An Essay on the Life of the Honorable Major-General Israel Putnam: Addressed to the State Society of the Cincinnati in Connecticut* (Hartford, CT, 1788), 16–26.
27. Cited in Livingston, *Israel Putnam*, 185.
28. *Connecticut Courant*, October 10, 1774.
29. Ibid., October 17, 1774.
30. Ibid., October 10, 1774. Smalley's problems with the town were not over; see ibid., October 17, 1774.
31. *Connecticut Gazette*, September 9, 1774.
32. Cited in Livingston, *Israel Putnam*, 189–90.
33. Ibid., 185.

34. Ibid., 188–89.
35. *Connecticut Gazette*, October 7, 1774.
36. Ibid., September 9 and September 23, 1774; and *Essex Gazette*, September 6–13, 1774; Sargent, ed., "Letters," 355.
37. Stiles, *Literary Diary*, 1:482–84, 457.
38. *Essex Gazette*, September 13–20, 1774; *Boston Gazette*, October 10, 1774.
39. Worthington Chauncey Ford, ed., *Journals of the Continental Congress*, 34 vols. (Washington, D.C., 1904), 1:39–40.
40. Reed, *Correspondence of Joseph Reed*, 1:80.
41. Smith, *Letters of Delegates to Congress*, 1:85–86.
42. Ibid., 87–88.
43. Ibid., 75, 80.
44. Reed, *Joseph Reed*, 1:79.
45. Davies, *Documents*, 8:186.
46. Ibid., 198–201; and Force, *American Archives*, 1:768–69.
47. Davies, *Documents*, 8:212, 215.
48. Smith, *Letters*, 1:157.
49. Ibid., 160–61.
50. Force, *American Archives*, 1:980.
51. Davies, *Documents*, 9:37–39; and Donoughue, *British Politics*, 212–27.
52. David Hartley, *Letters on the American War*, 3.
53. Force, *American Archives*, 1:980.

## 6: *The Association: The Second Stage of Insurgency*

1. Two notable exceptions to this generalization about the literature are David Ammerman, *In the Common Cause: American Response to the Coercive Acts of 1774* (New York, 1975); and Merrill Jensen, *The Founding of a Nation*.
2. For example, David Andress, *The Terror: The Merciless War for Freedom in Revolutionary France* (New York, 2005).
3. These issues are explored in T. H. Breen, "Where Have All the People Gone? Reflections on Popular Political Mobilization on the Eve of American Independence," in *War in an Age of Revolution, 1775–1815*, eds. Roger Chickering and Stig Foerster (Cambridge, UK, 2010), 210–26. See also Hermann Wellenreuther et al., *The Revolution of the People: Thoughts and Documents on the Revolutionary Process in North America, 1774–1776* (Göttingen, Ger., 2006); and Wellenreuther, *Von Chaos und Krieg zu Ordnung und Frieden: Der Amerikanischen Revolution erster Teil, 1775–1783* (Berlin, 2006), Anhange, 643–706.
4. Breen, *Marketplace of Revolution*, chap. 6. On the broader transatlantic development of a consumer economy in eighteenth-century Holland, England, and America, see de Vries, *The Industrious Revolution*.
5. The full text of the Association can be found in Merrill Jensen, ed., *English Historical Documents: American Colonial Documents to 1776*, 12 vols. (New York, 1969), 9:813–16.
6. Richard D. Brown, *Revolutionary Politics in Massachusetts: The Boston Committee of Correspondence and the Towns, 1772–1774* (New York, 1976); and Ammerman, *Common Cause*, chap. 6.

7. *Connecticut Gazette and the Universal Intelligencer* [New London], February 17, 1775.
8. William A. Benedict and Hiram A. Tracy, *History of the Town of Sutton, Massachusetts, from 1704 to 1876* (Worcester, MA, 1878), 91–95.
9. Force, *American Archives*, 2:2. See also ibid., 1:967 and 3:170–76; and Marshall, *Extracts from the Diary of Christopher Marshall*, 11–12.
10. Force, *American Archives*, 3:172.
11. Isaac Mansfield, Jr., *A Sermon, Preached in the Camp at Roxbury, November 23, 1775* (Boston, 1776), 20–21.
12. "Political Observations Without Order: Addressed to the People of America," [November 14, 1774], in Force, *American Archives*, 1:976–77.
13. Ibid., 1061–63. A thorough account of the social and political tensions in Virginia during this period can be found in Michael A. McDonnell, *The Politics of War: Race, Class, and Conflict in Revolutionary Virginia* (Chapel Hill, NC, 2007).
14. *Rivington's New York Gazetteer*, January 26, 1775.
15. Cited in Willard, *Letters on the American Revolution*, 53–56.
16. F. M. Caulkins, *History of Norwich, Connecticut, from Its Settlement in 1660 to January 1845* (Norwich, CT, 1845), 214.
17. The quotations in this section are taken from Ebenezer Punderson, *The Narrative of Mr. Ebenezer Punderson, Merchant; Who Was Drove Away by the Rebels in America, from His Family, and a Very Comfortable Fortune in Norwich, Connecticut* (London, 1776), 3–8, 15.

## 7: Schools of Revolution

1. The best account of "government by committee" remains David Ammerman, *In the Common Cause*, 103–24.
2. Breen, *Marketplace of Revolution*, chap. 8.
3. *North Carolina Gazette*, April 14, 1775.
4. Hermann Wellenreuther, "Associations, the People, Committees of Observation and the Culture of Right, 1774–1776," paper presented at a conference on the Languages of Rights During the Age of the American Revolution, Northwestern University, Evanston, IL, May 14, 2004.
5. Leora H. McEachen et al., eds., *Wilmington–New Hanover Safety Committee Minutes, 1774–1776* (Wilmington, NC, 1974), 77–78.
6. See Evangeline Walker Andrews, introduction to *Journal of a Lady of Quality; Being the Narrative of a Journey from Scotland to the West Indies, North Carolina, and Portugal in the Years 1774–1775*, by Janet Schaw, ed. Evangeline Walker Andrews and Charles McLean Andrews (New Haven, CT, 1934), 1–18. It should be noted that the editors of Schaw's *Journal* fully understood how sources like this might force a radical revision of traditional interpretations of the Revolution. "Such contemporary evidence," they noted, "makes us realize that our forefathers, however worthy their object, were engaged in real rebellion and revolution, characterized by extremes of thought and action that always accompany such movements, and not in the kind of parlour warfare, described in many of our text books, in which highly cultivated and periwigged American gentlemen of unquestioned taste and morality, together with farmers of heroic mould, engaged life and limb for princi-

ples of democratic government, which developed in fact, only during later periods of our national life." Ibid., 9.

7. Ibid., 5–6.
8. McEachen, *Wilmington–New Hanover Safety Committee*, 1.
9. Saunders, *Colonial Records of North Carolina*, 10:65.
10. Ibid., 9:1109–10.
11. Ibid., 1084–85.
12. Ibid., 1091.
13. McEachen, *Wilmington–New Hanover Safety Committee*, 18–19.
14. Ibid., 19.
15. Ibid., 21.
16. Ibid., 19, 21.
17. Ibid., 14–15.
18. Ibid., 22.
19. Ibid., 23–24.
20. Schaw, *Lady of Quality*, 191–92.
21. Ibid., 191–92.
22. Ibid., 192.
23. Ibid., 194.
24. Ibid., 190. Major General James Wolfe died of wounds received during the Battle of Quebec in 1759. He quickly became an iconic figure for those who celebrated the military power of the British Empire. See Simon Schama, *Dead Certainties: Unwarranted Speculations* (New York, 1991).
25. Schaw, *Lady of Quality*, 190–91.
26. Ibid., 191.
27. For example, in his masterful study of popular politics in New Jersey, Larry R. Gerlach explains, "the profusion of grass-roots committees brought a remarkable degree of community involvement in and commitment to the protest movement. Men who had previously been excluded from positions of leadership now found themselves exercising political authority. In all, some 450 men served on the various committees. The county committees of correspondence remained dominated by an elite; the local committees represented all but the lower social strata and thus may be said to have accurately reflected the will of a considerable segment of the population." Larry R. Gerlach, *Prologue to Independence: New Jersey in the Coming of the American Revolution* (New Brunswick, 1976), 233–34. See also Anne M. Ousterhout, *A State Divided: Opposition in Pennsylvania to the American Revolution* (New York, 1987), 56; and David H. Villers, "'King Mob' and the Rule of Law: Revolutionary Justice and the Suppression of Loyalism in Connecticut, 1774–1783," in *Loyalism and Community in North America*, ed. Robert M. Calhoon et al. (Westport, CT, 1994), 17–30.
28. Jensen, *The Founding of a Nation*, 516–34; Lemuel Shattuck, *History of the Town of Concord* (Boston, 1835), 82–85.
29. "Minutes of the Committee of Safety of Bucks County, Pennsylvania, 1774–1776," *Pennsylvania Magazine of History and Biography*, 15 (1891): 259–60. See also Force, *American Archives*, 2:1050–55 and 3:112–18.
30. On this point, see Jackson Turner Main, "Government by the People: The American Revolution and the Democratization of the Legislatures," *William & Mary*

*Quarterly* 23 (1966): 391–407; Jerrilyn Greene Marston, *King and Congress: The Transfer of Political Legitimacy, 1774–1776* (Princeton, NJ, 1987), 74–75; and Ammerman, *In the Common* Cause, 103–5.

31. Force, *American Archives,* 2:3.
32. Gerlach, *Prologue,* 208–12.
33. Force, *American Archives,* 2:276.
34. *Virginia Gazette* (Pinkney), December 1, 1774; and *New-Hampshire Gazette,* December 2, 1774.
35. *Maryland Gazette,* December 15, 1774; Force, *American Archives,* 1:1031–32.
36. *New-Hampshire Gazette,* December 16, 1774; Gerlach, *Prologue,* 248–49; and Force, *American Archives,* 2:1745.
37. The two quotations and statistics on committee size appear in Ammerman, *In the Common Cause,* 106–108.
38. Force, *American Archives,* 2:34–35.
39. *Maryland Gazette,* December 21, 1774.
40. Ibid., June 15, 1775.
41. Marshall, *Extracts from the Diary of Christopher Marshall,* 51–53.
42. Gerlach, *Prologue,* 274.
43. Cited in ibid., 250; Force, *American Archives,* 2:701.
44. Force, *American Archives,* 2:284–85.
45. Ibid., 3:151–54.
46. Saunders, *Colonial Records of North Carolina,* 9:410–22; and McEachen, *Wilmington–New Hanover Safety Committee,* 73, 75, 77–79.

## 8: Insurgents in Power

1. On the contagion of violence in rebellion and civil wars, see Stathis N. Kalyvas, *The Logic of Violence in Civil War* (Cambridge, UK, 2006); Jeremy M. Weinstein, *Inside the Rebellion: The Politics of Insurgent Violence* (Cambridge, UK, 2007); and Stathis N. Kalyvas et al., eds., *Order, Conflict and Violence* (Cambridge, UK, 2008). Richard Maxwell Brown provides a useful overview of the problem in *Strain of Violence: Historical Studies of American Violence and Vigilantism* (New York, 1975).
2. John L. Brooke, *In the Heart of the Commonwealth: Society and Political Culture in Worcester County, Massachusetts, 1713–1861* (Cambridge, UK, 1989); and Richard D. Brown, *Revolutionary Politics in Massachusetts,* 201–7.
3. Albert A. Lovell, *Worcester in the War of the Revolution . . .* (Worcester, MA, 1876), 29–31. See also Kenneth J. Moynihan, *A History of Worcester, 1674–1848* (Charleston, SC, 2007), chap. 4.
4. Lovell, *Worcester,* 34–42; and Worcester Society of Antiquity, *Collections* 4 (1882): 225–39.
5. Late in 1775, Clark Chandler had another confrontation with a Worcester committee. His behavior led to a brief imprisonment. In September he formally apologized and asked for mercy, and after reading his abject confession, the committee not only freed him but also allowed him to reside in the area. Lovell, *Worcester,* 40–41, 46–47, 71–79.
6. *Connecticut Gazette and the Universal Intelligencer* (New London), February 17, 1775.

7. Force, *American Archives*, 3:1571–76.
8. *Essex Gazette*, January 10–17, 1775. See also the proceedings against Adam Stuart before the Londonderry, New Hampshire, Committee of Safety and before the committee of the New Hampshire House: Nathaniel Bouton et al., eds., *Documents and Records Relating to New Hampshire, 1623–1800*, 40 vols. (Concord, NH, 1874), 8:52–53.
9. Force, *American Archives*, 3:59–60.
10. Saunders, *Colonial Records of North Carolina*, 9:1027–32.
11. Force, *American Archives*, 3:56–57.
12. "Minutes of the Committee of Safety of Bucks County, Pennsylvania, 1774–1776," *Pennsylvania Magazine of History and Biography* 15 (1891), 265–67.
13. Lawrence W. Towner, "True Confessions and Dying Warnings in Colonial New England," in *Sibley's Heir: A Volume in Memory of Clifford Kenyon Shipton* (Boston, 1982), 523–39; and Daniel A. Cohen, *Pillars of Salt, Monuments of Grace, New England Crime Literature and the Origins of American Popular Culture, 1674–1860* (New York, 1993).
14. Force, *American Archives*, 3:1173–74.
15. Force, *American Archives*, 2:1112–13.
16. Oliver, *Origin and Progress of the American Revolution*, 157; *Connecticut Gazette*, October 27, 1775.
17. *Connecticut Gazette*, February 10, 1775, October 27, 1775, and April 12, 1776. Another interesting case of a committee's struggle to persuade a person of his political errors and his eventual forgiveness occurred in Cumberland County, New Jersey. See Force, *American Archives*, 2:34–35.
18. One notorious case involving a minister of loyalist persuasion is the subject of Sheldon S. Cohen, *Connecticut's Loyalist Gadfly: The Reverend Samuel Andrew Peters* (Hartford, CT, 1976).
19. *New-Hampshire Gazette*, January 20, 1775.
20. Ibid.
21. Force, *American Archives*, 2:234–35. See also the ordeal of Reverend Mr. John Agnew. He was called before the Nansemond County, Virginia, committee for a number of indiscretions, the most serious being his claim that the Association reflected "the designes of the great men . . . to ruin the poor people; and that, after a while, they would forsake them, and lay the whole blame on their shoulders, and by this means make them slaves." Ibid., 226–28.
22. William Hand Browne, ed., *Journal of the Maryland Convention, July 26–August 14, 1775; Journal and Correspondence of the Maryland Council of Safety, August 29, 1775–July 6, 1776*, vol. 11, *Archives of Maryland*, 72 vols. (Baltimore, 1892), 11, 38–39, 49–51; and Force, *American Archives*, 3:52–56, 105, 128–29.
23. Force, *American Archives*, 3:105–6, 125–30; David Curtis Skaggs, *Roots of Maryland Democracy, 1753–1776* (Westport, CT, 1973), 150; Browne, *Archives of Maryland*, 11:9, 12, 44–48, 51–52.
24. Force, *American Archives*, 1:970–71; and Richard B. Harwell, ed., *The Committees of Safety of Westmoreland and the Fincastle: Proceedings of the County Committees, 1774–1776* (Richmond, VA, 1956), 32–35.
25. *Essex Gazette*, January 10–17, 1775.
26. Force, *American Archives*, 2:35–36; and Gerlach, *Prologue to Independence*, 238–39.

27. *Minutes of the Provincial Congress and Council of Safety of the State of New Jersey,* (Trenton, NJ, 1879), 37.
28. Ibid., 44.
29. Ibid., 53–54.
30. Force, *American Archives*, 1:1051–52.
31. Ibid., 1:131–33; see also page 1100.
32. *Minutes of . . . New Jersey*, 39–40.
33. Force, *American Archives*, 2:12–13.
34. Ibid., 836–37.
35. *Massachusetts Spy*, December 8, 1775.
36. For New York, see Force, *American Archives*, 3:582–620; for New Hampshire, Bouton et al., eds., *Documents and Records*, 8:204–96.
37. Force, *American Archives*, 3:141–42. See also Leora H. McEachen et al., eds., *Wilmington–New Hanover Safety Committee Minutes, 1774–1776* (Wilmington, NC, 1974), 83; and Force, *American Archives*, 2:606–607, 704, and 3:41, 99–100.
38. Force, *American Archives*, 3:107–12.
39. Ibid., 2:793.
40. Ibid., 700–701.
41. Ibid.

## 9: An Appeal to Heaven: Religion and Rights

1. My analysis of popular political culture owes a lot to David D. Hall's insights into the conversation between high and low religious culture in seventeenth-century New England. See Hall, *Worlds of Wonder, Days of Judgment: Popular Religious Belief in Early New England* (New York, 1989), 3–20.
2. Zabdiel Adams, *The Grounds of Confidence and Success in War, Represented* [sermon delivered to a company of militia in Lunenburg, Massachusetts, January 2, 1775] (Boston, 1775), 34.
3. Cited in J. M. Stowe, *History of the Town of Hubbardston* (Hubbardston, MA, 1881), 41.
4. Cited in Christopher M. Jedrey, *The World of John Cleaveland: Family and Community in Eighteenth-Century New England* (New York, 1979), 138.
5. The flag-raising ceremony was originally described in T. H. Breen, *The Lockean Moment: The Language of Rights on the Eve of the American Revolution* (Oxford, UK, 2001), 1–5.
6. *A Prayer, Composed for the Benefit of the Soldiery . . .* (Cambridge, MA, 1775), 3.
7. *New-England Chronicle or Essex Gazette*, July 13–21, 1775. George Washington later commissioned a similar flag to fly over two shore batteries and six armed vessels operating near Boston. See Edward W. Richardson, *Standards and Colors of the American Revolution* (Philadelphia, 1982), 59; and Alfred Morton Cutler, *The Continental "Great Union" Flag* (Somerville, MA, 1929), 27–28. Charles Royster provides a good account of Leonard's chaplaincy in *A Revolutionary People at War: The Continental Army and American Character, 1775–1783* (New York, 1979), 170–74.
8. Cited in Henry Belcher, *The First American Civil War: First Period, 1775–1778*, 2 vols. (London, 1911), 1:208.

9. John Locke, *Two Treatises of Government*, ed. Peter Laslett (Cambridge, UK, 1960), 445; also 300, 397–98, 404.

10. Peter Laslett, "The English Revolution and Locke's *Two Treatises of Government*," *Cambridge Historical Journal* 12 (1956): 40–55; and John Marshall, *John Locke: Resistance, Religion and Responsibility* (Cambridge, UK, 1994).

11. Locke, *Two Treatises*, 445.

12. John Dunn, "The Politics of Locke in England and America in the Eighteenth Century," in *John Locke: Problems and Perspectives*, ed. John W. Yolton (Cambridge, UK, 1969), 45–80. A different view of Locke's importance in America can be found in Isaac Kramnick, *Republicanism and Bourgeois Radicalism: Political Ideology in Late Eighteenth-Century England and America* (Ithaca, NY, 1990).

13. *Boston Gazette*, March 1, 1773.

14. Thomas Hutchinson, *The History of the Colony and Province of Massachusetts-Bay*, 3 vols. (Cambridge, MA, 1936), 3:388, 395. How Americans understood rights has generated a large scholarly literature. Titles that have shaped the discussion include John Phillip Reid, *Constitutional History of the American Revolution: The Authority of Rights* (Madison, WI, 1986); Jack P. Greene, *All Men Are Created Equal: Some Reflections on the Character of the American Revolution* (Oxford, UK, 1976); and Stanley N. Katz, "The Strange Birth and Unlikely History of Constitutional Equality," *Journal of American History* 75 (1988): 747–62. The most balanced examination of the language of rights on the eve of independence is Daniel T. Rodgers, *Contested Truths: Keywords in American Politics Since Independence* (Cambridge, MA, 1987), chap. 2.

15. Josiah Tucker, *The Respective Pleas and Arguments of the Mother Country, and of the Colonies* . . . (London, 1775), 16, 38–39; Richard Price, *Observations on the Nature of Civil Liberty* . . , in *Richard Price and the Ethical Foundations of the American Revolution* (Durham, NC, 1979), 113; Josiah Tucker, *Cui Bono?* . . . (London, 1782), 94; Ambrose Serle, *Americans Against Liberty: Or an Essay on the Nature and Principles of True Freedom* . . . (London, 1775), 37, 46; and John Roebuck, *An Enquiry Whether the Guilt of the Present Civil War* . . . (London, 1776), 67. In his *Letters on the Present Disturbances in Great Britain and Her American Provinces* (London, 1777), Allen Ramsay assured British readers that "the People of England will be able to see through all the sophistry of the American Pamphleteers, who, having no sense of their own, borrow some from Locke" (24).

16. Rodgers, *Contested Truths*, 50–53; Stephen A. Conrad, "Putting Rights Talk in Its Place: *The Summary View* Revisited," in *Jeffersonian Legacies* (Charlottesville, VA, 1993), 254–80; and Bernard Bailyn, *The Ideological Origins of the American Revolution*, Enlarged Edition (Cambridge, MA, 1992), 28.

17. *Pennsylvania Packet*, September 19, 1774.

18. Force, *American Archives*, 1:1350–51.

19. Samuel Williams, *A Discourse on the Love of Our Country* (Salem, MA, 1775), 7. See also Nathaniel Niles, *Two Discourses on Liberty* . . . *June Fifth, 1774* (Newburyport, MA, 1774), 9–11.

20. Samuel Lockwood, *Civil Rulers an Ordinance of God, for Good to Mankind* . . . [Election Sermon for Connecticut] (New London, CT, 1774), 17–18.

21. *Connecticut Courant*, May 8, 1775.

22. *Pennsylvania Evening Post*, February 27, 1776.

23. Dan Foster, *A Short Essay on Civil Government* [sermons delivered in Windsor, Connecticut, October, 1774] (Hartford, CT, 1775), 8.

24. Cited in Pierce, *History of the Town of Gorham, Maine*, 114–17.

25. Broadside, *At a Town Meeting Held at Newport on the 12th Day of January, 1774* (Newport, RI, 1774). Also, for Exeter, New Hampshire, see *New-Hampshire Gazette*, January 7, 1774.

26. Robert J. Taylor, ed., *Massachusetts, Colony to Commonwealth: Documents on the Formation of Its Constitution, 1775–1780* (Chapel Hill, NC, 1961), 27.

27. *Pennsylvania Evening Post*, February 27, 1776.

28. Lockwood, *Civil Rulers*, 5.

29. Williams, *A Discourse*, 8; Foster, *Short Essay*, 6–8.

30. For example, see Michael J. Sandel, *Democracy's Discontent: America in Search of a Public Philosophy* (Cambridge, MA, 1996).

31. Force, *American Archives*, 2:1557.

32. Niles, *Two Discourses*, 30.

33. Fiske, *The Importance of Righteousness*, 33.

34. Peter Whitney, *The Transgression of a Land Punished by a Multitude of Rulers* (Boston, 1774), 17.

35. Force, *American Archives*, 2:1558.

36. Eliot quoted in Fiske, *Importance of Righteousness*, 26.

37. Ibid., 27.

38. Ibid., 32.

39. Ibid., 18.

40. Lockwood, *Civil Rulers*, 15–16.

41. *Norwich Packet*, September 1, 1774.

42. *Connecticut Gazette and the Universal Intelligencer*, May 27, 1774.

43. Jonathan Parsons, *Freedom from Civil and Ecclesiastical Slavery, The Purchase of Christ* (Newburyport, MA, 1774), 18. Also, *Connecticut Gazette*, October 27, 1775; *Connecticut Courant*, May 8, 1775.

44. John Allen, *An Oration on the Beauties of Liberty, Or the Essential of the Americans* (Hartford, CT, 1774), 25–26.

45. Parsons, *Freedom*, 16–17. Also, Niles, *Two Discourses*, 12–15; *Connecticut Gazette*, October 27, 1775; *Connecticut Courant*, May 8, 1775.

46. Cooper, *A Friendly Address*, 5. There is some disagreement about the author of this title. Thomas Bradbury Chandler is often suggested.

47. Whitney, *Transgression*, 53–53.

48. Bailyn, *Ideological Origins*, 86–89; and Gordon S. Wood, "Conspiracy and the Paranoid Style: Causality and Deceit in the Eighteenth Century," *William & Mary Quarterly* 39 (1982), 401–41.

49. Cited in Harry S. Stout, *The New England Soul: Preaching and Religious Culture in Colonial New England* (New York, 1986), 284.

50. Force, *American Archives*, 2:1011–13.

51. *Boston Evening-Post*, March 6, 1775.

52. Cited in Sarah J. Purcell, *Sealed with Blood: War, Sacrifice, and Memory in Revolutionary America* (Philadelphia, 2002), 18.

53. For a complete listing of the publication of *The Crisis* in colonial America as a separate "periodic paper," see Charles Evans, ed., *American Bibliography*, 14 vols.

(Chicago, 1909), 5 (1774–75), 112–25. I have quoted in this chapter from John Anderson's New York City reprinting of *The Crisis.*

54. Paul Leicester Ford, "The Crisis," *Bibliographer* 1 (1902), 139–52; John Cannon, ed., *Letters of Junius* (Oxford, UK, 1978), 453; and C. W. Sutton, "Thicknesse, Philip 1719–1792," *Dictionary of National Biography,* ed. Sidney Lee, 22 vols. (New York, 1909), 19:612–13.

55. *The Crisis,* no. 1.

56. Cited in Ford, "The Crisis," 144. Also, *Journals of the House of Commons, from November 29th, 1774 . . . to October the 15th, 1776,* 56 vols. (London, 1803), 35:158–59; and *Parliamentary Register; Or History of the Proceedings and Debates of the House of Commons,* 17 vols. (London, 1775–80), 1:235. The extraordinarily shrill character of the popular press in London during this period is described in John Brewer, *Party Ideology and Popular Politics at the Accession of George III* (Cambridge, UK, 1976), 154–66, 252–54.

57. Ford, "The Crisis," 144.

58. Ibid., 144–46, 148; *The Crisis,* no. 3, 18, 21.

59. Cited in ibid., 146–48.

60. Cited in ibid., 148; *Essex Gazette,* April 18–25, 1775.

61. For the full list, see Evans, *American Bibliography,* 5:112–25.

62. Thomas R. Adams, *American Independence, the Growth of an Idea: A Bibliographical Study . . .* (Austin, 1980). We obtain a fuller sense of the sudden popularity of *The Crisis* from the unpublished records of Robert Aitken, a leading Philadelphia bookseller. During May and June 1775 he sold hundreds of copies, most of which were purchased by Benjamin Towne, printer of the *Pennsylvania Evening Post.* (Robert Aitken's Wastebook, Library Company of Philadelphia, 260–62). I want to thank Benjamin Ponder for sharing his research on Towne with me. Also, Marshall, *Extracts from the Diary of Christopher Marshall,* 16 (April 22, 1775): 24 (May 7, 1775).

63. *New London Gazette,* June 9, 1775. In addition, some numbers of *The Crisis* appeared in the following American newspapers: *Connecticut Courant* [Hartford], *Connecticut Journal* [New Haven], *Norwich Packet, Boston Gazette, Boston Evening-Post, Massachusetts Spy* [Worcester], *Essex Journal* [Salem], *Essex Journal* [Newburyport], *New-Hampshire Gazette* [Portsmouth], *Providence Gazette, Pennsylvania Evening Post* [Philadelphia], *Constitutional Gazette* [New York], *North Carolina Gazette* [New Bern], *Maryland Journal and the Baltimore Advertiser* [Baltimore], *South Carolina Gazette and Country Journal* [Charleston].

64. *Virginia Gazette* (Hunter and Dixon), April 1, 1775.

65. On the dramatic change in the political climate, see Julie M. Flavell, "Government Interception of Letters from America and the Quest for Colonial Opinion in 1775," *William & Mary Quarterly* 58 (2001): 411.

66. *Connecticut or New London Gazette,* June 9, 1775. Also, *Norwich Packet,* October 9–16, 1775; *New-England Chronicle, or Essex Gazette,* May 18, 1775; and *Pennsylvania Evening Post,* April 22, 1775.

67. *Pennsylvania Evening Post,* October 14, 1775.

68. *Massachusetts Spy,* May 17, 1775. Also, *Constitutional Gazette,* August 3 and November 8, 1775.

69. *South Carolina Gazette and Country Journal,* May 2, May 9, and June 6, 1775.

70. *New-Hampshire Gazette*, October 10, 1775.

71. Ford, "The Crisis," 139–52. *The Crisis* is mentioned in Wilson, *The Sense of the People*, 242–43; and Maier, *From Resistance to Revolution*, 257–58.

72. *The Crisis*, no.3, 22.

73. Ibid., no. 1, 6; no. 3, 20.

74. *The Crisis Extraordinary* (1775), 2–4.

75. *The Crisis*, no. 5, 36.

76. *The Crisis*, no. 22, 182.

77. Ibid., 183; no. 14, 116; and *Crisis Extraordinary*, 14.

## *10: Endgames of Empire*

1. The phrase comes from K. G. Davies, introduction to *Documents of the American Revolution*, vol. 10, 4, 7.

2. The two best accounts of the battles of Lexington and Concord are David Hackett Fischer's richly researched *Paul Revere's Ride* (New York, 1994) and Allen French, *The Day of Concord and Lexington, The Nineteenth of April 1775* (Boston, 1925).

3. "General Gage's Instructions to Captain John Brown and Ensign Henry De Berniere, February 22, 1775," *Massachusetts Historical Society Collections* 4 (1816): 205–15.

4. *Connecticut Courant*, May 29, 1775.

5. Force, *American Archives*, 2:523.

6. Clark, *The Fate of Blood-Thirsty Oppressors*, 31.

7. *Connecticut Courant*, May 8, 1775.

8. David Humphreys, *An Essay on the Life of the Honorable Major-General Israel Putnam* (Hartford, CT, 1788), 103.

9. Henry Clinton, *The American Rebellion*, ed. William B. Willcox (New Haven, CT, 1954), 14.

10. Force, *American Archives*, 2:359.

11. *PHILADELPHIA, April 24, 1775. An Express Arrived at Five o'clock This Evening . . .* (Philadelphia, 1775); Frederick W. Ricord and William Nelson, eds., *Documents Relating to the Colonial History of the State of New Jersey*, 33 vols. (Newark, 1880–1928), 10 (1767–76): 586–88; and Fischer, *Paul Revere's Ride*, 270–71.

12. Reed, *Life and Correspondence of Joseph Reed*, 1:104.

13. Clark, *Blood-Thirsty Oppressors*, 29–30.

14. *Newport Mercury*, April 24, 1775 (italics added).

15. *Essex Gazette*, April 18–25, 1775; and *New-Hampshire Gazette*, April 19, 1775.

16. Davies, *Documents*, 9:117–18.

17. *Lloyd's Evening Post and British Chronicle*, June 14–16, 1775, in Willard, *Letters on the American Revolution*, 97.

18. Ricord and Nelson, *Documents*, 503, 591–93, 603–604, 645–46.

19. "Letter to Lieutenant-General John Dalling From George Cuthbert," *Pennsylvania Magazine of History and Biography* 66 (1942): 207–209.

20. Richard B. Harwell, ed., *The Committees of Safety of Westmoreland and Fincastle: Proceedings of the County Committees, 1774–1776* (Richmond, VA, 1956), 67.

21. *Cape Fear Mercury*, July 28, 1775.

22. Davies, *Documents*, 9:133.

23. Force, *American Archives*, 2:442–45. Also, Anne M. Ousterhout, *A State Divided: Opposition in Pennsylvania to the American Revolution* (New York, 1987), 112–19.

24. William Stearns, *A View of the Controversy Subsisting Between Great-Britain and the American Colonies. A Sermon* . . . (Watertown, MA, 1775), 31–32.

25. Force, *American* Archives, 2:362–63.

26. Cited in Donoughue, *British Politics and the American Revolution*, 272–73.

27. Cited in ibid., 275, 278; Force, *American Archives*, 2:1755–56 and 3:6–7.

28. Force, *American Archives*, 2:1097.

29. *Connecticut Gazette*, December 1, 1775.

30. An excellent collection of letters from royal officials stationed in the American colonies to their superiors in London can be found in Davies, *Documents*, vols. 8–9.

31. Ibid., vol. 10, introduction.

32. Carole Watterson Troxler, "Martin, Josiah (1737–1786)," *Oxford Dictionary of National Biography*, Oxford University Press, Sept. 2004, online edition, Jan. 2008 (www.oxforddnb.com.turing.library.northwestern.edu/view/article/39777, Access Date: May 18, 2009); Vernon O. Stumpf, *Josiah Martin: The Last Royal Governor of North Carolina* (Durham, NC, 1986); Alfred Moore Waddell, *A History of New-Hanover County and the Lower Cape Fear Region* (Wilmington, NC, 1909), 73–74; Davies, *Documents*, 8:927–30.

33. Davies, *Documents*, 8:171–79 and 9:37; William L. Saunders, ed., *The Colonial Records of North Carolina*, 10 vols. (Raleigh, NC, 1886–90), 9:1029–30, 1051–56.

34. Cited in Hugh T. Lefler and William S. Powell, *Colonial North Carolina: A History* (New York, 1973), 266. Also, Saunders, ed., *Colonial Records*, 9:1029–30.

35. See Chapter 7.

36. McEachen, *Wilmington–New Hanover Safety Committee*, 18–19.

37. Saunders, *Colonial Records*, 9:1166–67.

38. Ibid., 1214–16.

39. Davies, *Documents*, 9:209–16. On the reaction to the news of Lexington, see McEachen, *Wilmington–New Hanover Safety Committee*, 31–32 (June 19, 1775).

40. Force, *American Archives*, 3:8–9, 62; McEachen, *Wilmington–New Hanover Safety Committee*, 43; and Waddell, *A History*, 131–32.

41. Schaw, *Journal of a Lady of Quality*, 205; Saunders, *Colonial Records*, 10:41–45, 113–14.

42. Force, *American Archives*, 3:61–64, 1135–36.

43. Lawrence S. Mayo, *John Wentworth, Governor of New Hampshire, 1767–1775* (Cambridge, MA, 1921); and Jere R. Daniell, *Colonial New Hampshire: A History* (Millwood, NY, 1981), chap. 10.

44. Force, *American Archives*, 1:1041–42. See also Richard Francis Upton, *Revolutionary New Hampshire: An Account of the Social and Political Forces Underlying the Transition from Royal Province to American Commonwealth* (Port Washington, NY, 1970), 21–23.

45. Force, *American Archives*, 1:1054–55.

46. Ibid., 1042, 1043. Also, *Essex Gazette*, December 13–20 and 20–27, 1774, and January 3–10, 1775; *Rivington's Gazette*, December 29, 1774.

47. Davies, *Documents*, 8:248–51.
48. Cited in Upton, *Revolutionary New Hampshire*, 24.
49. *New-Hampshire Gazette*, January 6, 1775.
50. Davies, *Documents*, 9:28–29.
51. Ibid. See also William P. Colburn, *History of Milford* [New Hampshire] (Concord, NH, 1901), 49.
52. Davies, *Documents*, 9:136.
53. Upton, *Revolutionary New Hampshire*, 30, 32–34.

# *Acknowledgments*

My father, George Edward Breen, did not live to see the completion of this book. During his last years, we had many conversations about the project, and he offered wonderful insights and welcome suggestions. Many others have shared in the process of turning rough ideas about the American Revolution into a coherent argument. Hermann Wellenreuther, Peter Onuf, Peter Drummey, Eric Slauter, Russell Maylone, Sarah Breen, and Woody Holton offered encouragement, while at the same time helping me avoid embarrassing errors. I enjoyed excellent research support from Laura Garofalo, Howard Pashman, Andrew Wehrman, Christopher Rogers, Kate Stephensen, and Christopher Hodson. Michael Guenther and Strother Roberts, Jr., assisted me in the dreary businesss of checking citations. And three friends volunteered to read the complete manuscript: Walter Woodward, Edward Stehle, and Patrick Griffin. At a key point in the research phase I received generous backing from the Alexander von Humboldt Foundation and the Max Planck Institute for History in Göttingen, Germany. From the start of this project, Northwestern University provided a splendid environment in which teaching and research came together to spark new perspectives on the past. In particular I want to thank President Henry Bienen and the former provost Lawrence B. Dumas, good friends and outstanding administrators.

Over the last several years I have learned a lot from men and women who attended my lectures and discussions on the revolution of the people. Their questions and comments helped me strengthen the argument. Let me thank, therefore, those who offered constructive criticism at the University of North Dakota, Southwest Missouri State University, Notre Dame University, the University of Vermont, Brigham Young University, the Rothermere American Institute (Oxford University), the German Historical Institute (Washington, D.C.), the International Center for Jefferson Studies (Charlottesville), the Massachusetts Historical Society, Ludwig-Maximilians-Universität (Munich), the National Humanities Center, and Western Connecticut State University.

One could not ask more from an editor than I did of Thomas LeBien. Like a good coach, he pushed, criticized, praised, and at the end of the day, helped me see dimensions of my own argument that had escaped me. At all stages, I was ably assisted by Susan C. Breen, a formidable and demanding editor who repeatedly reminded me that I had a responsibility to restore to the American people the story of their own revolution.

# Index

Jacobins, 258
James II, King of England, 37, 60
Jefferson, Thomas, 35, 100, 241; on
 Battle of Lexington, 279
Jephthah, story of, 245
Jewell, Moses, 14–15
Jews, 36
Johannes in Eremo, *see* Cleaveland,
 John
Johnstone, George, 68
Jones (tavern owner), 277
Judges, Book of, 245, 285

*Kentish Gazette*, 69, 265
Keyes, Capt., 141–42, 143
Killingly, Conn., 125
King, Richard, 97–98

Lane, Samuel, 13, 42
"Last Dying Speech of the Crisis The,"
 265
"Lawyer, A" (Fallon), 205
Lebanon, Conn., 119, 121, 124–25
Lee, Arthur, 285
Lee, Joseph, 93
Lee, Richard Henry, 98, 154–55, 156,
 158
Lee, Stephen, 145
Lee, William, 154–55
Leighton, Hannah, *see* Davis, Hannah
Leninists, 258
Leonard, Daniel, 93
Leonard, Rev., 244, 246
*Letters from a Farmer* (Dickinson), 266,
 285
*Letters on the American War* (Hartley),
 159
"Letter to the Inhabitants of
 Massachusetts Bay," 78–80
Lexington, Battle of, 3, 8, 24, 27, 35, 42,
 45, 48, 84, 148–49, 160, 180, 218,
 222, 239, 241, 244, 268–69, 292, 295,
 298; American cause and, 279; British
 reaction to, 286–87; British spy
 mission and, 276–78; Gage's

assessment of, 284–85; George III's
 reaction to, 286–87; importance of,
 281; Jefferson on, 279; mobilization
 spurred by, 285–88; nationalism and,
 280; news of, 275, 280–84, 286;
 popular reaction to, 278, 281–84;
 shared revolutionary identity and,
 279–80
Liberty Pole, 220
literacy, 29, 102
Livermore, Samuel, 297–98
Locke, John, 19, 144; influence of,
 242–43, 245–47
Lockwood, Samuel, 249, 252, 255
*London Chronicle*, 105
Loring, Joshua, 90–91
loyalists, 162, 163, 204, 252; committees
 of safety opposed by, 207–12;
 disarming of, 239–40; *see also* Tories
Lusk, David, 145
Lutherans, 33

Maddison, Lt. Col., 134
Maine, 27, 30, 49, 51; mandamus
 councilors protests in, 96–97, 98
mandamus councilors, 88–97, 98, 134
Mansfield, Isaac, Jr., 173–74
Marshall, Christopher, 132–33
Martin, Joseph Plumb, 27
Martin, Josiah, 189–90, 289–94, 297,
 300
Mary II, Queen of England, 37, 60, 66
Maryland, 112, 166, 169, 198, 199, 200,
 229; oath of allegiance in, 237–38
*Maryland Journal and the Baltimore
 Advertiser*, 106–107, 267, 321n
Massachusettensis (pen name), 176
Massachusetts, 4, 17, 51, 52, 61–62, 86,
 87, 98, 112, 132, 134, 137, 154, 166,
 198, 238, 246, 251, 257, 275; charter
 of, 66; Coercive Acts and, 52–53;
 Neck fortifications controversy in,
 157–59; provincial Congress of, 50,
 239, 260
*Massachusetts Gazette*, 210
Massachusetts General Court, 48